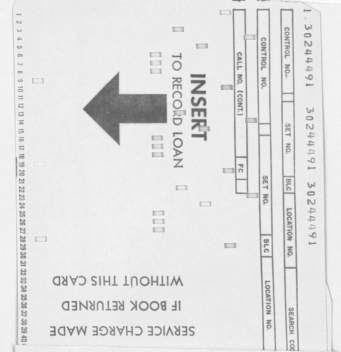

CAMBRIDGE STUDIES IN ECONOMIC HISTORY
PUBLISHED WITH THE AID OF THE ELLEN McARTHUR FUND

GENERAL EDITOR
M. M. POSTAN
Professor of Economic History in the University of Cambridge

MARSHALLS OF LEEDS
FLAX-SPINNERS
1788-1886

JOHN MARSHALL
Portrait by John Russell, 1802, in the University of Leeds.

MARSHALLS OF LEEDS
FLAX-SPINNERS
1788-1886

BY

W. G. RIMMER

Lecturer in Economic History at the
University of Leeds

CAMBRIDGE
AT THE UNIVERSITY PRESS
1960

PUBLISHED BY
THE SYNDICS OF THE CAMBRIDGE UNIVERSITY PRESS
Bentley House, 200 Euston Road, London, N.W. 1
American Branch: 32 East 57th Street, New York 22, N.Y.

©

CAMBRIDGE UNIVERSITY PRESS
1960

Printed in Great Britain at the University Press, Cambridge
(Brooke Crutchley, University Printer)

TO THE MEMORY OF
MY FATHER

CONTENTS

LIST OF ILLUSTRATIONS

PLATES

FIGURES

PREFACE

Less than twenty years after the erection of the first cotton-mills, efforts were being made to spin flax by similar machinery. Foremost amongst these pioneers was John Marshall of Leeds, a young man of twenty-three. When he died at the age of eighty in 1845, an obituary writer described him as 'one of those men to whom England owes so much of its commercial pre-eminence'. Since the outbreak of the French war in 1793, Marshall and Co. had been the largest spinners in the trade and the founder himself became a millionaire. This achievement places Marshall alongside other outstanding businessmen of that age, and in many respects he overshadows a fellow-townsman, Benjamin Gott, who pioneered the factory production of woollen cloth.

Recent business histories, particularly those relating to textile firms, have dealt with large concerns which outlive the nineteenth century and adapt themselves to the different conditions of the twentieth century. Anyone who has sampled directories knows that such firms are a rarity. Consequently a view of industrial development derived from such exceptional cases often appears to differ from assessments based on a wider analysis of the industry or economy. Because so many studies at the particular level of the firm do not reflect general trends, it is time that business historians restored the balance by examining firms which decayed and passed out of existence. Marshall and Co. provides such a case-study. Forty years after the founder's death, his grandsons closed the great flax mills and retired from business. And, although its size and position in the trade prevents Marshall and Co. from qualifying as a representative firm, its demise provides an opportunity to find out why one big firm fell by the wayside, an industrial dinosaur of the Darwinian Age.

This account of the business activities of a Yorkshire family over three generations is based on a dozen private ledgers and stock books, a few score letters, and a bundle of notebooks. Much of this material has been severely mutilated, probably by a member of the family who set about the task of writing the firm's history at the close of the nineteenth century with a pair of scissors. None of the routine records generated in running a large business—order-books, wage-books, journals, day-books—survive; and, because the family's numerous houses have passed into other hands, not many domestic records have been discovered, though more may yet come to light.

With such evidence relating chiefly to the family as businessmen, and covering for the most part the years 1806–46, it did not seem possible to attempt anything more than an analysis of various facets of the firm in turn—its markets, finance, machinery, mills and partnership arrangements. This proved a convenient way of arranging the material. But the result—a loosely connected set of essays—was disappointing. It was not only discontinuous, but such an arrangement also skirted many problems central to the understanding of a firm. Finance, machinery, labour were not important in themselves but assumed significance only when related together over time and viewed as the result of a businessman's effort or lack of it. Continuity lay not in the firm's buildings or products (some of which still survive in other hands), but in the activity of its owners who had a great deal of power to control what happened. The firm's history thus appeared to consist of a description of the interaction between the businessmen involved and their environment—their workpeople, the townsfolk of Leeds, customers, landowners of the Lake District and politicians at Westminster. By narrating such relationships, concentrating on those which seemed important at particular times, one tries to understand and perhaps convey something of a businessman's search for betterment and advantage in the nineteenth century.

Despite the shortcomings of the records, my aim was to write a narrative account of Marshall and Co. What may sometimes seem a preoccupation with certain episodes will often reflect the distribution of the evidence. Beyond that, two specific limitations require explaining. An account of Marshall's mill at Castle Foregate, Shrewsbury appears in the *Transactions of the Shropshire Archaeological Society*, volume LVI, and only passing reference is made to it here. Second, John Marshall's political activities have not been dealt with at length despite their relevance because Mr H. Fairhurst has already studied them in detail on the basis of newspaper sources and

Preface

will, I trust, soon make his findings available. Revision at this stage might improve some details and perhaps lead to a change of emphasis at certain points. But it would be more rewarding to investigate flax-spinning in centres other than Leeds in greater detail and examine the social adjustments of many more mill-owners. However, such a task is beyond my immediate purpose and would require a different type of book.

I am indebted to many people for assistance. The late Mr D. Marshall deposited records relating to his great-grandfather's mills in the Brotherton Library at Leeds University; the Editors of the Thoresby Society encouraged me to undertake this task; Mr and Mrs G. Ferrier kindly allowed me to consult material at Derwent Island, Keswick; and I was fortunate in being able to draw on the memories of Miss C. Marshall and Professor T. H. Marshall. I wish to thank those who read all or part of the text, and suggested improvements: Mr D. M. Joslin, Mr P. M. Sheard, Mr D. Sargan at an early stage, and later Mr C. H. Wilson and Professor Asa Briggs. The graphs were carefully drawn by two members of the Thoresby Society, Mr W. H. Connett and Mr M. S. Dougill; Mr F. Smith compiled the index; and I am grateful to Mrs B. Bardgett and Mrs E. Smith for typing the text. Professor A. J. Brown generously helped towards the inevitable and sometimes daunting burden of costs. And finally, I must thank my wife and Mr H. J. Hagedorn: the former for considerable indulgence in allowing the ghosts of past Marshalls to live with us and for helping with the more tedious tasks; the latter for stimulating criticism and warm friendship.

W. G. R.

THE UNIVERSITY OF LEEDS
14 June 1957

CHAPTER I

JOHN MARSHALL'S INHERITANCE

(i)

From east to west across the fields of northern Europe flax was grown by peasants. 'I suppose the cultivation here'—John Marshall wrote in Scotland at the beginning of the nineteenth century—'is much the same as in Russia. They scratch up a bit of ground and sow flax or corn without any sort of fence to preserve it from the cattle, and when that is exhausted they leave it and choose a bit somewhere else.'[1] For generations the occasional growth of flax had been part of farming. After the harvest, during the winter months, 'the country people...dress it, spin it, weave it and bleach it, all in their own families', making a coarse heavy cloth for domestic use.[2] In some places, making linens had ceased to be simply part of a peasant's provision for his family. Commerce penetrated first finishing, then weaving, spinning and even the growing of flax. The peasant's product—as cloth, and later as yarn or flax—went into the market, and districts in northern Europe acquired reputations for materials like Hessians and Osnaburgs which were exchanged at distant places.

The pattern is familiar. What remains obscure in England is the time and place of the transition from predominantly peasant to urban craftsmanship. At the end of the seventeenth century, both peasant and townsman made linens. In the shires, stretching from the southwest to the north-east, smallholders planted flax seed and made their own cloth. Apart from the manufacture of sails in coastal towns, linens were woven in such northern inland towns as Warrington,

---

[1] John Marshall, 'Tours' (Scotland, 1800). Unless otherwise indicated, all footnotes refer to the Marshall MSS. in the Brotherton Library, University of Leeds, or at Derwent Island, Keswick. Neither collection is indexed, and citations are based on the type of document and the date of entry. The business notebooks of John Marshall and his sons (including the former's experiment and tour books), the partners' private ledgers for the Water Lane and Castle Foregate mills, business correspondence and miscellaneous papers relating to the Kay case, the labour unrest of 1871-2 and the closing of the mills, are in the Brotherton Library. Correspondence and papers relating to family affairs are at Derwent Island.   [2] *Ibid.*

Knaresborough and Darlington. But whether located in town or countryside, England's linen manufacture was at that time small and relatively backward. Weavers and bleachers were not sufficiently skilled to produce the fine-spun, well-finished cloths made in parts of the Continent. Hence the upper orders of society in London and the provinces bought German cloth finished in Holland, or, when not prohibited, French linens. Moreover, trade across the ocean was largely in Dutch hands. A House of Commons committee heard in 1751 that 'none of the English Manufacture was exported until about twenty five years since'.[1] Domestic production therefore was limited by the demand for heavy linens at home, and a growing Irish industry, which in the early eighteenth century had free access to British and colonial markets, hastened to satisfy such demand in England. Despite long-standing encouragement by the state, English farmers remained obdurate and English merchants unwilling to plant more flax and make more linens. Yet within five generations, between 1700 and 1830, an English flax-spinning industry grew up which dominated European production.

England's linen industry began growing early in the eighteenth century and continued to flourish until the mid-nineteenth century. Two main factors account for its sudden, marked expansion before the introduction of mills and machinery: foreign flax and protection.

Linen weavers in the British Isles, except those in Ireland, depended for their raw materials on imports of either flax or yarn. If the cultivation of flax in England had once been widespread, the total amount produced could not have been very large.[2] Despite official encouragement and the exhortations of philanthropists and farming enthusiasts, the high cost of producing flax, set against the limited demand for it, priced it out of the evolving pattern of commercial farming.[3] The crop persisted on a limited scale in only a few areas

---

[1] *Report from the Select Committee Appointed to Examine the Petitions Respecting the Linen Manufactory*, 1751. First Series, vol. II, pp. 287–316, *passim*.

[2] J. H. Clapham, *A Concise Economic History of Britain* (1949), p. 190; A. J. Warden, *The Linen Trade* (1864), pp. 361–3; J. Horner, *The Linen Trade of Europe* (1920), pp. 216–18.

[3] Warden, *op. cit.* pp. 374–6. See also A. Yarranton, *England's Improvement* (1677), pp. 43–56; A. Young, *General View of the Agriculture of the County of Lincoln* (1799), pp. 161–4.

of the north and south-west, and in such districts spinners and weavers were to be found. In the seventeenth century, when woollens flourished in the western Pennines, linens dominated the domestic industry of the lowlands between Preston and Manchester.[1] There, enclosed smallholders and cottagers spun and wove flax grown locally. But, as the industry grew, additional supplies of flax and yarn had to be brought from Ireland and Germany.

Before the mid-eighteenth century, several expanding linen centres came to the fore, usually originating in close proximity to a local crop; 'eight to ten miles around Knaresborough', Cleveland, Stockton, and west across the dales to Carlisle and Whitehaven. To the south, Leicester, Derby, Bromsgrove and Reading and, in the south-west, Somerset and Devon had linen-weavers.[2] At that time, the native crop amounted to no more than a few thousand tons; hence, the development of the industry in the eighteenth century depended on imports, and this in turn promoted growth chiefly in the north. Imported yarns came from Ireland, Scotland and north-west Europe; flax came from Ireland, and especially from the Baltic, where Great Britain had a trading monopoly by the mid-eighteenth century.[3] West Riding merchants from Knaresborough and Barnsley rode regularly to Hull to buy Russian flax.

Imported flax and yarn was a necessary but not sufficient cause for growth. In addition the industry needed markets and ultimately, therefore, better skills. Technically, the British trailed behind continental producers, and even coarse native linens cost more to produce than their German counterparts. Consequently the initial growth of the English industry depended on protection to provide markets, although in the long run its fortunes would depend on being able to make better-quality linens.

From early in the eighteenth century, the government granted

[1] A. P. Wadsworth and J. de L. Mann, *The Cotton Trade and Industrial Lancashire* (1931), pp. 79, 90, 111. See also *Sel. Ctte. Rep.* 1751, p. 293, evidence of John Craven; 'The Manufacturers in Manchester depend on cotton as well as linen, but the cotton is only a temporary thing'.

[2] *Report from the Select Committee on the Petition of the Dealers in, and Manufacturers of, Linens*, 1744. First Series, vol. II, pp. 65–72. There were at that time a thousand looms in Knaresborough.

[3] C. Wilson, *Anglo-Dutch Commerce and Finance in the Eighteenth Century* (1941), pp. 51, 19.

3

English producers preferential treatment in colonial markets, and exports in general carried a bounty. On this basis the coarse-linen industry developed. Even so, expanding sales abroad was an uphill task. Heavy linens shipped from Whitehaven and Liverpool to the West Indies came into competition with Dutch goods. In 1744 British traders sought a monopoly in that market, and they secured a higher bounty. Irish and Scottish manufacturers also stood to benefit from trade with the colonies and, by the mid-eighteenth century, English producers wanted further discrimination, this time against Irish goods.[1]

Access to a growing and increasingly sheltered colonial market was an important factor in the rise of the industry at that time. No less important, especially after the mid-century, was the effort made by English producers to supply a larger proportion of the home market. There, the industry secured protection varying from the outright prohibition of French lawns and cambrics to stiff import taxes. The advantages derived from such trade barriers depended ultimately on the ability of English producers to make high-quality fashion goods, like checks for furniture coverings and table linens, as well as to increase sales of coarse sheetings, shirtings and towellings. Thus many rising linen centres began to specialise in lighter fabrics. The Scottish expansion of the 1730's consisted of fine linens made in the Clyde valley,[2] and weavers in Carlisle, Darlington, Stockton and Knaresborough began to make some lighter goods after the mid-century. But the industry was far from standing on its own feet. Complaints about Dutch competition in the home market continued in the 1770's, despite the fact that the Netherlands' industry had begun to decline.[3]

A third, more ephemeral factor in the rise of the linen industry was the short supply of cotton compared with that of flax in the mid-eighteenth century. The fortunes of cotton and flax were of course linked together, usually to the detriment of flax. For much of the eighteenth century, Lancashire manufacturers used flax yarns as warp in weaving union goods. In addition, under certain circumstances,

---

[1] *Sel. Ctte. Reps.* 1744 and 1751; Wilson, *op. cit.* pp. 56–7; Warden, *op. cit.* p. 665.
[2] *Sel. Ctte. Rep.* 1744. Glasgow had 1500 looms at that date.
[3] Wilson, *op. cit.* pp. 51–2, 57, 61–2.

all-linen goods could provide a close substitute for union cottons. Such a situation arose in the mid-eighteenth century. During the 1740's, when English cotton imports doubled, French, Dutch and Italian buyers entered the West Indian and Mediterranean markets, causing cotton prices to double.[1] For almost half a century, the demand for cotton rose faster than its supply, and this raised the demand for flax yarns and linen goods. In turn, linen prices rose, as for instance during the 1740's, when Irish prices went up by a fifth. But, for a generation, linen prices rose relatively less than cottons, and linen merchants managed to supplant cotton goods in some tropical markets.

The native linen industry had developed considerably by the third quarter of the eighteenth century.[2] The English domestic market consumed 80 million yards of cloth in 1756. Forty per cent of the supply was retained imports. Ireland and Scotland each provided 15 per cent. The remaining 30 per cent, some 26 million yards, was made in England, indicating an industry with about 10,000 looms. In 1773 Alexander Somerville valued the native flax crop at £300,000, equivalent to nearly 4000 tons of flax, enough to make 8 million yards of linen. The rest of the raw materials used by English workers came from abroad. From 1763 to 1771 imported yarn from the Continent *and* Ireland averaged 3000 tons a year, sufficient to make 17 million yards of cloth in England *and* Scotland. Flax imports of the order of 5000 tons or more would have been required to provide the balance of raw materials for current outputs.

Such dimensions are no more than a rough guide. But they illustrate both the relative importance of imported materials, and also the size of the English section of the United Kingdom industry, which John Horner claimed to be on a par with the Irish and Scottish sections by the mid-century. Indeed, at that time, the linen industry in the British Isles did not differ much in size from the cotton industry.

Growth was very rapid in the third quarter of the century. The weight of imported yarn, freed from import duty in 1757, doubled, especially after the duty on foreign linens was raised in 1767. Since

[1] *Sel. Ctte. Rep.* 1751, p. 291, Appendix III, p. 309.
[2] The following section is based on *Sel. Ctte. Reps.* 1744 and 1751; *Report from the Select Committee Relative to the State of the Linen Trade*, 1773, First Series, vol. III, pp. 99–133; Horner, *op. cit.* pp. 232, 238; Warden, *op. cit.* p. 370.

Irish yarn exports increased at the same time, it appears likely that the growing imports of continental yarns went to English and Scottish looms. (Yarn imports continued to increase until the last quarter of the century, when machine-spinning required the import of more flax. Only then did yarn imports fall—from 17,000 tons in 1771 to 1000 tons in 1830; and flax imports rose correspondingly—from 12,000 tons in 1787 to 50,000 tons by 1830.) Moreover, after 1750 the quantity of foreign linens imported declined whilst the amount re-exported remained constant. Assuming that domestic demand did not decline, this would give English weavers a larger share of the home market. Perhaps five-sixths of English output was by this time bought by fellow-countrymen.

England had a flourishing native linen industry by 1770. Despite its predominantly urban location, the recent growth of the industry saved it from gild organisation and control was in the hands of merchants, like J. J. Backhouse of Darlington who employed sixty weavers, or William Wilson who pioneered weaving and bleaching in Barnsley.[1] Such rapid expansion bred optimism, and this encouraged further growth.

In the last quarter of the eighteenth century this situation changed. Early in the 1770's there was a severe trading-recession followed by the revolt of the North American colonies. To offset their loss of trade, English linen-producers urged the government to raise tariffs on imports, a request that was not granted.[2] At the same time, the growth of the industry was beginning to affect its methods and location. A textile expansion based on higher productivity invariably disturbs the balance existing between spinning, weaving and finishing. It appears likely that when the flying shuttle increased a weaver's output and thus raised the already high ratio of spinners providing yarn, cotton and worsted manufacturers had some difficulty in finding the extra labour required. Indeed the flying shuttle could

---

[1] *Sel. Ctte. Rep.* 1773, p. 114; G. N. Clark, *The Wealth of England* (1946), p. 48; P. W. Matthews and A. W. Tuke, *History of Barclay's Bank* (1926), pp. 198 ff.; J. Burland, *William Wilson* (1860), pp. 7-40, *passim*; R. Jackson, *History of Barnsley* (1858), pp. 167 ff.; J. Wilkinson, *Families and Celebrities of Barnsley* (1833), p. 63; *Proceedings of the Geological Society of the West Riding of Yorkshire* (1859), pp. 580-3.
[2] *Sel. Ctte. Rep.* 1773, pp. 113-14.

only be fully exploited where extra yarn was forthcoming either from imports or by an increase in the number of native spinners, drawn perhaps from a wider area. What happened in the linen industry remains obscure: at Darlington and Knaresborough, merchants put out flax to domestic spinners farther afield, sometimes competing with cotton and worsted manufacturers in their search for labour. Concurrently, newer centres like Barnsley relied more on imported yarns, and this solution offered the best prospects for expansion. The disadvantage of 'putting-out' farther afield was not so much that it involved extra travelling, took more time and added to costs, because the marginal expenses involved in travel were not costed and consequently labour costs per bundle of output did not rise. The real shortcoming was that a weaving centre dependent on nearby rural spinners was more likely to be limited in the rate of its expansion.

More urgent and decisive in affecting the fortunes of the linen trade were the technical changes taking place in the cotton industry, whose growth had been held back partly by a limited supply of raw material and weak warp yarns. By the 1770's machinery was in operation which could spin this short, even and elastic fibre. Coarse yarns suitable for warp could be made on Arkwright's small multi-spindle frames, and the invention of the mule in the 1780's led to the production of fine yarns. Simultaneously, as plantations spread in central America, the supply of raw cotton increased. These changes affected linen interests in two ways. First, their customers had a substitute. Cotton manufacturers no longer wanted warp yarns, a loss felt mainly by spinners outside England. At the same time, cotton cloth routed linens in tropical markets and jeopardised the sales of some linens, chiefly foreign ones, at home. One merchant claimed that, at the light end of the trade, 'cotton goods are much used in place of cambrics, lawns and other expensive fabrics of linen'.[1] This was an ill omen. Later, when slavery flourished once again in the southern states of the U.S.A., cheap cottons imperilled linen production everywhere. Meantime, in the 1780's, though the sales of English linens were not immediately affected, the prospects of the industry were much less promising than they had been a generation

[1] D. Macpherson, *Annals of Commerce* (1805), vol. IV, p. 81, quoted in Horner, *op. cit.* p. 316.

earlier. Henceforth English linen producers would have to contend more with competition from native cottons than from foreign linens.

In the second place the swift expansion of the cotton industry, the increased output of goods at lower cost, and the fortunes made by such cotton manufacturers as Arkwright, were both an example and a challenge. By clinging to old methods, linen producers might last a little longer. By seeking new techniques, they could hope for riches; expansion, and ultimately survival, would depend on the manufacture of cheaper linen yarns.

This challenge was felt most in north-eastern England and Scotland. The growing cotton industry had a large appetite for productive resources, and mills in Lancashire, the Clyde and Lagan valleys employed women and children who had previously spun flax yarns at home. Linen producers did not offer such high wages as cotton manufacturers, whose labour cost per unit of output fell steeply with new methods. Accordingly the linen industry declined in Lancashire, north-east Ireland and western Scotland, a phenomenon duly noted by John Marshall on his early tours.

Since the cotton trade is introduced much less yarn is spun in the neighbourhood of Lisburn and Belfast....The cotton manufacture extends principally to the north of Carrickfergus, Coleraine, and some to Londonderry. It increases and will, in a few years, drive linen out of this neighbourhood...[and in the south-west of Scotland] the fine cotton and muslin manufacturers have nearly driven out linen from this side of the Island.[1]

Lanarkshire, which in 1727 produced 272,000 yards of linen cloth, more than a tenth of Scotland's output, made only 23,000 yards in 1822, less than 0·1 per cent of Scottish production.[2]

A response to these forces affecting the linen industry would not come from cotton towns like Belfast and Glasgow, nor from those districts in Ireland which still produced linens with cheap peasant labour. Those most sensitive to the expansion of linen production and the challenge of cotton, who discerned the probable direction of change and had the imagination and resources to bring it about, belonged to the weaving towns of eastern Britain.

Two lines of advance seemed feasible. Flax chemically treated

---

[1] Marshall, 'Tours' (Ireland, 1803); (Scotland, 1800 and Ireland, 1803).
[2] G. G. Bevan (ed.), *British Manufacturing Industries* (1876), p. 69.

could be made to resemble cotton. When flax was boiled in a saline solution, the gummy substance holding the small *ultimate* flax fibres together was neutralised and after that the fibres could be spun like cotton. But the effect was to halve the weight of flax, and turn 'good flax into bad cotton'.[1] Alternatively, existing cotton machinery could be adapted to spin a long, uneven, and inelastic fibre. This solution was pioneered in Darlington, where linen production had developed as a subsidiary industry during the eighteenth century about the time it waned farther inland at Barnard Castle. A linen merchant and banker in Darlington, James Backhouse, helped John Kendrew, a glass-grinder at the Low Mill, and Thomas Porthouse, a watchmaker, to register a patent in June 1787 for flax-spinning machinery. The equipment, comprising drawing frames with drums large enough to roll out long flax fibres and a spinning-frame with four spindles, was modelled on cotton machinery, which Kendrew knew about at first hand.[2]

Darlington, a town with only 4000 inhabitants, soon had a linen industry larger than that 'of any town in England'.[3] Spinning-mills on the river Skerne supplied some 500 weavers with yarns which formerly had been spun in the surrounding villages. 'Their yarns at the commencement were no better than those which were spun at the common hand-wheel; but they were produced at much greater abundance and at less expense.'[4] In the early 1790's weavers throughout Yorkshire and in Durham and Cumberland were using Darlington yarns.

Although Kendrew and Porthouse were the first to respond successfully to the challenge, they did not themselves benefit greatly. After a few years in partnership they separated; Kendrew had a mill at Houghton, and Porthouse one at Coatham. Neither became rich. The real beneficiary was a young man who in December 1787 sought their permission to copy the new patent machinery.

[1] Horner, *op. cit.* pp. 247–8.
[2] Warden, *op. cit.* pp. 690–2; *Gentleman's Magazine* (July 1787) cited in *Encyclopaedia Britannica* (1797) on flax; W. H. P. Longstaffe, *History and Antiquities of Darlington* (1854), p. 319; W. Fordyce, *History and Antiquities of the County Palatine of Durham*, vol. I, pp. 479 ff.; W. E. M., MSS., History of Darlington (n.d.) in Darlington Reference Library, pp. 8 ff. Both Darlington and Barnsley owed much of their development to Quaker families. [3] *Universal British Directory*, 2nd ed. (1790).
[4] Longstaffe, *op. cit.* p. 312.

9

(ii)

Towards the close of the sixteenth century the Aire valley in the West Riding of Yorkshire developed quickly. Villages became more thickly populated, the production of coarse woollen cloth increased, and Leeds, the market centre in the valley where cloth was exchanged and finished, doubled its population in the generation after 1580. When its merchants secured a royal charter of incorporation in 1625, the town had 6000 inhabitants.

The cloth traded in Leeds was made by rural clothiers dwelling in the Pennine foothills to the west of the town. In broad river valleys, families lived in scattered farmsteads and wrested a meagre living from the soil; but higher up the hillsides the soil swept by winds and rain yielded poor crops, and settlers there eked out a living by spinning and weaving wool. Typical of such villages was Yeadon, in the parish of Guiseley, seven miles from Leeds. At the edge of bleak moorland dwelt sixty families occupied as clothiers. Their small stone cottages, placed close together, formed a compact village without a church or overlord.

One family named Marshall multiplied rapidly in Yeadon during the seventeenth century, despite the waning prosperity of the local woollen trade. At the Restoration they occupied nine cottages and two substantial houses, and every year one of them would fill a common office in the township.[1] One Marshall household had in the early seventeenth century acquired a large dwelling, the Low Hall, situated in Nether Yeadon down the hillside. There, surrounded by the agricultural workers of Rawdon who lived in scattered farmsteads and labourers' cottages, they acquired the status of 'respectable country gentlemen'.[2] And in time, this branch of the family exer-

---

[1] Hearth Tax Return (Skyrack Wapentake), 1672, *Publications of the Thoresby Society*, vol. IV, pp. 29, 35; P. Slater, *History of the Ancient Parish of Guiseley* (1880), pp. 93, 184, 229, 265. MSS. Records of Yeadon Township; Overseers Accounts, 1753–1842; Minute Books, 1765–1857; Miscellaneous records, 1688–1752. (At the offices of the Aireborough Urban District Council, Rawdon.) See also Slater, *op. cit.* p. 184; and J. H. Palliser, *Rawdon and its History* (1914), pp. 19, 107.

[2] John Marshall, 'Sketch of his own Life', p. 4. (This 31-page document was 'extracted from the sketch of his own life', probably by his grandson S. A. Marshall, *c.* 1880.) See also Slater, *op. cit.* p. 184. The Low Hall was sold and re-bought by the family in the 1650's for £800.

cised considerable influence on the life of the valley. John Marshall (1661–1745) founded a village school in 1703. Nine years later he played a leading role in organising the first Baptist community in the West Riding.[1] A small meeting-house was built near the Low Hall which served the needs not only of the villagers but also of Baptists living as far off as Halifax, 10 miles away, dissenters who hitherto had been associated with a congregation in Lancashire. Through these institutions, the Marshalls and others contracted relationships which resulted in the families being spread over a wider area. The eldest son at the Low Hall, who inherited the family estate, usually married into a local gentry family. But his younger brothers and sisters together with their cousins in the village had no such prospects. Hitherto they had married the children of nearby villagers with the result that after a few generations many families were related in some degree to one another. Through the meeting-house and the commercial ties of parents, many Marshalls began to find partners farther afield, so that, by the later eighteenth century, the Low Hall family was related to a great many other households throughout the clothing district, all sharing in common their religion, sometimes their education, and often their interests in trade.

Both masters of the Low Hall in the first half of the eighteenth century were called John, and each had seven children. The second, who died in 1749 only five years after his father, had two sons and five daughters. The elder boy married the great-niece of Sir Walter Calverley, whose house and estates stretched along the far side of the river. The younger son, Jeremiah, was given £200 and sent to Leeds in the 1740's to serve an apprenticeship with Cloudsley and Stephenson, linen merchants, who were also dissenters.[2]

Jeremiah Marshall came to a boom town. Since the 1690's the

---

[1] Slater, *op. cit.* p. 248. The Rawdon meeting-house, of which John Marshall and Booth were trustees, began as an offshoot of the Rossendale Confederacy. By the mid-eighteenth century independent congregations had developed out of the Rawdon Chapel at Bradford and Halifax, and in 1779 at Leeds. (See *Baptist Quarterly Historical Society Transactions*, vol. VI, pp. 72 ff.) By implication, Baptists from all over the West Riding congregated at Rawdon early in the eighteenth century, and this interaction doubtless accounts for many connexions between families; and in the absence of a Baptist church in Leeds until 1779, members either had to journey to Rawdon or transfer to another denomination in the town.

[2] Marshall, 'Life', pp. 4–5; *Publications of the Harleian Society*, vol. XXXVII, p. 294. Cloudsley was a member of Mill Hill Chapel.

population of Leeds had grown from 6000 to 10,000.[1] The output of West Riding broadcloth, much of which passed through the town's markets and finishing shops, rose from under 30,000 pieces in the late 1720's to 60,000 pieces two decades later. By the new Aire Navigation, merchants shipped coal and woollens, and imported corn and raw materials. The built-up area of the town which covered 60 acres contained 2500 houses, those of the merchants dominating the skyline. Already the exclusive character of Newtown, the early seventeenth-century extension at the top of Briggate, was being compromised by the influx of newcomers, and merchants began to build westwards along Boar Lane towards the parks, erecting Trinity Church there in the 1720's. Though never a residence of gentry, Leeds with its markets, inns and shops, its assembly hall, library and local newspaper, had an air of provincial leadership.

For twenty years after the mid-1740's the expansion abated. Then began the tremendous growth that continued unchecked for nearly a century. In 1770 the town had 16,000 people: thirty years later twice as many. Physically, expansion took place on all sides. In the old inner wards, where no further space could be found for building, the subdivision of existing property was well advanced. In the outer wards, buildings went up rapidly; cottages for artisans spread east and north around the town, and middle-class squares were fashioned in the parks and hills to the north-west away from the bustle and noise of the port area. In 1770 Leeds had 3500 houses: by 1800, 6000. In the early 1770's, 100,000 pieces of broadcloth were milled yearly in the West Riding: a generation later the amount had trebled. Cheap coal from the Middleton Colliery encouraged such new industries as chemicals, potteries, glass-works and iron-founding. In 1771 the town consumed 28,000 tons of coal and a generation later something like 65,000 tons. Dye-houses sprang up along the

---

[1] The following paragraphs are based on Poor Rate Assessment Books for the Township of Leeds, 33 vols., 1713–1805; Apprentice Register of the Leeds Workhouse Committee, 1726–1809. (The above records are deposited in the Leeds City Archives.) See also the *Leeds Directory*, 1798; D. Defoe, *Tour through England and Wales* (1724–6), vol. II, pp. 204–8 (Everyman edition); H. Heaton, *The Yorkshire Woollen and Worsted Industries* (1920), p. 278; W. G. Rimmer, 'Middleton Colliery', *Yorkshire Bulletin*, vol. VII, pp. 41–57; F. Beckwith, 'The Population of Leeds during the Industrial Revolution', *Publications of the Thoresby Society*, vol. XLI, p. 177; Leeds Corporation Court Book, vol. III, 28 March 1793.

far bank of the Navigation; new trades emerged, printing, paper and machine-making; tanning and shoemaking became important, and the number of teamsters and shop assistants increased enormously as the town's commercial influence reached farther afield. The Corporation made no attempt to continue the gild organisation set up in the seventeenth century, and no obstacles were set before newcomers. Members of the Corporation, an oligarchy consisting of the principal merchant families and their satellites, were very prosperous and saw no reason to interfere in the town's development. Indeed they sometimes publicly deplored trading monopolies and regulations which touched their particular interests. Thus apart from a brief lull in the mid-century Leeds was one of those exhilarating towns full of opportunity and with visible signs of success, one where some men were, and others hoped to become, rich.

Having finished his apprenticeship and set up as a linen draper in Cloudsley's shop, Jeremiah Marshall sought a wife, and at the age of twenty-nine wed Mary Cowper of Guiseley, a great-niece of his grandmother. She was 'an agreeable young Lady with a handsome fortune' of £1200, and this enabled Marshall, who had earlier suffered a trading setback and been rescued by his former master, to open shop at No. 1 Briggate.[1]

At that time Leeds had few linen drapers and virtually no linen industry. Perhaps half-a-dozen merchants had warehouses in the town, some of whom finished linens woven elsewhere. Wilsons of Water Lane, founded in 1752, bleached and stiffened coarse Scottish linens which they sold over a growing area of northern England, especially Lancashire.[2] Marshall dealt in Irish linens. Both businesses prospered. Wilsons, who began with £600, accumulated assets worth £80,000 by 1806, two-fifths of which were held in stocks. Marshall, by 1787, was worth nearly £10,000. In the late 1770's he considered moving to new premises in the fashionable west end of the town, and when, at the age of fifty, he built one of the largest houses together with a warehouse in Mill Hill, Jeremiah

---

[1] *Leeds Intelligencer*, 2 September 1760; Marshall, 'Life', p. 5; John Wray MSS., Diary, vol. I, p. 167 (in Leeds Reference Library).

[2] Wilson and Sons, Linen Merchants, 1754–1832; and records of an anonymous linen merchant, 1773–1813. (These business records are deposited in Leeds City Archives.)

Marshall could look back on a successful business career.[1] He had a modest fortune, and a reputation for integrity and diligence. As a newcomer of little substance and a non-conformist, he did not gain acceptance amongst the town's merchant dynasties and their followers. But Marshall had many friends amongst dissenters, especially those neighbours whom he met at Priestley's chapel.[2] For Jeremiah Marshall, a Baptist of the old connexion, on finding no Baptist chapel in the town, had some time after his arrival in Leeds become a Unitarian like his master, joining a religious community that suited his new station in life.

Marshall's first two children, both boys, died in infancy. Then, in 1765, Jeremiah's wife had a third son, named John. Five years later the child fell ill after a smallpox vaccination and he was sent to a maternal aunt, Sarah Booth, in Rawdon. This relative, an 'elderly lady' of forty-three, had recently lost her only son at the age of twenty-one, and willingly undertook to look after her nephew.[3] For the next five years of his life, the child lived in Rawdon, meeting his aunts, uncles and cousins, attending the meeting-house (which had been rebuilt and enlarged), taking lessons from the minister, and attending the village 'Grammar School'. At eleven, he left to begin training with a view to becoming a merchant. First, he boarded eighteen months at Hipperholme School, two miles from Halifax, 'then a good classical school'. After an interval of eighteen months in Leeds, he went to Mr Astley in Derbyshire whose 'plan of instruction was well calculated for giving a taste for general knowledge and literature'. On his return to Leeds, John Marshall learnt French and merchants' accounts and, before he was seventeen, entered his father's business.

[1] Leeds Poor Rate Assessment Books, 1790, p. 31. Marshall's property in Mill Hill was assessed at £15 the house and £5 the warehouse. The dwelling was retained by Jeremiah's widow, and sold shortly after her death in 1799 to a Mr Carbutt.

[2] L. W. Schroeder, *Mill Hill Chapel, 1674–1924*, pp. 50 ff. William Wood, Priestley's successor, set out to foster the social life of his congregation during his long tenure. In the 1780's, young members had fortnightly lectures, in which Wood probably communicated something of his enthusiasm for natural science. In the 1790's Marshall's son attended scientific lectures in Leeds (see John Marshall, *Philosophical Lectures and Extracts*), and it seems likely that his interest in science was derived partly from the chapel, both from Wood and also the renown of the former pastor, Priestley.

[3] This and the following quotations are from Marshall, 'Life', pp. 1–3.

CHAPTER II

MAKING A FORTUNE, 1788–1815

(i)

At the age of thirty-two, John Marshall began an autobiography. 'I sit down this 18th day of September 1796 to write a sketch of my past life. My chief object is, by taking a connected view of past events, to form a better judgement of my future prospects, and to ascertain what propensities ought to be checked or encouraged.'[1] Believing as he did that worldly success depended not on a man's birth or connexions but on personal endeavour, he thought about his past from time to time to see what progress he was making. The key to a man's position was his character, the assortment of traits which each person made for himself as he passed through life. Success, according to this view, was due to the development of good qualities—perserverance, hard work, judgement. In Sir Peter Fairbairns's words:

> To rise in the world three qualifications are necessary: truthfulness, a sound judgement, and persevering industry.... Some may think they have no chance, that no opportunity of distinguishing themselves offers itself; but this I do not believe.... I can more readily believe that they have not sought opportunity, nor availed themselves of it when fortune has thrown it in their way.[2]

If a man failed, therefore, he had only himself to blame, and looking at the mass of mankind it was simple enough, if one considered them individually responsible, to attribute their condition to want of ambition, lethargy and ignorance. A prudent man felt obliged to pause, sort out the trends in his past, match them against his ambitions, and so measure his progress. For this reason, John Marshall took his bearings at three points during his life.

---

[1] Marshall, 'Life', p. 1. In this document, John Marshall stands out as the inner-directed character-type described by D. Riesman in *The Lonely Crowd* (1950). This offers a useful key to the understanding of Marshall. But it is necessary to go farther than this and observe him in a concrete environment.

[2] Sir Peter Fairbairn, *Useful Information for Engineers*, quoted by G. Meason, *The Official Illustrated Guide of the Great Northern Railway* (1861), p. 394.

Valuable as such a record is, it suffers from important limitations which should be made explicit. Looking back on his career and accounting for his achievement, Marshall prided himself on having a full complement of success-making qualities and the ability to seize opportunities that came his way. Such an explanation is unsatisfactory for two reasons.

In the first place, it limits itself to those events which Marshall considered important, and then gives only his view of them. To reassure himself about the progress he was making, Marshall could not do otherwise than view his actions in a favourable light. To have admitted that he realised his ambitions by superior wile and craftiness would have tarnished his character. As a result, whenever he came into conflict with others, he presented his opponents as either ignorant, wicked or presuming. Throughout the autobiography, virtue brings its own reward. Marshall could not have explained his achievement in any other way, and this view of his success certainly satisfied his contemporaries who believed in simple, personal causes. But early nineteenth-century business folklore is too shallow an explanation of what happened, and even sympathetic Victorians were sometimes critical. One editor, writing Marshall's obituary, had some reservations: 'He carried on business in an era more favourable perhaps than the present for accumulating wealth.... Still, no doubt his great success was attributable mainly, if not entirely, to the energies of his personal character.'[1] Moreover the abilities conducive to success emphasised by Marshall, such as perseverance and judgement, describe activities which without further qualification could be morally either good or bad. A man who amassed wealth on such a scale was bound to be subject to criticism, much of it relating to the methods he used. Marshall was undoubtedly a domineering man, one who used other people like puppets, casting them aside as soon as they had outlived their usefulness. The *Leeds Intelligencer* accused him of using 'fair or unfair' means to accomplish his ends.[2] He was not above intrigue, spying on his competitors, exploiting his accumulated powers to crush whoever threatened what he conceived to be his own interests at any particular time. However much he

[1] *Leeds Times*, 14 June 1845.
[2] *Leeds Intelligencer*, 17 July 1828.

welcomed competition in public, he never allowed others to exploit opportunities near his own concerns. Watt saw one aspect when he described Marshall as 'an arrant Jesuit', and Alaric Watts later used the same epithet.[1] On the other hand, surrounded by his family, Marshall could appear 'so gentle, so mild, and with so much genuine feeling, simplicity and good sense'.[2] Marshall's supporters and critics naturally described different facets and chose different words; and the autobiography was written by a convinced admirer.

In the second place, even if it is read literally, the autobiography does not account for the magnitude of Marshall's achievement as 'one of the most remarkable instances, even in this commercial county, of *men who have risen* by their own talents, perseverance and enterprise from moderate circumstances'.[3] There was, of course, no reason why it should explain the degree of Marshall's success. In referring to the qualities which helped him the author was not trying to explain why he was more successful than others. The only division that he and others like him made was the one between success and failure.

The importance of this record both on account of its factual content (which is not always accurate) and for the insight it gives into Marshall's motivations and reactions in certain situations far outweighs these limitations. And in the wider context of the relation between a businessman and his environment it shows how a mill-owner, crystallising the experience he derived from this new form of production, began formulating something approaching a social philosophy. In addition it sheds some light on the social changes taking place during the industrialisation of a mercantile town. In the society of a provincial town the new factory-owners were in many instances outsiders on account of their origins, religious affiliations, place of birth or simply the status attached to their particular occupation. In Leeds, which had been a corporate town for five generations,

---

[1] James Watt, jr., quoted in W. B. Crump, 'The Leeds Woollen Industry', *Publications of the Thoresby Society*, vol. XXXII, p. 189; *Leeds Intelligencer*, 17 July 1828.

[2] Letter from Dorothy Wordsworth to Jane Marshall, 10 September (1800), quoted in E. de Selincourt (ed.), *The Early Letters of William and Dorothy Wordsworth, 1787–1805* (1935), p. 252.

[3] R. V. Taylor, *Leeds Worthies* (1865), p. 412. See also H. R. Fox Bourne, *English Merchants* (1866), vol. II, pp. 226 ff.

even rich dissenting families, like that of Armitage, had no place within the merchant oligarchy which formed the social *élite* of the town. A small group, perhaps a score of families, drawn together by a common interest in the woollen-cloth trade and related by inter-marriage, had run the town for over a century in furtherance of their own interests, exploiting the power both of their individual businesses and that conferred on them by membership of the Corporation.[1] This clique was the effective ruling-class in a town that numbered around 6000 families, and they stamped certain activities with approval and withheld their sanction from others. A nonconformist —who would probably be a shopkeeper, a tradesman or a small merchant—a stranger, a man who followed a calling not connected with the woollen trade, was suspect as long as the oligarchy's authority prevailed until he had established his respectability to their satisfaction; and even then, his disabilities of birth or religion usually barred him from inclusion in the ruling-class, however wealthy he became. Towards the persons of the town's leading merchant families, an out-sider had to show polite deference and conduct himself with a wary eye, unless he was prepared to accept the consequences of disrespect.

When late in the eighteenth century established woollen merchants saw outsiders like Marshall or the Benyons or Humble or Bowers or Armitage (a long list could be made) amass wealth quickly, they were inclined to attribute such gain less to simple virtues of character than to sharp practices and risky undertakings.[2] The newcomers were seldom respectable townsfolk of good character in the eyes of the town's established families; and in this situation the rising genera-tion of mill-owners, particularly those who, unlike Benjamin Gott, were outside the oligarchy, strove to accomplish two things. First, they had to establish their characters; explain their rise as the result of commendable business activity, and protect their integrity. In the second place, at some point in their rise they had to invest in respect-

[1] For the seventeenth-century Borough Charters, see J. Wardell, *The Antiquities of the Borough of Leeds* (1853). For reference to Dissent in Leeds, see the bibliography in Leeds City Archives compiled by H. Taylor. These aspects of the town's development will be dealt with in my forthcoming study on Leeds.

[2] Letters of James Watt, jr., to M. R. Boulton, reproduced in E. Kilburn-Scott (ed.), *Matthew Murray* (1928), Appendix B, pp. 33–43. These letters, written shortly after the expiry of the Watt patent show a man opposing newcomers with the sanction of established authority.

ability, buy a large house, entertain, become local benefactors, perhaps take a discreet part in politics. In this way they would anchor themselves socially in the town either by coming to terms with the existing society where this was possible or by developing their own social hierarchy. Apart from the social standing it conferred, a *rapprochement* with the town's *élite*, or the establishment of their own groups, was a sound business investment for the newcomers. Acceptance meant that their character was endorsed either by the town's ruling-class or by a socially coherent section of townsfolk; either gave a rising mill-owner wider sanction for what he did. Once established, he could proclaim his views on success and at the same time exploit his newly acquired support to further his own business ends against competitors. In each town both the old and the new thus interacted and often changed to accommodate one another; the old endorsed the new values; the new imitated the old and even shared in many existing social arrangements.

Marshall rightly judged himself to be an ambitious and capable man. In every situation he saw how to advance his own interests and that was his immediate objective. Not that he behaved rationally; on the contrary, he sometimes acted compulsively, but always in pursuit of his declared goals. Unlike his mother, he showed little consideration for others. 'She seemed to enter intuitively into the feelings of the person with whom she had intercourse, and justly to appreciate their talents and dispositions. This faculty arose in great measure from the minute and unremitted attention she paid to the feelings and happiness of all around her.'[1] Marshall could no more spare the time for this than for gaming and assemblies. He had so much to accomplish in this span of life. Even when a rich man, he preferred work to the companionship of people. When at Westminster he wrote : 'I should rather wish for employment than not, when I do attend Parliament.'[2] And when he found time could be spared from business he used it in improving activities.

The improvement of land by draining and fencing and the increase of its value by planting have been useful objects of pursuit and continue to be both a satisfactory and pleasant occupation of my time. The study

---

[1] Marshall, 'Life', p. 12. [2] *Ibid.* p. 28.

of Political Economy, and the moral improvement of society have always been my favourable pursuits.... The time occupied by troublesome office is well repaid by the insight which it gives into human character and motives of action.[1]

Likewise reading and walking were 'pleasurable excitements to the mind' and body.

To some extent, Marshall was temperamentally too reserved to enjoy the company of others and his domineering manner daunted them. Apart from Peter Garforth, a Shipley cotton-spinner, and David Wood, a machine-maker, he made no enduring friendships. It was not of course easy for a man who climbed so rapidly to make lasting associations. At the same time, Marshall's well-known quiet shyness could be a useful mask. Never altogether sure of his place or how to conduct himself in situations where his authority did not reach, he escaped from his inability to make polite conversation and he avoided *faux pas* by cultivating this reserve; and, of course, silence saved him from committing himself on many issues, thus making it easier to gain acceptance in new social circles.

As a youth he wanted to become famous and rich, both regressive goals never quite reached in life. Equipped with the qualities conducive to success—ambition, perseverance, judgement (needless to say the emphasis changes according to the time and place)—he journeyed through the years gathering riches, power and self-confidence. This was his manifest destiny and he would not be distracted from it. *En route*, he imagined himself like Christian, beset by temptations and obstacles to be overcome, and each victory sped him on his way. But the Puritan warp in Marshall's writing is interlaced with Utilitarian weft. Outsiders by birth and religion were rising in society and enjoying the fruits to which their wealth entitled them. Marshall was no exception and sought to buy the best in life. Such indulgence not sanctioned by a self-denying ethic, he soon justified by a calculus of pain and pleasure.

It is true that I have gone through an uncommon share of labour and pain, but it has not been altogether unattended with pleasure; and I had an active mind which would have been miserable in idleness, and which courted

---

[1] Marshall, 'Life,' pp. 30–31.

difficulties for the pleasure of overcoming them. I have undergone a discipline which will enable me to bear the common accidents of life with fortitude and will give a higher relish to the pleasures of prosperity.[1]

Later in life, he turned intellectually as well as socially towards the Benthamite circle in London, acquiring the reputation in Leeds of being a 'political economist'. And to his sons he bequeathed a philosophy which allowed them to be insensitive to the condition of others and which brought no reassurance when economic and social changes threatened their position.

Looking back at the start of the journey in order to account for his achievement, Marshall visualised himself above the average run of boys. Early experience, he decided, set him apart from other children and endowed him with a strong character and intense sense of purpose. He remembered how frail and how ill he had been until at seventeen 'the swellings in my neck... were at length entirely removed by drinking Thorparch waters'.[2] He remembered how he suffered acute loneliness, 'the deep dejection of spirits I have sometimes felt on returning to my solitude [in Rawdon] after a visit to Leeds where I had young companions'.[3] These instances he singled out as examples of obstacles overcome, as victories of his youth. Far from causing him distress, separation, illness and solitude provided opportunities to strengthen his character. He scorned the pursuits of playmates who idled away their time; 'having scarcely an associate of my own age I contracted a strong degree of social gravity, & rather a distaste for the active amusements of boys which have never entirely worn away'.[4] Confined to mixing with adults, he found satisfaction in their company, and naturally felt a close attachment to his aunt,

...a woman of uncommon strength of understanding, correct judgement and most benevolent heart. I am indebted to her for a great part of whatever is good in my character, and never was there a stronger mutual attachment between two persons of such different ages.... She made a companion of me though a child. We read everything together, which gave an interest to our books and gave me a thirst after improvement and knowledge, which in a young mind is so essential to future usefulness.[5]

[1] *Ibid.* pp. 9–10. [2] *Ibid.* p. 3.
[3] *Ibid.* p. 2. [4] *Ibid.* p. 2.
[5] *Ibid.* p. 2.

Thus Marshall visualised himself as having been a quiet, aloof, serious-minded boy, gifted with talent and propelled by ambition.

He recalled how at his entry into the family business at seventeen he had enjoyed himself. There was much to learn; in 1784 his father let him supervise the erection of the new premises at Mill Hill, and in 1785 business took him to Ireland. But, after a few years, this enthusiasm waned. He chafed at the dull routine and at the prospect of remaining a draper for the rest of his days. 'Had I been content to go on in the beaten track which my Father had marked out for me, I might have passed through life in a quiet regular way.'[1] The drapery trade 'might have satisfied a moderate man', like his father, who had 'always lived plentifully and hospitably' but who was 'not eminent for abilities or mental acquirements'. Like Mr Astley, the school-teacher, Jeremiah Marshall was in his son's eyes 'a very amiable man...not a man of much learning or strength of understanding'.[2] They were both ordinary people without the ambition and ability to become great. John Marshall wanted to achieve more in his own lifetime. 'I longed for an employment where there was a field for exertion and improvement, where difficulties were to be encountered and distinction and riches to be obtained by overcoming them.'[3] To judge from his father's experience the career of a Leeds draper promised no such reward. Of course, Jeremiah was merely 'average'; his 'integrity and diligence in business could not fail to increase his property'.[4] Even as a linen draper, John Marshall would have wanted to do better. But he saw more exciting, quicker ways to get on in life. Across the Pennines, men were making fortunes in new mills.

Early in December 1787 Jeremiah Marshall, who had 'scarcely suffered from any illness', died suddenly from a stroke.[5] He was fifty-seven. His material possessions comprised the new house and warehouse, and £7500 in the business; in all, an estate worth £9000. John Marshall's prospects and plans changed overnight. From being a draper's assistant he became, at twenty-two, controlling partner in the family business, and had surplus resources to use as he saw fit.

---

[1] Marshall, 'Life', p. 5. Cf. Fox Bourne, *op. cit.* vol. II, p. 226.
[2] Marshall, 'Life', pp. 5, 4, 3.   [3] *Ibid.* p. 5.
[4] *Ibid.* pp. 4–5. See Wilson, *op. cit.* pp. 56–7.
[5] Marshall, 'Life', p. 4.

'My father left no will, and my mother and I made no division of the property, which with the profits of the trade produced above a thousand pounds a year.'[1] With household expenses amounting to only £500 a year, John Marshall had an annual windfall of £500. This he subsequently regarded as a turning-point in his career; his father's death set him free and also provided the means for him to pursue his ambitions at a very propitious moment.

Marshall had no hesitation about what to do. Six months earlier Kendrew and Porthouse had taken out a patent for spinning flax by machinery. Marshall decided to try it out. He knew something about the trade, and he saw what was possible for a man of enterprise. He had resources to spare, and as a sensible businessman ventured them in a way that he expected to pay.

My attention was accidently turned to spinning of flax by machinery, it being a thing much wished for by the linen manufacturers. The immense profits which had been made by cotton spinning had attracted general attention to mechanical improvements and it might be hoped that flax spinning, if practicable, would be equally advantageous. It would be a new business, where there would be few competitors, and was much wanted for the linen manufacture of this country.[2]

Success—and, despite his ignorance of machinery, he felt sure that he would succeed at once—would bring a fortune and renown. 'Nor was it with the mere desire of getting money, that I entered into more hazardous schemes, but with the ambition of distinguishing myself.'[3] Should he fail—he never confessed to such weakness—he would have squandered his surplus and had the drapery trade to fall back upon. He stood to gain, but not to lose.

[1] *Ibid*. p. 5. On a fragment of paper, written in the hand of John Marshall, is the following statement:

I began to spin flax 1788. My father left	8,000
Mrs Booth	3,000
Profit of linen trade	3,000
	14,000
Lived on Int. of Capital. 1802 in 14 Years	14,000
	28,000

Marshall's net effects according to his private ledger were £26,451 on 4 January 1802. However the point here is that Mrs Booth, his aunt, appears to have loaned or bequeathed £3000 to John Marshall which he used for his initial venture. There is no confirmation of this fact elsewhere, and it suggests that Marshall's early losses were larger than the first ledger entries indicate.

[2] *Ibid*. pp. 5–6.   [3] *Ibid*. p. 5.

A few weeks after his father died, this young man, full of enthusiasm and eager to refresh himself in action, hastened to Darlington to inspect the patent machines.[1]

In order to follow Marshall's initial progress as a spinner, it will be useful to have some idea of the situation confronting him. Mule spinning in the 1780's enabled cotton manufacturers to produce fine yarns and this adversely affected the trade in light linens. However, the chief losers were continental weavers who lost ground in the English domestic market. There was no imminent danger that the demand for coarse and medium linens would collapse. Consequently the first objective of a machine flax-spinner in the late 1780's was to displace the coarse yarns made by hand-spinners, not to compete in price with cotton yarns.

Hand-spinners could be displaced in two ways. Any restriction in the supply of hand-spun yarns left the market open to mill-spinners. The spread of cotton production in Ireland and the wartime dislocation of European trade had this effect. Closer to the situation of the late 1780's was a second possibility, that mill-spinners would make cheaper yarns of equal quality.

Using machines to produce cheaper yarn does not seem a difficult feat. But technically it was at the time far from simple. Mill-spinners made little headway before 1800 and they did not triumph finally until the 1830's.[2] On his side the hand-spinner initially had two advantages over mill-spinners. By hand, a spinner could make yarns of any weight. Machines could spin only heavy yarns, about 5 leas, at the start. This severely restricted the market for machine yarns and a long time elapsed before medium and fine yarns could be made by machines. Second, hand-spinners were part-time workers. Their families had other means of subsistence. Consequently a hand-spinner's labour could be secured for a few pence per day. On the

---

[1] Jeremiah Marshall died in December 1787, and before 5 January 1788, when John Marshall leased a mill, he had been to Darlington.

[2] This partly explains why many writers date the effective mill-spinning of flax from the 1820's. See *Leeds Mercury*, 23 July 1836, or Greenwood on flax machinery in the *Proceedings of the Institute of Mechanical Engineers* (1865), pt. 1. After the mid-1820's all except the finest hand-spinners (making upwards of 400 leas) were driven out of the trade and mechanisation spread rapidly in the traditional linen districts of continental Europe.

other hand, townsfolk who worked in mills had no subsidiary occupation and needed a subsistence wage, around 6s. a week for a young woman. In addition, mills had elaborate machines which cost much more than the manual implements of a cottager. Cheap labour and equipment are not, of course, absolute advantages. More important than the level of wages is the cost of labour per unit of output, and the whole aim of machinery was to raise labour productivity. But that took time. To begin with, machine-spinners had high labour and capital costs compared to hand-spinners and they found it very difficult to price hand-spinners out of and gain a foothold in the heavy end of the market.[1]

The real problem of an early spinner was to stay in business until he could press home his potential superiority. He had to develop techniques which could be used to commercial advantage. Machine-spinners would in time achieve higher production ratios. Where a hand-spinner using a distaff or wheel made only a single length of thread, a mill operative tending frames might make ten, a hundred, even a thousand lengths in the same time. Machine-spinners would also devise machines to supplant other manual operations such as hackling, roughing and carding, and eventually they would design a system of continuous production, feeding fibres direct from one machine to the next. Such changes would raise productivity and number the days of hand-spinning. Also on a technical plane, machine-spinners would find ways of making lighter yarns, at first by improved methods of preparing and ultimately by a new way of spinning. They would use cheaper flax than hand-spinners to make yarns of equal quality, and an important step forward was made once mill-spinners began

---

[1] As Marshall and Co. used hand-looms, costing 35s. to 50s. each in 1794, the main test of relative costs lay in spinning. The average cost of a mechanical spindle at Marshalls in 1793 was 15s. to 25s.; in addition, a carding engine cost £30 and a roving frame £40. To this must be added the expense of prime movers and fabric. By contrast, a hand-spinner could buy a wheel for a few pounds. Cf. Horner, *op. cit.* pp. 251–3, cites a memorandum of Joseph Nicholson on Ireland, where in 1811 hand-spun yarn cost less than English mill-yarn. Comparing these labour-costs with those at Marshalls in the same year, the latter were slightly lower, owing of course to much higher productivity; but once fixed costs and preparatory costs are added, Irish hand-spun yarn made by women earning 2d. to 5d. a day was cheaper. See also Horner, *op. cit.* p. 253, on the importance of quality of flax used. Unfortunately there appears to be no adequate series for a useful comparison between hand- and mill-spun prices in the 1790's, a decade of rising flax prices.

to use Baltic flax, which cost about half as much as the native crops used by west-European hand-spinners. They also found ways of spinning tow, small lengths of fibre generated during the scutching and milling processes; just how important this would be can be judged from the fact that over half the flax used in linen production was turned into tow. Eventually, all these things were possible. But so far as the pioneer mill-spinner was concerned they were objectives and his survival depended on attaining them.

This is merely one aspect of the situation confronting a pioneer. There were other problems—raising money, organising production in a mill, keeping accounts, and so on. But a basic problem was to displace hand-spun yarns, and without protective tariffs the outcome remained unsettled for a generation despite a long period of war.

Marshall asked Samuel Fenton, a junior partner in the drapery business, to join him in the new venture. Fenton, a distant cousin and a co-religionist, had entered the firm in 1785 at the age of twenty-four, soon after the move to Mill Hill, investing £2000 in return for a quarter share of profits. He was a young man and, on the understanding that he looked after the drapery trade, raised no objections to Marshall's project. A third person, Ralph Dearlove, a Knaresborough linen merchant, also entered the scheme, advancing £700 in return for a fifteenth share. With £500 a year of his own, Dearlove's £700 and, as a last resort, the drapery business, Marshall started as a flax-spinner.

In January 1788 the partners leased from James Whitely, a Leeds dyer, 'a New Erected Water Mill called Scotland Mill together with two closes of land situate in the Parish of Addle to the North of Leeds'.[1] They hired the premises for thirty-three years at an annual rent of £109, inserting an escape clause which allowed them to quit after three years. The mill stood in an isolated spot, 5 miles from the

[1] The 'Opinion of Mr Thomas Fenton' of Lincoln's Inn, 21 March 1790. Thomas Fenton was Marshall's partner's brother, 'an attorney well skilled in all the nefarious practices of his profession', according to J. Watt, jr. (Kilburn-Scott, *op. cit.* p. 40). Marshall sought advice on a tenant's right regarding fixtures when quitting Scotland Mill. (The interests of the Fenton family in Leeds extended to coal, sheep, linen and glass in the mid-eighteenth century and a generation later spread to South Yorkshire. Many were Unitarians attending Mill Hill Chapel.) See Hunter's *Familiae Minorum Gentium*, vol. I, p. 289, *Publications of the Harleian Society*, vol. XXXVII.

town and not within easy reach of a road. At first sight the two-storey building and its outhouses might have been taken for a moorland farm. But closer inspection would have revealed water-wheels, one dipping into Meanwood Beck, the other fed by a goit inside the mill, and a new building, one end used for a machine shop, the other as a stable. Early in 1788 Marshall, Fenton and Company, directed by John Marshall, began to spin flax yarns.

Their success depended entirely on the performance of the Darlington machinery which Marshall had secured permission to use in return for royalties. After the flax had been cleaned and hackled by hand, a spreader laid it on the apron of a drawing frame and the fibres passed through reducing rollers into a can. After repeating this process several times, the flax formed a uniform band or sliver and passed on to the spinning frames.[1] The results were anything but impressive. The drawing frames could not reduce tow, and only heavy (5–7 lea) line yarns could be spun. Breakages frequently occurred and the yarn came out lumpy and hairy. More expensive flax was used than a hand-spinner needed for a similar yarn, and there was little economy in labour. Apart from drawing and spinning, the other processes remained manual; and the fibre passed from one machine to another in cans which were carried by hand. Like many others, Marshall found that he had acquired the right to use unpromising machinery. He would in normal times find it impossible to compete with hand-spun yarns in local markets.

By June 1788 Marshall realised that he had to improve the Darlington machinery. Since he could at least produce line yarns he concentrated on trying to spin tow, and in the next five months made seventeen experiments with that aim in view.[2] At first he tried modifying the Darlington machinery. He altered the distance between the rollers of the drawing frame, inserted carding rollers, and twisted the sliver to prevent the short fibres slipping and patching, only to find that he could not draw them out. Later he concentrated on carding and set up a model comprising a carding engine, drawing and spinning frames. This produced better results but he

[1] See Horner, *op. cit.* pp. 248–51, for the details of the process.

[2] The following sections are based on John Marshall's 'Experiment' books: vol. I: 'Spinning', June 1788–July 1790; vol. II: 'Spinning', July 1790–June 1801; vol. III: 'Spinning', August 1803–23; 'Bleaching', October 1788–January 1803.

ran into difficulties over the width of the cards. When, on 11 September, he tried the tow machinery in the mill, it proved unsuccessful. A month later Marshall used a hackle to draw out *shorts*, fibres 12 in. to 16 in. long 'into a sliver like worsted...it drew rather better but still the ends of the fiber did not hand forward from one roller to another but frequently fell down'.[1] At this point, he concluded that 'flax will not spin with rollers the common way because the fiber will not stick together so much as to hand forward from one roller to another especially at such distances as the length of the fiber requires them to be.... It will be spun best from a sliver drawn from the heckle in the same manner as worsted if that be practicable.... It will not draw after it has got much if any twine.'[2]

Marshall's first attempt to spin tow and shorts ended in failure and eight months passed without further experiments, during which time he spun poor-quality line yarn on the Darlington plan. In June 1789, when he resumed experimenting, Marshall sought to improve his line yarns. In the Darlington frame, the sliver passed over a damp cloth just before spinning on the flyer. Marshall now replaced the cloth by a pair of rollers which wet and slightly drew the sliver. Consequently 'the sliver was made evener and smoother, the rough thick places being drawn out'.[3] Unfortunately the new method had a disadvantage. Once half full, the reeling bobbins pulled the sliver forcefully through the new rollers, causing the yarn to break. At this juncture, mid-July 1789, Marshall returned to Darlington only to find that as little progress had been made there. He tried to card line at Porthouse's mill but failed to doff the sliver: 'the greatest difficulty seems to be to get the sliver to leave the teeth of the cards clear'.[4] Back at Scotland Mill, he laid out line by drawing it through a hackle. 'It answered the purpose of clearing the yarn from those knots which the card cylinder produces—but it could not be drawn from the heckle sufficiently even, nor to an even length, and sometimes a small bunch of fibers slipped through....'[5] Again without achieving any practical improvements, Marshall concluded this group of experiments

[1] Marshall, 'Experiments', vol. I, October 11.
[2] *Ibid.*
[3] *Ibid.* Memorandum, June 1789.
[4] *Ibid.* 25 July 1789.
[5] *Ibid.* 12 August 1789.

uncertain whether to hackle by hand or whether to use a carding engine.

There appears to be no chance of spinning line without having previously obtained a regular disposition of the fibers so that there may be a regular succession of ends and not too many come forward at a time. The card cylinder in the manner we use it has the desired effect as to the disposition of the fibers, but it has a very great fault in producing an infinite number of knots upon the line and likewise breaking the fibers which makes bad yarn and appears to be the chief cause of the great number of breakages in spinning.[1]

During these early years Marshall was learning a great deal about the properties of flax and the possibilities of machinery. But, working by rule of thumb, he often failed to connect cause and effect. As a result Marshall and his assistants took a long time discovering by trial and error what seems in retrospect to be the obvious next step. Sometimes they neared a solution only to find the machinery which had been designed too expensive or too complicated to operate. For they had one measure by which to judge their efforts, namely making yarns that were an immediate commercial proposition. At the end of nearly two years, however, Marshall had made no significant advance in either spinning tow or preparing line.

In the autumn of 1789 Marshall surprisingly records a series of weaving experiments. Having made little headway with spinning, he transferred his hopes to a power loom. Edmund Cartwright had taken out four power-loom patents between 1785 and 1788, and in 1787 he set up a factory at Doncaster with twenty looms, including one for weaving coarse linens.[2] In December 1788 Marshall installed four looms at Scotland Mill. 'Found them very liable to be out of order which was in part owing to the badness of the workmanship.' His weavers each produced 'in general only abt. 3 pieces week'.[3] Preoccupied with spinning improvements, Marshall did nothing to rectify the shortcomings of the looms until September 1789, when 'we gave over spinning and set Matt Murray to work on a new loom'.[4]

---

[1] *Ibid.*

[2] P. Mantoux, *The Industrial Revolution in the Eighteenth Century* (1928), p. 247; J. Burnley, *The History of Wool and Woolcombing* (1889), pp. 111–12.

[3] Marshall, 'Experiments', vol. 1, December 1788. I would like to thank Mr D. C. Snowdon of Leeds University for advice about these experiments.

[4] *Ibid.*

This is the first reference to Matthew Murray, the young metal-smith of Stockton-on-Tees who migrated to Leeds. It is not possible to say when he found employment at Scotland Mill and began to influence Marshall's experiments.[1] Probably Murray came late in 1788, and had a voice in affairs several months later. There can be no doubt, however, that many of the experiments recorded by Marshall after September 1789 (until 1794) were inspired and conducted by 'Matthew' who was responsible for the main inventions of the period. On this particular occasion, Murray made no progress. From the description of the protector motion, it seems that he simply copied Cartwright's patent of 1 August 1787 (no. 1616); and by December 1789 he gave up, defeated, so that the firm used only hand-looms for the next twenty-five years.

Marshall had been at Scotland Mill for two years spinning heavy line yarns. Sometimes he came near to spinning tow and improving the quality of line yarn, but he never quite succeeded. Nor was he consoled by the fact that other spinners had made no more progress; indeed, he would have seized any invention that met his needs. Soon he would have to decide how much longer he could afford to persevere without more definite promise of success, and more particularly whether he intended to quit the mill at the end of three years' tenancy. Meantime, he resumed his efforts to make better line and spin tow.

New experiments began where the previous ones left off, and on this occasion Marshall had Murray who could see what went wrong and devise progressive modifications. They started in January 1790 carding long tow, but 'could not get an even sliver'. On 6 February, they used a hackle roller once more:

The heckle seemed to be large enough for that length of fiber but the rollers had not twine enough to pull it out of the teeth of the heckle and it frequently went round with the heckle...Matthew proposed...to move the fluted roller in the usual way and cut a part of it away so that the twine from the roving spindle might pass the roller and get hold of the ends of the fibers that were drawing, then the roller would draw them out taking hold of the ends that were twined together, which would answer the same end as twining and drawing at the same time....[2]

[1] R. V. Taylor, *op. cit.* pp. 298 ff.; Kilburn-Scott, *op. cit.* pp. 7–8; *Dictionary of National Biography* (1894), vol. XXXIX, p. 398. Stockton, near Darlington, was amongst the towns which pioneered the use of flax-spinning machinery.

[2] Marshall, 'Experiments', vol. I, 8 February 1790, no. 2.

Three days later, they 'tried a fluted roller with one side cut away', but it 'did not answer'.[1] So Murray placed the hackle roller

in a right line between the feeding and drawing rollers....It [the sliver] came very well off the heckle roller, and drawing and twisting by hand produced a perfect roving, it therefore appeared certain that the principle of it would answer—and the fault of the drawing roller seemed to be solely its running forward over the twined part and swallowing up the twine....[2]

At last they appeared to be making some progress, and Murray next inserted a wire 'rising up at the point of drawing...to push the sliver out of the teeth of the heckle'.[3] Realising that they were making progress, Marshall immediately widened the scope of their experiments to include spinning as well as preparing, thereby hoping to secure improvements all along the line. 'Sent Murray into Cheshire to enquire into their mode of spinning worsted', a fibre about 16 in. long, quite similar in length to long tow.[4] But Murray 'could not get into their mills' and from hearsay decided that the Cheshire method was not suitable. So Marshall proposed a new spinning frame 'upon the old plan of twisting and drawing at the same time'.[5] This done, they found that the yarn 'seldom broke, and when it did it was owing to a soft twined place in the roving which went round with the card'.[6]

Up to this point Marshall had been experimenting with tow. Towards the end of March he applied the new system to line yarns where each fibre is about 2 ft. long. Within ten days Murray produced the machines that he was to patent in June 1790.[7] In this set of experiments, two important alterations were introduced. First 'Matthew proposed to draw the sliver thro' 2 revolvg. sheets of

[1] *Ibid.* 11 February 1790, no. 3.
[2] *Ibid.*
[3] *Ibid.* 20 February 1790, no. 3.
[4] *Ibid.*
[5] *Ibid.*
[6] *Ibid.* 12 March 1790, no. 4.
[7] Patent no. 1752, 1 June 1790. For a description of this machinery see Horner, *op. cit.* pp. 254–6. I would like to thank Dr P. P. Townend of Leeds University for helping to confirm the fact that the experiments recorded by Marshall foreshadow this patent.

leather instead of the Card, because the sliver has so great a tendency to go round with the card...',[1] and second,

Made a drawing frame with the delivering rollers working at right angles to the drawing rollers which had the effect of perfectly contracting the sliver without doubling back any of the ends of fibers which any sort of fixed contractors will unavoidably do....It does not seem necessary to twine and draw at the same time in the preparing frames because it may be drawn perfectly without twine—and it might be spun the same way with the rollers at right angles.[2]

With this machinery a spinner had better fibre-control. He could reduce flax to a more uniform sliver and spin slightly lighter yarns. Thanks to Murray, Marshall had taken an important step forward and he now decided to begin manufacturing on a larger scale.

The problem outstanding at this time was tow-spinning and in June 1790 Marshall returned to this task. The difficulty lay in doffing the carded sliver: 'We never yet could get a sliver from the cards either tolerably even or that would hold together to hand up to the rollers of the drawing frame.'[3] They made several carding-machines in the next six months, but met with so little success that, in January 1791, Marshall wrote: 'The above expert[s] fully convinced us that tow...cannot possibly be taken off the cards in a level sliver, and the fibers straight.'[4] Then, unexpectedly, they designed a satisfactory carding-machine.

We then set the fillet Cylr. to doff the main swift the same way as the main swift doffs the trimmer, we took away the fancy roller and placed the working roller upon the fillet Cylr. which roller was doffed by the main swift....This plan answered every end we wished, the sliver was level and without patches, the fibers were taken off straight, and we thought it was carded as well as possible.[5]

With the technical bottlenecks broken Marshall ended his experiments for the time-being and turned instead to the task of organising a larger output.

It had taken Marshall three years, much longer than he had expected, to solve the minimum number of technical problems

---

[1] Marshall, 'Experiments', vol. I, 25 March 1790, no. 6.
[2] *Ibid.* 5 April 1790, no. 9.
[3] *Ibid.* June 1790, no. 13.
[4] *Ibid.* vol. II, January 1791, no. 30, p. 24.
[5] *Ibid.* p. 25.

necessary for survival. Although he pinned his future on new methods of production, he inherited a merchant's attitude to machinery as something subsidiary to the main task of buying, selling and making a profit. He had acquired the Darlington system confident that it would spin good yarn and, when it failed, Marshall ventured into activities for which he had neither training nor aptitude. The technical objectives stood out clearly enough: but Marshall failed to get the results he wanted. The answers were provided by Murray, although they might just as well have come from inventors elsewhere. This does not mean that Marshall played a passive role in the process of invention. He collected and ventured the resources in the first instance. He had the idea and the faith, and persevered until a way was found. In 1790 he earned his reward with Murray's patent, an invention which made his survival as a spinner highly probable.

When Marshall saw Murray's experimental machines he decided to terminate the lease at Scotland Mill in 1791 and move nearer to Leeds. In May 1790 he paid William Naylor, a Leeds merchant, £600 for just over an acre of freehold land in Water Lane. This site, although it lay in open country mid-way between Holbeck and the township of Leeds half a mile to the east, was expensive because it was in an area of potential development. Except for residential suburbs on the north-east fringes of the township, the physical growth of Leeds in the eighteenth century took place around the port area and east along the north bank of the Navigation.[1] (With only one bridge across the river at the bottom of Briggate, little development took place at any distance along the south bank.) Then in the 1770's work commenced on a canal running west to Liverpool, and the land in the valley west of the town suddenly acquired commercial importance. Marshall was one of the first manufacturers to buy a site in this district. On the south boundary of his land flowed Hol Beck and immediately beyond was Water Lane; north, less than a hundred yards away, was the canal already navigable to

---

[1] The following paragraphs are based on Beckwith, *op. cit.* p. 177; *1801 Census of Population*; Rimmer, *op. cit.* pp. 46, 50; *The Watson Papers*, North of England Institute of Mining and Mechanical Engineers; Leeds Quarter Sessions Order Books, 11 January 1790, pp. 102–5 and 29 July 1793, pp. 160–1; T. Bradley, *Old Coaching Days in Yorkshire* (1889), pp. 136–237; *1798 Leeds Directory*; *A Plan of Leeds*, by Netlam and Giles, 1815.

Skipton, and beyond the river Aire at Bean Ings, Benjamin Gott began to build a woollen mill in 1792.

The Water Lane site had distinct advantages over Scotland Mill. Only a few hundred people lived in the farming district of Adel, and Marshall would have had to recruit labour from farther afield. Then he would have found it necessary to provide accommodation near the mill, and in time he would have been faced with problems raised by the age and sex distributions of a mill village. By contrast, Holbeck had a population of 6000 and Leeds of 30,000. Male hand-loom weavers dwelt in the villages nearby, and their women-folk together with a rapidly growing local male population wanted work. So labour rarely presented a problem at Water Lane. At Water Lane, moreover, the firm was at the hub of a transport system the equal of any then in existence. Continental flax came to Leeds along the Aire Navigation, the terminus of which was half a mile away; and once the Liverpool canal was completed, Irish flax came by water almost to Marshall's warehouse. Goods sent overland were taken by carriers who provided a rapidly expanding service for the town after 1770. In addition, at Water Lane, Marshall had easier access to the town's banks, dyers, iron-founders and machine-makers, all businesses of recent origin; and, since the site lay beyond the town-ship boundary, the firm escaped the poor-rate prevailing in Leeds. Finally, coal could be bought much more cheaply in Leeds. At the Staithe, a quarter of a mile away, Middleton Colliery sold coal for 58d. a ton. Out at Adel, borings in the 1770's at Black Moor yielded negative results, and coal carted from Leeds Staithe to Scotland Mill would have doubled in price according to the tariff laid down by the Quarter Sessions. Moving close to Leeds reduced several costs and forestalled difficulties that would have arisen in the country.

Marshall's first task at Water Lane was to build and equip a mill as quickly as possible in order to make the most out of Murray's invention. By September 1791 a four-storey building—Mill *A*, as it was later called—had been erected.[1] Though small by later standards,

---

[1] See the plan on page 35. I am indebted to Professor A. W. Skempton of Imperial College, London, for having this plan drawn on the basis of an illustrated auction catalogue annotated by S. A. Marshall in 1886. For John Marshall's attitude towards steam power, see the letter of Marshall and Fenton, 25 February 1789, in Portfolio 89, *Boulton and Watt Collection*, Birmingham Public Library.

it was much larger than Scotland Mill. It covered an area 50 yards long by 15 yards wide and provided about 9000 sq. ft. for plant. Believing that steam did not produce a drive smooth enough for spinning flax, Marshall persisted in using water power. An atmospheric engine housed in a building at the east end of the mill raised

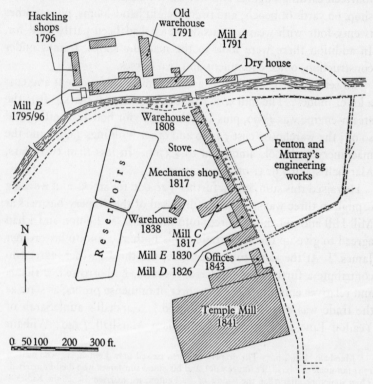

Fig. 1. Diagram of Marshall's mills in Water Lane, Leeds.

water which on its fall turned a wheel. However, in a matter of months, Marshall changed his mind and in March 1792 began negotiating for a 20 horse-power Boulton and Watt steam-engine which William Murdock installed the following September.[1]

---

[1] *Ibid.* Marshall and Fenton letters, May–August 1792. S. A. Marshall later recorded some facts about the installation of the first engine: '5 September 1792, paid Mr. Murdoch for completing the engine £2–2–0...15 September '92 Paid men for supper engine completed, £7–18–0.'

Several other buildings went up before the end of 1792; a large flax warehouse, a counting house, stables, a dry house, shops for smiths and joiners, and several cottages. The mill yard was paved and walled around. Inside the mill, there were by April 1793 fourteen spinning frames (one of which came from Adel) carrying 832 spindles; fourteen carding engines and five drawing frames; in the hackler's shop, 60 yards of bench; and twenty-eight hand-looms, plus another twenty-four with weavers outside which had been partly paid for. In addition there were tools in the machine shops, frames under construction, office equipment and two horses.

To set up on this scale was a considerable achievement and cost a lot of money. The mill cost £1600 (about 2s. 2d. per sq. ft.); the steam-engine was £800, plus a further £200 for boilers, shafting and so on; the warehouse cost £1440 and other buildings £993; and the machinery and tools amounted to £3709. In less than two years, Marshall spent £9241 on fixed capital.

He raised this sum, plus a further £10,000 for stocks and working capital, in three ways. First, he disposed of the drapery business at Mill Hill and put the resources into the mill. 'S. Fenton and I had agreed to give up the linen trade to his Father...and to his brother James.'[1] At the same time, Dearlove, the third partner, agreed to contribute a further sum of £210. Second, he borrowed. Friends and relatives enticed by the 'prospect of immense profits, as soon as the trade was established' lent £5000.[2] Marshall's aunt Sarah of Yeadon Low Hall sent £100; William Marshall £140; William

[1] Marshall, 'Life', p. 7. The drapery business passed to S. Fenton, sr., who died in 1794 (an uncle of Marshall's future wife), and his eldest son James who died unmarried. Then sometime after 1806 the widow of S. Fenton, jr., married Benjamin Sadler—the brother of Michael Sadler—who came from Derbyshire, and the business continued as Fenton, Sadler and Co. See R. V. Taylor, *op. cit.* p. 359; and *Publications of the Harleian Society*, vol. XXXVII, p. 289.

[2] Marshall, 'Life', pp. 6-7. The following information is derived from Ledger no. 1; Leeds Poor Rate Assessment Books, *op. cit. passim*, 1790's; *Leeds Directory* 1798; Papers relating to the descendants of Edward Armitage of Farnley Hall (in the Yorkshire Archaeological Society). There are two further points of interest with regard to these loans: (1) despite the fact that three water-driven woollen mills were built in Rawdon during the 1790's, the Marshall and Booth families took no part in those ventures, instead supporting John Marshall in flax-spinning; and (2) a striking feature of the loans made by friends and co-religionists was the number of women lenders. Wealthy widows, aunts, or spinsters in Leeds and Rawdon were in this instance a very useful source for initial capital.

Pollard, a distant relative and merchant of Halifax, sent £400. On this and on later occasions his relatives, whose means came from the woollen industry or farming, never failed when asked to provide small sums of money. Other loans, each of a few hundred pounds, came from neighbours in Mill Hill—John Simpson, Ann Johnson and Miss Smith. The largest loan of all came from James Armitage of Carr Hall, Hunslet, head of a wealthy local family of merchant clothiers who were also ardent nonconformists, mostly Baptists. He granted Marshall a mortgage for £2500 at 4¾ per cent and later added a bond for £750 at the usual 5 per cent. Marshall's third source of capital was the bank of Beckett and Co., whose founder had recently come from a Barnsley Quaker family of linen bleachers.[1] In April 1793 Marshall, Fenton and Co. had an overdraft of £3783, which helped considerably to finance the purchase of flax. Thus Marshall encountered no great difficulty in securing risk capital. Resources and institutions were at hand able to finance the scale of operations at which he aimed. His only problem was to persuade those who knew him to part with their money when he wanted it.

Having built a mill and equipped it, Marshall next had to spin and sell yarns as well as weave and sell cloth. Unfortunately there is very little indication of the firm's performance at this time. On the whole the early 1790's were good years for trade, and Marshall quickly stepped up the production of yarn and cloth. In April 1791, at the time of moving, the firm made two grades of cloth, and only eleven pieces in that particular month. The following April, they made six grades and 255 pieces. Early in 1793 they were producing between 6000 and 7000 pieces a year. More important than weaving was the manufacture of sale yarns. Early in 1793 the firm used flax, cheap Königsberg flax, at the rate of 230 tons a year; 85 tons eventually became cloth for sale; the remaining 150 tons went on to the market as 10,500 bundles of line or tow yarn. With this scale of operations, employing over 200 hands at the mill and weavers outside, Marshall, Fenton and Co. seemed well on the way to success.

No doubt Marshall found this aspect of their progress reassuring. But there was another factor to consider. In the year ending March

[1] See Wilkinson, *op. cit.* pp. 36–86, for the Beckett family, and especially pp. 72–3 for the origin of the Bank.

1792 the firm spent over £10,000 and derived only £1500 from sales. This explains not only Marshall's haste to raise a mortgage and to dispose of the drapery business at that particular time, but also a debit entry in his ledger for a 'supposed loss...£2000'. Marshall understood that they would have a tight period until production got under way and brought returns, the profits of which would finance the expansion. His partners read the situation differently, however, and arrived at another conclusion.

At the end of 1792 Fenton and Dearlove had been associated with the venture for five years. Between them, they had given Marshall about £3000. So far they had not received a penny profit, and at times they feared that they would lose their capital. The Darlington machinery had not proved a good investment. Two years had now passed since Murray's patent and Marshall still wanted more money, offering nothing in return except more promises. Fenton could raise no more: Dearlove had no desire to involve himself any further. The conduct of the concern pointed to the fact that Marshall was a headstrong, inexperienced young man with no special aptitude for business. Relatively heavy stocks of warp and flax suggested either over-investment or failure to sell as much as he had hoped. Neither explanation brought reassurance. Dearlove began to withdraw his assets from the business and Fenton sought to rejoin the drapery business which had passed to his father. Then in March 1792 Marshall surprised his partners unpleasantly, when without drawing up a balance he debited the firm with this 'supposed loss...£2000' and in due course charged Dearlove £143. This confirmed the partners' doubts that the business was mismanaged and unprofitable.

The sudden and arbitrary declaration of loss in 1792 shows Marshall's business acumen. To pay for his schemes he had to persuade others to dig into their pockets, and he was not yet in a position to countenance any withdrawals. By announcing a heavy loss, Marshall tried to frighten his partners into either raising more capital or (what is more likely) separating from him, thus leaving him free to find new partners who had money. If Fenton and Dearlove could not raise funds, if their enthusiasm had waned, it would serve Marshall's interests best if they left—if possible, without their capital.

Relations between the partners reached a climax during the commercial crisis early in 1793. The outbreak of war with France placed Marshall in a difficult position.

The sudden shock that was given to mercantile credit brought us to a stand....We had a large stock of flax, the payments for which were becoming due, our book accounts were of small amount, and in the entire stagnation of trade which ensued, we could neither sell our goods nor obtain payments. Our Bankers called on us to reduce our account which we were unable to do and equally so to provide cash for the workmen. At first my spirits sunk under my situation, and I shall never forget the remorse which I felt, at thinking of the hazardous situation into which I had brought my Mother, who had entrusted me with her all.[1]

To find out how they stood, he made a list of the firm's assets and liabilities for the first time and, in April, struck a balance. The results, in a summary form, appear below:

Assets	£	*Liabilities*	£
Land, fabric and plant	7,937	Bank overdraft	3,783
Stock of metal, wood, machines in progress	1,214	Loans	5,517
Stock of Russian flax	7,734	Trading debts due to creditors	5,915
Stock of yarn and cloth	2,926	Partners share capital	10,149
Outstanding debtors	2,320		
Cash in hand	191		
	£22,322		£25,364

From this reckoning the firm's deficit amounted to £3042. Characteristically, Marshall later exaggerated the loss when he wrote 'at the valuation we then fixed our loss was above £8000'.[2] However, the size of the deficiency matters less than its impact on the partnership and on Marshall himself.

In the first place the crisis gave Marshall an opportunity to bring the partnership to a close. He shared out the loss: £287 to Dearlove, £426 to Marshall, Fenton and Co., and took the rest himself. This wiped out his partners' investments, and in Fenton's case 'all he was

[1] Marshall, 'Life', pp. 6–7.
[2] *Ibid.* pp. 7–8. On several occasions, Marshall's recollection of events differs from his ledger entries. But this is the sole instance of such a large discrepancy. The above version of the balance-sheet shows the position *before* the sale of flax at Hull; and Marshall's alleged loss 'above £8000' may represent a cumulative total since January 1788.

worth'. Marshall could exploit them no further and so they separated. 'As they could neither of them be of any further use, I released them from the concern and took the whole upon myself.'[1]

In the second place, so far as Marshall himself was concerned the crisis served as a warning. Retrospectively he considered it the second turning-point in his career. The situation stunned him because he had not been prepared for it; and being unprepared implied that he had not run the concern in a businesslike manner. 'We were aware of the great sums we had spent'; and had been ready to wait for 'immense profits'.[2] Suddenly, the firm seemed to be on the rocks. 'If the concern had been broken up and the Mill and machinery sold, I must have lost all I had, and probably there would not have been enough to pay my creditors.'[3]

At a later date Marshall naturally depicted the situation as more perilous than it really was. In fact, he had little difficulty in surmounting the liquidity crisis. After selling flax lying at Hull (at a loss of £500), he 'paid some of [his] most pressing creditors'.[4] At the same time he laid off many workers and reduced output. Then, in the general settlement that followed, his share of the loss came to £2727, and this left him nearly £7000 plus outstanding loans to carry on the business. To return to full capacity production again he needed more money and turned once more to relatives and friends. 'I borrowed £1200 from Mr Garforth upon the security of my house in Mill Hill.'[5] Over £700 came from neighbours who went to Mill Hill Unitarian Chapel and others who lived close by, like Joseph Wright and Abraham Rhodes. And the same amount came from relatives in Rawdon, together with a sum of £50 from the Baptist meeting-house there.[6] Thus the commercial crisis of April 1793 did not seriously jeopardise Marshall's business.

[1] Marshall, 'Life', p. 8. [2] *Ibid.* pp. 6–7.
[3] *Ibid.* p. 7. [4] *Ibid.* pp. 7–8.
[5] *Ibid.* p. 8. 'He was of great use to me by his advice and encouragement.' Peter Garforth, both father and son, were closely associated with John Marshall. In 1785, Peter Garforth, sr., a Wesleyan miller at Skipton, had in conjunction with John Blackburn and William Sedgewick leased a mill for cotton-spinning at Skipton; see W. H. Dawson, *History of Skipton* (1882), p. 280. Peter Garforth, jr., joined Marshall in 1800 in establishing Edward Baines as editor of the *Leeds Mercury*; see Edward Baines, jr., *Life of Edward Baines* (1859), pp 39–41.
[6] Investors were identified on the basis of the sources cited in note 2, p. 36 above. The loans at 5 per cent were repaid within a decade.

He exaggerated its severity simply because it caught him unawares. Two years later he could congratulate himself on his escape and point out how useful the experience had been: 'I have reason to think that the breaking out of the war at that time, the most fortunate event that could have happened for me. If we had not received some such check, we should have gone on thoughtlessly with a ruinous expense, which we should probably have been unable to retrieve.'[1] The real shock at that time lay not so much in the loss of a few thousand pounds but in the damage to Marshall's self-esteem. His description of the way in which he reacted to the situation confirms this. 'I set my shoulder to the wheel in good earnest. I was at the Mill from six in the morning to nine at night, and minutely attended to every part of the manufactory.'[2] As if it had been a religious conversion, this episode was a watershed in his life. He remembered how his father had faced and overcome a similar situation. He looked back on the period before 1793 as a time of floundering and mismanagement. His reputation for probity, integrity, and enterprise had been at stake, and he nearly became the laughing-stock of the town, a headstrong young upstart who tried to become rich overnight by venturing into a new type of business which he failed to conduct in a sound manner. But having escaped such humiliation, Marshall believed more strongly than ever in his capabilities.

Once he had warded off his creditors, Marshall had good reason to feel optimistic. Yarn imports dropped sharply owing to deflationary forces at home but it seemed likely that, once demand recovered, the war would restrict yarn imports from the Continent.[3] This would provide machine-spinners with a golden opportunity, and Marshall lost no time preparing for it. He had borrowed in order to run the plant at full capacity, and now in order to expand further he needed more money than family or friends could provide, especially as he was mortgaged up to the hilt. So he sought new partners.

The new associates would have to be men who could pay a high price. Marshall reckoned that the business had excellent commercial

[1] Marshall, 'Life', p. 8.   [2] *Ibid.*
[3] A. D. Gayer, W. W. Rostow and A. J. Schwartz, *The Growth and Fluctuation of the British Economy* (1953), vol. I, pp. 27 ff.; for yarn imports at Hull, see John Marshall's 'Notebook', *c.* 1790–1830, p. 54.

prospects and, technically, Murray had been making small, worth-while improvements. Nearly a third of the spindles made heavy tow yarns and the mill spun line yarns up to 12 leas. This represented a considerable step forward, particularly since, on arriving at Water Lane, Marshall had suffered a temporary setback. The carding engine which he expected to prepare tow slivers proved disappointing. In September 1791 he wrote: 'In our new Engines...we found that after some weeks working we could not card the tow...so as to spin at all.'[1] This was a serious blow and he immediately made a deter-mined effort to solve this fundamental problem. In October a new carding engine was made which 'answered extremely well. It was very well speeded and carded the tow very well....We found no fault with it but that the wheels of the fillet Cylr. made a great noise.'[2] However, as soon as they began to produce tow yarns, they encoun-tered difficulties in drawing; 'the yarn was very full of patches which was caused by the tow being too much drawn...whether it is that the long fibers are drawn and the short ones not...or from what cause we cannot tell, but the fact is certain'.[3] Three months later, in January 1792, they solved this problem by taking the carded slivers direct to the roving frame 'and not going through the Draw-ing frame at all'.[4] At long last, Marshall spun tow yarns and began to install carding engines and tow frames.

For a year they did not progress beyond this point. In May 1792, Marshall made a new carding engine to produce a first sliver of line. 'If the waste be not too great it will certainly be preferable to any hand spreading.'[5] He fed the machine with 'coarse 12 head Petg. undrest flax...to spin it to a thread of 7 or 8 leas in the pound to do for canvas warps, as, if it would answer, there would be a prodigious saving in using it instead of shorts as it costs about 31s. per cwt, and shorts 51s.'[6] Despite the fact that the results were disappointing, Marshall persisted in carding line to produce a sliver. However, he was far from satisfied with the method for he realised that carding

[1] Marshall, 'Experiments', vol. II, September 1791, no. 32, p. 29.
[2] *Ibid.* vol. II, October 1791, no. 33, pp. 30–2.
[3] *Ibid.* October 1791, no. 34, p. 32.
[4] *Ibid.* January 1792, no. 37, pp. 34–5.
[5] *Ibid.* May 1792, no. 39, pp. 37–9.
[6] *Ibid.* May 1792, no. 40, pp. 39–40.

'cannot split the fibers like a heckle but breaks them short and makes them chiefly into Tow'.[1] In the autumn of 1792 they applied card clothing to the drawing rollers, for they were 'more convinced than ever that flax could not be drawn even...with rollers...we again recurred to our old idea of drawing by cards'.[2] This experiment failed, although they 'were still satisfied that the principle was a good one. A card seems the only contrivance that can draw a substance of unequal length to perfection.'[3] And when an elaborate drawing frame with six pairs of rollers failed, he concluded that 'fibers of irregular lengths could only be drawn by some kind of points'.[4] Yet in this they consistently failed, and Marshall reconciled himself to this fact in December when he wrote 'this experiment appeared to us decisive that flax cannot be drawn by cards or points in a sufficient quantity at a time to make a perpetual sliver'.[5] Nearly thirty years passed before he discovered gill frames.[6]

In 1793 Marshall no longer sought to improve the line-preparing frames. Instead he spun better yarns as a result of two other modifications. In May he reverted to the Darlington method of spreading a sliver of line on a board by hand. 'It made full as good a sliver as the Carding Engine and quite as free from patches and seemed to waste and injure the line less, but took more time as a girl cannot spread more than 20lbs per Day and a Cardg. Eng: with 2 spreaders and 1 Doffer does 1 cwt....Spreading on a board is certainly better for fine line.'[7] Also copying the methods of Darlington's spinners 'who are said to spin very well', he put a twist in the sliver making

[1] *Ibid.* vol. ii, June 1792, no. 40, p. 42.

[2] *Ibid.* October 1792, no. 41, p. 43. He refers here to flax suitable for line yarn.

[3] *Ibid.* October 1792, no. 41, p. 47.

[4] *Ibid.* November 1792, no. 42, p. 50.

[5] *Ibid.* December 1792, no. 43, pp. 51–2. At this point, Marshall made a detailed comparison between cotton, wool, silk and flax fibres, indicating the peculiar problems confronting a spinner of each fibre. For instance, preparing was the main problem facing woollen and flax-spinners; Marshall, 'Experiments', vol. ii, pp. 52–7.

[6] Horner, *op. cit.* pp. 259–61. The first patent registered for a gill frame was in 1795. See below, chapter iii.

[7] Marshall, 'Experiments', vol. ii, May 1793, no. 44, p. 58. As a result of reverting to the Darlington plan, Marshall had to defend a suit for non-payment of royalties to Kendrew and Porthouse. This was settled out of court for £500, but it moved the Corporation of Leeds to seek Parliamentary annulment of a patent so 'prejudicial to the millowners and trade of Leeds', and Benjamin Gott presented the petition. See *Leeds Corporation Court Books*, vol. iii, 1773–1835, p. 106, 12 April 1794.

a roving 'which confines the fibers from coming irregularly forwards', and 'altered the spinn^g. Box to a draw of 18 instead of 9. It spun better and made better yarn from the same flax.'[1] Then in August he 'tried to wet the yarn on a new plan. We made the front roller of the Spinning Frame of Brass and wet the top Roller by a Spunge... supplied with water...from a trough placed behind'.[2] The important point was to get 'an exact degree of moisture—too much or too little spoils it'. When they succeeded in regulating the moisture exactly, it 'had the desired effect of making the yarn smooth and strong, and saved about half the breakages—a roving spun wet breaking 12 times a day when a dry one broke 25 times'.[3] Thus by hand-spreading, twisting, finer drawing and damping, Marshall could spin smooth line yarns up to 10 or 12 leas by the autumn of 1793.

At this point, in December 1793, Marshall persuaded Murray to take out a second patent which included a carding engine and a wetting sponge for the spinning frame.[4] On the strength of this patent, Marshall enticed two of his customers, Thomas and Benjamin Benyon, Shrewsbury woollen merchants, to join him in partnership. They were to advance £9000, 'a capital equal to mine', in return for a half-share of the profits.[5]

(ii)

Between 1793 and 1800 Marshall's business grew rapidly. In the four years before 1798, fixed capital at Water Lane—fabric, machines and tools—rose in value by more than £20,000. In 1796 the partners established a new plant a hundred miles away on which they spent £17,000 in buildings and equipment before 1800. Despite the fact that money measures incorporate the effect of rising prices, an investment of £37,000 in fixed capital and over £30,000 in stocks within six years was no mean achievement. With the plant capacity

---

[1] Marshall, 'Experiments', vol. II, May 1793, no. 44, p. 59.

[2] *Ibid.* vol. II, August 1793, no. 46, p. 61.

[3] *Ibid.*

[4] Patent 1971, 18 December 1793. In his 'Life', p. 8, Marshall wrote that after the crisis 'Matthew Murray exerted his talents and made some great improvements'.

[5] Marshall, 'Life', pp. 8–9. The agreement with Benyons was signed on 16 December 1793, and they eventually invested, from outside sources, £17,000 at Water Lane and Castle Foregate, *ibid.* p. 4. For the Benyons' backgrounds, see below, chapter II, section (iii).

built up in these years, John Marshall would shortly become a very wealthy man.

Work on a larger second mill at Water Lane began early in 1794, soon after Marshall had found new partners. Four-to-five acres of land were bought from David Rider for £2300, on which Marshall paid a deposit of £1300. About half the land joined the mill *A* site to the west; the other two acres were directly opposite on the south side of Water Lane, a convenient nearby place for future expansion. When complete mill *B* (as it was named) had five storeys and a total floor area of 29,000 sq. ft., between two and three times the size of mill *A*. In June 1794 Marshall ordered a 28 horse-power steam-engine from Boulton and Watt for delivery in the New Year but it arrived in April, four months late, and mill *B* did not start spinning until September 1795.[1] At the end of the year, 1200 spindles were already at work in the new mill.

Early in the morning of 13 February 1796, five months after completion, mill *B* was totally destroyed by 'the most dreadful fire we ever remember to have happened in this country'.[2] The blaze began in the dry house or store and swept through the hackling shops and mill. A wall collapsed, killing seven and injuring twenty workers. And the damage was so extensive that a London paper reported the firm as a total loss, a view which the *Leeds Intelligencer* expeditiously corrected: 'The Mill which was burnt down was only partly filled with machinery. Their old mill which was full of machinery and the flax warehouse escaped any damage.'[3] Marshall assessed the damage at £10,000, half of which was covered by insurance; and the rest could easily be raised from current profits which ran at a high level between 1794 and 1796. Rebuilding started immediately. In this respect, the fire did not lead to a critical situation. Nevertheless it was a severe setback for, although it came at a time when the partners could afford such a loss, it coincided with a buoyant market for machine yarns. Marshall tried to fulfil his orders and maintain a

[1] Marshall and Benyons–Boulton and Watt, October 1794–March 1795. They state on 4 April, 'Our engine has now arrived', and commenced to pay their premium on 18 September 1795.

[2] *Leeds Intelligencer*, 15 February 1796.

[3] *Ibid.* 22 February 1796. See also Selincourt, *op. cit.* pp. 146–52. These letters of Dorothy Wordsworth suggest two fires occurring within a few months.

high level of output by transferring the hands from the burnt-out mill to mill *A* where they worked through the night, the sole occasion when the firm ran a two-shift system around the clock. And by protesting to Boulton and Watt that his new engine 'has stood still about six months', Marshall persuaded them to waive the premium.[1] On 11 July, four months after the fire, mill *B* stood rebuilt and ready for occupation, and by the end of the year it had 1800 spindles at work. At the same time the hackling shops and dry house were replaced, and two new buildings—a smith's shop and a yarn warehouse—were put up in the yard. Also in 1796, the firm set up its own bleach-yard at Wortley, a few miles away. At this point the expansion stopped; no further building of importance took place at Water Lane until 1806. The only significant addition to the fabric and fixtures was a new 30 horse-power Murray engine in 1799, bought to provide the extra power wanted for 500 more spindles. In four years (1794–8) Marshall and Benyons had spent £7543 on fabric extensions at Water Lane.

During the same period the cost of new machines and equipment came to £13,329. The largest item and the best single measure of expansion was the expenditure of £6504 on spindles. In December 1793 the firm had 832 spindles; in January 1798, 3964. However, the real change in spindleage was more than the difference between these figures. Only twelve frames, all made in 1793, survived to 1798. Those made earlier were scrapped and 113 new frames were installed. The older frames carried between forty-eight and sixty-four spindles and in 1794 they were modified to incorporate Murray's sponge patent. The new frames carried only thirty spindles, each one of which averaged twice the cost of a pre-1793 spindle. By 1798 mill *B* had been filled with plant and the expansion eased off, except for 500 extra spindles which were installed when Murray delivered the new steam-engine.

The money to pay for this expansion came from two sources; the Benyon brothers and current profits. Marshall's partners provided £3888 in December 1793, and nearly £4000 when they sold their woollen business in 1794. Beyond these sums, fresh capital came

[1] Marshall and Benyons–Boulton and Watt, 27 August 1796, 7 October 1796; Marshall, 'Life', p. 9.

from profits. Between December 1793 and July 1804 the profits declared at Water Lane totalled £70,899. In addition to his share of this sum, each partner received 5 per cent interest (charged as a cost of production) on the value of his capital. No partner drew heavily on his earnings, and consequently their share capital increased rapidly. Marshall withdrew an average yearly sum of £1800 between 1795 and 1802, a figure swollen by two large withdrawals in 1795–6 when he married and moved to a house in Meadow Lane, a few minutes' walk from the mills.[1] Over the same period the Benyon brothers took out between them £1500 a year (excluding a special transfer of £7448 to a mill in Shrewsbury in 1800). In all, the partners withdrew about a third and left two-thirds of their earnings in the business. Thus the pace of expansion was governed largely by the rate of profits. For instance, between 1794 and 1797, profit per spindle was high and the partners' savings went into new plant and fabric. When the rate of profit fell, they curtailed physical expansion at Water Lane, and their savings (which continued to accumulate) went into stocks for the enlarged plant. From 1794 to 1798 investment in fixed capital was two and a half times greater than investment in stocks; between 1798 and 1803 stocks rose by £15,000 and fixed capital by £12,000. The business was now independent of external sources of capital for growth: in future, the firm generated its own capital for expansion and, for the next fifty years, Marshall and Co. had no difficulty in finding capital. Instead, a new problem arose: a high level of earnings and a low level of withdrawals resulted in over-capitalisation, and the burden of interest charges—paid at the rate of 5 per cent on invested capital—grew to such an extent that it became necessary for the partners to find outlets outside the business for their savings.

Running at full capacity, the Water Lane mills made 100,000 bundles of yarn a year by 1800. Over half of this output was sold to weavers, about five times the quantity sold in 1793. In the early 1790's Marshalls had supplied heavy line yarns to local weavers in Knaresborough and more especially in Barnsley where linen production grew rapidly. Developing out of that situation, there were

[1] Marshall, 'Life', p. 11. See p. 68 below.

three ways in which the firm could increase its sales. It could sell heavy yarn to weavers farther afield; it could increase its sales of heavy yarn in local markets, which would not be difficult as the linen trade expanded; and it could make lighter yarns and displace more hand-spinners, which would be the most profitable course of expansion. All these tendencies, the widening and deepening of markets, were apparent by 1800.

On his travels, Marshall kept his eyes open for new markets. In 1800 he noticed that Cumberland check-weavers 'get nearly half the yarn spun in the neighbourhood and make out with Scotch, Irish hanks and Hambro' yarn.... They can work our yarn without starch-ing it, which may probably introduce it.'[1] Sometimes he looked a long way ahead. Thread-makers in the Lake District used 30–35 lea yarns and Marshall, who could not yet spin such fine counts, observed 'we might have a good demand for these sizes'.[2] In Scotland, the firm sold yarns to the growing linen industry around Dundee, and Marshall found a small Glasgow mill selling 'line up to 16 leas...at Dundee 10 per cent below our prices'.[3] Of course, the farther afield Marshalls sold their yarns, the more they could expect to meet com-petition. But this prospect did not seriously concern Marshall for by 1800 the firm had begun to edge into the market for medium yarns, and expansion north of the border did not impinge on their interests. 'There have been no attempts lately [in Scotland] to spin small— The Scotch mills in general do not spin smaller than our 16 lea— I do not find that any of them are increasing much or making much profit by it.'[4] By 1804 the firm spun line yarns ranging from 12 to 20 leas, and tow from 3 to 12 leas. Six years earlier Marshall had spun 30 lea line experimentally although he had not yet turned it into a commercial proposition.

The production of lighter line yarns was a real achievement. Not only could the firm penetrate more deeply into local markets, but its margins widened once production costs fell by perhaps a third owing to flax being stretched twice as far as it had been ten years earlier. Making these yarns was not the outcome of any new method.

---

[1] Marshall, 'Tours' (1800 Cumberland and Scotland), *c.* 15 September.
[2] *Ibid. c.* 15 September.
[3] *Ibid. c.* 30 September at Glasgow.
[4] *Ibid. c.* 30 September at Glasgow.

The techniques and machines employed were known in 1793, and from that time Marshall made fewer experiments, especially after Murray left in 1795 to join James Fenton and David Wood as machine-makers.[1] Between 1788 and 1794 Marshall averaged eight spinning experiments a year: from 1795 to 1823 the number fell to two. For a brief period, 1801–3, he intensified his efforts, trying to follow up steps which he had outlined four years earlier. But on this occasion he burst into activity partly because of the advances he noticed in other mills and partly to secure a tactical advantage over his partners. He had no flair for fundamental invention and simply aimed at some modifications bearing on quality and costs. In 1802, for example, he spread line from a hackle, finding that

It cost twice as much as spreading on tables, but saved weighing which costs as much as spreading. The yarn appeared to spin better and to be freer from fishes than table spreading. Good 16 lea line spun well to 18 leas and made good yarn, when carefully prepared, but it requires great attention to bring the fibers forwards and not knot them in the heckle.... After a tryal of half a year and frequent examinations of the yarn, we found the quality of it not so good as from table spreading....It requires too much nicety and care to be practicable by hand labour only. It must have some mechanical assistance before it can answer.[2]

Earlier, he constructed a combing machine similar to and immediately after Cartwright's patent for Big Ben. The aim was to improve long tow, and in this case Marshall found that the machine called for too much concentration by the operative and promised no reduction

---

[1] Fenton, Murray and Wood began at Mill Green, Holbeck, and in 1802 built the Round Foundry just outside the Leeds township boundary on Marshall's land, opposite his mills in Water Lane. David Wood, a close friend of Marshall, was according to J. Watt, jr., 'a steady man of business who directs the works', and later he specialised in textile machinery (Kilburn-Scott, *op. cit.* pp. 8, 34–5). Matthew Murray was the firm's inventor and sales manager, 'a great scoundrel but a very able mechanic' (J. Watt, jr.); he was a newcomer to the town who rose from the labouring classes and did not have a reputable character for many years. Murray was to the fore in freely borrowing and developing the ideas of others. The third partner, James Fenton, was 'a man of property and was Marshall's partner....Mr Gott speaks well of him...but his character is not very respectable' (J. Watt, jr.). Watt continues 'Marshall provided him [Fenton] with a share in the business [the Foundry] to get him out of his own the linen trade'. Fenton attended to the financial side of the business in the Counting-House. Of this firm, and other machine-makers in Leeds, J. Watt, jr., speaking as an established machine-maker, observed, 'they are men without character and without means'. In short the machine-makers consisted of new men who had no position in the regular society of the town.

[2] Marshall, 'Experiments', vol. II, June 1802, no. 73, pp. 109–10.

in costs.[1] The firm's success in spinning medium yarns weighing as little as 10 lb. a bundle was the result of other changes—better combinations of machinery and manual work, the more exact construction of frames (now supplied by Murray who extracted patent fees), and to a labour force gaining in skill.

To guard against exaggerating their progress, it is important to indicate the limits of their achievement. In December 1798, when John Marshall took his bearings, he claimed advances on only two fronts. By that time, Marshall thought that, thanks to hand-spreading and some minor improvements in preparing and spinning, they spun 14–20 lea line yarn better than hand-spinners. In the higher counts, they were still at a disadvantage:

We spin from 20 to 30 leas good yarn but require for those sizes a superior quality of flax to what is used by hand spinners. Our 25 lea line would be spun [by hand] to 30 or 35 and our 30 to 50 or 60. This imperfection in our fine spinning we attribute to the defect of our first preparation. Line cannot be spread on a board without great injury to its quality.... The remedy we propose is to produce our first sliver from a heckle or something with points, which may deliver the fibers straight and unbroken, and leave the broken parts or refuse in the heckle. If a sliver with a regular disposition of fibers can be obtained by this means, we may spin our 16 lea line to 20, and our 30 to 60 which would make a great difference in the profits of the business.[2]

However, Marshall failed to draw from a hackle when he tried in 1802. As for shorts (fibres 12 in. long) he conceded first place to hand-spinners, who managed to spin 12 lea yarn compared with his 10 leas; and from long tow, Marshall produced 5–7 leas and hand-spinners 5–10 leas. Apart from spinning line up to 20 leas, Marshall's performance compared favourably with hand-spinners only in spinning short tow into 'as well and as small a thread as handspinners, say from 3 to 4 leas per lb.'.[3]

In the late 1790's the increase in yarn output created a pressing technical problem for the firm. The end-process of bleaching threatened to become a bottleneck on production. In the past, grey yarn had

[1] Marshall, 'Experiments', vol. II, November 1799, no. 68, pp. 100 ff.; J. Burnley, *op. cit.* (1889), pp. 112 ff.
[2] Marshall, 'Experiments', vol. II, December 1798, no. 66, pp. 95–6, 'General State of the Business'.   [3] *Ibid.* p. 99.

been exposed to the sun for several months on a bleach green, occasionally being watered to remove dirt. It was a slow operation involving a large piece of land and the process had passed into the hands of bleachers, men of substance who dominated the hand-spun trade in Barnsley just as they did in Ireland. To handle a larger volume of yarns the number of bleach greens could have been increased, and to some extent this did happen. But from the point of view of machine-spinners who wanted to undertake all the processes of yarn production, natural bleaching took too long and tied up too much capital. Their aim was to discover a new and cheaper method. So Marshall entered the bleaching business, bought a bleach-yard in 1796 a few miles away at Wortley, and began experiments to find a new method as cotton-spinners had recently been doing.[1]

A flax-spinner who tried chemical bleaching had to solve two problems. Could he use the same methods as cotton-spinners? They used ashes and vitriol, and increasingly from 1787 a chlorine bleach produced from vitriol, salt and manganese. Second, could he overcome the difficulty perplexing chemical bleachers everywhere, namely securing a uniform whiteness *throughout* each hank of yarn?

Marshall began using ashes and vitriol, the method practised at Barnsley and Wigan.[2] Then he found out from books about Berthollet's method of oxygenated muriatic acid (hydrochloric and manganese). The idea of a chlorine bleach appealed to him, but he visualised a number of practical difficulties and drew up a list of eleven queries which he wanted answering before going farther. The questions related to such points as the size of vessel for making the liquor, whether the bleach had to be thrown away after use, how to measure its strength, what length of time the yarn should be

---

[1] See A. and N. L. Clow, *The Chemical Revolution* (1952), ch. 9; C. Gill, *The Rise of the Irish Linen Industry* (1925), pp. 245–6, 247 ff.; Horner, *op. cit.* p. 65; 'Letters of Charles Bage to William Strutt' (1802–1818), MSS. 2685 in Shrewsbury Reference Library, 11 February 1802, 23 October 1808, 21 March 1810, 5 August 1810, 14 November 1810, 26 February 1815. (This correspondence shows that Bage, who was in charge of the bleaching for Benyons at Leeds, depended on advice from Strutt, a cotton-spinner, and technically that Benyons and Bage did not surpass Marshall—indeed, in 1815 Bage wrote 'nothing will be made of linen bleaching in simple water impregnated with gas', a conclusion reached by Marshall much earlier.)

[2] Marshall, 'Experiments', 'Bleaching', 1788–1803.

4-2

immersed, and so on. To get answers, Marshall visited Mr Wood at Bolton, and was so satisfied that he bought some bleaching liquor from Ainsworth and Vallet, nearby at Halliwell. When he tried this out on his return, he found that very diluted liquor turned flax yarn yellow and cost 3s. a bundle which was too expensive. So he diluted the bleach with only four parts of water; the result was a perfect white, but the cost even more prohibitive.

Satisfied that the method would work, Marshall wondered whether he could turn it into a commercial proposition. He might try some combination of natural and chemical bleaching which would reduce costs to 1s. a bundle, or he might produce his own chlorine more cheaply and economise on labour:

...it seems that Linen Yarn will bear a very strong liquor without injury. The same liquor undiluted acts upon our yarn without injury, which Ainsworth and Co., for their cotton yarns dilute with 14 parts water. On the other hand it has very little effect on our yarn when diluted with more than 4 parts water. If this be the case, the disadvantage of it requiring such powerful liquor may possibly be more than counterbalanced by its being able to bear it so strong as to produce a colour at 1 or 2 operations, and thereby produce a greater saving in labour than the extra expense of the chymical liquor. If yarn could be made white with one regular work, then bouking and steeping in the liquor once, and if a pint of liquor would do for a score, and it could be made for a 1d a pint, it would be nearly if not quite as cheap as the common mode of bleaching.[1]

The problem was similar to that which Marshall faced when he first began spinning, namely finding a new method as cheap as the traditional one. Again he persevered, for good bleaching not only promised to improve the quality of their yarn but also result in the sale of more white and less grey yarn. So he read J. Curry and T.L.Rupp on bleaching, invited Mr Vallet of Ainsworth and Vallet to Water Lane, and took the latter's advice to use more manganese because 'manganese in England is very inferior in quality to that of France and Germany'.[2] Yet despite these efforts, chemical bleaching remained expensive and Marshall produced off-white yarns bleached unevenly in patches.

Shortly after 1800 Marshall decided that an even whiteness might be obtained in two ways. The first consisted in hanging hanks of

[1] Marshall, 'Experiments', 'Bleaching', 1798, pp. 27–8.
[2] *Ibid*. August 1799, p. 44.

yarn on a roller which rotated in the liquid bleach. The results were good, the cost too high. (About the same time, he tried the new patent bleaching powder made by Tennant and Knox. This proved both expensive and ineffective.) The second method involved a new principle, invented by Chaptal. 'After a common boil with an alkali, hung [the yarn] twenty four hours in a steam engine boiler.'[1] Pleased with the result, Marshall built a brick shed with 20-in. walls at the bleach-yard; 'We set a 5 horse Steam Engine boiler on the outside of the building and conveyed the steam through a lead pipe into round tubs in which the yarn was hung.'[2] This time the results were not encouraging. 'It seems that no great progress can be made in bleaching by the application of alkalies alone. Too intense an action of them, without the alternate action of acids reduces and injures the yarn.'[3]

Without properly solving the problems involved, Marshall ended these experiments in order to turn to more pressing matters. About a fifth of the yarn spun at Water Lane was bleached during the next decade, most of it Suffolk colour. And until 1815 at least, the firm used a combination of methods: chemical bleaching with potash and chlorine (made on the premises out of salt, vitriol and manganese), boiling in an alkali, and also the traditional method of exposure in fields, for which Marshall rented more land in Wortley.

Besides spinning and bleaching yarns for sale, Marshall and Benyons' produced heavy linens. In the four years from 1794 the number of looms increased in the same ratio as the number of spindles. In March 1793 the firm had forty-three hand-looms; by the end of that year eighty-one: at that point the entry ends but, according to the growing value of stock out in weavers' hands, there were by 1798 about 150 looms weaving for the firm. At that capacity, the expansion of this process also ceased. The firm put out nearly half its yarn— all its tow and some line—to weavers in nearby villages who bought their looms on instalments from the mill. At first, only coarse cloth was woven—canvas, hessian and raven-duck—but by 1804 the firm produced not only an extended line of heavy linens in bears and ships,

---

[1] *Ibid.* January 1802, p. 63.   [2] *Ibid.* p. 64.
[3] *Ibid.* March 1802, p. 70.

but also lighter cloths, such as ducks and linens made from their 15–20 lea yarns.

Sometime in 1795 the Benyon brothers had wanted to begin manufacturing thread, a trade that was growing rapidly in the north. Marshall had never twisted thread at Water Lane, and his partners, who then had a larger share of the capital and a controlling voice in the affairs of the business, chose to build a third mill at Shrewsbury rather than at Leeds. There they would be near the carpet weavers of Bridgenorth and Kidderminster who would buy the tow yarns generated as a by-product of thread-making. The Ellesmere canal, then under construction, offered a link with the north and an alternative route to the River Severn for incoming flax. Coal came by water right to the door of the site they chose at Castle Foregate. And their schemes depended above all on the fact that Benjamin Benyon very much wanted to return to his native town.[1]

After the fire at mill *B*, the Benyon brothers decided to erect a fire-proof mill and put the Salop design in the hands of Charles Bage, a Shrewsbury wine-merchant. Bage, a keen student of new engineering methods, had been in communication with Jedediah Strutt about the fire-proofing of his cotton factory at Belper. The mill at Castle Foregate, the first multi-storey building with iron beams and columns, was one of Bage's more successful achievements, and in return for his services he became a partner in the Salop branch of the business.[2]

Work on the new mill began late in 1796 and was completed early the following year. It stands, an immensely impressive structure, showing how, within a short span of years, the large buildings so

[1] In many respects the least mobile factor of production at that time was the entrepreneur, not least because 'character' and 'connexions' counted for so much. This situation changed during the next half-century. The introduction of thread-making did not necessarily show enterprise. On 27 September 1814 Bage wrote to Strutt, *op. cit.* 'If you cotton gentlemen would be so good as to give up thread, we might look to it; but you have complete possession of the Ladies, and we are not likely to dispute the prize with you'. Until the 1830's when flax-spinners could make very light thread there was no obvious case for expansion in this direction. In 1797, the Benyons might have been more sensible extending their grip on the yarn market.

[2] T. Minshull, *The Salopian Guide* (1804), pp. 47–8; Bage–Strutt, 29 August 1803, 11 August 1818; H. Owen, *Some Account of the Ancient and Present State of Shrewsbury* (1808), p. 61. For the mills, see H. R. Johnson and A. W. Skempton, 'William Strutt's Cotton Mills', a paper delivered to the Newcomen Society in December 1956. For the finance of the Castle Foregate Mill, see the deeds, dated 20 September 1796, 1 February 1797, 1 July 1797, at the Shrewsbury Reference Library.

characteristic of the nineteenth century supplanted the small chapel-size mills which Marshall and Co. first constructed. The Salop mill stood five storeys high and held approximately as much machinery again as mill *B* in Water Lane. To drive its machinery, a 20 horse-power engine had been ordered in May 1796 from Soho; it was delivered in July 1797, and production started at the mill two months later.[1] In the mill-yard a flax warehouse and dyehouse were built, and later an apprentice house for mill children, and outside the gates several rows of workers' cottages. Then in 1799 Benjamin Benyon added an imposing north wing and installed a second engine, this time from Murray at Leeds.

Between 1796 and 1800 the partners put more into expansion at Castle Foregate than at Water Lane. Unfortunately no records survive to show the precise nature of the early financial arrangements in Salop. At the start, this side of the business owed much (probably about £8000) to the resources which the Benyons received from the sale of their woollen business, and to a mortgage of £6000 at 5 per cent granted by a firm of London bankers. Marshall, who disapproved of the venture, subscribed nothing at this stage. Amongst other reasons, he felt that further expansion at Leeds where he had land awaiting development would have offered a better financial return: but this was little more than a rationalisation of his opposition to an offshoot beyond his control. By 1800, however, largely as a matter of personal strategy, he showed more interest in the Salop mill, though to some extent this interest may have been inspired by impressions of the thread trade which Marshall gained on his travels. Once the firm spun lighter yarns, thread-making brought new market opportunities. On his tour of Cumberland, Marshall noticed that 'the thread manufacture has increased very much...they make chiefly 3 cord coloured thread...and sell it in the north of England and Scotland'.[2] The largest production of thread took place in Scotland, where Marshall estimated the weekly output to be 13 tons. On the east coast from Berwick to Aberdeen, $7\frac{1}{2}$ tons of coloured and 3 tons of bleached thread were made each week; and in the west at Paisley very fine

---

[1] Marshall and Benyons–Boulton and Watt, *op. cit.* 2 May, 13 May, 24 May, 10 June, 10 December 1796; 16 February and 16 June 1797.

[2] Marshall, 'Tours' (Scotland and Ireland, 1800), *c.* 15 September.

threads were made, though the weekly output of 2½ tons consisted chiefly of 40 lea thread twisted from yarns hand-spun in Aberdeen or imported from Hamburg. The Irish made poor threads and would have to buy Scotch or English goods. Signs such as these show Marshall developing an interest in thread-making. And when Mary Marshall, his mother, died in November 1799 leaving him £5000, he invested this sum in the Salop concern. (In effect, Marshall transferred £5000 from the Water Lane to the Castle Foregate business. On leaving home in 1795, John shared with Mary Marshall the property they had inherited from Jeremiah Marshall, and Mary Marshall left her share in the business.) In the following year, 1800, the Benyon brothers transferred over £7000 from the Leeds to the Salop mill. With these resources, there was sufficient to finance expansion until capital could be generated out of profits. In the three years 1800–3, profits at Castle Foregate amounted to £20,020, and John Marshall's capital there doubled.

Marshall and his partners had tasted success. Early in 1803, their joint capital amounted to between £80,000 and £90,000. They had earned 15 per cent on their outlay.[1] And John Marshall had a net estate of £33,211. More impressive than the financial record and a better indicator of their future prospects was the relative scale of their operations. They employed over a thousand hands; their engines rated over 150 horse-power; they had nearly 7000 spinning spindles. No other spinner approached this class. The rest, as Marshall's travels show, were small firms with a few frames turned by water-power. Not that the use of water-power limited the scale of operations at that time. A giant water-wheel generated 100 horse-power, sufficient to drive 4000 cotton spindles, or slightly fewer worsted and flax spindles on account of their heavier weight.[2] Early steam-engines could not rival this performance in power and cost. Few streams provided so much power, however, and the cotton manufac-turers took advantage of the best sites. Even so, quite a small stream

[1] That is, 15 per cent on investment. Between 1792 and 1807 Benjamin Gott averaged 19 per cent on outlay. In the late eighteenth century, the Bean Ing woollen mills used about three times as much capital and made about four times as much profit as the Water Lane Mills. Gott MSS., in the Brotherton Library, University of Leeds.

[2] Marshall, 'Notebook', 1790–1830, pp. 1, 4.

would turn a wheel 16 ft. high and 9–10 ft. broad, enough to drive 2000 flax spindles. Few flax mills had so many spindles by 1800; indeed, most had less than a thousand. Coates's mill at Ripon was quite typical at the time. It had

3 spinn^g. frames of 30 Sp^s. at work. 6 D^o. standing, spinning line 13 leas per lb. very badly—The spinning frames are copies from ours in every respect, and wet the same.... The tow yarn I saw of 8 to 10 leas per lb. from long white tow, only a few hanks, was very good, the finer sorts 12 to 14 leas bad and uneven. Mr Coates is not at all calculated for such a business and it must be a very losing one.[1]

Near Ambleside, Benson and Braithwaite's mill had three tow frames each with twenty-four spindles, and they produced between a half and a ton of tow a week.

One would imagine that if it answered they would increase their machinery as they have plenty of power.... They sell 10 lea tow yarn at 12½ per lb. which would pay a great profit if the process was not an expensive one.... They are going to spin line and intend to draw it out of the strick without spreading it on a table.[2]

It is most unlikely that Marshall failed to visit or at least refer to the larger flax mills then in existence. (Indeed, large mills indicated success and merited his attention; and on two occasions he visited the great cotton mills at New Lanark.)[3] This being the case, the largest flax mill seen by Marshall at the beginning of the nineteenth century belonged to Hornby, Bell and Birley of Egremont near White-haven, the centre of an old linen district. This firm had 1500 spindles and used 8 tons of flax each week.

They are building another mill which will do as much more.... They spin very well with very few breakages, particularly the heavy line yarns 5 to 10 leas per lb. of which they spin a great deal, and run their frames at the speed of 15 or 16 leas per day per spindle... Their machinery is rough and clumsy compared with ours, but much better than the Darlington machin-ery.... They produce their first line sliver by drawing it out of a heckle.... When the Girl is very carefull a very good sliver is produced better than

---

[1] Marshall, 'Tours' (Scotland and Ireland, 1800). Ripon, 4 September.

[2] *Ibid*. Ambleside, 8 September.

[3] *Ibid*. (Cumberland and Scotland 1800, 1807). 26 September 1800, 3 August 1807. (Marshall appears to have been almost as interested in the beauty of the falls at Cora Lin as in Owen's mills, which employed 1600 at a time when Marshall hired 1100.)

by spreading on a board. It is a little more labour but that is no object. One great disadvantage is that they cannot lay out the first sliver to any exact weight. They are tolerably exact from habit....[1]

From all sides, the evidence points to the same conclusion. Their financial record, size of plant, technical progress, and to credit Marshall's remarks, their efficiency, placed Marshall and Benyons on a plane above other spinners. They had laid the foundations for making a fortune.

(iii)

The partnership between John Marshall and the Benyon brothers lasted for ten years. In many respects they were men of similar stamp. Their upbringing and Unitarian religion saved them from the ignorance and roughness that marked so many self-made business-men. All had uncommon mercantile ability, employed new methods, seized a favourable opportunity, and exploited to the full the resources they had available. Marshall justly claimed that he never relaxed from business matters until he was forty, and even on his holidays he visited mills and pondered the commercial possibilities elsewhere in Britain.[2] Business was just as much a consuming passion with the Benyon brothers, especially Thomas who had the ability and energy so often associated with success. Their father, a Shropshire attorney, came from a family that had been engaged in commerce for several generations.[3] When his eldest son entered the legal profession, in due course becoming attorney-general to the Duchy of Lancaster, the younger boys, Thomas and Benjamin, born in 1762 and 1763, were apprenticed to a Shrewsbury draper. After putting out yarn in the neighbourhood of their native town for a decade, they had earned £13,000 besides the reputation of being very able businessmen. They had therefore climbed as far as Marshall in the same span of years when they entered his flax business in 1793.

Charles Bage, the Shrewsbury wine-merchant who became a junior partner in the Salop concern, was altogether different. He was ten years older than his partners, and since he belonged to St Chad's

---

[1] Marshall, 'Tours' (Scotland and Ireland, 1800). Egremont, 15 September.
[2] *Ibid.* (Cumberland and Scotland, 1800.) Ripon, 4 September.
[3] I wish to thank Mr L. C. Lloyd for drawing my attention to several sources relating to Marshall's partners.

Church, recently erected in the new fashionable quarter of Shrewsbury where he lived, he did not share their Unitarian affiliation.[1] Nor did he have the interests of a growing family at heart, at least not until a second marriage very late in life. On the other hand, like Marshall and the Benyons, he wanted to be rich and distinguished. Yet despite the fact that he came from a family which had for two generations been paper manufacturers in the Midlands, he had singularly little talent for business. All his associates decried his services as a manager, and Bage betrayed part of the reason why in a letter to Strutt: 'I can hardly understand the satisfaction you take in continual labour of mind, and since you are ambitious of continuing in this world as long as you can, you should not work on the machine too hard, but give it occasionally a little relaxation oil.'[2] Charles Bage had no enthusiasm for business as a way of life, preferring local politics and the study of modern science as ways of spending his time. Nevertheless, the Benyon brothers needed him in his capacity as an engineer just as Marshall used the talents of Murray. But whereas Murray was an artisan who could be hired for a wage, Bage, a gentleman with an established position in society, could only be secured by a share in the partnership.

Employing Bage was something of a gamble. Inspired by Strutt's work at Belper—'How much we are obliged to you for teaching us to make build^{gs}. fireproof'[3]—he constructed several iron-frame buildings for the Benyons. And it is clear that Bage calculated the strength of his mill beams and proved them by full-scale tests.[4] In this, and in other fields like bleaching, he was abreast if not ahead of current developments in science and engineering. But he failed to help Benyon in the way that Matthew Murray had helped Marshall. In 1815, at the age of sixty-three, he left Benjamin Benyon in order to invent a power-loom. 'Being no longer a spinner, and

[1] *Salopian Shreds and Patches*, vol. III, pp. 150, 153 in the Shrewsbury Reference Library; J. Marns, 'The Mayors of Shrewsbury', *Transactions of the Shropshire Archaeological Society*, 44th series, vol. IX, pp. 8–9, described Bage as 'a talented member of a very talented family'; Bage–Strutt, 14 July 1816 reveals an interesting difference of opinion about the treatment of the lower orders. Bage thought that the leanings of Strutt, Benyons and Marshall towards working-class improvement would foment unrest and must result in harsher laws.

[2] Bage–Strutt, 11 August 1818.

[3] *Ibid.* 28 October 1811.   [4] *Ibid.* 29 August 1803.

having little else to do, I have been constructing a loom on a plan quite new, and am about to try it with four horse power. Linen has not been advantageously wove by power looms, and having the weakness of other projectors, I flatter myself I shall succeed better.'[1] But success never came and Bage died disappointed in 1822. It was inevitable that he should fail. Not only did he choose a treacherous path, but as an inventor he lacked the purpose of Matthew Murray, who concentrated on developing what was wanted as an immediate commercial proposition. Bage would gamble on a long shot in a way that no sensible man of business would have done.

Bage's partners did not share his illusion about how to make money. They were hard-working men of action steadily augmenting their resources and using them to attain the limited ends which they had in view. But before they had gone very far in enlarging their business, indeed after only eighteen months together, they were jostling with one another for control and inevitably came into collision.

This struggle for power broke the surface of their relations when the third mill was built at Salop. In 1793, Marshall had no alternative but to seek partners who could furnish resources for a second mill. He could only hope that, like Fenton and Dearlove, they would not interfere with his management of the business. At first sight the Benyon brothers appeared likely to fit this situation. They lived a hundred miles away and they had their own woollen business. Then, to make it appear that his capital equalled what his partners offered in December 1793, Marshall debited the loans made by friends and relatives to his own private account and, since he could hardly do otherwise, charged the business with only the Armitage mortgage. As a result Marshall's capital in the firm appeared as £10,546 at a time when his net estate was £7180. At first the Benyon brothers invested only £3889 and promised to raise another £6000 in the future. Marshall's predominance seemed assured for the time being

[1] Bage–Strutt, 27 June 1816; see also 14 July 1816, and 11 August 1818, 'After many attempts and successive alterations and improvements, always pursuing the same principle, I have produced the only loom so far as I know and believe, that answers for linen.' Bage had ten looms at Coleham; C. Hulbert, *History and Description of the County of Salop* (1837), p. 308, footnote. For other efforts to invent a loom at the same time, see Warden, *op. cit.* pp. 457, 461, 462.

and in 1794–5 he drew heavily on his assets, taking out £3203, to furnish a new house and also acquire extra land.

From the start the Benyon brothers had no intention of being passive partners and planned to take over at Water Lane themselves. Within a year, they sold the woollen business at Salop and moved to Leeds in order to assist in the management of the mills. They could afford to increase their capital in the firm by £4000 so that, together with untouched earnings, they had assets of £12,889 in the Leeds firm at the end of 1795, compared with Marshall's £9635. In 1796, instead of a half share of the profit, Marshall had to accept two-fifths; and, as the financially stronger partners, the Benyon brothers insisted on producing thread and building a third mill at Shrewsbury. Naturally Marshall opposed the scheme because it meant that control over the business was passing into other hands. In practice he had no option but to acquiesce, although he claimed that he did so only because in return 'the Benyons...now gave up a larger proportion to me at Leeds, in consideration of the establishment of this concern [at Shrewsbury], and their having a larger share in it'.[1] But in the agreement of 1797, made for a term of seven years, the Benyon brothers took the larger part of the profits, which were divided on the following basis:

	Leeds	Shrewsbury
J. Marshall	$\frac{9}{20}$	$\frac{2}{8}$
T. and B. Benyon	$\frac{11}{20}$	$\frac{5}{8}$
C. Bage	—	$\frac{1}{8}$

Benjamin Benyon returned to Shrewsbury where, assisted by Bage, he managed the new thread-mill. Marshall together with Thomas Benyon ran the Water Lane mills, each of them pushing for supreme control.

At once Marshall began scheming to re-establish his position. The new partnership agreement satisfied nobody and the next round in the struggle started with complaints about their respective shares of profit. 'The difference of our shares was a continual source of jealousy.'[2] The Benyon brothers complained that Marshall with a third of the capital at Water Lane took nearly half the profits; further, with no capital at all at Salop, he was entitled to a quarter share once profits were made. Marshall, whose position was weaker, protested

[1] Marshall, 'Life', pp. 12–13. [2] *Ibid.* p. 13.

that the Leeds mills under his management made a net profit of
£6000 a year whereas the Salop venture was a fiasco and had not
made a penny, and he came as near as he could to suggesting that
he was lining the Benyons' pockets with riches.

As output increased total profits rose to a higher level and Marshall
drew less from the business, with the result that the share capital of
the partners at Water Lane increased rapidly, and the disproportionate ratio between their assets diminished. Indeed, after transfers
to Salop in 1800 both parties had fairly equal amounts of capital at
Leeds. So Marshall pressed for a fresh division of profits in the next
partnership agreement due in 1804. He proposed that the Benyon
brothers should have a half share in each concern, the other half to
go to himself and Bage whose 'services to the concern were at least of
equal value'.[1] This was exaggerating the role of Bage, but it suited
Marshall's purpose and he later wrote as if he would have sacrificed
his own interests in order to ensure that Bage got what was due to him.
'This would have been disadvantageous to me because it was reducing
my share in the more profitable concern, but it was no more than
just to Mr Bage who had given up his own business and devoted
himself to ours.'[2] Not knowing the share that Marshall proposed for
Bage, it is difficult to evaluate his self-denial. An agreement of the
kind Marshall probably had in mind would certainly have been in his
interest. He had ostensibly altered his view towards thread-making
and staked his claim to the profits which he anticipated at Castle
Foregate. But, even more important, he would have an equal weight
with the Benyons in the conduct of affairs. Assuming that Bage
gained from the scheme, he would be indebted to Marshall, and his
half-hearted attention to business affairs made him a pliable partner.
'Mr Bage was possessed of talent and understanding but was not a
man of business. He had not the steadiness and perseverance which
the management of a large manufacturing concern requires, nor a
sufficient knowledge of commercial transactions, to form a correct
judgement of the mode of conducting them.'[3]

As it turned out, Marshall misjudged the reactions both of Bage
and the Benyon brothers. The latter did not intend to share their
authority and countered every move Marshall made; and Bage,

[1] Marshall, 'Life', p. 13.   [2] *Ibid.* pp. 13–14.   [3] *Ibid.* p. 13.

Marshall complained, was 'completely under the control of Mr B. Benyon' in Shrewsbury.[1]

If he had not done so earlier, Marshall began at this juncture to think of a separation. Before 1800 he had insufficient resources to carry on alone, but in that year he had £16,000 of his own and four years later when the current agreement lapsed he had £45,000. With this money he could go his own way, and he later betrayed his real reasons for wanting a separation when he wrote: 'I was determined never again to make a connexion for the sake of capital.... I was confident in my own abilities for conducting the concern.'[2] In his autobiography, he could not attribute his action to his loss of control. Instead he stressed the fact that Castle Foregate was 'badly managed and of course unprofitable'.[3] Had he wanted to, Marshall might have remembered that at the start Water Lane also ran at a loss. He could not really expect an immediate return on the outlay (in which he had no share), and after 1800 (when he lent financial support to the venture) the Salop mill yielded a good profit. Perhaps Marshall felt that a larger return could have been obtained at Leeds—15 per cent instead of 7 per cent on outlay—and in the short run this may well have been the case. But apart from the purchase of land in 1794 and again in 1801 to the south of Water Lane, there is no evidence to suggest that he contemplated any increase in productive capacity there before 1812. The criticism of the Salop venture was a personal attack on Benjamin Benyon, who managed a distant mill in the direction of which Marshall had very little influence; and his plea of 'bad management' provided a pretext for a course of action he had already decided upon.

Marshall could disentangle himself from his partners in one of three ways. He could sell out to Benyons, a possibility which he did not consider. Conversely, Benyons could sell out to Marshall; this assumed that Marshall would have more capital than either he or they thought likely. Finally, the business could be divided out; and both parties expected that this would happen. Benyons and Bage would take Castle Foregate and compensate Marshall for his share there; Marshall would take Water Lane and compensate the other partners. On the understanding that this would happen at the end

[1] *Ibid.* p. 13.   [2] *Ibid.* p. 15.   [3] *Ibid.* p. 13.

of the present partnership, each party began to manoeuvre itself into a more favourable position. For example, in August 1802, soon after Marshall had bought 5 acres south of Water Lane, the value of the land at Leeds was raised from £5000 to £7000, and the write-up distributed between the partners in proportion to their shares. Marshall retaliated, buying all the firm's land at its new book-value and allowing the use of the occupied portion in return for an annual rent.[1] Part of the remainder he sold and rented to Fenton, Murray and Wood, who constructed the Round Foundry on it in 1802, and in this way Marshall aligned them behind him at a time when his own partners contemplated a new plant of their own at Leeds a few hundred yards south across the fields.

When the time came to arrive at terms, the negotiations foundered. The Benyon brothers (perhaps with justification in view of Marshall's remarks about Castle Foregate) offered less compensation for Marshall's Salop interest than he would accept: 'I would have con-

---

[1] In 1790, Marshall had bought 1 acre north of Water Lane for £600 on which he built mill *A*. Four years later he bought a further 4 acres from David Rider for £2300, on which he paid a deposit of £1300 and the rest over ten years. This purchase comprised 2 acres north of Water Lane for mill *B* and 2 acres south of Water Lane. Then in 1801–2 Marshall spent £3610 on a further 5 acres south of Water Lane. Thus the firm had 10 acres, 3 to the north and 7 to the south of Water Lane. (This corresponds with an entry in the Leeds Ledger, 1793–1804, for 5 August 1802.) Part of the land south of Water Lane he sold and rented to Fenton, Murray and Wood where, as J. Watt, jr., saw, they built the Round Foundry in 1802 (Kilburn-Scott, *op. cit.* p. 34). Marshall probably sold 2 acres to the machine-makers, whose plant covered 3½ acres and they added further buildings on the other 1½ acres by 1815.

Several points in these transactions deserve comment:

(1) Land prices in the district were rising rapidly as Watt's letters show, and Marshall was prudently providing for expansion on adjacent sites. In 1803 he had 3 acres vacant south of Water Lane and began to build there in February 1805. Moreover, in 1804–5, he spent £5000 on 7 acres to the west as far as Silver Street, and there he constructed cooling reservoirs between 1816 and 1819 and later his son erected the Derwent Street cottages. (John Marshall, 'Private Ledger', pp. 37, 35; 'Leeds Ledger', 1793–1804, 2 July 1806.)

(2) By helping Fenton, Murray and Wood, he enlisted them in his cause at a time when he was in the process of separating from Benyons and Bage. It was obviously in Marshall's interest that they should give him primacy of service.

(3) According to the letters of J. Watt, jr., it seems that the Soho firm wanted information about their Leeds competitor and considered setting up there because of the volume of trade in Leeds. There was no intention of hindering further expansion by Fenton, Murray and Wood who had recently occupied their new site. In any case, Marshall, who had land to spare, stood behind Murray. Boulton and Watt, whose first patent had expired, would naturally use their superior power to crush a new rival, but the way to do this was to take Murray's business away from him. Hence Watt's concern to acquire land by the canal, and his view that 'there is sufficient opening here for another works'.

fined myself to the Leeds concern, if the Benyons would have given a fair value for the Salop factory; but as they would do not that, I was determined to show how it would answer with good management, for I thought the thread manufactory which we had there might be made profitable.'[1] As a result of this uncompromising attitude, Marshall committed himself to buy out the other partners at both Leeds and Salop.

He undertook to pay his associates the book-value of their assets in the mills on 1 July 1804, the last day of the current partnership agreement.[2] According to his recollections, Marshall owed Benyons and Bage £70,000. 'I was not a little anxious about providing the sum of money which I had to pay my former partners. It appeared a large sum to pay at once.' So he 'took precautions to be prepared'.[3] Once more he offered Bage a share in the firm, pretending that he did so 'more from a wish to act honourably towards him, than on account of his value as a partner';[4] but he found no financial relief in that quarter. Next in 1802 Marshall took £13,000 out of the business which he lent to friends—Samuel Fenton, Peter Garforth, then a cotton-spinner in Shipley, and Joseph Wright, a Hull flax merchant: 'I made use of my surplus capital in accommodating some of my friends who returned the obligation when I afterwards wanted it.'[5] Another change in the situation which eased Marshall's burden was the fact that Benyons took out part of their assets in both cash and kind before July 1804. In order to finance and equip the new mills which they were building at Meadow Lane in Leeds and at the canal terminus in Shrewsbury, the Benyons withdrew £10,000 in cash alone. As a result, in 1804, Marshall owed his partners less than £60,000. Moreover, since they took more than £23,000 worth of plant and stock from Water Lane and an unknown amount from the Castle Foregate mill, Marshall had to find at the most £37,000 in cash—plus whatever profits were declared at a final reckoning when all debts were settled. Again time was on Marshall's side. The final settlement took eighteen months to complete, and under it Marshall owed his former partners £15,000. In short, over a period of two years,

[1] Marshall, 'Life', p. 14.
[2] Articles of Agreement, Benyons and Marshall, 29 June 1802.
[3] Marshall, 'Life', p. 15.
[4] *Ibid.* p. 14.   [5] *Ibid.* p. 15.

Marshall had to find £50,000 at the outside and enough capital to keep the mills running with less plant in them than before. He met the situation partly by calling in loans worth £13,000 and borrowing a further £13,000—including £4000 from his brother-in-law, Mr Jones, a Manchester banker. The rest he met out of his own resources: at the final settlement in 1806 he received £12,000, and in eighteen months' operation (July 1804 to December 1805) he made a net profit of £22,000 from the mills. What seemed a formidable task went through without difficulty, though it meant that Marshall put every penny into fixed capital and left himself with no reserve for a few years; but he kept the mills running, and at the same time made a down-payment on another piece of ground south of Water Lane costing £5000.

One easy solution to this financial operation Marshall did not entertain. He had many offers of capital on the basis of partnership and refused them all. In future he intended to have complete control himself over the firm and to ensure this he had in mind junior partners who would carry out his orders exactly and efficiently without questions or any show of initiative on their part. For these roles he selected two employees, John Hives and William Hutton. They were capable men with experience of the flax business. By 1804 Hives, who joined the firm as a clerk in 1798 at a salary of £150, had after many years of thrift saved £1000. But Marshall was interested more in the 'character and ability' of these men than their resources. Hutton, his chief traveller, 'having been married early had saved nothing'.[1] To each Marshall gave a twelfth share: he sent Hutton to Shrewsbury to manage the thread-mill, and Hives took charge at Water Lane. From Marshall's point of view it was an excellent arrangement. 'Hutton was an excellent manager of the manufacturing part of the concern, and Hives of the mercantile part; and I could bring into full activity the experience and knowledge of the manufacture which I had gained, unclogged by the interference of partners whose views differed from mine.'[2] In 1810, when Hutton's health began to fail, Marshall provided for the future by elevating John Atkinson, the chief clerk at Leeds, to the partnership. Atkinson, who was only twenty-seven, went to Shrewsbury and took over after Hutton retired in 1815.

---

[1] Marshall, 'Life', p. 15.   [2] *Ibid.* p. 16.

In several respects, the separation from the Benyons and the new partnership arrangements mark a turning-point in Marshall's life and business career.

First, for the next twenty years, Marshall had as partners men of lower social standing, men of his own creation who were indebted to him. This was important in view of his inability to persuade and compromise with people. Marshall knew what he wanted to do, and forced his views on other people. He treated Hives and Hutton, who had a very small share in the concern, like employees; and they responded with loyal and efficient service. The profits of the business were no longer equally divided but went mostly to Marshall. Only after many years, when the partners began to provide for their families, was there any clash of interests.

Second, with the mills in the capable hands of his lieutenants, Marshall found that he 'could with propriety relax a little from [his] attendance on business' and he could no longer ascribe his mounting wealth to hard work at the factory.[1] Instead he emphasised a new quality for success, *judgement*: 'a concern directed, in the general plan of conducting it, by a good judgement, may be well and profitably managed in the detail by servants, and that good servants cannot make up for want of judgement in the chief'.[2] As he advanced in years and became richer, Marshall became convinced that this was the way to manage a business. Only one other attribute was necessary for success, *concentration*. 'By pursuing any one object with steadiness or perseverance either as a profession or a trade, a man with common abilities will almost always succeed....By the steady pursuit of one undertaking for a series of forty years, I have acquired a large property and have established manufacturing concerns.'[3] Such opinions committed to writing at this time by the founder became family heirlooms, and his sons had an image of the great businessman directing his interests from afar (before the days of telephone and tape) and managing at the same time to lead the life of a country gentleman, patron and politician.

Once he was relieved from long hours and daily attendance at the mills, Marshall pursued other interests. In 1805 he removed to New Grange, a substantial estate formerly occupied by a rich woollen

---

[1] *Ibid.* p. 17.   [2] *Ibid.* p. 22.   [3] *Ibid.* pp. 24–5.

merchant, away from the smoke and bustle of the town. He now
had the interests of a growing family to consider, for in August 1795
'finding my concerns going prosperously, and that I ran no risk of
involving a wife and family in difficulties', he married a distant
cousin, Jane Pollard, the daughter of an eminent merchant and
Unitarian in Halifax whom Marshall had known since his schooldays
at Hipperholme.[1] By March 1797 Dorothy Wordsworth was congratulating her school companion 'upon the health, strength, live-
liness and activity of your little boy.... I find that you do not view
him merely with the doating eyes of a mother. You can perceive that
he is not handsome; this is a strong presumption that you are not
deceived when you please yourself with discovering in him all the
more essential qualities to be desired in a child of his age.'[2] In 1805
they had six children, and more were to follow. 'A family of five
sons and six daughters...made the acquisition of property, and
advancement in society, matters of greater interest.'[3] In addition
Marshall began to serve in the 'common offices' of society, as chapel-
trustee, overseer and volunteer. He subscribed to the Leeds Library,
new public buildings and utility companies in the town. Along with
Peter Garforth and a small group of Unitarians, he helped to re-
establish the *Leeds Mercury* under the editorship of Edward Baines.
In the summer the family took longer holidays, and Marshall found
out a great deal about how other people lived. Thus, from the age of
forty, he began to concern himself more with his social position and
his interests broadened considerably. Mounting wealth enhanced
his stature; a large house, patronage, and public service brought
gains in character, respectability and wider social support. Apart from
being a dissenter and joining in the recent trend of dwelling outside
the township, Marshall's social activities did not differ from those of
an established merchant in the town—except in one respect. Either
he did not seek, or could not secure, a foothold within the town's
ruling class. Probably he did not seek to enter into its ranks, for by

[1] Marshall, 'Life', p. 11. Jane Pollard was the fifth daughter of William Pollard, a
member of Northgate-end Unitarian Chapel. Not only was Marshall distantly related
to his wife, but they shared the same school and religious background. For their honeymoon, they spent three weeks in the Lake District.
[2] Selincourt, *op. cit.*, Dorothy Wordsworth to Jane Marshall, 19 March (1797), p. 164.
[3] Marshall, 'Life', p. 11.

PLATE I

JANE MARSHALL
Portrait by John Russell, 1802, in the University of Leeds.

the early nineteenth century there was a small group of well-off dissenters, sufficient in numbers to create their own small social hierarchy and institutions, around which they would eventually rally opposition to the oligarchy in the town. The Marshalls played a leading role in this assault during the 1820's and 1830's, along with Thomas Benyon, Tottie, Goodman, Baines, and perhaps a score of leading families who were for one reason or another outside the pale of the merchant corporation.[1] However, in the early 1800's John Marshall was only starting to make his first investment in social standing; not only were his efforts local, but they were largely confined to the dissenting community and ordinary offices of society. Up to this time he was (outside the society of his own chapel) a newcomer, seeking to establish his claim to social respectability; hence the reticence, the wary manner, and often the uncertainty as to how to behave. Whether he would, as an outsider of growing fortune, seek to join the town's ruling class by wresting power from the oligarchy, or whether he would transfer his social aspirations elsewhere (and, as many businessmen have been accused of doing, seem to neglect the town) were questions that belonged to the future.

(iv)

In 1804 John Marshall had nearly £40,000; at the end of 1815 he had nearly £400,000. During the years between the renewal of the French War in May 1803 and its conclusion in July 1815 he made a fortune as a flax-spinner.

The total earnings of the partners during these years were about £446,000. Of this income 71 per cent came from profits: £238,000 at Water Lane and £82,000 at Castle Foregate. 18 per cent came from interest on capital in the business: £55,000 at Leeds and £24,000 at Shrewsbury. 11 per cent came from rent: £24,000 at Leeds and £23,000 at Shrewsbury.

The lion's share, on an average £39,000 a year, went to John Marshall. As owner of the land, fabric and engines, he took all the rent; 7½ per cent on existing fixed assets in 1804 (rounded off at £2000 a year for Water Lane and £1500 for Castle Foregate), plus

[1] Baines, *op. cit.* pp. 39 ff.; A. S. Turberville, 'Leeds Parliamentary Reform, 1820–30', *Publications of the Thoresby Society*, vol. XLI, *passim*.

10 per cent on new outlays of £37,000 during this decade. As the supplier of all except £1000 of capital in 1804 and supplier of three-quarters in 1815, he had most of the interest. Finally, by the articles of partnership, he took $\frac{10}{12}$ of the profits until 1810 when Atkinson became a partner, $\frac{19}{24}$ until 1812 and then $\frac{35}{48}$. So that despite withdrawals of £3000 a year for household expenses—twice as much as in the 1790's—his estate increased tenfold.

Marshall's partners also did well, much better than they could have hoped for as clerks and travellers. At first Marshall restricted their spending by a clause in the partnership agreement stating that no partner 'could take out more than £400 per annum till the capital of each partner amounts to £6000 per share'.[1] However, by 1810, when Hives and Hutton had accumulated such sums, this clause had lost its significance. 'We were in no want of capital for a gradual increase of the concern.'[2] Once Atkinson joined the partnership the number of shares was increased without any amendment regulating withdrawals, and in theory the newcomer who soon had three shares could have drawn £1200 a year. In practice, Hives and Atkinson took out on average £900 a year; and by 1815 Hives had a capital of £23,402 and Atkinson, after four years as a partner, £4000. Hutton on the other hand had only £14,000 in the business, mainly because failing health after 1810 led him to take out £3000 a year. Such income enabled Marshall's partners to take larger houses in fashionable quarters of the town and to aspire to an upper-middle-class style of life.

How did Marshall make so much profit at a time when war stifled the English flax industry? Marshall attributed what was later regarded as the period of his greatest success to good management and a 'demand for our yarns...at that time very great'.[3] It is a pity he was not more specific, for it is impossible to know whether or not the causes revealed by studying his accounts also reflect the view he took of his success. The striking fact about profits at Water Lane —and what follows refers only to that plant—is that they rose from £7000 a year between 1800 and 1802 to £16,000 in 1803 and an average

[1] 'Leeds Ledger', 1806–71, bk. 4, p. 294.
[2] Marshall, 'Life', p. 16.   [3] *Ibid.* p. 16.

of £20,600 a year from mid-1804 to the end of 1815. This sudden increase was not due to any proportionate expansion in plant and output. Nor did any innovation take place during these years to account for such a rise. Nor, as Marshall perhaps thought, could it be attributed to more efficient management after separating from Benyons and Bage, for the rise began earlier. In fact the rise in profits coincided with the renewal of the French War, and high profits were the product of higher prices and margins all along the line. For a decade, woollen manufacturers like Gott and flax manufacturers like Marshall, who mastered the turbulent conditions of these years, had an advantage over cotton manufacturers whose raw material prices did not rise in the same degree.[1]

Throughout the 1790's Marshall and Co. made slightly less than 2s. profit on a bundle of yarn and total profit rose with output. In 1794 profits amounted to about £2200 on an output of 16,000 bundles, some of which was woven into canvas for sale; in 1798, 63,000 bundles produced a profit of £6524 and in 1802 output rose to 85,000 bundles and profit to £7600. Profit margins did not change a great deal during this decade. This did not mean that production costs per bundle of yarn were constant, but rather that changes in one direction were neutralised by changes in the opposite direction. Between 1793 and 1802 flax prices doubled. For several years, Marshall more than off-set the extra cost by making thinner yarns and stretching flax twice as far. Then, after 1797, when flax prices rose more steeply, the firm reached its full capacity output and the incidence of overhead costs fell. Even so its profit margin contracted by a sixth, chiefly because the level of yarn imports was recovering and also because the firm could not at the time pass on its higher costs through higher prices. But, broadly speaking, in the 1790's the level of profits varied with changes in plant, and unit profits remained fairly constant.

This situation changed when England declared war against France in 1803. At an early stage Napoleon prohibited trade with England and prepared to invade the country. In August he tried to close the

---

[1] Wool and flax prices were very high after 1800. Between 1803 and 1808 Gott's trading profit averaged £35,000 a year; Gott MSS. For a diagram of flax prices, see Gill, *op. cit.* p. 223.

Elbe and Weser to English navigation. Apart from the commercial excitement roused by the imminence of fighting on British soil, these actions imperilled England's supply of linen yarn and to a lesser extent part of her flax supply. Prices, steadied by fourteen months of peace, rose precipitously, and nearly two years passed before buyers took a more calculated view of the future and prices stopped soaring. However, the important fact is that for twelve years after 1803, with one exception, the price of flax remained *over* £70 a ton. Against a potential British demand of nearly 30,000 tons in 1803–4, imports from 1803–15 averaged less than 20,000 tons a year. Flax was scarce and prices remained high, so high that English farmers raised their output from 3000 to 5000 tons.[1]

Because mills spun heavy yarns, the price of flax more than at any other time determined the price of yarn. The fall in yarn imports meant that the total supply from home and overseas sources contracted more sharply than demand and higher flax prices could be passed on to the consumer. Yarn selling from 12s. to 14s. a bundle in 1793–4 was 18s. by 1803. After 1804 Marshall never sold 16 lea line during the rest of the war for less than 22s., and the average price for their whole output stayed *above* 25s. a bundle. As a result, the profit on yarn rose from 2s. a bundle in the 1790's to at least 4s. after 1803. On an output of 80,000 bundles, total profits went up £8000 a year.

Having accounted for £14,000 of the firm's £20,000 annual profit in terms of wider margins on a constant output, owing chiefly to the higher prices of flax and its products, there remains some £6000 a year more profit, above the level prevailing in the 1790's, to explain by variations in output and to some extent by lower factor costs. How these changes increased profits will be considered presently. Meantime, in order to appreciate Marshall's behaviour and account for his success during these years, it is necessary to consider his activities as a speculator.

Flax accounted for four-fifths of Marshall's total costs and each year he spent around £75,000 on it. Buying on such a scale at a time

---

[1] W. Marshall, 'Report on Tour in Yorkshire and Scotland,' 1817, Appendix, pp. 13–14; J. Warnes, *On the Cultivation of Flax* (1846), p. 75.

when prices fluctuated considerably had an important bearing on profit. The gain that might result could be realised in one of two ways. The flax when used could be priced at historic cost and the profit gained by shrewd buying would appear in the final balance where total expenses are set against revenue. Alternatively, stocks might be revalued and carried forward at current prices in which case the margins in the final reckoning would appear smaller because an unrealised profit had previously been declared on stocks.

In trying to account for Marshall's high profits between 1804 and 1815, it matters little in the long run which of the above methods he adopted. In fact, he was somewhat ahead of his day and used a system of process accounting at current prices, thus securing a very realistic representation of the position of his business. In 1811 the firm's closing flax stock was valued at 87s. a cwt., and carried forward to 1812 at 104s. a cwt.; this added £8000 to the profit of that year. Quite apart from the revaluation of stocks in the bi-annual checks on which profits were based, Marshall kept track of the more spectacular inventory gains and losses in a rudimentary profit and loss account which he began to keep from 1806. In years of acute famine, the flax, yarn and canvas in stock would be marked up to current prices; at the end of 1808 he 'advanced' his stock by £28,590 and in 1811 by £8295. When prices fell, he wrote his stock down; in 1809 the firm lost £4575 and total profits dropped to the low figure of £5028; and in 1812 he depreciated 200 tons of Baltic flax by £10 a ton, took 10 per cent off the stock of bleached yarns, bringing the loss to £4270 and in addition he lost a cargo of flax at sea worth £2350; finally, towards the end of the war, when prices began their long fall, he lost £2000 on the flax he held.

From these entries, it is clear that Marshall thought of inventory profit (or loss) as something distinct from manufacturing profit (or loss). The question arises: to what extent did advances on stock account for Marshall's large wartime profits?

According to his profit and loss account, which shows only the more important gains and losses, Marshall's *net* gain from this activity was £23,690. However, this version of what happened is not sufficiently comprehensive to be conclusive. Flax, yarn and canvas prices continually bobbed up and down. Concealed in the half-yearly *spinning* and *weaving* accounts for 1812–15 (when prices fell) are small losses totalling £4200, which Marshall did not enter separately as inventory losses in the general statement, although they were taken into account in arriving at profits. The same applies to the earlier period when prices rose. How important these omissions were as a source of profit can be assessed by applying the proportions of profits on goods manufactured each year to the firm's opening and closing annual stocks. This shows that as *yarn* prices and stocks rose between 1806 and 1808, the firm made considerable inventory gains which were nearly all forfeited when prices fell in 1809. Thereafter Marshall kept yarn stocks at a lower level and price changes made correspondingly less impact on profits. In the long run (from January 1806 to December 1815), the firm's *net* inventory *gain* on *finished* goods amounted to only £350. Gains and losses almost cancelled each other out. But if finished goods are separated from flax in Marshall's own statements of inventory gains and losses, it appears that *net* gains on *flax* stocks amounted to some £16,000, about £1400 a year. Thus not only do changes in stock values explain why profits appear very high one year and very low the next, but they also go a little way towards accounting for the higher level of profit the firm made.

Carrying flax, yarn and canvas cost money and space, and it might be argued that the firm really made no profit from holding large stocks. To store more flax Marshall built a new warehouse which cost £2400, and the business had to pay a yearly rent of £240 for its use. In addition, the cost of additional circulating capital added at least £1400 a year to the firm's expenses. Taking one year with another, the firm's inventory gain did not cover the cost of holding extra stocks. As merchants, the partners would have failed dismally on this performance. But Marshall bought and held large stocks during the war for manufacturing, not for re-sale.

The Water Lane mills used about 17 tons of raw material each week, and to operate smoothly stocks had to be carried. The very nature and origin of the crop complicated this process even in ordinary times. Each season, in each market, the quality of each grade of flax varied in a way which directly affected spinner's profits; a good crop well-dressed would yield a higher proportion of line yarn and less waste. Further, most of the flax consumed in Britain came from the eastern Baltic. English orders placed early in September were executed immediately the flax harvest reached the ports late in October, before winter ice stopped shipping, and the rest of the crop was held over until the following spring. Consequently there were two buying seasons, and manufacturers took this into account in planning their raw material supplies. In the 1790's Marshall generally had about three months' supply on hand at the end of the year. When Napoleon's authority spread across Europe, the normal operation of this market ceased. In some years only 10,000 or 11,000 tons of flax reached Britain.[1] As a result Marshall increased his stocks after 1803 out of proportion to working-needs, never having below six months' supply and in 1811 holding a full year's requirements.

To make sure of adequate raw material supplies, Marshall had two alternatives. He could buy from merchants as need arose, in which case the importers took the risks and called the tune. Many small spinners were in this position and suffered severely; at one time they faced prices of £150 a ton. Marshall avoided such dependency and his inventory profits indicate, in fact underestimate, what the firm would have paid for flax at current prices. The other course was open to Marshall as soon as the firm made substantial profits; if the partners limited their withdrawals, he could invest the balance in stocks and guarantee supplies for the mills. This is what happened. No partner drew heavily on his share of profits, and Marshall held the growing balance either as flax or cash until 1814 when, after two years of falling flax prices, he transferred his part of these assets into consols. The possibility that savings would be used to enlarge the plant did not arise. Expansion would have aggravated the raw material situation; nor was there any point in increasing output until the volume of sales rose to a permanently higher level, and that came when prices fell after 1812. Instead, by exploiting his financial power and buying sensibly, Marshall kept the firm supplied with flax and stayed away from the market when prices rose very high.

[1] Warden, *op. cit.* p. 111; *A Statistical Display of the Finances, Navigation and Commerce of the U.K.* (1833), part II, 121; John Marshall, 'Notebook, 1790–1830, p. 54, for imports of yarn and flax at Hull after 1790; Horner, *op. cit.* ch. LIII. For the view that wartime fluctuations nearly ruined the flax-spinning industry, see W. Charley, *On Flax and its Products* (1862), p. 24.; and Warden, *op. cit.* p. 616.

Twice he misjudged events and failed to realise much of his potential gain. Nevertheless, the spectacular advances of some years may have convinced Marshall that, as his resources grew, he could gain most by speculation.

How far Marshall succeeded in safeguarding his material supplies and the benefits that followed may be judged from events. In 1804, when Marshall was buying out Benyons and Bage, he bought only a small quantity of flax, less than 300 tons, just sufficient to feed the reduced amount of his machinery for half a year. In order to lessen his dependence on Baltic sources and more easily to spin medium yarns, an eighth of Marshall's purchases comprised expensive English flax costing £80 to £90 a ton; such flax by virtue of its quality yielded a higher, more profitable proportion of line yarn. However, in 1805 he failed to get equally good yields from that season's English crop and decided to buy only Baltic. Trade with north-eastern Europe had improved once Britain established command of the seas, and importers eagerly flouted Napoleon's boycott. As flax prices fell to less than £80 a ton, English merchants built up their depleted stocks and a record level of 6000 tons came to Hull in that year. Marshall bought some 500 tons, just enough to meet his current needs. He had not finally settled with Benyons and Bage, besides which he would lose by holding stocks if prices continued to fall.

Next year, 1806, when English merchants were well-stocked and no longer so eager to buy, prices fell a further £5 a ton. Marshall bought 1000 tons, over a third of Hull's flax imports, at a very low average price of £62. In 1807 Napoleon, triumphant in central Europe, imposed a stringent embargo on British shipping. Yarn imports at Hull fell from 1500 tons in 1806 to 600 tons in 1807. Merchants who had refrained from buying in 1806 were again forced on to the market; over 4000 tons of flax came into Hull and its price rose sharply. A fire-proof warehouse capable of carrying 500 tons of flax had just been erected at Water Lane, and for the second year running Marshall bought heavily, taking 1155 tons of flax. In 1808 Russia, defeated, agreed to close Baltic ports to British shipping, and later that year trade came to a standstill. Yarn imports dwindled to less than 300 tons at Hull, and flax prices accelerated upwards. Earlier in the year Marshall had bought a full year's supply, taking

855 tons at £79½ per ton, half the flax imported at Hull. In addition he bought 53½ tons of United Kingdom flax at prices varying from £109 to £125 a ton. At the end of the year, when the price of Baltic flax rose above £100 per ton, Marshall had sufficient in stock for a full year's work.

Trade was possible for a few months during the spring of 1809. Spinners and merchants, desperate for supplies, imported at famine prices all the flax and yarn they could obtain. Marshall bought only 177 tons at £112 a ton.

This sudden sortie to the Baltic undermined some of the gains that Marshall might have expected to come his way. In a situation fraught with uncertainty, he had differed from others in his view of what would happen and until 1809 proved more accurate in anticipating events. He could afford and had a full warehouse; others faced famine prices and actual shortages. But as soon as more flax came into the country prices eased off, and at the end of the year Marshall had to write down 200 tons of flax remaining in stock by £20 a ton.

After 1810 a similar cycle of events occurred. The Russian economy began to suffer because it lacked a market for primary products, and the government started to relax trading restrictions. Flax prices therefore continued to fall. However, since the English linen industry had shrunk after its experience in the last few years, merchants probably hesitated to take advantage of the opportunity and raise their stocks. They waited for prices to fall further. Again Marshall acted differently. He bought 1023 tons of flax, 36 per cent of Hull's imports, at £88 a ton. Prices fell further in the following year and Marshall bought 1320 tons, 85 per cent of the flax imported into Hull, at £75. Once more the firm had 500 tons of flax in store when, in the summer of 1812, Napoleon set out to punish the Tsar, partly for lifting the counter-blockade against Great Britain. Flax prices jumped to more than £100 a ton, and remained high until the military issue was settled in favour of the allies late the following year. In 1812 only 800 tons of flax and 5 tons of yarn reached Hull. Late the following year, the situation improved a little; 3000 tons of flax and 500 tons of yarn were imported. Marshall produced on the basis of his stocks and bought lightly—in 1812, 468 tons of Baltic and 156 tons of Irish flax, and in 1813, 445 tons of Baltic and 223 tons of Irish flax. However, events again reached a climax sooner than Marshall had expected. After Napoleon's retreat from Moscow, flax prices fell and the warehouses at Water Lane were fairly full. Once again ships began to sail freely in the Baltic and flax prices fell continuously for the next twenty years; it was no longer prudent or necessary to hold large stocks. Marshall bought over a thousand tons of flax in 1814 and in 1815, and he used it all. Yet even with 300 tons on hand, less than three months' supply, the firm lost £2000 as prices tumbled down.

If in some years Marshall made spectacular inventory gains, his *net* profit from this source was not large in the long run and it accounts for only a small part of his wartime gains. His real achievement lay in using spare resources to safeguard his flax supply and maintain output even in such critical years as 1808–9 and 1812–13. Marshall never once had to cut production on account of a flax shortage, though had the famine continued he must surely have been affected. As it was, by running at or near full capacity he strengthened his position in the market and gained from rising yarn and linen prices.

What other factors contributed to the high average level of Marshall's wartime profits? At the level of output reached by the Peace of Amiens, the firm would alter its annual profits (at the margin then prevailing) by £1000 with a 5 per cent variation in production. Alternatively, a 3*d.* variation in the profit margin, due to a change in costs or prices, would also have altered profits by £1000. The fact is that higher profits came from a combination of increased output, the higher product prices previously referred to and falling labour and overhead costs.

Sales were the result on the one hand of economic facts—incomes, tastes, substitutes—things for the most part beyond the direct control of an entrepreneur; and on the other hand of a businessman's response to these facts. In a period of rapid technical change and wartime scarcities, this response will be shown by a readiness to alter prices, products and markets. In the 1790's Marshall was keen to improve the quality of his goods and alert to new market possibilities. Less progress was made in these directions during the last decade of the war; for instance, 'line [was] not in general spun to a smaller thread than it was in 1798'.[1] Instead, Marshall first varied the composition of his end-product to suit the market; then after 1812, when yarns were in great demand, he increased output from the existing plant. Radical improvements in technique and a search for new markets came again after the war.

As soon as Marshall had replaced the plant removed by Benyons and Bage, yarn prices rose but his sales did not increase. The number of bundles disposed of by the firm on the market was 63,000 in 1806 and only 64,000 two years later. (These figures do not include an increase in yarn supplies to the firm's own weavers, and they may reflect the impact of Benyons entry into the local trade as a separate firm.) Consequently Marshall's stock of yarn began to grow; by the end of 1807 it amounted to 36,000 bundles and at that level the firm had no alternative but to reduce output. A quarter of the labour force was turned off; the rest worked fewer days (300 in 1808, compared with 316 in 1807) and shorter hours. By 1809 the firm reduced its output to 62,000 bundles of yarn. This contraction meant a fall in *manufacturing profit* from £21,700 in 1807, when 88,000 bundles had been spun, to £18,000 in 1808 and £18,500 in 1809.[2]

To compensate for the sharp decline in the demand for yarns Marshall made more linen for sale in London and Manchester. If Yorkshire weavers were going out of business or could not afford to hold as much yarn as they had formerly, Marshall turned instead to consumers. The general buying public had not reacted so quickly to rising prices and they still wanted canvas and linens. The average price of a piece of canvas at Marshall's was about 28s. 6d. in 1806; prices rose slowly at first, then jumped late in 1808 and reached a peak of 44s. 6d. early in 1809 when sales levelled off and gently fell. Thus Marshall saw how to gain from the rise in incomes which inflated demand. He hired more weavers—152 in 1806, 175 in 1808—and increased the proportion of yarn woven by the firm on

---

[1] Marshall, 'Experiments', vol. III, December 1810, no. 103, p. 50, 'General State of the Business'.

[2] *Manufacturing profit*: Marshall *sometimes* distinguished between inventory gain and other profit and I have tried to do this systematically. This produces a profit figure in which inventory fluctuations have been discounted. Information on time worked is derived from departmental accounts and from the *Factory Inquiry Commission*, Supplementary Reports, Part 1 and Part 2, North-eastern District, C. I. Part 1 and C. I. Part 2. Sess. 1834 (167), vols. XIX and XX.

its looms from 45 per cent to 50 per cent. Canvas sales rose from 22,000 pieces in 1806 to 26,000 pieces in 1807, a level maintained for the next two years.

At the same time, in view of a rising demand for thread, Marshall expanded the output of thread (and therefore tow yarn) at Castle Foregate. In 1808 the business made a profit of £64,544 at Leeds and Salop, and Marshall went beyond restoring the depleted plant to creating additional capacity. By the end of the war yarn spindles at Salop had increased by a third to 2424. Tow yarns, sold to carpet makers for backing, accounted for a third of the output; the rest was line yarn twisted into thread, and the number of twisting frames was doubled.

Whilst other spinners and weavers were hard pressed and even put out of business by famine flax prices, Marshall, secure in his supply of flax, maintained a fairly high level of output until 1808–9. He could not sell all he made and had to reduce yarn output; but to compensate for this he began to weave more canvas and make more thread. Moreover, had the famine continued into 1809 he would have made an even larger profit out of his stocks.

Once flax and yarn prices eased off later in 1809, Marshall cleared the existing stocks of finished goods before stepping up output. He had overcome the test of war and could turn it to his advantage. Imports of foreign *yarn* were still jeopardised and the native spinning industry had suffered many setbacks. The result was that Marshall could sell as much as he could make at Water Lane for the duration of the war. 'The demand for our yarns was at that time very great.'[1] He brought to an end the increase in linen production, diverting only 35 per cent of the firm's yarn to weavers who had a few years earlier taken 50 per cent; and within five years the quantity of yarns sold increased by a fifth to reach 77,000 bundles.

The rise in yarn output (to 86,000 bundles in 1810 and 100,000 in 1811) took place without any increase in plant, simply by employing more labour and working longer hours. In 1810 he took on over a hundred hands at the Water Lane mills, bringing the labour force there up to 584, and they worked 347 days in that year. In 1811 the firm had 700 workers; they also worked 347 days but their working

---

[1] Marshall, 'Life', p. 16.

week averaged 80 hours instead of the usual 72. In both years Marshall sold more than he made and yarn stocks fell to less than a month's supply. As a result *manufacturing* profit reached almost £24,000 in both years.

The high prices of 1812 reduced yarn sales to 77,000 bundles, and canvas suffered similarly. Stocks rose; forty-four workers were dismissed and the firm worked only 304 days. But by the end of 1813 peace was in sight, prices began to fall and sales picked up. Marshall immediately cleared his stocks and raised output the following year. In the boom of 1814–15, when the demand for yarns was such that new firms began to enter the industry, Marshall and Co. worked to the utmost and raised output by a third. Four old frames were scrapped in 1814 and thirteen new line spinning frames carrying 270 spindles were squeezed into mill *B*. A hundred workers were taken on, and a labour force of 692 worked an average of $13\frac{1}{2}$ hours a day for 353 days. This great effort produced 107,000 bundles of yarn. But it could not meet the back-log of demand waiting to be satisfied, and for a time yarn prices rose whilst flax prices fell. The following year, 1815, five more spinning frames were fitted into mill *B*. An extra fifty hands were taken on, and the mills worked for 355 days —during three months at $84\frac{1}{2}$ hours a week. In that year Marshalls produced 120,000 bundles of yarn; and again, despite falling flax prices, yarn prices remained steady. In these two years, the firm's *manufacturing* profit amounted to £49,000. Then in 1816 the boom came to an end. Forty hands were dismissed, the mills worked for 291 days, 65 hours a week. Output dropped to 96,000 bundles and the firm suffered its first loss for over twenty years.

A buoyant demand and high prices certainly swelled profits and in most years between 1810 and 1815 must have been a decisive influence. More pervasive and less spectacular was the effect of reductions in cost due to mechanical improvements and the spread of overheads. Gains secured by increases in efficiency demonstrate a systematic search for profit by improvements within the firm, and in some years cost reductions made a significant impact on profits. For example, in 1807, despite rising flax prices and higher charges for rent and interest, the firm produced an extra 5000 bundles of yarn and 4000 pieces of canvas more cheaply than the output of the previous year; the cost of flax per bundle of yarn fell by spinning lighter counts and the productivity of the hacklers, especially the boy apprentices, rose. Indeed in that year the whole rise in profits came about by increases in efficiency.

The cost of spinning a bundle of grey yarn in this decade is shown graphically in an appendix.[1] There was no consistent trend either up or down between 1806 and 1814; the cost hovered mostly around 22s., although in some years (1809, 1812 and 1813) it rose substantially. However, since the prices of many things rose considerably at this time, to keep costs fairly constant was something of an achievement. What happened can be seen by considering the three principal expenses—flax, labour and overheads.

Raw materials accounted for nearly four-fifths of the cost of spinning a bundle of yarn. Flax cost per bundle varied for two reasons: the price of flax rose and fell; and the amount of flax required to spin a bundle, that is 60,000 yards of yarn, changed if the output comprised chiefly heavier or lighter yarns. By far the most important fact during the war was the price of flax. Reference has been made to the fact that the price Marshall paid for flax doubled between 1806 and 1809 and during the rest of the war it never became as cheap as it was in 1806. Other things being equal, the cost of flax per bundle of yarn would rise or fall in proportion to the price of raw flax and there was a fairly close correspondence during these years. Changes in the size of yarn did not greatly affect the cost of flax per bundle. The number of bundles spun from a ton of raw material rose before 1809 and then remained around a hundred. The average fineness of yarn spun increased from just below to just over 10 leas per lb. (This could have been due to improved machinery, or more simply to the quality of flax. Expensive grades of flax were expected to warrant their price by yielding a higher proportion of line yarn, and if this happened changes in the price which the firm paid for flax cover changes in the length of yarn spun.) However, at this time no pronounced change took place either in spinning-machinery or in the fineness of yarn produced.

According to Marshall, labour costs, between a seventh and a

---

[1] See Figs. 9, 10.

tenth of total costs, became a little lower between 1796 and 1809, and then stayed remarkably constant at 2s. a bundle.[1] The initial decline was not the result of lower wages. These actually increased, though very slightly considering the rising prices of many necessities during the war. Bleachers, skilled men who commanded high weekly wages of 21s. in 1806, received no increase during the war. The price a weaver received for a piece fell by 1d. though the length of cloth woven in a week did not change. Only the unskilled machine operatives gained; spinners were paid 6s. a week in 1806, an additional 3d. in 1809 and a further 3d. in 1813. This rise in wages showed in higher labour costs of 1½d. a bundle for spinning after 1809. To offset this Marshall tried to raise output per spinner but made no real progress until 1813. Between 1806 and 1812 whenever a spinner attended more spindles, which she did if finer yarn was spun, *her* output fell because the yarn had more twist and was slower in spinning. Conversely, when coarser yarns with less twist were spun at a quicker pace, the girl watched fewer spindles and the quantity that came off each spindle, and therefore *her* output, rose. The results of such attempts to improve the productivity of capital or labour are not important in this perspective—in one year an 8 per cent increase in the number of spindles tended by a spinner resulted in a 5 per cent decline in her output. They are interesting simply because they represent continuous attempts to raise efficiency. But, after 1812, increased output per worker went hand in hand with the production of predominantly finer yarns. To some extent this progress was due to improved hackling which produced a smoother sliver, less liable to break; and at the same time a spinner, instead of tending thirty spindles each making 10 leas a day, now watched sixty spindles making 15 leas or 120 making 12 leas.[2] (Probably this involved watching two sides—a feature of the Leeds mills which William Brown noticed in 1821—and it coincided with an increase in spinner's wages of 3d. a week.) However, the higher output per operative had no immediate impact on unit labour costs. Only line spinners produced more and even then the advantages that could be obtained from better slivers awaited the introduction of new spinning frames. Marshall began to attend to this task in 1811; for example,

[1] Marshall, 'Experiments', vol. III, December 1810, no. 103, p. 50.   [2] *Ibid.*

in that year all the old frames, about half of those in Room 7, were scheduled for breaking up, but two years passed before they were replaced.[1]

If spinning labour costs tended to rise, the downward pressure on labour costs can be attributed to a saving in the hackling process. In fact the firm saved £1500 a year on wages when labour costs for hackling fell from 1s. 5d. a bundle in 1806 to 9d. in 1810. The reason for this was the mechanisation of hackling, a technical change induced by a production bottleneck.

Hackling is, after sorting, the first factory process in producing yarn. Adult males pulled bunches of flax through combs by hand in the hackling sheds, straightening and cleaning the fibres, separating them into long lengths that became line yarn and shorter lengths for tow. It was a skilled and very important job because the proportions into which the hacklers split the flax determined the relative quantities of the final product, and line yarns sold at twice the price of tow.

For some years mill-owners like Porthouse sought without success to design a hackling machine. After 1800 such efforts increased because hand-hacklers had to work more slowly in order to further the production of slivers sufficiently smooth for making medium yarns. Trouble arose when hacklers began to exploit their position, insisting on a long apprenticeship for recruits and demanding a higher wage, despite the fact that by 1808 they earned over £2 a week. This stimulated the invention of several machines. Marshall had a machine in 1808, for which John Hives took out a patent in the following year, and the latter was promptly challenged by Matthew Murray who had made six machines for another Leeds spinner, James Tennant. Within a decade machines displaced hand hacklers in the larger mills, though many small firms continued to use manual labour until the late 1820's.[2]

---

[1] Cf. Marshall, 'Experiments', vol. III, April 1811, no. 114, p. 52. 'Our old frames, being much worn and not worth replacing, we break up all made previously to 1801, and replace with them the new ones. Those made since 1801, we refit with new plates and spindles to the plan of the new ones.'

[2] Hives patent 3527, 12 August 1809. On 10 February 1809 Murray sent a model of a hackling machine to the Society of Arts for which he was awarded a gold medal (Kilburn-Scott, *op. cit.* p. 51). In the depositions, Hives v. Benyon 1818 (Marshall Collection), it appears that Tennant, a spinner who had been helped financially by John Marshall in 1804, had Murray's machines in 1808. The feeling in 1818 was that on this

Marshall had two hackling machines at work in Water Lane in 1809, twenty-two in 1810, and thirty-two in 1815. The number of hand hacklers employed dwindled from seventy men and thirty apprentices in 1806 to forty-two men and twenty-six apprentices in the slacker year of 1808, and to only five men in 1809. By 1810 their places had been taken by 124 workers: eleven men sorters; nine men and forty-two boy roughers; and sixty-two boys and girls on the new machines. Wages for hackling fell from £4458 in 1808 to £3126 in 1810, a saving which in one year would have bought nearly seventy machines, the number installed by 1825. Just as important was the effect of the new machines on productivity. Reference has already been made to their effect on spinning. As regards hackling itself, where hand workers formerly hackled 4 cwt. and their apprentices 3 cwt. of flax in a week, a machine attended by a child separated at least 14 cwt. In addition, whereas a craftsman produced *less* than 50 lb. of potential line from a hundredweight of flax, a machinist averaged 56 lb.[1]

The third element of expense is the miscellany of charges labelled 'General Expenses' which could amount to as much as a fifth of total costs. They contained a high proportion of fixed costs, and the expense per bundle fell whenever output rose and vice versa. It is not possible to be certain about the magnitudes of all the items under this heading, but it seems fairly clear that, despite rising rent and interest charges, sales and manufacturing expenses remained fairly constant around 4s. a bundle.[2]

Interest charges grew from £1662 in 1806 to a peak of £8885 in 1813 and then as capital diminished fell to £6602 by 1815. Nearly £10,000 spent on fabric and power at Water Lane increased the rent from £2000 in 1806 to £2958 in 1815. No new buildings had been erected with a view to increasing output. The principal additions

occasion Murray deserved credit and Hives's solicitor advised against taking Benyons to court. For workers' combinations, see J. G. Marshall, *Report of the 28th Meeting of the British Association*, 1858, Statistical Section, pp. 184–8.

[1] Marshall, 'Experiments', vol. III, December 1810, no. 103, p. 50. Marshall claimed that 'Heckling machines save one third of the expense of wages, cut the line better than it is done by hand, and make 5 lb. per cwt. more yield'.

[2] These costs, which are itemised only for 1806 and 1811, were arrived at in an arbitrary manner. However, major items such as rent and interest can be derived from the partners' yearly accounts.

consisted of three low buildings at the north end of the new site across Water Lane. They included a dry house, a more impressive counting house and a mechanics' shop and, most important of all, the three-storey warehouse costing £2400, erected in 1806. This row of buildings was fire-proof in construction and cost more than earlier fabric at Water Lane: the warehouse, for instance, cost 4s.10d. per sq. ft. Other spending on the fabric at this time was for power and lighting. In 1814 a 56 horse-power engine costing £2782 was erected in mill *B* in place of the original 28 horse-power engine which could not supply sufficient power for the extra line spinning placed there when hackling machinery, carding and tow spinning were reorganised and placed in mill *A*. Between 1810 and 1814 Marshall installed gas lighting, erecting gas houses and gasometers in the yards, north and south of Water Lane, at a cost of £2721. Hitherto the firm, which did not work night shifts, had used candles to avoid the smell of oil lamps. The advantage of gas lamps lay in providing an intenser light at dawn and dusk during the winter at a lower cost. Marshall, like Clegg at Manchester, probably reckoned to use lights about 400 hours a year. He estimated that 100 lb. of coal, costing 4½d., gave 320 cu. ft. of purified gas, equivalent in illumination to 16 lb. of tallow candles at 6d. a pound. Having deducted receipts from the sale of by-products, namely 64 lb. of coke and 5·4 lb. of tar, and added the cost of wages and gas plant, Marshall expected to light his mills at the same intensity as before for a fifth of the cost—or provide five times as much light for the same cost.[1]

The most obscure items in 'General Expenses' are the omnibus costs covering manufacturing overheads such as coal, machine repairs and engine men, and sales expenses consisting of travellers, offices and discounts. These two categories were of the same magnitude and together amounted to £10,000 in 1806 and 1811. Subsequently they fell until 1814, offsetting higher rents and interest; then for a few years after the war an additional £6000 a year was spent on sales.

By analysing unit costs in this manner it seems clear that, except for the introduction of hackling machinery, no changes in productivity occurred which reduced costs significantly. The same conclusion

[1] John Marshall, 'Notebook', 1790–1830, p. 64. Cf. Bage–Strutt, 5 March 1808, for Clegg's Mill at Manchester.

arises from an examination of other processes—weaving and bleaching. The predominating and decisive factor influencing total costs at this time was the price of raw materials, particularly flax in the spinning process.

No single cause wholly accounts for Marshall's fortune during this decade. That he did so well was due in the first instance to price inflation and to foresight in the purchase of flax. So far as Marshall was concerned there was no corresponding wage inflation; and the demand for linens before 1809 and for yarns afterwards remained buoyant. He had the enterprise and resources to benefit from a situation which injured others; as he put it, 'the times have been favourable, and our profits have been proportionately great'.[1]

There is a further question that must be raised even if it cannot be adequately answered: did Marshall's success depend on a monopolistic position? Of course Marshall never confessed to being a monopolist, although in 1820 he boasted that 'It is rather singular that in a period of 30 years, there have not been more men of talent engaged in [flax-spinning], whose competition would have produced a more rapid advance in the manufacture.'[2] As Marshall became rich and distinguished, others might have followed in his footsteps.

There were of course other mill-spinners. On his travels Marshall visited at least a score of flax-mills, describing most of them as inefficient and unprofitable. Certainly they were small and from Marshall's viewpoint may not have counted as rivals. None had the resources to follow him. Moreover, during the war few newcomers entered the trade and many spinners failed. So Marshall did not encounter serious competition until other urban spinners emerged after the war. Nevertheless, even during the war he was not alone in the market. His output met only a small part of the needs of Yorkshire weavers. Slightly over half his sale yarn went to Barnsley in 1812, where he supplied a sixth of the master weavers' requirements. They bought the rest of their yarns from hand-spinners at home and, whenever possible, abroad. A further 8 per cent of the sale yarns made at Water Lane went to north Yorkshire towns such as North-

---

[1] Marshall, 'Life', p. 16. [2] *Ibid*. p. 17.

allerton and Brompton which drew most of their machine yarns from Darlington. The rest of Marshall's output, 38 per cent of the sale yarn made at Water Lane, went to London, Bristol, Norwich and the principal towns of south-east Lancashire and the West Riding: in none of these places did this yarn amount to more than a very small fraction of the total supply. Likewise Marshall's output of canvas was less than 1 per cent of United Kingdom production. In the raw material market, he bought only 6 per cent of the United Kingdom's imports, and not until the 1840's did foreign growers complain that the price of flax was fixed at Leeds. By the ordinary tests Marshall did not have the substance of a monopolist. Nor is there any evidence to show that he acted in concert with Benyons, the other main spinner in Leeds after 1804; indeed, it is unlikely that he would have found it worth while to do so in a period of inflation.

Notwithstanding these facts, there were times during the war when Marshall was in a very commanding position and he could have taken the opportunity to force prices up. No evidence survives to show whether he did. However, there can be no doubt that Marshall was becoming the acknowledged leader of the industry. He set the pattern in offering credit and the pace in innovations. Others watched what he was doing and tried to follow suit. On at least one occasion Marshall, by ignoring a new technique, helped to retard its adoption for a decade. In this sense, he dominated the industry and influenced what went on.

(v)

Twenty-five years have passed, and John Marshall has gone a long way towards realising his ambitions. Nobody could any longer regard him as a headstrong young man whose future hung in the balance. At fifty, he is a pillar in local society, respected and feared for his wealth and position, praised for his benevolence, and an example to be followed:

To a person wishing to be conversant in flax spinning the investigation of Marshall's works could not fail to be useful and interesting. These works are the most extensive and the best regulated of the kind in Britain, and their eminence has been entirely brought forward by the exertions of a single person viz: John Marshall who has entirely raised himself from a humble individual to possess an income of not less than a hundred thousand pounds per annum. I would do well to acquaint myself particularly with his personal character and habits through life—his education—his abilities —his capital at beginning—the prudence or rapidity of his career in extending the different checks he met with—his method of experimenting and executing improvements in the machinery and organisation—his method of interesting able people in his service, and at great length the present state of all his mills and machinery, with their teams of managers, clerks, overseers and hands.[1]

How did Marshall reach such a position? He was ambitious, capable, and realistic in the path which he chose. The first important step was his perception of a route, based on the experience of Lancashire's spinners. After that he was favoured by circumstances and had the ability to overcome the obstacles which he encountered: his father died and left him the means to start; others provided financial or technical assistance to speed him on his way. Then in the 1790's whilst other spinners remained small, Marshall pushed ahead at a rapid rate until his partners became a millstone around his neck. With the same resolve that enabled him to deal with the 1793 commercial crisis and two years later minimise the effects of a fire, he undertook a considerable financial transaction to free himself from the Benyon brothers. Finally he was in a position by 1803, as some people always are, to gain from war; when the French flag spread across Europe and flax prices rose, he made his fortune as a flax-spinner.

In short, an explanation of Marshall's success involves both the character of the man and favourable, even fleeting, features in his environment. He sensed what would be to his advantage, reacting quickly to any changes which affected his methodical search for profit. Apart from the war, the prevailing situation was relatively straightforward; although the institutional framework was parochial and in some respects undeveloped, Marshall thought that on the product side he operated in what was essentially a free market;

---

[1] William Brown, *Information Regarding Flax Spinning at Leeds* (1821), p. 252, in the Leeds Reference Library. Carlyle in his *Reminiscences* refers to John Marshall as a man who 'by skilful, faithful and altogether human conduct in his flax and linen manufactory at Leeds had made a large fortune and as a man worth having known, evidently a great deal of human worth and wisdom lying funded in him'.

secondly, in a clearly structured society in which criteria regarding status were generally shared, there was no difficulty in measuring one's position and progress. Apart from income tax he did not have to contend with state intervention and, being a pioneer, he never clamoured for the protection that has accompanied industrialisation elsewhere; nor did he have to come to terms with organised labour. His only concern was to develop a new technique and organise factory production on an increasing scale. Once he had done this, his fortune grew and he built up his social position in local society. As the autobiography shows, he had no doubt about his achievement. A century and a half later, it is more difficult to measure success in England, not least because achievement on such a scale no longer seems possible.

CHAPTER III

GENTLEMAN FLAX-SPINNER, 1815–1826

(i)

After the war Marshall's style of life changed. When he considered the course of his life in 1828 at the age of sixty-three, he looked back contentedly on a decade full of new experience:

New scenes and situations in society, give a new interest to life. A variety in a man's objects of pursuit, keep up and in some degree renews, that freshness and novelty of feeling which gives so great a charm to youth. A taste for paintings has been productive of considerable pleasure to me, though it has been somewhat displaced by other pursuits. A taste for natural scenery and for laying out ornamental grounds, has been a source of high enjoyment. The improvement of land by draining and fencing, and the increase of its value by planting, have been useful objects of pursuit and continue to be both a satisfactory and a pleasant occupation of my time. The study of Political Economy, and the moral improvement of society, have always been my favourite pursuits, and are subjects which will never be exhausted. The novelty of a change of dwelling is a source of pleasurable feeling, and I have experienced this more particularly, because I have made frequent changes for the better....New acquaintances, new situations, (a new country to explore) are pleasurable excitements to the mind.[1]

No longer did Marshall devote himself solely to business: he aspired to a social standing higher than that attached to being a successful mill-owner. While keeping the business intact for his sons, he deployed his wealth and energy to foster many new interests. The possession of country estates and town houses bore witness to both his purse and social position. He thought more about the problems of society, became an educational pioneer, a patron, a member of Parliament, activities which cost money and brought social recognition and influence, tangible assets in a society of landed gentlemen where family and its connexions went much farther than they do now towards charting a man's fortune in life. Association with the aristocracy conferred a prestige which made him well-nigh invulnerable to the

---

[1] Marshall, 'Life', pp. 30–1.

back-bitings of merchants, manufacturers and the lower orders. At the same time, Marshall sought to provide for the future of his children who were coming of age.

Consequently, from the end of the war, Marshall's activities out-side the mills and, in particular, his family ambitions, bear upon the fortunes of the firm. He had founded a successful business, and went on to promote the interests of his family. Should the security or the well-being of the firm and of the family conflict with one another, John Marshall and his sons would have to choose between them. Henceforth the activities of the Marshalls as flax-spinners and as a wealthy middle-class family are themes which run together and alternate in any explanation of events.

Marshall outgrew the flax-mills as a source of wealth at the end of the war. The firm continued to have a call, but only a limited call, on his resources. Between 1815 and 1842 (the year he effectively withdrew from the business) Marshall spent over £50,000 on new buildings and engines in return for a 10 per cent rent until 1824 and then $7\frac{1}{2}$ per cent. Since these assets were not depreciated and since the firm usually shouldered the cost of maintenance, Marshall got an average yield of $8\frac{1}{2}$ per cent from this investment in the 1820's; and, even after taking a third off the rent in 1831 and eight years later a further £1000, his return amounted to practically 5 per cent. He had no second thoughts about these outlays because they brought a good return. In contrast he did not invest any more in the trading-capital and machinery of the firm. Other partners paid for plant worth almost £200,000 between 1812 and 1842 from their accumulated profits, while John Marshall's share of the capital steadily dwindled. In 1804 he had supplied virtually all of it, and in 1815 83 per cent; never again did his capital in the mills rise above the £200,000 of 1813. In the mid-1820's when other partners increased their share, Marshall's portion fell below 80 per cent; after 1830 he withdrew two-thirds so that in 1842 his sons, with a capital of £216,000, had three times as much as their father. Marshall had decided not to increase his capital because he could make more money, more easily, in other ways.

To appreciate why Marshall invested outside the business, compare the relative returns he could have expected. If he left his profits in the firm, for each £100 added to his capital, he earned £5 interest *and* (according to the operative partnership agreement) between two-thirds and three-quarters of marginal profit due to the extra capital. If the firm failed to make extra profit, Marshall earned £5 interest, and lost his share of an extra £5 which would have been paid as profit if he had not invested £100 and drawn interest on it. In other words, by investing £100 outside the business he lost £5 interest and earned the lion's share of the extra £5 that would be declared as profit. Consequently, without a major technical change or a very large expansion, Marshall, though not his partners, fared best by keeping the firm's capital constant and helping himself to the largest share of profits. Since he received between 66s. and 75s. for each additional £5 of profit before 1830, he had only to make 1½ per cent using his money in other ways to break even; more would be a net gain.

Naturally he kept intact the capital which he already had in the business, at least until the 1830's. This assured his control over Hives and Atkinson, and after 1824 he had to leave his capital in the business until his sons had accumulated enough to stand on their own feet. But the fact that Marshall gained most by higher profits strained relations between the partners after the war. Hives and Atkinson received a small part of the profit and increased their incomes by adding to their capital and drawing interest; and they complained about the amount Marshall was taking as rent. It did not suit Marshall to raise the firm's interest costs, so he tried to increase profits—and thereby his own income—through speculating in stocks. There was no longer any need to invest in flax as there had been in wartime, and Marshall had to operate on a long-term falling market. According to his son John Marshall II (who did not perceive his father's real purpose) the policy did not succeed, and until the 1830's the business had more capital than it needed for the scale of its operations.

People say, and say truly of our firm, that we have too much capital in our business. I remember in the beginning of 1826 to have come to a good resolution in my own mind to keep our concern moving with a smaller capital; being convinced from my own recollection and observation of the speculations that had been made by us since 1815, when I first knew the trade that we had suffered from having too much capital. I cannot recollect our ever speculating in holding a stock of yarn or manufactured goods, without losing by it.[1]

Marshall, it seems, had not been able to change the partnership terms to suit himself when they came up for renewal in 1818. Hives and Atkinson were quietly critical and in a stronger position than before. Sometime in the future they would have to go. But Marshall was not ready then to dispense with their services; he waited, trying in the meantime to advance his own interests by speculation, and complaining whenever profits and therefore his share of total earnings were low.

If Marshall invested a diminishing part of his earnings in the mill after the war, what did he do with the remainder? Much was spent on his family and houses, an outlay that will be considered presently. But this expenditure could be paid for out of the *interest* which he received on existing assets. The assets themselves and the profits generated by their investment kept on accumulating—with the result that Marshall's interest-income rose, enabling him to finance a more expensive way of life.

Finding outlets for the investment of profits *outside* the mills did not present a serious problem, but its solution inevitably had a bearing on the future of the family and the firm. Not only did Marshall set his sons an example but he also provided them eventually with an alternative source of income, and neither was in the best interest of the firm.

To use his spare resources, Marshall could choose between three possibilities. In the first place he could have set up a new business or developed an old one. He saw many an inviting opportunity, as for instance at the lead mines in Wharfedale.

In one instance a drift was taken a mile and a half underground from the level of the valley to drain a mine. It cost £10,000 and was seven years in cutting. What a saving would the present state of knowledge in mechanics have made them. A steam engine that cost £600 would have been put up in a few months, and not only drained the mine of water, but have drawn up all the ore....It is surprising that Steam Engines have not yet been applied to lead mines...an immense fortune might be got.[2]

---

[1] John Marshall II to John Marshall, 16 September 1827.
[2] Marshall, 'Tours' (Cumberland and Scotland, 1800). Ripon, 4 September.

To have entered this field or any other would have violated the precept which he constantly enunciated as a condition for success, namely concentration on one task. Much more likely, however, he preferred at the age of fifty to expatiate on the merits of hard work rather than indulge in it. A second possibility would be to lend his money to those—and there were many who asked—who wanted to exploit the miracles of machinery. In the 1790's the Benyon brothers had helped to finance him, and despite disagreements they fared well together financially. But the trouble with lending on a substantial scale was that it really involved managing, and Marshall did not want to burden himself. It was too risky to lend large sums of money and remain a sleeping partner. Marshall himself had first-hand knowledge of the tragedy that could follow. His father-in-law, William Pollard, had agreed in his old age to take a share in the Bradford bank of Leach and Hardcastle, 'who wanted the credit of his name but he took no part in the management of the concern'.[1] A few years later, mining speculations ruined the bank, and Pollard lost the 'greater part' of his property, died of the shock and left his wife and unmarried daughters dependent upon and perpetual reminders to their brothers-in-law. So Marshall only lent small sums to close acquaintances. To use his spare resources profitably, he chose a third possibility on the basis of his wartime experience, namely the stock-market.

In June 1813 when flax prices gave every sign of continuing their fall, he invested his bank balance, £26,361, in Exchequer Bills; fourteen months later he sold them for £26,595, and, with interest, made $4\frac{1}{2}$ per cent on the transaction. Straightway he plunged deeper, buying £95,000 3 per cent Reduced Stock at an average price of $65\frac{1}{2}$; and even after selling at 62 two years later, he made, counting interest, nearly 2 per cent on the operation, enough to make it worth while. After that Marshall bought steadily. To begin with he acquired foreign bonds, usually well below par: in 1816 he put £18,500 into 5 per cent French funds; the following year £83,000 into 6 per cent American bonds; by 1822 he had £31,000 in the issues of liberated Spanish colonies in South America. However, the bulk of Marshall's holdings were North American: in 1822 he had £212,000 invested there, and a decade later, £277,000. When the Federal Government

---

[1] Marshall, 'Life', p. 19. Leach was in fact related to Pollard, Fenton and Marshall.

refunded and converted its debts early in the 1820's, Marshall moved his resources into the Second Bank of the United States and into States' securities issued to finance public improvements. By 1829 he had $300,000 in Bank funds; and to his stocks of New York, Pennsylvania and Ohio which promised at least 5 per cent, he began adding bank and canal shares from growing areas in the deep south, Alabama, Mississippi and Louisiana. All except 3 per cent of Marshall's investments were abroad in 1832, yielding in some cases an effective interest rate above 20 per cent. At home he had £4000 in local turnpikes and utilities which paid 5 per cent but offered little chance of speculative gain and, as a wealthy citizen of Leeds, he subscribed £2000 to local issues on behalf of cultural societies and commercial buildings, outlays which promised little reward.

The coming of the railways modified the composition of this portfolio. Between 1832 and 1838 Marshall invested equal amounts at home and abroad. By 1836 he had £100,000 in railway shares, and when early in that year the investment fever reached its height, Marshall thought about selling out. 'Speculation is going on so madly that I am inclined to do my share towards reducing it, and selling some of my railway shares, with a view to buying in again when any useful one wants support, which time I am persuaded will come.'[1] He left it too late, however, and subsequently entered his railway holdings as £38,000 shares and £59,000 debts.

By 1840 Marshall had invested £½ million in funds. There is no evidence of his total earnings—as interest and from capital transactions—from this source. The South American stocks yielded 8 per cent from 1820 to 1822. Of his railway shares in eight companies, three paid no dividends before 1840, another he sold at a loss, and the rest yielded no more than 4 per cent. A million pounds, which is more than he derived from the mills after 1815, would be a conservative estimate of his capital gains and income from this source. In the early 1820's his *interest* from securities brought him almost as much income as the flax mills in Leeds and Salop; ten years later, he earned nearly twice as much from funds.

Marshall not only diversified the employment of his resources by speculating, he also used them in such a way as to limit the demand

[1] John Marshall to Henry C. Marshall, 27 April 1836.

on his time and the liability of his purse. But he was tireless in his calculating pursuit of gain. Whilst he looked out for big opportunities, he did not neglect details. In 1829 he instructed his son to find out whether the firm received more in interest than it paid as commission to Beckett's Bank. If it did, the firm lent money to the Bank for 2 per cent.

Rather than lend money at 2 per cent, I would take out some cash now, as I can invest it at 5 per cent as I told you. We had about 30.000 in their hands 1 Jan. and though we owe them 12.000 now, it may not be in cash soon enough to balance the interest. You may easily calculate from the present face of the account what the balance of interest will be on 1 July and what the Commission will be to that time.[1]

As soon as he had a house in London, Marshall opened a Bank of England account which reduced bank charges on transfers to Leeds and abroad.[2] And when the builder erecting his sons' house sought an advance of payment half-way through the construction, Marshall refused except on the basis of a loan at 5 per cent.[3] The coming of old age, advancement in society, and severe losses at times, never sapped Marshall's unflagging urge to make money. He did not, as he himself stated, behave like this 'for the mere desire of getting money' but because it gave him satisfaction as a man of business, and in the long run his accomplishment as such would to a large extent be measured by the fortune he made.[4] At his death in 1845, the press guessed his wealth to have been between £1½ and £2½ million.[5] From the mills at Leeds and Shrewsbury he derived very nearly £1 million, and as much again from his investments; in addition he made something from farming and planting.

In middle age, Marshall grew increasingly aware of the social limitations of self-made wealth. Riches alone did not confer prestige and advance his status. Therefore he used his wealth to improve his own social position, and in the process to discharge the duty which

---

[1] John Marshall to John Marshall II, 8 April 1829.
[2] John Marshall II to John Marshall, 16 September 1827, 20 September 1827.
[3] John Marshall to John Marshall II, 8 April 1829.
[4] Marshall, 'Life', p. 5.
[5] *Leeds Intelligencer*, 14 June 1845; *Leeds Times*, 14 June 1845. The largest unknown is Marshall's income from securities: for instance, how much did he lose in the Second Bank of the United States in 1841? Nine years earlier his funds there amounted to half a million dollars.

he felt towards his offspring. In pursuit of these goals he spent nearly £1 million in the last thirty years of his life, as much as he paid out in wages to the labour force of his mills. More than a third went on household expenses, at least a fifth on gifts to his family, and nearly a tenth on property. The rest, some £¼ million, he disbursed on paintings, patronage and politics.

For the first decade of their married life the Marshalls had lived in Meadow Lane, a sparsely built suburb protruding south from Leeds township, near the Water Lane mills and the bustle of the Navigation. With an estate of over £70,000 in 1805, Marshall was on an equal financial footing with many of the richer merchants in the town and he decided to leave neighbours like Murray, Taylor and Wordsworth and to live, like Gott at Armley, in a more becoming residence. He chose an old farm in the hills to the north-west of the town, an area where many prominent citizens were starting to live. New Grange was fashioned out of what had once been abbey estates beyond Headingley village, and Wade's trustees asked a high rent—£500 a year for the first five years and then £200; but the house and its extensive lands provided the Marshalls with the status they sought locally. John Marshall became a spare-time farmer, laying out the grounds near the house and rearing sheep in the fields. The year they moved in he bought a hundred beasts, wethers and ewes, and on an outlay of £374 he calculated his profit from the sale of wool and lambs to be 10 per cent. Later he extended the farm, renting adjacent fields from the Earl of Cardigan. The house itself was large, indicating a man of substance. Its staff numbered more than a dozen servants—housekeeper, butler, maids, grooms and gardeners. The cellars were well stocked with wine, and Marshall began to spend on books and paintings. (Portraits of him and his wife had already been painted in 1802 by John Russell, styled painter to the king.) By residence as much as wealth, the Marshalls ranked amongst the foremost families of Leeds, and in keeping with their position they patronised the local library and educational ventures, and supported Baines in his exposition of Whig principles.[1] New Grange was also the home of a growing

---

[1] Baines, *op. cit.* pp. 39–41. Two of Marshall's associates who helped to revive the *Leeds Mercury* were Peter Garforth, jr., and James Bischoff, both related by marriage to the Stansfeld family, who were Mill Hill Unitarians.

PLATE II

HALLSTEADS
Photograph: G. P. Abraham Ltd, Keswick

DERWENT ISLAND

family. Twelve children were born between 1796 and 1815, and a succession of nursery maids and well-paid governesses were a permanent feature of the establishment. Marshall no longer lived as he and his mother had done at Mill Hill on £500 a year, nor even the £1000 a year spent at Meadow Lane in the 1790's: New Grange cost at least £3000 a year in household expenses, and in addition Marshall helped to support his wife's relatives who had moved to North Hall in Leeds after William Pollard's death in 1798.

At the end of the war the Marshalls had a second house, a summer residence called Hallsteads, hidden amid the trees of a promontory jutting out from the west bank of Ullswater in the Lake District. It formed 'as beautiful a situation as any upon the Lakes'.[1] The house, modest in size, two storeys above ground, and built in a light stone, cost £11,800. The principal rooms overlook the lake, beyond which rise the majestic fells of Martindale Common. A furlong away, out of sight by the water's edge, Marshall converted an old church into a house for his wife's kin, and when a large company gathered at Hallsteads, Old Church served as an annexe. Henceforth the family spent its summers in splendid isolation surrounded by picturesque scenery and the silence of mountains.

Several factors explain the choice of the Lake District for a country residence. The Marshalls first went there on their honeymoon and the notebooks kept by John Marshall on his early tours show a passionate, if not very articulate, sentiment for natural scenery. Nothing gave him more pleasure than rowing across a lake, especially in the quiet of moonlight. Water frothing over falls held him spellbound. He walked over the hills, along valleys, awed by the grandeur of the views. 'From Keswick went through Wattenlath and Borrowdale and came down by the foot of Honiston crag to the top of Buttermere—a very fine view of Borrowdale coming down from Wattenlath—Honiston and the other crags at the head of Buttermere are the most grand of any—the crags near Wythburn are perhaps more beautiful, from the mosses with which they are covered.'[2] On his way through this countryside Marshall found peace and tranquillity. The realities of town life, its long hours of daily toil and

[1] Marshall, 'Life', p. 18.
[2] Marshall, 'Tours' (Scotland and Ireland, 1800; Scotland, 1807 and 1821).

the dreary spectacle of human helplessness, seemed for a time so far away and unimportant. Even the Cumberland people, renowned for their independent spirit, had a special appeal in contrast to the lethargic factory hands who always seemed so overwhelmed by their environment. Not that Marshall admired the rural scene indiscriminately. He writhed when he came across peasants miserably chained to an unwilling soil, nor did he relish the dirt and squalor of a small country town. It disturbed him to find people so far behind the times. But away from people, alone or with a few acquaintances in the wilderness, 'the whole scene is wild and savage, with scarcely any trace of cultivation', he refreshed his solitary nature.[1]

At one time he felt the views at Loch Lomond to be 'the most beautiful I ever saw—so much more extensive than any of the English lakes', but Scotland was too far away to become a refuge from Leeds.[2] So he contemplated buying an estate in the Lake District. As early as 1800 he kept an eye on likely bargains, such as this one at the foot of Crummock: 'A fine estate on sale, £300 rent...some of it beautifully wooded, will sell for ab^t 30 years purchase.'[3] But at that time he felt that 'the most desirable place to live would be at the head of Windermere—it is in the centre of the lakes, & less out of the world —many families have lately built houses and settled near the lake, & particularly near Ambleside, & the value of land has advanced rapidly. It is odd enough that the greater part of them have no taste for the beauties of the country but spend their time in visiting and card parties.'[4] However, as his fortune mounted, Marshall aspired to something more and thought of buying a large country estate where he could dwell for a part of each year and pursue his interests in progressive agriculture. In 1810 he and his wife went to Watermillock near Ullswater for the summer. 'A principal inducement was the delicate state of my wife's health, which I hoped a change of scene and air would restore; to which was added a partiality for that country and a great enjoyment of lake scenery.'[5] This holiday, which

---

[1] Marshall,'Tours' (Cumberland and Scotland, 1800). Workington he described as 'a dirty, ill-built, disagreeable town' in contrast to Whitehaven built on the American plan and the 'regular streets' of Maryport, a new town of the last thirty years.
[2] *Ibid.* (Scotland, 1807).   [3] *Ibid.* (Scotland and Cumberland, 1800).
[4] *Ibid.* (Scotland and Cumberland, 1800).
[5] Marshall, 'Life', p. 17.

'answered our utmost expectations both as to health and happiness', became an annual event, and 'induced me to purchase land in the neighbourhood'.[1] By 1812 Marshall had spent over £10,000 on estates which he stocked with sheep at Huddlesaugh and Knot. The following year he decided to build Hallsteads.

Personal preference, Jane Marshall's health, his acquaintanceship with Foxcroft who had lived there and Mrs Marshall's longstanding friendship with Dorothy Wordsworth explain the choice of Ullswater as a residence. But there was perhaps a further reason. Marshall never intended once he was rich to remain a townsman like Gott. Although he did not rise from the humble origins sometimes claimed, his background excluded him from the small circle of related families which formed a social oligarchy in Leeds. Eventually he might gain acceptance, for there were cracks in the ice of their exclusiveness as their economic security melted in the later eighteenth century. But Marshall, who had swiftly rivalled them in wealth, could not be sure that in a small town community, criss-crossed by powerful petty interests, he would get a place in their society. For long he was just a draper's son, and even longer a dissenter and a Whig. Spinning flax and not being a merchant, it was alleged that he 'treated his LONG WOOL friends with scorn'.[2] For his part Marshall wanted to be more socially than a big fish in a provincial pond. He harboured no eccentric notions about society, and had no urge to reform or reject it. Like most newly rich he accepted English society as he found it, and simply aimed to rise as high as he could.

A rapid ascent in the social scale was not a straightforward proposition like producing yarn. Money would buy some ladders like land, houses and servants. But he could never be certain that his neighbours would not push him back where they thought he belonged. He had heard about but, unlike Gott, did not know any of the gentry families in Yorkshire, and he hardly dare set himself up there uninvited as a landed proprietor. At the start he had to climb alone and, as if he had been repeating his early spinning days, he knew what he had to do. By going to Cumberland, a district almost bereft of

---

[1] *Ibid.*

[2] From a political squib, 'The House that Jack Built'. Matthewman Collection, vol. I, 'Old Leeds', p. 52, in the Leeds Reference Libarary.

old and powerful landed families, and generously sprinkled with the new middle classes, he would quickly be accepted. So he bought extensive properties, worth £66,500 by 1826, mostly at Loweswater, Buttermere and Ullswater. He went to settle there as a wealthy businessman interested in farming and public service. Before long he became Deputy Lieutenant and in 1821 High Sheriff, and ranked with the 'aristocracy' of the county, though by contrast, he remained personally unknown to the Yorkshire gentry for many years to come.[1] Time and money were on his side, however, and like a spider weaving its web, he assiduously made connexions, so that in 1842 his son-in-law wrote: 'Today we will dine with Lord Fitzwilliam whose family are old friends of the Marshalls.'[2]

The move to Hallsteads, like Marshall's investments in funds, was in retrospect a turning-point in the family's fortunes. Intended as a summer residence, it became more important in Marshall's life than his house in Leeds. He gave up New Grange and its farm, buying Headingley House close by the Grange from James Bischoff, a woollen merchant, for £7500, and he added a west wing in 1819 costing £2753. There the family stayed during the winter months. But Marshall's delight and the family home was Hallsteads.

A second house doubled his domestic expenses; between 1815 and 1828 the annual cost of Hallsteads was £3000, so that on both houses Marshall spent £6000 annually. In those days this was a princely outlay, and it reflects the extent to which Marshall's habits of consumption changed as he climbed the social scale. And important for the future was the fact that the family no longer felt it belonged to Leeds. The children naturally thought of themselves as part of the gentry society around them, and they came to expect much the same things in life, education, occupations, sports, and in time, husbands or wives.

As Marshall's interests broadened, his activities extended into new fields. He visited the houses of gentry, many of whom he met at Westminster, but he was inhibited by his background and interests

<hr />

[1] Marshall, 'Life', p. 29.
[2] W. Whewell to his sister, 7 May 1842. I would like to thank Miss C. Marshall for granting me access to this correspondence, covering the years 1811–64.

from cursing the Catholics, calling for corn laws, and opposing Parliamentary Reform like so many of his new acquaintances.[1] If in outward forms he imitated his social superiors, his real sympathies sprang from his own singular experience. He remained, as Whewell noticed, a north-countryman, reticent, awkward and ill-adjusted in society, plain in his manner, and earnest in all that he undertook. Though not content to remain a mill-owner, he did not become a crusty country gentleman. Both as regards the place he sought for himself, his manner, and the ideas he held, he was something of a new phenomenon in English society.

Before the age of forty his intellectual interests had revolved around the mills and new scientific techniques. He studied science because it helped him: a knowledge of chemistry was useful in bleaching, the theory of machines in providing power, the properties of materials in construction. Beyond this, he took lecture-notes on optics, electricity and astronomy.[2] He studied and talked about geology. He tried out the latest techniques in farming. In short he wanted to keep up with the rush of modern knowledge because it could be useful. As a man of action, he was never so foolish as to confuse knowledge with power. At the same time keeping abreast of the latest developments in other fields gave him the particular satisfaction of always being one step ahead of most other people. Such interests gave him confidence, compensating in most situations for his social shortcomings. The deadweight of tradition, the technical ignorance and superstitious religions of the past, he brushed scornfully aside.

Engrossed in business problems, no more than an overseer in the public service, Marshall had little occasion to develop his views for many years. As he became richer he grew self-conscious of his provincial shortcomings. 'The first effects of newly acquired wealth are always seen in the buildings of a town. Refinement of taste and manners are of slower growth. It is the next generation which must spend what their fathers have learnt to accumulate.'[3] So far as he himself was concerned, however, Marshall believed in improvement

---

[1] Turberville, *op. cit.* pp. 23, 28, 34; Marshall, 'Life', p. 28; J. S. Mill, *Autobiography*, 1873 (World's Classics Edition), p. 99.

[2] John Marshall, 'Philosophical Lectures and Extracts'.

[3] Marshall, 'Tours' (Scotland, 1807). 5 August.

there and then. By finding out something about art, old buildings, traditional ceremonials, and above all the way in which aristocrats laid out and planted their estates, he sought to compensate for some of the cultural deficiencies of his provincial-town background and make himself socially more acceptable. At the same time, he developed a deeper interest in social problems and had an urge to air his views. He could diagnose the widespread misery he saw in peasant economies, especially Ireland, with a clear grasp of the essentials—a growing population, late marriages, subdivided holdings and concealed unemployment, potatoes, mud cabins and beggary.[1] Improvements, he believed, depended on raising productivity, and to do this the Irish must give up the enforced idleness of Saints' days and precarious dependence on one crop. To start afresh they would first have to improve their transport; then landowners should offer shorter leases until they had accumulated enough capital to work their estates by new methods, at which point they must push the peasantry off the land into towns. Invited to address the Leeds Philosophical Society, Marshall chose such themes as 'The relative happiness of cultivated and savage life', 'On the production of wealth, and the propriety of discussing subjects of political economy as distinguished from politics', and 'The present state of education in England as a preparation for active life'. And in 1828, he wrote a book, '*The Economy of Social Life*', 'intended to explain . . . to the working-classes, some of the most important doctrines of political economy'.[2]

Having confined his activities to the provinces until he was fifty, Marshall decided in 1821 to venture into London society. In the spring of that year during his term of office as the High Sheriff of Cumberland he rented a house in London, and each year returned at the same season. Then in 1825 he leased 4 Grosvenor Square for seven years at a cost of £13,000, and after the expiry of the lease acquired 34 Hill Street, Berkeley Square.

Finding a place in London society was more expensive and fortuitous than anything Marshall had so far attempted. Apart from any preconception about the rank of those best fitted to wield power, Marshall was too old to be very ambitious for himself in politics and

---

[1] Marshall, 'Tours' (Scotland and Ireland, 1800, and Cumberland and Scotland, 1800, 1807).   [2] R. V. Taylor, *op. cit.* p. 412.

simply sought to widen his social web. But this did not prove easy at first because he had few useful connexions and no position to exploit, save that of patron. His preference for new ideas in political economy drew him towards the group of men interested in Utilitarian philosophy. They could use financial support, and Marshall thought it would be worth his while to provide it. In three years (1825–8) he spent £3000 on the *Parliamentary History and Review* under the editorship of Bingham. In its pages, he encouraged James Mill and others to lay bare the fallacies of speakers at Westminster.[1] And, eager to support Bentham's schemes, he subscribed on behalf of himself and his sons to a new University in London and became a member of its council.

Turning aside for the moment from his career in London, Marshall's associations there and his interest in social problems led him to practice his own version of Utilitarianism in Leeds in the early 1820's. He had long been connected with local educational ventures, the founding of a Lancasterian School, a Mechanics' Institute, and a Literary and Philosophical Society in Leeds; later, in 1826, he proposed the establishment of a university in the town.[2] He was also aware of experiments by other factory-owners, Dale, Owen, Strutt, and his former partner Bage, to set up schools at their mills, and in 1822 Marshall persuaded owners of other firms around Water Lane to join him in managing and paying for a school in Holbeck. During the day, girls and boys in the neighbourhood were taught how to read and write for 2d. a week. In addition the girls learnt to sew, and for an extra 1d. boys could be instructed in accounting. Each night from 7 to 9 p.m., evening classes served 'those young persons... engaged in the Manufactories...during the course of the day';[3] if the pupil brought his own candle, the charge was 2d. a week, otherwise 3d. Financially the school soon ran a deficit; and Marshall's associates, considering this to be the result of working-class indifference,

---

[1] Mill, *op. cit.* pp. 99–100.   [2] *Leeds Mercury*, 14 January 1826.

[3] The following paragraphs are based on loose papers and a book containing information on labour, in the Marshall Collection. See also G. Ward, 'The Education of Factory Workers', *Economic History* (1935), pp. 110–24; Bage-Strutt, *op. cit.* 22 July 1812, for their schools; Marshall, 'Tours' (Scotland, 1800), 26 September for Dale at New Lanark; *Factory Inspector's Report 1836* (78), vol. XLV, p. 155, for Hives's school. There were four teachers at Marshall's school on 30 September 1826.

withdrew their support. Although Marshall felt that educational institutions should be self-supporting, he was not prepared to end the venture so abruptly: instead he doubled the charges for day students, and provided a free night school for four months a year, presumably during the summer. Then in May 1825 he began an experiment of sending children from his mills to the day school. At first he allowed twenty 'most deserving boys in the mill' to attend each Saturday. This upset labour arrangements in the mills and the children gained little from erratic attendance at school. Marshall, who was aware of the difficulties, abided by his resolution and soon more than thirty girls and boys went to the school. They were mostly between the ages of eleven and twelve, chosen so that 'it would be desirable to send the same if we can i.e. if they merit it'. Before long the number attending rose to sixty, a quarter of those under thirteen. The next step was to let fifty older children attend classes 'after work hours' every Monday evening, and each overseer was instructed to send 'the well-behaved who wanted to go'. As a result, before a separate infants' school was built in 1832, nearly two thousand children, a high proportion of those employed, passed through the school, being taught by monitors under the eye of a schoolmaster and mistress.

Marshall certainly had no need to offer free education to his young employees. Except perhaps for mechanics, the firm had no apprenticeship schemes. Three-fifths of the labour force were women and children who stepped straight into their jobs of minding machines without training. Promotion to a higher-paid task came when a vacancy occurred and depended on proficiency, in other words devotion to duty and concentration on one's work. Furthermore, the rate of turnover was so high that the business could have gained very little from training-schemes. The average length of service in 1831 was sixty-one months: at one extreme were the skilled mechanics and sorters who had been with the firm an average of thirteen years; and at the other extreme young machine-minders who never stayed more than five, and only three years in the hackling and roughing departments.[1]

[1] 'Labour Book', cited in note 3, p. 105 above; *Factory Inquiry Commission* Supplementary Report, Part 2, C. I., Part 1, pp. 75–79, Question 66. (A copy of the return is in the Marshall Collection.)

If his purpose was not to train his employees, why did Marshall spend on factory schools and to some extent sacrifice the interests of his business in this way? The answer lies in the fact that as a man of wealth and action he wanted to put Bentham's doctrines into practice and set others an example.

As he grew older Marshall became increasingly convinced that education was indispensable to successful living. His own success was the product of his values and knowledge. In his younger days these two qualities—the one moral, the other intellectual—had been fostered by parents, relatives, chapel, schools and public lectures. Naturally he thought that the only way 'to promote the improvement of the rising generation' and hence society at large was through education.[1] So much of the misery afflicting mankind was generated by ill-disposed and ignorant people without a care for the morrow.

Marshall knew from experience that more than three out of every four families in Leeds lived in labourers' cottages and neglected the education of their offspring. Each day parents went to work, leaving their children to roam the streets and 'contract habits of idleness and vice'.[2] The well-intentioned efforts of those who tried to do something for their children produced undesirable results. 'The neglect or indulgence with which children of the poor are usually treated, or what is worse, the unsteadiness and caprice, the mixture of kindness and undue severity, produces a degree of bad temper, which makes the adult miserable to himself, and a cause of wretchedness to others.' So much social evil sprang from this source that until those in authority provided training for the young the next generation would be as helpless and miserable as the present one. The first requisite, a 'moral education' or the cultivation of proper dispositions must be undertaken before a child reached five for 'much may be learnt at this age'.

...we must admit that the moral character of every human being, the habits of thinking and feeling, begin to be formed very early in infancy,... [when] the mind is untainted with vice, its habits are unformed, and it is most susceptible of deep and lasting impressions. It may then be trained to every right disposition and habit.... Good habits may at this age [2–5] be formed, which ordinary care in after years will render permanent and invincible.

[1] *Leeds Mercury*, 14 January 1826.
[2] *Ibid.* 11 February 1826. All Marshall's views in this paragraph are from this source.

To attain this end, infant schools must be established where 'the minds of the infant poor' would be set in 'a right temper and disposition'. In this way the younger generation would 'cultivate kindly feelings towards each other', display obedience and affection towards their masters, enjoy the health that comes from a well-disciplined life and be fitted 'to fulfill the duties of their several stations in after life'. For these reasons, he advocated the development of this branch of education in Leeds.

After such moral improvement, the child next required an 'intellectual education'. In a progressive society dependent upon accounts and machines, it was as important for men and to a lesser extent for women to be literate as it was for them to have a steady hand or strong arm. Everybody in a wealthy country should be given the opportunity to read, write and do sums, and so have a chance to get on in life. Therefore at this stage a child should learn about the contemporary world and become ambitious. Tests and marks kindled a sense of accomplishment and rewards such as a scholarship went to the best pupils. In this way people learnt 'to make the right use of their advantages, and to apply their new powers to the service of the community'.[1]

It was in this frame of mind that Marshall started his factory school in order to provide an opportunity for children of some merit. Hence the recurrent emphasis on sending only the *deserving* workers. Select every Saturday morning those hands who have attended well, conducted themselves well and tried to work well: and be extremely particular in examining who are the most deserving hands in each room who should be sent to school. A great proportion of the good will depend on the judgement exercised in the selection of the hands. And send as many as you can spare.[2]

At the school these children were taught to read and write, a few did sums, and all learnt about the Bible, especially the New Testament, the Book with a message.

Marshall's mill school was an experiment, the practical expression of his faith in education as a social function. Whether he was convinced of its success it is difficult to say. The results of education cannot be measured objectively, like a firm's profits. Records were kept during the 1830's to show the literacy and in some cases the

[1] *Leeds Mercury*, 11 February 1826.   [2] 'Labour Book', 8 June 1825.

scholastic achievement of the mill-hands. To some extent this may have been done to furnish favourable evidence in the public debate on factory conditions. In so far as the hands worked diligently, remained submissive and moderate in their demands, read the books placed in the mill library, attended church each Sunday, and by their behaviour distinguished themselves from other workers, Marshall no doubt felt that he had achieved something worth while.[1] Other flax-spinners like John Hives, Benyon and Titley soon followed his example, and his son, John, pointed out that by comparison country landlords did nothing to educate and improve the condition of their workers, keeping them chained to a traditional routine and a superstitious religion.

Once, John II questioned the wisdom of educating the lower orders; 'Are they not the great, perhaps the *too* great readers of newspapers?'—for instance, the *Northern Star* a few years later.[2] But the existence of the school was never in jeopardy. A separate infants' school was erected in 1832 and ten years later a new junior school. What had originated as a pioneer experiment continued because it met the requirements of the law, and in the 1840's a third son, James Marshall, became an outspoken advocate of compulsory State education for the working-class, contesting a parliamentary election on this issue.

John Marshall's views on education reflect a social philosophy grounded in his experience. It was no doubt convenient to believe that the labouring class willed their own misery and to advocate education as a panacea. But if such a diagnosis and cure were much too simple, they at least show a genuine awareness of conditions and the will that something should be done to improve them. In this Marshall set an example which others followed, with the result that mill-schools contributed much to the very widespread literacy of the urban masses before the introduction of compulsory elementary education. There was here an honest attempt to make town life more viable for the labouring class, giving many the chance to stand on their own feet.

---

[1] John Marshall II to John Marshall, 16 September 1827: 'Some of the members of our Holbeck book club are becoming a little more energetic.' In June 1832, 964 out of 1303 workers at the Water Lane Mills attended chapel; 'Labour Book', 1.

[2] J. Marshall II, draft speech for the House of Commons, May 1833.

At the same time Marshall was not radical in his approach to social problems. Twice he visited the great cotton mills at New Lanark, but made no effort to imitate Robert Owen's paternalism. Of course, in Leeds he did not have the same control over his workers. They passed their lives in well-established neighbourhoods and spent only a few years at his mills. But even in the isolation of Hanwood or at the apprentice house at Castle Foregate, he did not interfere in people's lives beyond offering education and preaching temperance.[1] Marshall did not seek to change human nature nor alter society, but to introduce useful improvements. In this, he took a very broad view. For he proposed the provision not only of working-class but also of middle-class education in Leeds. 'Leeds which may justly be considered the capital of the North eastern part of England ought to take the lead in the introduction of every useful institution; and assuredly there is no institution which can more advance the character and respectability of the town itself, or be of more value to society at large, than such as promotes the improvement of the rising generation.'[2] There were, he reckoned, 600 middle-class families in the town with 'on average each one boy at school in different parts of the country, at an annual expense of £50. This large sum might be kept at home.' It could finance a self-supporting university whose professors 'would form an agreeable addition to the society of the town'. Entry would be open to all, whatever their religion, who could pay the university fees. Students would live at home, attending until the age of sixteen or eighteen 'when they enter business', and would receive instruction in arts, literature and science. The proposal did not bear fruit in Marshall's lifetime; but a generation after his death, his grandson served the Yorkshire College in its early years.

After several seasons in London, Marshall decided, like others in his position, including an erstwhile partner, Benjamin Benyon, to enter Parliament.

---

[1] Hanwood, the bleaching establishment 10 miles outside Shrewsbury acquired in 1811, no longer survives. Marshall himself was not a teetotaller; needless to say, different standards applied to those who could afford a 'higher life'.

[2] *Leeds Mercury*, 14 January 1826. The remaining quotations in this paragraph are from this source.

My chief motive for having a seat in the House of Commons is a wish to see the mechanism by which the affairs of a great nation are conducted and to study the characters of the men who take the lead in public life, and the principles on which they act. I also desired it as being creditable to my family and an introduction to good society.... These measures would be in a great measure obtained by a seat for a close Borough, which involves but little of labour or attendance upon business.[1]

Acquiring a rotten borough proved more difficult than Marshall anticipated. He agreed to pay £4500 for a seat at Rye, when he discovered that the agent had no authority to sell it. This was an unexpected setback to his plans. At a loss how to conduct such negotiations, and impatient with intrigues, he soon decided to go no further with his scheme. 'I was so disgusted with the manoeuvring and jobbing which it seemed necessary to go through, that I determined to give up the thoughts of it.'[2] However, the Broughams, who were his neighbours in the Lake District, eventually came to the rescue and secured him a seat at Petersfield for 5000 guineas.

Meantime, after the disenfranchisement of Grampound, Yorkshire received two extra seats in the Commons. The Tories offered four candidates and the Whig interest, represented by the Fitzwilliams, sought a partner for the young Lord Milton. Lord Morpeth, who advocated religious toleration, freer trade, the repeal of the corn laws, the abolition of slavery and a measure of parliamentary reform, was approached but declined to bear the expense of a contested election. Thereupon Baines suggested John Marshall as a candidate. The latter having already perceived the singular opportunity at hand, had begun to seek nomination himself in June 1825, 'twelve months before the election'.[3] In this he had the ardent support of the *Leeds Mercury*. 'Is there no other man in addition to Lord Milton, that they can invite to stand forward at the next election as the organ of these principles?...We think that we could suggest a name that would ably maintain the interests of trade and commerce, and support the principles of civil liberty.'[4] At this time Marshall was

---

[1] Marshall, 'Life', pp. 25–6; for Benjamin Benyon's parliamentary career, see H. T. Weyman, 'Members of Parliament for the Borough of Shrewsbury', *Transactions of the Shropshire Archaeological Society*, 4th series, vol. XII, pp. 247–8.
[2] Marshall, 'Life', p. 25.   [3] *Ibid.* p. 27.
[4] *Leeds Mercury*, 21 January 1826.

very active not only in his educational schemes, but also in the anti-slavery and civil liberty causes. Moreover an 'extreme depression' of trade early in 1826 made local business interests solicit relief through government action, and this helped Marshall's cause because he could fairly claim to be a spokesman for their interests and the vote of the West Riding towns could affect the outcome of the election. When asked by a deputation of Pontefract burgesses to stand for that borough at the next election, Marshall declined, letting it be known instead that he would be available as a county candidate and he 'was not afraid of the expense'.[1] After devious negotiations, in which Marshall characteristically exaggerated his value, he agreed to stand, having informed the Fitzwilliams that 'when in Parliament I should act upon my own opinions respecting Parliamentary Reform and the Corn Laws, which I apprehend were somewhat different from those of the Party'.[2] On account of his age and deficiencies as a public speaker, he refused to 'undergo the fatigue of a contest'.[3] But the occasion did not really arise because Wortley, the Tory who favoured civil liberty, was elevated to the Upper House and his partner Bethel withdrew. Thus Marshall and Milton were returned in June 1826 without a poll. Even so the joint expenses of the election Marshall reckoned as £53,000, though according to his private ledger *his* expenses were less than £10,000.

The honour of being the first mill-owner to represent the commercial interests of the West Riding was not lost on Marshall;

...to have the public business of a large county to transact, and important interests to represent, leads to a more complete attainment of these objects [namely participation in public affairs and social advancement] and gives a weight and influence, which the representative of a rotten Borough, without superior talents, would never possess.[4]

As a result of his election, Marshall made his début amongst the Yorkshire gentry. But in Leeds his prestige waned. If his assault on the Establishment angered the Tories, his diffident, remote manner did not inspire his own supporters. Thenceforth, he 'seldom came before the public without committing a *faux pas*'.[5]

---

[1] Marshall, 'Life', p. 27.
[2] *Ibid.* p. 28.
[3] *Ibid.* p. 27.
[4] *Ibid.* p. 26.
[5] *Leeds Intelligencer*, 17 July 1828.

In Parliament he made little impression. He had, according to an obituary notice, 'little capacity for mixing in the arena of legislative and party politics'.[1] He had never contemplated political action as a way to further his own ends, simply because he never felt the need for such help. To him, politics was simply administration, little different in his recollection from running a factory: 'Such business [Parliamentary business] occupies a considerable proportion of a man's time, but to one accustomed to the management of extensive commercial transactions, is not likely to be either difficult or oppressive, and I should rather wish for the employment than not, when I do attend in Parliament.'[2]

In the spring of 1827, after years of good health, Marshall fell seriously ill. Having achieved his purpose, he resolved to retire from politics, and in 1830 when Parliament was dissolved he gave up his seat. Dorothy Wordsworth lost no time in congratulating his wife,

Upon Mr. Marshall's withdrawing from the very arduous office which he has so honourably and usefully held...another parliament would have been too much to look forward to!—health and strength for the fatigues, anxieties and late hours of another six or seven years! Besides, while in the country his quietly active mind always finds sufficient employment...*even in London*, when I consider the variety of his tastes, and the multiplicity of his affairs and his connections, it seems to me that he will have more than enough of salutary employment to satisfy the craving of any mind however active that has borne the Brunt of sixty years...I can fancy Mr. Marshall the gladdest of the glad on returning to his beautiful home among the mountains...free to stay in the quiet retirement that you all love so much, till winter storms drive you away.[3]

Retirement from Parliament did not mean the end of Marshall's active life, although he added no fresh laurels to his achievements. For another ten years he divided his time between Hallsteads, Leeds, London and resorts like Leamington and Bath. Not until 1840 did Marshall and his wife spend a winter at Hallsteads.[4] Then towards the end of their lives, when Marshall was nearly eighty and his

---

[1] *Ibid.* 14 June 1845.

[2] Marshall, 'Life', p. 26.

[3] E. de Selincourt (ed.), *The Letters of William and Dorothy Wordsworth, The Later Years, 1821–50*, vol. I, pp. 495–6.

[4] W. Whewell to his sister, 9 April 1840, 5 July 1843. (I have not found any evidence that Marshall refused a peerage in his later years. Cf. Taylor, *op. cit.* p. 415.)

wife over seventy, they spent their time in the Lakes, withdrawing into the company of their family and watching their grandchildren grow up.

Marshall never intended that his own children should make their way in life in quite the same way as he had done. Perhaps he believed in some mysterious process of heredity which transmitted qualities necessary for success. Certainly as he grew older, his ambitions widened to include the future of his offspring. He saw to it that they did not lack opportunities, and treated them in every way like an indulgent parent. In return he had the great satisfaction of seeing his children well established in society during his lifetime.

William, the eldest, would inherit the estates and become a landed proprietor, a squire in the villages near Ullswater, and spokesman of the county's gentry. After a private education, William entered the Inns of Court and in due course was called to the Bar. During his residence in London, he lived in style, drawing £700 a year from his father apart from the cost of fees, books and lodgings. On his twenty-eighth birthday in 1824, his father gave him Patterdale Hall, an estate stocked with sheep at the southern tip of Ullswater, worth £13,000. Two years later his father gave him the seat in Parliament which had cost 5000 guineas; and for the rest of his active life William sat in Parliament, representing the constituency of Carlisle and East Cumberland for a generation after 1832. In 1828 he married Christiana Hibbert, the seventh daughter of a very elderly and eminent West Indian proprietor in London, whereupon his father 'fitted up and furnished the house...where he intends chiefly to reside'.[1] Later William Marshall received other gifts: £5000 in cash in 1830, £20,000 of Louisiana stock in 1832, and property worth £15,000 by 1839. All told, William received by gift and bequest £150,000 in stocks and most of his father's property in the Lake District.

The four younger sons—John II, James, Henry and Arthur—were destined for the flax business. As they approached manhood, Marshall's partners, Hives and Atkinson, grew apprehensive about

---

[1] Marshall, 'Life', p. 21. For G. Hibbert (1757–1837) see *Dictionary of National Biography*, vol. XXVI, p. 343. Before training for the law, William Marshall was educated by the Rev. Dr Whitaker of Holme for £200 a year, including board.

their own position. John Marshall II entered the family business as his father had done at the age of seventeen. Five years later, in 1820, his father gave him a capital of £5000 and made him a partner. This brought matters to a climax with Hives, who wrote to Marshall:

I do not think it likely that we shall go together again after our present Term is expired, for in making any new arrangements I have no prospects that any of my sons would ever be admitted into the Trade, nor indeed of continuing in it myself, longer than I was useful to the concern...I am quite undetermined as to the course I should pursue if I left the Concern at the end of the present Term, for my property is more than equal to all my wants without business, and nothing would induce me to embark in a new concern but that of establishing a Trade for my children.[1]

To this Marshall replied: 'I am sensible that at your time of life you naturally look forward to the future settlement of your sons.... You are aware of the situation in which I am placed with two sons capable of conducting the business, and how differently I was situated eight years ago when our present arrangement was made.'[2] So Hives and Atkinson left to set up their own flax mills in Leeds. Hives bought land at the Far Bank and, when the partnership agreement with Marshall ended in 1823, they withdrew their capital of £60,000. From then on Marshall and Co. remained a family firm; and in the next decade three other sons, each with a share of £5000 from their father, joined the partnership. Justifying his action in 1828, Marshall sought to blame Hives and Atkinson for the separation. 'I was desirous of separating from Atkinson, because the Salop concern under his management, had become less profitable than before, or than it ought to have been.'[3] Such an allegation was in fact not fully justified, and in the case of Hives, a partner of twenty years' standing, Marshall found nothing to complain of other than Hives 'presuming on his own value...demanded a larger share than I thought reasonable'.[4] As if to support what he did, Marshall observed: 'They have succeeded in their new concern, and the separation has been advantageous to both parties. For though our profits were less for a year or two than with good management they might have been, that has

[1] J. Hives to John Marshall, 18 December 1822.
[2] *Ibid.* Marshall's reply is written on the reverse side. The partnership had three years to run when Hutton retired in 1815. The three surviving partners renewed their agreement for a further term of six years in 1818, but separated in January 1823.
[3] Marshall, 'Life', p. 22.   [4] *Ibid.* pp. 22–3.

been more than compensated by the intimate knowledge of the manufacture, which John [II] and James have acquired, by their being
early placed in the responsible management of it.'[1] This was perhaps
the first occasion of any importance when family interests took
precedence over those of the business.

In 1828 Marshall's second son, John II, married the daughter of
John Ballantine Dykes of Dovenby Hall. This match united the
Marshalls with an old gentry family of Cumberland and gratified
John Marshall very much.[2] The following year he built Headingley
Lodge near his own residence in Leeds for the young couple at a
cost of £6000. However, when his son sought to acquire New Grange
nearby at the end of 1829, John Marshall demurred: 'I do not feel
any wish for New Grange.'[3] He suggested instead that John II might
acquire 'a country residence at some future time', and early in 1832
helped him to buy one.

Acquiring an estate was as expensive as building a new mill, and
John Marshall behaved in a thoroughly business-like manner. Early
in 1832 he found out what estates in the Lakes were up for sale, and
narrowed his preferences to two properties fronting Derwentwater.
One belonging to Lady William Gordon lay 'towards the middle of
the lake...unannoyed by the Town' of Keswick.[4] It covered 529
acres, was overplanted, and valued at £14,000, about the sum John
Marshall II could afford. The other estate, which once belonged to
the Earls of Derwentwater and passed with their treason in 1715 to
the Greenwich Hospital, was at the north end of the lake, between
the shore and the town. It covered 2000 acres and was valued at
£61,600.[5] In order to secure a second opinion on the relative merits
of these properties, John Marshall asked William Wordsworth, a
friend of nearly forty years' standing, to view them for him. The
latter favoured the Greenwich Hospital estate.

---

[1] Marshall 'Life', p. 23.
[2] Bulmer, *Directory of Cumberland* (1901), pp. 721, 773.
[3] John Marshall to John Marshall II, 2 October 1829. Incidentally, at that time
Marshall's former partner, T. Benyon, lived at New Grange and his son at Gledhow
Hall; earlier they had lived in Park Place, Leeds.
[4] Selincourt, *op. cit.* p. 613.
[5] Valuation of the Lady Gordon and the Greenwich Hospital Estates, February 1832,
in Marshall Collection, on pages torn from a John Marshall II notebook. Cf. Selincourt,
op. cit. p. 612 footnote.

Were it not for the State of the Times, I should say without scruple that unless the price were very high with reference to the present rents, the purchase of the Derwentwater Estate, to sell out again in parcels would be a promising speculation—providing the Purchaser did not care about disfiguring the Country when he came to divide it. If he should have any reserve of this kind, even in favourable times—there might be a doubt then of him making much of a bargain.[1]

Wordsworth knew of a buyer who proposed to build on the site, and feared that it might be broken up for 'paltry cottages, rows of lodging houses, and inns and stables, etc., which would be the most likely way to make money of the thing'.[2] Obviously he hoped that Marshall would take the land and permit the building of no more than a few gentlemen's residences on it. John Marshall II could build a house by Friar's Crag, some distance away from the town end of the property where 'people and strangers...range over it in all directions'.[3] Such an estate had not only 'picturesque beauty above all praise', but its owner might 'erect a House correspondent to the dignity of the situation...sufficient to give...considerable influence over the Town'; in addition, 'at present no doubt it will be bought much lower'. At an auction in April, John Marshall bought the property for £49,800, a fifth below his valuation, and Wordsworth promised to suggest ways of improving its beauty. 'Mr Southey will be pleased to hear that you are the Purchaser, as will all men of taste, especially when they know your chief inducement for buying the property.' For though Marshall had been shrewd enough to buy a property that would increase in value, he intended for the present that it should remain intact and go to his son. But with a capital of £30,000 and an income of no more than £6000, John Marshall II could not afford such an estate. So he paid his father £20,000 and promised the rest with 3 per cent interest at the end of three years.

Two daughters also married at this time. The third girl, Jane Dorothea, gave her hand to an army captain when she was twenty-four. Her husband, who later rose to the rank of colonel, was the second son of Sir Granville Temple, a resident of Florence, and Marshall settled £13,000 on her. A younger sister, Julia, met Henry

---

[1] Selincourt, *op. cit.* p. 612. [2] *Ibid.* p. 612.
[3] *Ibid.* p. 636. The remaining quotations in this paragraph are from the same source, pp. 612 and 636.

Venn Elliott, a clergyman of good family, when she accompanied her father on his convalescence to Brighton in 1827. Five years later they married, but there is no record of the gifts presented on this occasion. However, John Marshall's generosity did not end with marriage. In 1840 Mrs Elliott and Mrs Temple received £3000 each and by his will both gained £20,000.

Marshall gave generously to his family, particularly in his later years. From time to time his unmarried daughters received presents, for instance in 1839 four of them received £3000 each; and he bequeathed to Ellen, an invalid who remained unmarried, £30,000. During his life Marshall gave more than £200,000 to his children. Not counting property and funds, he had at his death £170,000, of which £60,000 went to his wife and the rest to his daughters.

By the early 1830's his ambitions for his family were only partly fulfilled. Some had yet to marry and others to distinguish themselves in society. But in the fifteen years after the war Marshall had achieved a great deal: he had increased his wealth, ranked amongst the Cumberland 'aristocracy', represented the county of Yorkshire in Parliament, and launched his children on their careers.

Meantime what happened to the business? In November 1821 William Brown, the Dundee spinner, wrote

Mr. Marshall's great success, and prodigious extension, are said to have arisen from the indefatigable perseverance and great abilities of himself, and the late Mr. David Wood [a textile machine-maker] who were constantly in co-operation for improvement—but as the latter is now off the stage, and the former closely following, it is not impossible that the immense concern may be past its meridian.[1]

(ii)

After twenty-five years as a flax-spinner, John Marshall had built up a very large business. The three mills at Leeds and Shrewsbury had a quarter of a million pounds capital and employed nearly 1200 workers. Towards the end of the war Marshall had bought 1500 tons of flax a year and spun 150,000 bundles of yarn. From an annual revenue of a quarter million pounds he made a profit of 10 per cent,

[1] W. Brown, *op. cit.* p. 252.

plus 5 per cent on invested capital and 10 per cent (less maintenance) as rent on the fabric. By any measure, his achievement was remarkable. The trade paid its tribute by considering Marshall to be its founder; those outside were impressed by the extent of his concerns and wealth.

Businessmen admired not merely the magnitude of Marshall's achievement, but also his methods. His most visible accomplishment —and in common with most outstanding businessmen he took pride in it—was the organisation of his mills. As William Brown noticed:

In Marshalls every man chases his business—in the others every man's business chases him.... The hands had very particular printed instructions set before them which are as particularly attended to...so strict are the instructions that if an overseer of a room be found talking to any person in the mill during working hours he is dismissed immediately—two or more overseers are employed in each room, if one be found a yard out of his own ground, he is discharged. No overseer is allowed to touch a tool or shift a pinion with his own hands, on pain of dismissal—everyone, manager, overseers, mechanics, oilers, spreaders, spinners and reelers, have their particular duty pointed out to them, and if they transgress, they are instantly turned off as unfit for their situation.[1]

Such a large business would obviously require careful organisation if it was to be run successfully. Even if it had been their intention, the personal supervision of much that went on in the mills was beyond the capacity of the partners. Moreover, as he advanced in age, the founder spent less time at the plant. To ensure order and secure efficiency Marshall relied instead on an elaborate system of rules and accounting. In the first place, he took advantage of the fact that as the use of machinery spread he could define and regulate closely the repetitive tasks called for in spinning yarn. By the 1820's (perhaps earlier) two-fifths of the labour force at Water Lane consisted of young girls between thirteen and twenty, and one-fifth of children under thirteen, all of whom were machine-minders. It was a relatively simple matter to draw up rules governing their duties. Work began at 6 a.m. each day, and each operator tended a certain amount of power-driven machinery for 72 hours a week. An overlooker seated at a desk at the end of each room watched the hands at work. If a worker transgressed by being late or inattentive, she was

[1] *Ibid.* p. 244.

punished. In the 1820's a first offender was fined 1*d*. to 6*d*.; next time her wage would be cut, perhaps permanently; after that, she lost her place. At the same time economic incentives were used to foster diligence at work. Each quarter those in the most efficient department earned a bonus, £10 for the overlooker and about a week's wage for each hand.

The organisation of Marshall and Co. impressed contemporaries because firms of this size which called for detailed regulation were rare in the early nineteenth century. Later factory regulations would proliferate far in excess of those devised by Marshall. But the initial novelty of his system lay in the fact that duties and penalties were formally put on record and this enabled his rules to be both comprehensive and progressive in a way that was impossible where discipline was maintained by personal improvisation. By comparison with others Marshall's rules were far from being repressive. Like everybody else, he not only knew what was good for other people but what was best for himself, and he realised that nothing would be gained by pushing the hands too far. Usually he copied his working arrangements from practices current in the cotton industry, modifying them according to local custom in such matters as holidays. Enlightened self-interest taught him independently where to draw the line at hours of work, to install fans, regulate room temperatures, and later provide changing rooms, stoves and baths. Those in authority were expressly forbidden to use corporal punishment such as schoolteachers meted out with public acquiescence. Some trouble was unavoidable but, apart from a few incidents which allegedly occurred at Castle Foregate, Marshall's opponents found little evidence of cruelty or vice. Most critics confined themselves to general issues of inhumanity, like the political rhymer who wrote

> These are the children all forlorn,
> Who toil and slave from night to morn,
> In spinning the flax all heckled and torn,
> That lays in the House that Jack built.[1]

---

[1] 'The House that Jack Built', Matthewman Collection, vol. I. 'Old Leeds', p. 52, in the Leeds Reference Library. For an alleged incident of cruelty at Castle Foregate, see P. Horsman to Marshall and Co., 16 February 1833. In this letter Horsman, the manager in Salop, answered questions raised in the Select Committee on Labour of Children in Mills and Factories, 1831–2, about the treatment of the hands at Castle Foregate.

For discovering cases of brutality or misconduct, adversaries of the factory system fared much better at smaller factories where either discipline was lax or physically administered.

Indeed, Marshall made an effort to improve the status and welfare of his employees, particularly in the 1820's. But even in the 1790's, he had encouraged the adult males in the mills to form a friendly society. By subscribing each week to a common fund which they administered themselves, the men put something by to meet the natural calamities of sickness and death. They thus learnt to shoulder their own responsibilities as Marshall believed they should. For half a century at least the men at Water Lane and Castle Foregate ran these societies, making their own rules, choosing their own officers, and dutifully fining themselves for rowdy conduct at meetings.[1]

One important feature of Marshall's organisation which outsiders did not see—though doubtless they would have liked to—were his records. Apart from the ledgers, wage-books, letter-books and so forth (none of which survive) necessary for the daily conduct of an extensive business, the proprietors required at least a straight-forward aggregate financial account of each year's trading. But John Marshall wanted more than this. Not only did he try to keep the hands busy at their frames by factory regulations, but he also wanted to know if they processed the precious flax efficiently. This proved easy to arrange. Each machine turned out a standard product and its performance could be measured. In time every frame had a card to record its daily performance. Exactly when this system started it is not possible to say. The records of the steam-engines were allegedly not as full as they ought to have been in the early 1820's. On the other hand, there was no major alteration in plant between 1793 and 1822, and in choosing new machines the founder showed concern not only with a low level of operating skill for women and children machinists, but also with simplicity for the measurement of performance. It is reasonable to suppose therefore that machine records were started soon after 1804, though it is conceivable that the system of accounts which Marshall evolved was based on *estimates* of performance cal-culated by the overseers. In any case, every overseer submitted a

[1] 'Mill Club Rules.' Four books survive between 1795 and 1850.

report on the work performed in his room to the factory manager; the clerks in the mill's office then condensed the records of the four main departments—hackling, spinning, weaving and bleaching—on a half-yearly basis showing the inputs and outputs by quantity and value for each grade of raw material processed, constructing in effect a set of process accounts. Finally Hives and Marshall compiled a departmental abstract indicating average performance in physical and financial terms for both workers and machines, together with average factor prices. Simultaneously, John Marshall began a rudimentary profit and loss account, although to the end of its days, the firm's declared profit was calculated in customary merchant manner as the excess of assets over liabilities at the annual stock-take.

Compared with the private accounts of the 1790's, those introduced after 1806 were tantamount to developing a radar system for the business. Obviously Marshall wanted more than an exact annual *financial* summary of the firm's transactions. In the first place he sought to acquaint himself with the firm's position at shorter intervals than a year. Between 1804 and 1806 he experimented with periods of two and three months, and thereafter decided on a six-monthly account. In the second place the time span between the purchase of flax and the payment for finished products was at least fourteen months and Marshall wanted a frequent realistic picture of how the business stood. Process accounting in which current inputs and outputs were marked at current prices provided an estimate of the firm's unrealised profit and also indicated which particular operations were currently most profitable. There was no other way of being sure about this. Finally, by keeping a record of average performance, Marshall could compare year by year the output of the machinery, labour and the yield of each season's flax. On this basis he could if he wanted keep laggards up to scratch and see how innovations such as hackling machinery, faster speeds or different loads worked out in practice.[1] Only in this way, by reducing a mass of data to a few dimensions, could a change in one part of the mills be seen in the perspective of the whole. These accounts therefore provided Marshall with information which could be useful in making decisions.

A final aspect of Marshall's organisation which outsiders envied

[1] See for instance John Marshall II to John Marshall, 15 March 1827.

was the calibre of his overlookers, agents and managers. Marshall paid well and chose carefully. An overseer earned the handsome wage of £4 a week. A chief traveller, chief clerk or principal mechanic, would be hired on a seven-year contract and might receive as much as £400 a year in the 1820's, twenty times more than the average worker earned. Several of these senior employees had proved their worth; Hives, Hutton and Atkinson became partners and events fully justified Marshall's choice. They were very able, trustworthy executives, 'confidential servants who would follow the plans chalked out for them', and they established a tradition later carried on at Shrewsbury by Whitwell and Horsman.[1] Twenty years of delegating authority convinced Marshall that 'a concern directed, in the general plan of conducting it, by a good judgement, may be well and profitably managed in the detail by servants'.[2] The major decisions bearing on profit and calling for the bold judgement and vision which is supposed to distinguish a successful businessman Marshall of course reserved for himself. Each year he bought flax worth £70,000, fixed the prices of their products and decided what machines to install. David Wood, a partner in the Round Foundry across the street, helped with the machinery, which had changed little since Murray's inventions in the early 1790's. In his other functions Marshall was largely a buyer and seller and, despite a few miscalculations, he had acquitted himself with distinction in this role after leaving the Benyons and Bage in 1804.

At the end of the war therefore Marshall had a great engine at his disposal. Its strength lay in its size, resources and personnel. Internally its organisation would need careful watching to prevent deterioration. All systems have flaws and this one would eventually prove to be no exception. Overseers could conceal much that went on in the mills. Accounting became an end in itself. In the absence of the proprietors, the senior executives ran things as they wanted. However, since 1804 the organisation had shown no sign of serious internal stress. Hives and Atkinson would continue to serve Marshall well as long as he served their interests. So far the founder had placed the interests of the business before everything else. In the past decade he had proved himself capable of exploiting wartime

[1] Marshall, 'Life', p. 22.   [2] *Ibid.*

conditions; the plant was kept fully active and an interest was shown in raising its efficiency. But after the war external conditions changed, and Marshall's reaction to this situation would be the principal factor affecting the mills in the next decade.

The climate of business was never again so favourable for Marshall as it had been during the war. After five years of peace, he confessed that 'the trade has been overdone by many new adventurers entering into it', a reference directed to those spinners whose recent rise made Leeds the foremost town for the manufacture of flax yarn in the country.[1] Apart from a few sacking and buckram manufacturers weaving yarns spun elsewhere or stiffening canvas shipped from Scotland, Leeds had no linen industry in the late eighteenth century. Several years after Marshall's venture, a thread-maker and several weaving firms sprang up in the town.[2] After leaving Marshall, Benyons and Bage began in 1803 to spin and weave on Little Holbeck, where Meadow Lane joins Sweet Street. Two more spinners appeared in 1808: James Tennant at the Far Bank, and Titley, Tatham and Walker (an alliance of Staffordshire Quaker and Nottingham brass founder) at Water Hall Mill, where Hol Beck enters the river Aire. But at this time a traveller would have found more flax mills at Darlington, around Dundee, or in the valleys between the Wharfe and the Nidd.

At the end of the war a handful of new firms sprang up. In 1814 there were *seven* spinners, and *six* spinners and weavers in the borough. Two years later five of them fell victims to the recession. Flax imports at Hull fell two-thirds on the previous year and, except for 1812-13, yarn imports had never been so low within living memory. However, in 1817–18 seven newcomers replaced these casualties. Then in 1819 prices of flax imports again fell sharply and in 1821 William Brown stated that '...in England, scarcely any extension has been made

[1] Marshall, 'Life', p. 17.

[2] The following sources have been used for tracing the development of the Leeds flax industry: W. Brown, *op. cit.*, and *The Factory Inquiry Commission*, Supplementary Reports, Parts 1 and 2. (These documents show the industry after the French War and in the late 1820's.) J. Mayhall, *Annals of Yorkshire*, 3 vols., in reporting calamities gives information about the size of mills: e.g. 5 November 1824, 13 June 1826, 9 February 1829, 26 August 1874. See also *Leeds Directories* dating from 1797, and H. Grothe, *Philippe de Girard* (1873).

within the last two years, either of new erections or in the enlargement of old ones'.[1] Business picked up in the next few years and at the peak of the boom in 1825, 11,500 tons of flax came into Hull despite its high price. Three newcomers at least set up in these years, all in the east end of the town where Irish immigrants eked out a living as hand-loom weavers. Hives and Atkinson, Marshall's former partners, built great mills along the north bank of the river in 1824, employed 500 hands and used a 75 horse-power engine. Moses Atkinson in East Street had 200 hands and a 50 horse-power engine. Samuel Lawson, further up Sheepscar Beck in the Mabgate district had fifty hands and a 20 horse-power engine. By the mid-1820's Leeds had seventeen flax-spinners with 50,000 spindles, 800 horse-power, and a labour force of 5000. It had become the most important spinning centre in the country. Not counting a native crop of 3000–5000 tons most of which was used in Yorkshire, English spinners used between 10,000 and 12,000 tons of imported flax in 1817. Of this sum 7000 tons were spun in Yorkshire, the rest in Lancashire and the south-west. Within Yorkshire, 57 per cent went to Leeds, 29 per cent to Knaresborough, and the other 14 per cent to spinners in a score of old weaving towns dotted across the north of the county.[2]

The development of this industry was closely associated with its structure and this is not revealed by the mere enumeration of firms and total spindleage. The Leeds industry consisted of a few large, secure firms surrounded by a swarm of small, unstable competitors. William Brown counted nineteen mills in Leeds in 1821; five belonged to Marshalls and Benyons, who between them had half the horse-power and a quarter of the spindles in the town. Five years later, De Girard put the output of the big three—Marshall, Benyons and Hives—at double that of 'une vingtaine d'autres fabriques

---

[1] W. Brown, *op. cit.* p. 3.

[2] John Marshall, 'Notebooks', 1790–1830, p. 66; 1812–31. See also *Persons Employed in the various mills and Factories of the U.K.* 1836 (138), vol. XLV, p. 51; Pigot and Co., *Directory of Yorkshire* (1830); Baines, *Directory of the County of York* (1822), pp. 274, 400, 409. Later in 1836 there were sixty-four flax mills in the West Riding, thirty-four in Somerset and Devon, and fifty-four elsewhere in England. Leeds had thirty-four mills with an average labour force of 200; elsewhere in the West Riding, the average labour force was sixty-six, and in the south-west of England, thirty-one. In 1830, thirty towns had flax-spinners or weavers in Yorkshire: at Northallerton, for instance, 'the manufactures carried on here are linen...confined to supplying the inhabitants of the town and its vicinage with the usual articles of domestic consumption'.

plus petites'.[1] Apart from Marshall and Co. these big firms were founded by men whose initial capital was at least £50,000 and who quickly ran 10,000 spindles. Two, Benyons and Bage, and Hives and Atkinson, derived their resources from partnership with Marshall, and their entry into the trade as independent producers was determined by their relationship with John Marshall. In addition to these large spinners, three were of medium size, each having some 5000 spindles. The initial resources for one came through inheritance from a former woollen merchant in the town. The others, established in a small way before the end of the war, grew gradually in the subsequent decade.

Numerically greater than the large and medium spinners combined, particularly when failures are taken into account, were the small spinners. Some used 'a range of old dwelling houses...extremely mean and inconvenient' as premises, others built tiny two-storey mills.[2] These firms, William Brown noticed, struggled along on the edge of bankruptcy, 'their hands under no sort of methodical arrangement whatever...leading their lives in the midst of dust, waste, confusion and discontent'.[3] It was easy to begin in this way. Many ambitious overlookers or mechanics who had been employed in the larger mills saw an opportunity to set up on their own after 1812 when the manufacture of linens at Barnsley, 20 miles to the south, grew rapidly.

In 1770 Barnsley had only 400 families, and although linens had been made there for more than a generation the trade was still on a small scale.[4] However, in the next fifty years the population of the town trebled. Lancashire and Cheshire weavers displaced by the cotton industry were encouraged by local bleachers to settle in the town, to be followed in their turn by Scottish and Irish migrants. The common was enclosed in 1777 to provide space for the erection of weavers' cottages; and in 1789, five years before the opening of

---

[1] De Girard to Constant Prevost, 11 October 1826, cited by H. Grothe, *op. cit.* p. 14.
[2] W. Brown. *op. cit.* p. 3.   [3] *Ibid.* p. 244.
[4] J. H. Burland, *William Wilson* (1860), pp. 7, 11, 40; Jackson, *History of Barnsley* (1858), pp. 166 ff.; J. Wilkinson, *Worthies, Families and Celebrities of Barnsley*, pp. 63 ff.; *Proceedings of the Geological Society of the West Riding*, vol. III, pp. 580–83; E. Baines, *Directory of Leeds*, 1822, p. 134; W. White, *Directory...of the Clothing Districts of the West Riding*, 1847, p. 310; J. G. Marshall, *Report of the 28th Meeting of the British Association*, 1858, *Statistical Science*, p. 185; John Marshall, 'Notebook', 1812–31.

the canal, Barnsley had seven master-manufacturers supplying 500 hand-looms with 100,000 bundles of yarn a year. For the next forty years this industry continued to expand and in 1836 there were thirty-six master-manufacturers and 4000 hand looms in the town.

The period of the town's most rapid growth lay towards the end of the Napoleonic wars. In 1812 nineteen master-manufacturers put out nearly a quarter-million bundles of yarn to 800 looms and collected 100,000 pieces of heavy linen—towellings, sheetings, dowlas and ducks for making smock frocks; in 1818 2000 weavers used half a million bundles of yarn, twice the quantity used six years earlier, and in 1822 3000 looms wove nearly three-quarters of a million bundles of yarn. Within a decade the consumption of yarn at Barnsley increased by half a million bundles. As the linen producers in Barnsley concentrated on weaving and finishing—there was only one small mill-spinner in the town—their yarns came mostly from outside. It was this demand which provided the basis for the expansion of the Leeds industry. Flax imports at Hull rose significantly after 1815 and in the 1820's ran at three times the level of the 1790's, a rough measure of the growth of spinning at Leeds. Most of the additional yarn produced went to Barnsley to satisfy the growing demand there and also to displace yarns hitherto supplied to these local weavers by hand-spinners. In 1811 mill-spinners supplied all the heavy yarns, about 70 per cent of those woven in Barnsley. The lighter yarns used for huckaback, diaper, fine broad sheeting and later drills were made by hand-spinners and imported from the Continent. After the war, Barnsley manufacturers sought to exploit the buoyant domestic market for light linens and increased their demand for medium yarns. Within a few years mill-spinners at Leeds supplied what was wanted and monopolised this end of the trade. There was an absolute fall at Hull in the level of imported handspun yarns, which in the 1820's averaged a thousand tons yearly, half the level of the 1790's.

Thus the growth of spinning at Leeds and weaving at Barnsley were intimately connected. In the 1790's the heavy yarns produced by Marshall and Benyons gave Barnsley houses an advantage at the coarse end of the trade. Improvements in weaving subsequently encouraged Barnsley houses to make lighter, patterned linens. This in turn compelled Leeds spinners to spin medium yarns with the result that they fostered further expansion at Barnsley. Until the later 1820's, there was an auspicious alliance between these two sections. Having pushed past their Scottish competitors at the heavy end of the trade, Barnsley manufacturers surpassed north Yorkshire producers at the light end; and since cheap cottons for domestic use had not yet been extensively produced, the low prices of Barnsley's household linens attracted many new buyers in the home market.

These developments at Barnsley gave many newcomers the chance to enter the trade as spinners. The demand for additional yarn was beyond the output of large spinners in Leeds and neither Benyons nor Marshall added extra capacity before 1817. Indeed, Marshall and Co. contributed nothing to the increasing needs of Barnsley because until 1817 they produced chiefly heavy yarns, weighing on average 18 lb. a bundle. About half their output was sold to the largest weaving houses in Barnsley in 1812; the rest—including nearly all the increase which Marshall squeezed from his existing plant between 1812 and 1815—went to London, South Lancashire and elsewhere in the West Riding. Both old and new firms in Barnsley faced with a seller's market which lasted for three years sought yarns within the range of 12–40 leas wherever they could be bought. Consequently yarn prices remained very steady at a time when raw material prices began falling sharply, and this encouraged newcomers to try their luck. Buying a few frames and renting a room presented no difficulty, and the newcomers immediately began to devise ways of spinning medium yarns within the range of, say, 15–30 leas. Thus a swarm of small spinners appeared when effective demand outstripped capacity both at the end of the Napoleonic wars and again in the 1830's. But few had a long existence. Most of them entered the trade after several years of prosperity, and had no time to accumulate sufficient resources to withstand the next commercial setback. Many went out of business in 1816, and several others 'disabled from purchasing flax on the common terms of three or four months' credit, and selling their yarns at nine months' survived only by spinning on commission for Hull merchants.[1]

Yet despite their small size and short lives, these spinners influenced

---

[1] W. Brown, *op. cit.* p. 250.

considerably the development of the local industry. First, in order to secure a foothold in the trade, they sought new methods; 'the inferior mills almost all tried them [gill frames] but few...approved', and one spun *wet* French yarn ahead of the large firms who seemed more preoccupied exploiting their existing plant and markets.[1] Second, when the larger spinners eventually extended their capacity and manufactured lighter yarn, their output plus that of the small firms in Leeds grew faster than Barnsley's demands and price competition ensued. At Marshall and Co., between 1815 and 1820 when average costs fell 8*s*. 8*d*. a bundle, average prices fell by 10*s*. As John Marshall confessed, owing to the small newcomers, 'profits [were] so much reduced as to be a stimulus to greater exertions'.[2] Of course, small spinners could not in the long run survive in a fighting market. Their yarns cost a third more to produce than those of Marshall and Co. and were inferior in quality—having less twist they were weaker and also badly finished.[3] On a rising market Marshall and Co. were undersold by 6*d*. a bundle, but by accepting such a narrow margin small spinners could not accumulate resources to develop or survive a prolonged period of bad trade. Despite their efforts to pioneer new methods, it was the large firms which successfully developed them. As Brown noticed in 1821, 'Gill machines... are chiefly confined to the largest mills which are inaccessible..[it is] chiefly an argument in their favour that all the best mills have adopted them and consider them an improvement'.[4] In addition only the large spinners had hackling machinery: 'Two or three of the principal mills dress their flax by machines, the chief advantage of which is the getting rid of troublesome hacklers....No access is allowed to the works where the hackling machines are used, and of course I did not see any of them.'[5] Thus the big firms became the pace-makers, not the small ones which passed away. However, since some small spinners displayed such ingenuity, it is not surprising to find them developing their foundry work and surviving very successfully in an allied field. By the second quarter of the nineteenth century, textile engineering became a specialist activity easily undertaken by men

---

[1] *Ibid*. p. 7. See chapter IV, pp. 171–3, below.
[2] Marshall, 'Life', p. 17. [3] W. Brown, *op. cit.* p. 248.
[4] *Ibid*. p. 7. [5] *Ibid*. pp. 242–3.

with small capital and guaranteeing a fairly sustained demand from one branch or other of the textile industry. Samuel Lawson of the Hope Foundry was the best known of several flax-spinners who prospered this way.[1]

Not all yarn made at Leeds was sold in Barnsley. The larger spinners put some out to weavers in Leeds. And, towards the end of the war, Marshall and Co. sold half their sale-yarn in London, northern Yorkshire, Bristol, Liverpool, Norwich, the towns of south Lancashire and the West Riding. Then with the subsequent growth of the Leeds industry and competition in Barnsley, spinners sought markets farther afield. Their success in each case varied depending on alternative sources of supply. For instance in Ireland, Marshall's agent reported that local handspun yarns were cheaper than first- and second-quality medium yarns spun at Water Lane.[2] Progress in the Irish market therefore awaited either a considerable increase in demand beyond the capacity of native hand-spinners or the production of lighter as well as of cheaper mill-yarns. Both conditions were satisfied by the later 1820's and Ireland became an important market for Leeds yarns.

In Scotland and northern England, Leeds spinners encountered competition from Scottish yarns, particularly those spun in Dundee. William Brown, a spinner in that town, visited England in the autumn of 1821 to find out where spinning 'has chiefly taken root and where it is most likely to flourish'.[3] In September, he spent a week at Leeds studying the industry which he regarded as the most formidable obstacle to the expansion of spinning in Scotland. Several factors favoured flax-spinning at Leeds compared with Dundee. First, there was the cheaper price of coal which determined the size of engine used.

---

[1] See the *Factory Inquiry Commission*, Supplementary Report, Part 2, North-eastern District, C. I, pp. 43, 51, 66. Broadly speaking, two kinds of firm developed: some made the whole range of machinery used in processing one particular fibre; the other type specialised in one machine for all firms, e.g. combs, looms. The former flourished so long as the fibre was in demand, and with regard to flax, this led to the association of Fairbairn, Lawson, Combe, Barbour by the late nineteenth century. However, such firms soon wanted to sell machinery abroad in order to secure business. By contrast the second type of firm remained small and usually secured a more even demand from one or other branch of the textile industry at home.

[2] John Marshall II, 'Notebook', 1821–5, p. 24.

[3] W. Brown, *op. cit.* p. 1.

Coals in Leeds are only two-thirds the cost of coals in most parts of Scotland, one being about 8s. (including delivery) and the other about 12s. a ton at the furnace door.... The steam-engines used for flax-spinning in Leeds are much larger than those in Scotland their average size being 30 horse-power, whilst in Scotland it is only about 11 horse-power. This circumstance operated materially in favour of the Leeds mills for large engines are proved to furnish power much better than small ones. In Dundee, a 6 horse-power engine is found to require about double the proportion of fuel to a 20 horse-power. From this it may be inferred that the Leeds engines are fed upon 2/3 fuel of...the Scottish engines in quantity...it appears that the expense of fuel for the engines in Scotland is fully double that in Leeds, or in the proportion of 9 to 4.[1]

John Marshall too was very conscious of this advantage at Leeds. On his travels in north-eastern Scotland he immediately noticed 'a want of coals which are brought from Newcastle', an expensive mining area apart from the extra cost of freight and taxes.[2] Again in 1825, he reckoned that his coal bill of £1850 at Water Lane would have cost £9000 in Belfast.

Second, labour costs were lower at Leeds. Brown noticed that Leeds workers enjoyed a higher standard of living, being 'more comfortably lodged than in Scotland. Their houses are but two storeys high and each family occupies a whole house, cooking and eating in the lower flat or room, and sleeping in the upper. They seem comfortably clean and few are without neat and substantial furniture....'[3] This might have been the result among other things of higher wages, which for 'spinners in Leeds seldom or never vary from 6s. per week per spinner for two sides or sixty-four spindles. No mill gives more or less for good or bad hands—no piece work—no engagements but on two weeks notice—no money advanced—wages paid weekly.... Masters put little value on old trained spinners as green hands are easily trained to slow driving.'[4] But even if money wages were higher in Leeds, this was offset in the determination of labour costs, first by the fact than an operator tended twice as many spindles and produced 50 per cent more yarn than his counterpart in Dundee, and

---

[1] *Ibid.* pp. 4–5.
[2] Marshall, 'Tours' (Ireland, 1800, and Scotland, 1800). 'Coals are chiefly imported from England and sell in Dublin from 30s. to 40s. per ton, very few are got in Ireland, and those are bad—some in the North-Western side, but none got on the north eastern coast.'
[3] W. Brown, *op. cit.* pp. 6–7.   [4] *Ibid.*

second because of 'the greater proportion of young girls and boys, from nine to ten years of age' employed at Leeds at 4s. a week.[1]

Leeds spinners had further advantages which Brown omits to mention; their association with Barnsley's progressive linen trade, their proximity to the home-market, the excellent transportation system of northern England. Scottish spinners, according to John Marshall, suffered from 'the want of inland navigation—a bar to any rapid advance', and from difficult roads: 'It is a great pity that the military gentlemen who made these roads did not know better than to carry them over every hill that came in their way.'[2] Flax-spinning had of course developed in Leeds because a score of enterprising businessmen exploited factors such as these which *for the time being* worked in their favour. But such advantages were not likely to last for long, nor were they in themselves decisive reasons for the progress of spinning at Leeds. As Brown pointed out, Scottish producers had countervailing advantages. In the first place, Dundee, which developed its facilities as a port rapidly after the war, was better placed for importing flax.

I reckon this advantage more than equals the superiority Leeds professes in the way of coals. The Baltic flax is all imported at Hull, chiefly by Hull merchants, who sell it to Leeds spinners at prices similar to those of Dundee, the quality similar.... To bring [the flax] from Hull, a distance of sixty miles, creates an expense of fully 20s. per ton for canal dues besides the expense and disadvantage of dealing with such a distant market.[3]

In the second place, Dundee spinners gained from certain differences in practice, 'all of which though apparently of little consequence individually bear seriously on the profits'.[4] Slow driving and the longer credits granted at Leeds added to the amount of capital required there. In addition Leeds spinners generated more waste, hackling added 'an additional expense...equal to 20s. a ton', and 'the expense of spinning [was] a little higher'. When everything had been taken into consideration, Brown believed that 'the profits on spinning in Leeds I reckon considerably lower than in Scotland.... Some years ago the Leeds spinners surpassed the Scotch in every

---

[1] W. Brown, *op. cit.* pp. 6, 241.
[2] Marshall, 'Tours' (Scotland, 1800 and 1807).   [3] W. Brown, *op. cit.* p. 247.
[4] *Ibid.* pp. 250–1. The remaining quotations in this paragraph are from Brown, *op. cit.* pp. 250–2.

particular, but as the Scotch have improved and the English have not, the case is now reversed.' He therefore predicted 'an increase of spinning in Scotland and a decrease in England'. Though he exempted nearly half the spindles in Leeds from this verdict with the proviso 'I must be understood however to allow that Mr Marshall and one or two more in Leeds keep equal to the Scotch and probably will continue to do so', Brown's prophecy was neither fulfilled nor invalidated by future events. The spinning industries of both Leeds and Dundee subsequently increased, but on complementary rather than competitive lines. In the post-war decade, however, an urban industry grew up in Dundee.[1] Twenty-five of the thirty-one mills operating before 1812 were sited outside the town, twelve of the twenty newcomers in the following decade were within it. Their mills were small, the average size of those in the town being 450 spindles in 1822 whilst those in rural districts had only half as many. Some of the Dundee mills, however, were big, and Marshall was sensitive to their competition. Not only did they prevent Leeds firms from making headway with heavy-yarn sales north of the border but in the later 1820's Leeds spinners and Barnsley weavers found difficulty in meeting competition in England from cheap Scottish linens.

Leeds spinners seeking fresh markets in northern England had to face another challenge—mill-spinners using water-power. Isolated firms situated in the wilderness proved no obstacle because they seldom survived long. John Marshall smiled at the gentleman who 'built a cotton mill in the Highlands expecting to have labour cheap, but nobody would work at it and he was obliged to abandon it'.[2] Typical of several flax-mills between the Wharfe and Nidd, Colbeck, Ellis and Willis of Fewston had abundant water-power from the Washburn valley, but they had to depend on child apprentices and foundered on labour difficulties.[3] River towns like Darlington and Knaresborough where labour did not prove an insurmountable barrier and weaving was undertaken nearby offered better prospects for success. Despite poor communications and lack of coal, Knaresborough, 20 miles north of Leeds, flourished as a linen centre until

[1] Warden, *op. cit.* pp. 592–4; W. Brown, *op. cit.* p. 2. In 1821, the Leeds industry had three times as many spindles as that of Dundee.
[2] Marshall, 'Tours' (Scotland, 1800).
[3] W. Grainge, *The History and Topography of Harrogate* (1871), pp. 483–4, 456.

the mid-1820's.[1] In 1790 the town had a thousand looms; in 1818 1300. Once machine-spinning was feasible, flax dressed in the town was no longer put out to hand-spinners up the valley to Pateley Bridge, but spun by master-manufacturers in their own mills along the river. Robinson and Dearlove (Marshall's former partner) rented two-thirds of West End mill in 1827, spun a quarter of the flax coming into the town and sold 60,000 bundles in a good year. The yarn may have been poor stuff as Marshall alleged and production may have been seriously handicapped by drought in summer and floods in winter, but the integration of spinning and weaving in this fashion made such a market difficult for Leeds spinners to penetrate. It took time for the shortcomings of their linens and the limitations of water as a source of power to seal the fate of such towns. Meanwhile they grew, though not so rapidly as towns using steam-engines, a more mobile and potentially greater source of energy. Thus the weavers of such river towns never bought much Leeds yarn even in their heyday and subsequently when they stagnated they did not want any at all.

Peace, then, brought Marshall a new set of problems. Hitherto he had displaced hand-spinners of heavy yarn, met a limited amount of competition from Darlington yarns and exploited the acute scarcities of war. Now he had to compete in the Barnsley market with other mill-spinners in Leeds; the rising urban industry in Dundee sought to supply the Scottish demand for heavy yarns and penetrate into northern England where it faced the same barriers of integration and parochial loyalties that confronted the Leeds industry; and Marshall's yarns were too heavy and expensive for Irish weavers. Finally, in 1819 raw cotton prices fell 40 per cent and power-looms were rapidly introduced into the cotton industry. Consequently Barnsley linens, which were 'not exported but confined to the domestic trade of this country', and Leeds yarns were exposed to a mounting assault from cotton producers in the 1820's.[2]

[1] Baines, *Directory of Leeds*, 1822, p. 224; White, *Directory*, 1837, vol. I, p. 718; H. Speight, *Nidderdale*, pp. 304–5; E. Hargrove, *History of Knaresborough*, *passim*; *Visitors' Handbook to Knaresborough*, 1854; J. S. Fletcher, *History of Harrogate and Knaresborough* (1920), pp. 118–19; Grainge, *op. cit.* pp. 420, 438; and Marshall Collection, John Marshall II, 'Notebook', c. 1825–7.

[2] E. Baines, *General and Commercial Directory of Leeds* (1817), p. 40.

The first important post-war change at Water Lane was the construction of a third mill. The last addition, mill *B*, had been added twenty years earlier in 1795. After that Marshall had acquired land south of Water Lane for further expansion; and at any time after 1806 he could have financed extensions of plant without difficulty. But during the war he extended the Castle Foregate thread-mill, and yarn production at Leeds did not reach a permanently higher level until prices fell after 1810. By 1814–15, however, Marshall ran the plant at its utmost capacity in order to meet the post-war rise in demand. Working 12 hours a day on nearly every day of the year, the Water Lane mills produced over 100,000 bundles a year. But it would not have been possible to maintain such a performance for long. Since the trade was expanding and since John Marshall obviously took an optimistic view of his future prospects, he decided to add extra capacity. In January 1814 he began to inquire about the prices of steam-engines, and in July the following year he ordered machinery from Fenton, Murray and Wood for a new mill. Construction probably began towards the end of 1815 and was complete a year later. At his Meadow Lane mill, Thomas Benyon made a similar decision at the same time, so that the two largest spinners in Leeds simultaneously extended their plant.

Mill *C*, as the addition at Marshall and Co. was named, was built on the south side of Water Lane, abutting the long line of low buildings —counting house, dry house and warehouse—that had been built (in what became Marshall Street) about 1804. The new mill was a lofty six-storey building, constructed in a fire-proof fashion around iron beams and columns, and with large rectangular windows lighting every bay. The floor-space available for machinery amounted to 3120 square yards, three times as much as mill *A*. In the north-east corner of the mill, traversing several strongly reinforced storeys, was a large 70 horse-power engine made by Murray, 'the finest in Leeds', its flywheel being 30 ft. in diameter and weighing 14 tons. The cost of this mill with its engine and shafting, built at a time when prices were still high, came to £16,500, and at 5s. 1d. per sq. ft. it was for its size the most expensive the firm built. Production began in 1817 with eight hackling machines, fourteen carding engines, and 1500 line and tow spindles. Before the end of the following year the mill had been filled to capacity with eleven hackling machines, twenty-one carding engines and 2166 spindles, and kept this plant until a reorganisation in 1822. This addition increased the firm's spindleage by 55 per cent, and in a fairly busy year like 1821 over 150,000 bundles of yarn were spun without the strain of long hours, every day of the year.

During the construction of the new mill, John Marshall suffered his first trading loss in twenty years. In the recession of 1816 the average price of their yarns fell by 7*s.*, resulting in a deficit of £3464. Although the value of sales rose by two-fifths the following year, the average price of Marshall's grey yarns fell still further by 1*s.* 2*d.* a bundle, owing to the fact that Marshall and Co. concentrated on heavy yarns which were no longer very profitable. In 1816 over nine-tenths of their output was 16 lea yarn or heavier; only 3 per cent of the yarn produced in mill *C* early in 1817 was lighter than 16 leas.[1] At the same time the price of line yarn above 18 leas and of light warp yarn was rising owing to the demand of Barnsley weavers. To take advantage of this trend, John Marshall ordered Hives late in 1818 to 'spin all our 12 to 14—14 to 16—16 to 18—18 to 20'[2]. Such a measure improved their standing and their sales but it could not be considered as more than an interim expedient because of its effect on costs. To spin lighter yarns by existing methods the mill-spinner had to pay more for a higher grade of flax, subject the sliver to more rolling and drawing than a thicker yarn, and put more twist into it—at Water Lane a 30 lea yarn had twelve twists per inch compared with eight for 16 leas—thus spinning more slowly. All of these requirements added to costs and had not made it profitable in the past for a mill-spinner to compete with handspun medium yarns. But on the one hand faced with the fall in heavy-yarn prices owing to the production of lighter, patterned linens at Barnsley and also perhaps to a decline in the demand for sailcloth made in some of the weaving towns supplied by Marshall and Co., and on the other hand

---

[1] Bage–Strutt, 27 September 1814. Benyons and Bage spun up to 25 lea yarn and Bage claimed 'if we thought it our interest to spin 4 or 5 times as small we should find no difficulty in constructing machines for that purpose....We do not look to any improvements in flax spinning, except some means of spreading it with greater accuracy.'

[2] J. Marshall, 'Notebook', 1810–23, p. 20, 4 December 1818.

confronted with a buoyant Barnsley market for 20–40 lea yarns, the big spinners in Leeds were challenged to make medium yarns by a different, cheaper method. And since lighter yarns had to have more twist, their immediate objective was to find a less expensive way of preparing flax so that it could be spun into a finer yarn.

There is a certain unintentional irony in John Marshall's comment of 1820 that 'it is rather singular that in a period of thirty years, there have not been more men of talent engaged in it [flax-spinning] whose competition would have produced a more rapid advance in the manufacture'.[1] For apart from the mechanisation of hackling and some minor improvements in their spinning frames, Marshall and Co. were using the same methods for preparing, spinning and weaving in 1817, and even in 1820, as they had in 1794, and such advances as John Marshall sought and introduced were copied from others at his behest, particularly from small spinners in the district. When Charles Bage, his erstwhile partner, invented a power-loom in Shrewsbury, Marshall's partner at Castle Foregate, John Atkinson, began power-loom experiments there; had they succeeded, the competition between linens and cottons would have been much less one-sided than it became by the later 1820's. The previous year, in 1815, Marshall assisted by David Wood copied part of Horace Hall's patent specifications for gill-roving and wet-spinning, but at that time there had been no collapse of heavy-yarn prices and De Girard's method did nothing to improve the weight of yarn produced at Water Lane.

At times, Marshall sought to improve their preparatory stages. Ever since 1793 his flax had been spread by hand and then drawn by rollers into a roving. Often he felt that if the flax could be drawn over pins it could be spun to between 20 and 30 leas without any alteration in the spinning frame. But in 1801 and again in 1810 he failed experimentally to draw a first sliver from a hackle: 'We have not succeeded in introducing any machine with points to produce the first sliver instead of the spread board, but still think such a machine is much wanted.'[2] From the intervals between these attempts it is

[1] Marshall, 'Life', p. 17.
[2] Marshall, 'Experiments', vol. III, December 1810, no. 103, p. 50; Horner, *op. cit.* pp. 259–60.

clear that Marshall did not consider the matter one of urgency. The mills were fully occupied and very prosperous, and a major change might not have been wise. However, at the end of the war, there were rumours that small local spinners 'at some flax mills' had produced a first sliver by points, and not to be outdone John Marshall and David Wood tried again. Once more they admitted failure after a few months and refused to credit the claims of others, concluding that 'the system of drawing flax through hackles is in no way superior to that of drawing it through rollers. And if ever that question should be again agitated and these results should be doubted, this seems to be the fairest experiment to try over again, because you begin with the material in the very best state, perfectly free from knots.'[1] Instead he again tried Cartwright's combing machine as he had promised to do five years earlier once the patent expired; but Big Ben did not serve for flax. In April 1816 he made a good first drawing from a hackle but failed to devise a practical machine. Although 'on the old system with hand-hackling or imperfect and partial machine hackling and with roller drawing, a fine roving and good could not be produced', he knew no practical alternative.[2]

Two years later, in 1818, when heavy-yarn prices had fallen, Marshall decided that he must spin medium yarns and searched earnestly for a new method. He agreed with Thomas Benyon and Anthony Titley that they should collaborate in discovering the preparatory methods allegedly used by the small spinners who made light yarns.

Eventually Marshall found what he sought at a rural mill in Darley Dale, a valley south of Barnsley. The spinner there employed a method which had been kept secret for several years before it 'was generally known and introduced by other spinners'.[3] Late in 1818 John Marshall went to examine the process.

Dakeynes...used the plan of drawing through what they called Gills....
Between the front rollers and a single pair of back rollers placed at 21 in.

---

[1] Marshall, 'Experiments', vol. III, pp. 45–9, 62–3, 66–7, 69; J. Marshall II, 'Notebook', c. 1816, pp. 13–14, 23–7.

[2] J. Marshall II, notes relating to the case of Kay v. Marshall.

[3] Marshall, 'Experiments', vol III, February 1819, no. 124, p. 84; Horner, *op. cit.* pp. 259–61.

ratch, or more or less according to the length of the staple, 22 small hackles 1½ in. broad revolved, carried by a chain or leather belt which passed over two rollers. The hackles had each five rows of pins 2 in. long, 18 pins in a row of 3½ in. As soon as the sliver passed the back rollers, the hackles were pushed up perpendicularly through it, and before it reached the front rollers, they fell down perpendicularly and the sliver was left free and did not follow them.[1]

Shortly after, Titley erected a prototype at Water Hall mill and Marshall declared himself fully satisfied with the result. As he subsequently stated, 'Gill machines effected what we have so long aimed at producing, a good first sliver, and have overcome the radical difficulty of spinning an unequal and branchy material'.[2] At once he ordered a frame from Fenton, Murray and Wood, and early next year, 1819, asked for thirty-three more at £50 apiece.

Introducing gill frames meant reorganisation on a scale that John Marshall would have found difficult to recall. Hackling machinery had by comparison been easy to install: it was the first process in the mill and so dusty that it had to be kept by itself in the under-drawings or in a separate shed out in the yard.[3] But gill frames came in the sequence for preparing line yarns and to ensure a smooth flow of work machinery had to be moved around. In 1820 there were six new frames at work, in 1821 fourteen. In 1822 seventy-one more were delivered and the whole layout of the plant was altered to accommodate them. Mill *B* and two-thirds of mill *C* were rearranged for spinning medium yarns; the rest of mill *C* and mill *A* specialised on tow yarns. In 1821 a new 40 horse-power engine was fitted in mill *A* and 1250 extra tow spindles put in place of hackling machinery. At this point John Marshall had to decide whether to carry the transformation even farther. The average price of his 16 lea yarn had fallen 2s. 8d., about a seventh, in the previous five years. Even in a year

---

[1] *Ibid.* vol. III, February 1819, p. 84.

[2] *Ibid.* vol. III, 1822, p. 51. The first frame made in 1819 by Murray had '5 rows of pins 2 in. long. . . . The line spread from the strick by hand on long boards; then drawn a second time, then roved', see J. G. Marshall, 'Notebook', 1826–9, p. 15. For a description of the two methods of preparing then in vogue, that is, roller drawing and gill frames, and cylinder preparing, see W. Brown, *op. cit.* pp. 7–8.

[3] W. Brown, *op. cit.* p. 4. 'Heckling rooms. . .often at an awkward distance from the spinning frames. . .in an outhouse or a distant wing.'

of good trade this yarn brought little profit. A 12 lea yarn yielded
1s. 11d. profit a bundle on an outlay in flax alone amounting to 11s.11d.
On the other hand, the flax in 20 lea medium line cost 8s. 7d., in 30
lea line 7s. 1d., in 50 lea line 5s. 5d.; and although these yarns cost
between 6d. and 1s. a bundle more in the labour cost necessary for
extra preparing, they brought a profit of 5s. in 1820 and their prices
showed no sign of falling in the next two years. Clearly it was to
Marshall's advantage to increase the firm's output of medium at the
expense of its heavy yarns. Alternatively, if gill frames could be made
to improve the preparation of tow, he could spin a lighter tow yarn as
a substitute for heavy line yarn. This course would have considerable
advantages. First, heavy yarns would be spun from a very much
cheaper raw material and thus yield a wider margin; second, in the
hackling process alone the firm rendered 59 per cent of its flax unfit
for line yarn, and this either had to be used as tow or sold outside; and
third, Marshall and Co. could still profitably serve customers wanting
heavy yarns which would not have been possible had they concentrated on manufacturing medium yarns—'Though we may also
look forward to the line being spun much further, yet it cannot
probably be done till the tow has been spun so fine and so well as
to supply the place of coarse line yarns'.[1]

Much depended therefore on whether gill frames could effectively
prepare tow, and the founder together with his son James, who entered
the firm in 1820 as a trainee, began to tackle the problem. Hitherto
tow had been carded prior to spinning, like short wool, and then
drawn much more than line, the fibres being straightened by short
draws in the first frames and pulled out later. 'In 1821 and 1822, we
began to apply gill-preparing to tow; we first used it in mill *A*, to
replace the worst roller roving frames as they wore out. In these
frames the great distance between the hackles, the small number in
action at once and the width of the tools were great imperfections.'[2]
In face of this setback, they tried to improve the carding and spinning
of tow in order to produce a lighter yarn. At the end of 1823 the
firm began to sell 4 lb. tow, twice as fine as any made three years

---

[1] J. Marshall II, 'Notebook', 1821–5, p. 43, 29 January 1824. J. G. Marshall,
'Notebook', 1826–9, p. 10.
[2] J. G. Marshall, 'Notebook', 1826–9, p. 18.

earlier. Whereupon John Marshall II urged 'we ought to go forward as fast as possible in making new tow spinning frames...as quickly as we can. Being so short of tow spinning we ought on no account to break up any of our old frames but let our new frames form a clear addition.'[1] But the expansion of tow-spinning only raised a fresh problem. In 1823

we found that we had overloaded our tow-preparing machinery by extend-ing the spinning without a corresponding extension of preparing: we were obliged to card very heavy: the yarn uneven and the quality complained of: it therefore became evident that a great extension of tow-preparing was necessary. We proposed to make the cards more effective by giving them two workers, and cheaper and simpler by using a doffing cylinder and crank instead of a flexible sheet and rollers. The two workers were found advantageous, though not to any great degree: the cylinder after a variety of trials we finally concluded not to be effective or perfect for the length of staple our tow has, as the flexible sheets.[2]

This difficulty was overcome by doubling the number and raising the speed of the cards;

This increased speed was a very great assistance in rendering our carding at once nearly twice as effective as before. The speed of the feeding and the doffing we kept nearly as before; and afterwards as we increased our cards and diminished our weights we made our feeding sheets and rollers go twice as slow as at first, and one hand which at first spread only for one sliver eventually spread for 2.[3]

Thus a larger quantity of tow was prepared and in the next few years improvements through finer hackling, lighter loading and slower speeds rapidly followed one another. In 1826, according to James Marshall, they introduced 'a much better card: more efficient in splitting and penetrating the tow and more easily doffed and kept clean'.[4]

A similar problem of balance and the introduction of further improvements occurred also in the line department. Drawing there increased 'till at one time we had 7 or 8 drawing operations previous to roving in mill *C*, and 4 or 5 in mill *B*'.[5] The result was that the

[1] J. Marshall II, 'Notebook', 1821–5, p. 43.
[2] J. G. Marshall, 'Notebook', 1826–9, p. 10.
[3] *Ibid.* p. 10.   [4] *Ibid.* p. 11.
[5] *Ibid.* p. 15. The remaining quotations in this paragraph are from the same source.

machinery did 'a great quantity of work and spreading heavy'. But 'we soon found heavy spreading injurious to the yarn: and increased the number of machines and spread lighter'. Simultaneously the mode of hackling needed revising: '...coarser hackles had been introduced along with the heavy weights...we were using coarse tools in the hackling and making a great yield. But we were at the same time trying to spin the flax further than before, and soon found that quite incompatible with coarser hackling and preparing.'[1] In 1823 more hackling machines with finer tools were installed, although doffing continued to be done by hand. In 1821 there were ten frames with sixteen tools and one with twenty-four: four years later, thirty-two had sixteen tools and six had twenty-four. Finer pins and narrower tools split the lighter stricks more effectively and consequently improved the quality of the spinning.

Thus in the early 1820's there was a radical change at Water Lane. In four years, 1822–6, the number of tow spindles increased 10 per cent and the number of line spindles 52 per cent. By a careful use of space, 500 more line spindles were squeezed into mill *B* and over 1400 into mill *C*. In a busy year like 1825 the mills produced an extra 75,000 bundles of yarn, a 50 per cent increase in output. Furthermore, during 1823 Marshall and Co. shifted noticeably into the manufacture of lighter line and tow yarn. From 1814 to 1818, 1 per cent of output was 20 lea yarn or higher; from 1819 to 1823, the proportion over 20 lea rose to 15 per cent and 1 per cent was finer than 30 lea; from 1824 to 1828, when all line yarn was prepared by gill frames, the proportion over 20 lea rose to 53 per cent, over 30 lea to 12 per cent. As John Marshall II wrote, 'finer hackling and gill roving enabled spinners to make yarns twice as fine in 1826 as they did in 1816 on the old kind of spinning frame'.[2] For an outlay of no more than £5000 on gill frames, Marshall and Co. had taken an important step in the direction of becoming medium spinners.

As if to signal their intention of specialising on the production of sale yarn at Water Lane and confining their activities to mechanised operations which could be carried on inside a mill, the firm curtailed its weaving in 1822. Towards the end of the war, Marshall and Co.

---

[1] J. G. Marshall, 'Notebook', p. 15. Cf. Marshall, 'Experiments', vol. III, 1823, no. 128, p. 91. [2] J. Marshall II, notes relating to the case of Kay *v.* Marshall.

had sold between 50,000 and 80,000 bundles of yarn a year and put 40,000 out to local handloom weavers who made some 20,000 pieces of heavy canvas, numbers 50, 31 and 41 weighing respectively 35, 30 and 27 lb. After the war, when Charles Bage left Benjamin Benyon to start his own power-loom factory at Shrewsbury, John Marshall instructed Atkinson to set up a pilot scheme at Castle Foregate.[1] In 1789 the founder and Murray had not succeeded in making a satisfactory power-loom, but since then cotton manufacturers had made considerable progress and Marshall wanted to see if there was anything in it for him. The new power-looms effected an important saving in labour costs in the production of heavy linens, but their performance required improvement. By 1821, however, John Marshall had decided that weaving heavy linens had become increasingly unprofitable. The price of 31 canvas which had been over 30s. towards the end of the war had fallen to 24s., and heavier linens such as ships had fallen 15s. in the same period. In the year 1821, 120,000 bundles of Water Lane yarn were sold direct, and 40,000 bundles still put out to Holbeck weavers. But on an outlay of £23,248 the value added in this process was £1731, less than 7 per cent. The prospects in weaving heavy linens no longer seemed attractive and the amount of yarn put out was drastically reduced in 1823 after the reorganisation of the mills.

To what extent did the introduction of gill frames revive the fortunes of Marshall and Co.? Between 1816 and 1825 profits at Water Lane fell 38 per cent and at Castle Foregate 25 per cent compared with the previous decade. Despite the fact that output doubled the partners got £100,000 less. In 1816 and again in 1819 the Leeds mill declared no profit; in the five years 1816–20, total profits amounted to only £45,000. In the next quinquennium (1821–5) profits came to £83,000; but three-fifths of this sum was made in 1821–2 before the reorganisation. The yield of Marshall's Shrewsbury mill where no addition was made to the fabric between 1811 and 1821 followed similar lines. Between 1816 and 1820 profits fell to £3000 per year. After Atkinson's departure two new engines were installed, gill frames introduced and the number of line spindles

[1] C. Hulbert, *History and Description of the County of Salop* (1837), p. 308 footnote; Marshall, 'Life', p. 15.

increased. From 1821 to 1825, average profits rose to £9,000 a year, the most profitable years being 1824–5.

So far as John Marshall was concerned the outstanding feature in the commercial climate of the post-war decade, depressing as a steady downpour of rain, was the fall in price. Average yarn prices at the Water Lane mills fell from 331*d*. a bundle in 1815 to 252*d*. in 1816, less than 200*d*. by 1819, 162½*d*. in 1824, and rose in 1825 to 172*d*. only because 'our former prices of line are too low, if we must continue to pay so high for our flax'.[1] The price of heavy 10 lea tow and 12 lea line fell continuously after January 1814, fetching only half the price ten years later. Line yarn of 16 leas sold for 21*s*. a bundle early in 1816, held its price until November 1818, then dropped to 15*s*. by 1824. Medium yarns from 20 to 30 leas eventually shared a similar fate; in 1816 their price was 20*s*. 6*d*.; by the end of 1819 it had risen to 22*s*., until 1823 it remained steady, then it 1824 it fell to 13*s*. 6*d*. (Canvas and thread prices followed parallel courses.)

The fact that prices fell would not in itself bring a spinner to disaster. If costs had fallen as fast as selling prices, average profits would not have declined and the trade as a whole may have gained. But this did not happen at Marshall and Co. Whereas their average yarn prices at Water Lane fell 51*d*. a bundle between 1816 and 1820, their average costs fell only 46*d*. The most important factor in this reduction was a drop in flax costs from 149*d*. to 107*d*. a bundle—a drop of 42*d*. To a very slight extent this was the result of spinning lighter yarns—the number of bundles produced from a ton of flax rising from 105½ in 1816 to 107¼ in 1820. The principal cause was a fall in flax prices. The average price which Marshall and Co. paid for their flax in 1816 was £65·3 a ton; in 1820, a year in which flax prices again fell sharply owing to the spectacular descent of cotton prices, they paid £47·9. But the post-war drop in European flax prices was insufficient to compensate Marshall and Co. for the decline in their product prices; and according to his son, John Marshall failed to improve the position by speculating in raw materials. The costs of labour and overheads also fell after the war, from 80½*d*. in 1816 to 77*d*. in 1820, a reduction of 3½*d*. a bundle. Despite the fact that labour productivity (measured by the number of bundles a

---

[1] J. Marshall II, 'Notebook', 1821–5, p. 67.

worker produced in a year) was about 7 per cent lower in 1820 than it had been in 1816, labour costs declined owing to lower wages and the employment of a higher proportion of children. Earnings at Water Lane averaged £22½ in 1815, £19½ in 1816, and thereafter fell steadily to a low point of £13½ in 1820. Although the productivity of the *spinning* department declined from a weekly output of 4·6 bundles per hand in 1816 to 4 bundles in 1820 (owing to the slower driving necessary to spin yarn a few counts finer), labour costs fell from 17·7*d*. a bundle to 15·8*d*. Average earnings per hand declined from £18 in 1816 when 290 days were worked to £13·5 in 1820, a working year of 322 days. If the wages of young female spinners remained constant at 6*s*. a week, Marshall and Co. must have employed a much higher proportion of young women and children in their spinning department by 1820 than during the war; perhaps many of the additional 230 workers engaged to staff mill *C* came within these categories. Even so, when product prices fell sharply in 1819 owing principally to a strike in Barnsley, the mills were closed for a month; and Marshall ordered a general reduction in wages in order to avert another deficit. During the same period overhead expenses rose £5300 to the figure of £28,200 in 1820; the addition of mill *C* added £591 to Marshall's rental, and interest on extra capital amounted to £1500. However, although overheads rose by 23 per cent, output rose 35 per cent and average fixed costs fell.

Thus in the immediate post-war period when product prices declined, John Marshall met the situation until 1818 by reducing wages, employing cheaper labour and speculating in flax, and then he looked seriously for a more profitable product. In 1821 and in 1822, when the Round Foundry was making gill frames for Marshall and Co., heavy-yarn prices continued to fall. But flax prices fell faster and Marshall and Co. produced over 150,000 bundles of yarn in both years, about 25 per cent above their recent levels. The result was that with temporarily wider profit margins, the firm's net gain from two years trade amounted to £49,251.

By 1823 the effects of the reorganisation became apparent. Where Marshall and Co. obtained 107 bundles from a ton of flax between 1816 and 1820, they spun 117 bundles in 1823, 140 in 1824 and 159 in 1825. To do this, besides using gill frames and improved hackling

machines, they bought finer flax: 14 per cent came from Holland and
Flanders in 1821–3 (equal to the proportion of medium yarn spun)
and it cost £10 a ton more. So apart from the fact that the recent fall
in flax prices halted when the momentous drop in raw cotton prices
eased off, the average price paid by Marshall and Co. rose after
1822 through the purchase of more Flemish flax. In 1823 and
1824, they spent £53 a ton on flax, and at the height of the boom
in 1825, £65, which according to John Marshall II was £10 more
than its real value. The net effect of these two opposing forces was
a drop of 8*d*. in flax costs per bundle from 107*d*. in 1820 to 99*d*.
in 1825.

In the same period total average costs fell 24½*d*. to 159½*d*. The most
important cause was a drop in overhead costs from 52½*d*. to 39½*d*.;
concurrently labour costs fell by 4*d*. to 21*d*. Since annual earnings
in the yarn departments increased after 1820 to reach £18 per head
five years later, lower labour costs were achieved by higher productivity. In 1825 the Water Lane plant employed six more workers,
and produced 80,000 more bundles of yarn than in 1820. The average
output per worker had risen from 127 to 204 bundles a year. In
some respects 1825 was an exceptional year but yarn output did not
subsequently come down. The cause of the fall in average labour
costs arose out of the production of medium yarns. From 4½ bundles
a day before 1820 (a fraction more in a busy year and less in a slack
one), preparers and spinners averaged over 6 bundles in 1825. Preparing actually took longer because more twist had to be put into a
medium yarn and output per spindle fell from 14 to 13 leas per day.
But labour productivity rose as each hand tended more spindles. After
1820 preparers and spinners (averaged together) looked after a third
more spindles than they had a few years earlier; and in 1825 new iron
frames were introduced carrying between 50 and 120 spindles. In
the hackling department too, output per hand rose more rapidly
than earnings after 1820. At the same time an increase in capital
per worker—over 2000 extra spindles without any additional labour
—helped to raise the cost of general expenses. Between 1820 and
1825 these increased by £5900, or a fifth, to £34,100. But output went up by three-fifths with the result that average overhead
costs fell sharply. (The accounts of Marshall and Co. which show

an *increase* of $8\frac{1}{2}d$. a bundle in these miscellaneous costs are misleading. Their method of accounting was altered in the early 1820's, and the items comprising 'sales and manufacturing' expenses suffered most in the change.) During this quinquennium, interest charges rose by £4500, because the partners added £91,000 to the firm's capital: £11,000, or a cost of $\frac{2}{3}d$. a bundle on the 1825 output, was spent on new plant and the rest invested in stocks. Except for alterations to engines and the construction of a stamping shed in 1823, few changes were made to the fabric and rent rose by only £300 a year. The remaining rise in general expenses, some £1000, cannot be accounted for although part of it would certainly accrue from the cost of additional travellers and discounts and carriage which varied with output.

Together these changes brought about a reduction in total average costs of $24\frac{1}{2}d$. per bundle between 1820 and 1825. But prices, even of medium yarns, fell faster and profit margins narrowed from an average of $45d$. (1811–15) to $25d$. (1816–22) and then $16d$., 10 per cent on outlay (1823–5).

As a realist Marshall could not have expected wartime profits to continue once inflationary forces spent themselves. Falling prices and incomes affected everybody to some extent. But he was far from satisfied with their level of post-war profit and the reorganisation had barely improved matters, except perhaps in the negative sense of preventing further losses.[1] Of course, as John Marshall II argued, the abnormally high flax prices of 1825 seriously affected the profits which had been expected under the new system. Had flax been £10 a ton cheaper, Marshall and Co. would have gained an extra £13,000. But their profit margin was down by only $4d$. a bundle (to $1s.\ 1d.$) on the previous two years, and as 1825 was a good year for trade they had a larger turnover and secured the same level of total profit as in 1823–4. The real obstacle to their success appeared to be the continuous fall in product prices. From all sides came depressing reports of rivals selling and even producing more cheaply than Marshall and Co. A gill frame at £35 cost less than a ton of flax and might easily be bought out of savings on circulating capital because medium yarns required less raw material. The result was that a large spinner

---

[1] Marshall, 'Life', p. 22.

like Marshall and Co. lost a little of the power due to its superior financial weight. Not only Hives, but four medium-sized spinners in Leeds made lighter yarns and sold them at prices lower than Marshall and Co. at this time. Then in 1827, during the recession, John Marshall II confirmed William Brown's observation that small spinners in Leeds operated under a price umbrella. 'We are under-sold in coarse yarns by 6*d*. or 1*s*. per bundle, and unless the demand for yarn increases soon so as to raise the prices of the little spinners to our level, we must go down to their level without doubt.'[1] They also had to contend with increasing competition from Scottish spinners manufacturing at allegedly lower costs. Marshall and Co. paid 3*s*. 6*d*. a bundle for hackling and John II wondered 'how can flax be cut and cleared from knots at 2*s*. 3*d*. per cwt', as it was north of the border.[2] At the same time their progress in Ireland was far from encouraging. Early in 1822 Richardson informed them 'that Irish [handspun] yarn from 20 to 50 leas sells for . . . 12*s*. 6*d*. a bundle. Our [Marshalls'] price being best 16*s*. second 14*s*.'[3]. And Lancashire cotton manufacturers, whose raw material prices continued to fall, began producing cheap trousering.

That falling profits disturbed the founder suggests that there was another side to this story. Either John Marshall had failed to adjust his sights to the realities of the post-war situation and was not contented with a profit (exclusive of rent and interest) of £12,000 a year on an outlay of £125,000 (1823–5); or alternatively something was amiss inside the firm.

Looking back on the events of the post-war decade, John Marshall was far from satisfied with the performance of the mills. The chief beneficiaries had been the customers who secured a larger supply of yarn at much lower prices, not the spinners. And although he took the principal decisions affecting the firm's fortunes and was therefore responsible ultimately for its fate, Marshall tended to lay blame on

---

[1] J. Marshall II to John Marshall, 1 August 1827.

[2] J. Marshall II to John Marshall, 9 September 1827. A further difference between Scottish and Leeds spinners in the late 1820's lay in output per spindle owing to the contrast between dry and wet spinning.

[3] J. Marshall II, 'Notebook', 1821–5, p. 24. Cf. Gill, *op. cit.* pp. 247 ff.; E. R. R. Green, *History of the Lagan Valley, 1800–50* (1949), pp. 71–2. Richardson was Marshall's agent in Ireland for selling yarn and buying flax.

others. John Atkinson he accused of making 'the Salop concern...
less profitable than before, or than it ought to have been'.[1] Then in
the 1820's, when Hives and Atkinson decided to leave and the reorganisation for medium spinning brought no spectacular gain, the
founder thought that the fault lay in the inexperience of his sons,
'our profits were less for a year or two than with good management
they might have been'.[2] This he stoically regarded as the price which
had to be paid for 'John and James...being early placed in the
responsible management of it [the firm]'.[3] On the basis of their record
up to 1825, however, this judgement appears unwarranted and harsh,
suggesting that the founder censured others for his own shortcomings.

John Marshall II, who entered the business in 1816, became a
partner in 1820 at the age of twenty-three. In the same year, his
younger brother James, aged eighteen, joined the firm as a management apprentice. Without guidance from the experienced Hives,
without assistance in machinery from David Wood who had died,
John II and James depended wholly on directives from their father,
chiefly in the form of letters. It was far from satisfactory as an
arrangement. True, the business had been conducted in much the
same way whilst Hives had been in charge; but whereas the latter
had very considerable ability (as his subsequent career showed),
Marshall's sons were newcomers confronted with the task of managing the largest firm in the industry at the outset of their careers.
Moreover, whereas Marshall maintained a strictly business relationship and correspondence with Hives, expecting him to execute the
orders he issued, when his sons took over family and firm matters
got mixed together, and the founder expected them to show more
enterprising qualities than mere passive obedience. In these circumstances, more than may have been the case in Hives's time, the
founder's frequent absence from the mills seriously handicapped
the firm's prospects. He was interested in other things besides flax
and lost touch with the new personnel in the firm. His sons, jostling
for effective control, despatched partisan information which John
Marshall too readily interpreted in the light of his own earlier experience at Leeds. As a result it became increasingly difficult to reach
sensible business decisions at a time when they were very badly

[1] Marshall, 'Life', p. 22.   [2] *Ibid.* p. 23.   [3] *Ibid.*

needed. Subject to the shortcomings of this system John II dutifully and diligently carried out what his father wanted and within the province of his own authority displayed initiative by introducing several worth-while improvements.

The first task facing John Marshall II was the introduction of gill roving. In 1822 he reorganised the plant and by raising work loads effected a moderate reduction in unit labour costs. Much of his time at Water Lane was spent on the floor of the mills where he introduced various minor improvements in working arrangements. On one occasion, for instance, he watched a girl spreading flax and then shortened the spreading board. 'It seems to me much better to have the board only as long as a hand can just spread the handfull that she starts with. This will be about half the present length.... There need only be one board...because the machine can hardly draw what 2 hands spread....Thus the labour of walking round the frame is saved.'[1] His brother James, who was also keen to make useful changes, wanted to install smoke burners like those he saw at Manchester. According to his estimate, each would cost £45 and cut fuel consumption by a fifth, equal to £35 annual saving on a 30 horse-power engine.

General expenses in the early 1820's amounted to a sixth of total costs in John Marshall's profit and loss account, but John II reckoned them to be nearer a quarter, and believed that they must be reduced in a competitive world. This he did by employing the plant fully and also by seeking to lessen the amount of capital in the business. Accordingly, after the reorganisation in 1822, John II engaged John Farey to advise him on the capacity and performance of the firm's steam-engines because he wanted to offset the expense of slower driving by raising loads and lowering running costs. After a thorough investigation, Farey found that where the heavier yarns were spun in *A* and *C* mills, a horse-power turned under forty spindles and processed 6 tons of flax per year.[2] In *B* and *C*, where lighter yarns were made, each horse-power turned over fifty spindles but these used only 4 tons of flax per year. This was indeed a humdrum con-

---

[1] J. Marshall II, 'Notebook', 1821–5, 23 February 1822.
[2] J. Farey, Account of the Coals Consumed at Messrs Marshalls Flax Mills, Leeds, Yorkshire (1825); J. G. Marshall to J. Marshall, 21 February 1827.

clusion and he excused himself from undertaking the second part of his task, gauging capital efficiency by translating physical performance into financial terms, on the grounds of insufficient records. (He proposed being employed to put these right.) It was no fault of John II that Farey proved so unhelpful and subsequently he discovered with alarm that their engines were loaded several times more than cotton spinners dared work theirs in Lancashire. But the episode illustrates his awareness of the need to itemise and control the burden of fixed costs which rose as a proportion of total expenses when the prices of the variable factors fell. The founder had hitherto been content to make fairly generous rounded estimates of most items comprising fixed costs—such as 'discounts and bad debts £2000'—and these amounts were repeated year after year until he simply decided that it was necessary to alter the rate and perhaps carried out an investigation to provide a new basis. But within a year of Hives's departure, John II modified their system of accounting. The Departmental Abstract which John Marshall had introduced was superseded by an Annual Check Account, a new record with three sections.

1. '*The flax produce*' showing the proportions of line and tow separated, the length of yarn produced, its fineness, and the average output per spindle per day throughout the year.

2. '*Wages and Hands*' setting out for each operation the labour cost per bundle of yarn, the number of workers and their average weekly productivity for the year.

3. '*General Expenses*' breaking up overheads and by 1829 including depreciation cost for each unit of output.

These accounts had several virtues. In the first place systematic depreciation replaced the random methods practised by the founder to reduce the value of plant. A few years later when plant repairs were separately entered, the partners could more accurately evaluate the cost of machinery in each year's output. In the second place these checks were carried out by the partners themselves at Leeds. As a result, they were acquainted at first hand with what was happening. In 1827 James introduced the same system at Salop. 'I shall arrange a plan for the quarterly examination of machinery and distribution of labour in each department and go through each; and have a book to enter them in; similar to the one we were commencing at Leeds.'[1] On the basis of such records, they compared the relative performance of each department and mill at Leeds and at Salop, seeking to raise the laggards up to the best standards of operation.

Such activities as these bespeak the efforts of John II and to a lesser extent of James to make a success of their tasks as managers of these great mills. If sometimes they failed or made mistakes (as for example John II who allowed the sale of poor yarn in 1826) the founder might have recalled *his* early days, although these were now shrouded in an aura of glory. He might also have remembered that his sons began their careers in the atmosphere of competition that grew up in the post-war decade. John II was as disappointed as the founder that profits had not been higher after 1823, but except for the plaintive promptings of his father, the small margins produced by a fighting market would have been normal in his commercial horizons. Unlike his father who thought in terms of windfalls and imperfect competition and who for twenty-five years after 1793 made little effort to introduce new machinery and spin lighter yarns, John II laid considerable stress on continuous improvements in order to keep ahead of other spinners. As he explained to his father in 1827, the latest models were needed 'to enable us to do our work well', and in that year they planned 'a new edition of tow preparing'.[2] Moreover, if local machine-makers could not execute Marshall and Co.'s orders quickly—and their experience suggested this to be the case—then they would make some of their own plant. The Round Foundry took four years to deliver their gill frames, by which time other local spinners caught up with them; and although this did not affect the issue of competition in the long run, it may have affected the firm's profits in the short run. To avoid future delays, John II began to cast the fine gills that were wanted 'in a stock made of tin and lead mixed together', and he planned to set up a foundry at the Water Lane mill.[3]

This proposal formed part of a large scheme for expansion which

---

[1] J. G. Marshall to J. Marshall, 21 February 1827. Farey's investigation was an attempt to set up a standard cost and thus keep track of efficiency.

[2] J. Marshall II to J. Marshall, 14 April 1827; J. G. Marshall, 'Notebook', 1826–9, p. 18.

[3] J. Marshall II, 'Notebook', 1821–5, p. 31.

John II outlined in 1825 at the peak of the boom. The mills were at that time equipped to capacity. In 1824 he had found that 'our only spare room is in mill *C*, where we have about four arches unoccupied'.[1] Since then an extra thousand spindles had been installed, and though they were on new iron frames which carried twice as many spindles as wooden frames, there was an acute shortage of space. Iron frames carried 9 per cent of the spindles in 1825, 21 per cent in 1826 and 26 per cent in 1827. This eased the acute situation of space a little although room had to be found for additional preparing machinery to back up a net increase of nearly 2000 spindles in the two years after 1825. John Marshall II therefore devised a scheme for an 'Increase of the Manufactory'.[2]

Our manufactory is now nearly employed in spinning what we may call fine yarns, 10 lb. to 5 lb. per bundle and we can hardly supply the very great demand that there is. We are deriving a sufficient profit from the business and yet the raw material must be considered 8 or 10£ per ton above its fair average value. We must therefore expect it cheaper shortly, our yarn will then be cheaper and in greater request than now. We can also perceive that the improvements meditated in the hackling, breaking, preparing and carding processes must materially tend towards the spinning of both cheaper and finer yarn than we do now. If we could spin 4 lb. yarn, I believe we could sell a great deal at the present price 13*s*. 6*d*.; and at 13*s*. the quantity would be immense. A small improvement in the preparatory processes would instantly enable us to spin a large quantity. There is a large field open before us, for the application of more machinery and none in the trade better able to enter upon it than ourselves. It is likely to be the most profitable yarn to spin, its production being the most difficult. It is not desirable that our present machinery should be attempted to be changed so as to suit the produce of such yarn: it does very well for its present purpose and at remunerating prices. Under such circumstances it would be folly either to break it up or do anything more at it than keep it in good working condition.

Looking forward to the many improvements which we expect to make in the preparing processes, it does not seem right to have these improvements spread as soon as possible through the medium of the machine shop in which such machines might be made. We should therefore establish one of our own as quickly as we can and we have a right to expect great assistance from Mr. Farey in the organisation and direction of it. We must first get a manager of it; a man who will see the men do their work well and instruct boys who can readily understand plans and

[1] *Ibid.* p. 43, 29 January 1824.   [2] *Ibid.* p. 83, 24 April 1825.

carry them into execution. In the present state of the trade we should teach a good many boys. We must also get some work regularly laid out and planned for them, so that they may go straight forward with it. The repair of the spinning frames in Mill *B* is one stiff and constant job; the new work should be principally breakers and hackling cylinders. These are not yet sufficiently planned. It would be well to take this opportunity to alter those roving spindles in No. 35 with the moveable neck...Mr. Murray might be kept making spinning frames as fast as he pleased, and carding engines.

The further part of the yard in mill *C*, near the 8 Horse Engine, would be a very suitable place for machine shops and they should be planned and built this year and lathes should be got in readiness directly. Our fireman should be in training and our hands should be as numerous in our old shops as we can conveniently manage. Our machine shops should have the power of making about 3 or 4000 spindles a year with preparing nearly in proportion and we should look to establishing the iron work and the millwright work of the new mill ourselves.

How many hands and what sized buildings should we then require?

3 Model makers
8 Forgers
1 Caster
3 Millwrights
50 or 60 Filers
1 Book Keeper
1 Draughtsman
1 Fireman
———
about 70 people.

It seems desirable to cover the whole of that end of the yard of Mill *C* with building and 5 stories high; but it could not entirely be wanted for these machine shops. It would be 120 feet long. It might be a warehouse for the present.

70 people at 30s. equals £100 weekly £5000 per annum; they would make machinery worth £10,000 surely. Our foundry note has been I think £5000 a year for some time.

Suppose them built this summer and to be got into reasonable action by next spring; and that they made about 3000 spindles of machinery a year; they would fill a mill of 10,000 spindles in about 3 years; sooner if it were wished. The mill should be planned and begun next spring [i.e. 1826] the Engine made during the winter and fixed in summer; and a portion of the mill at work in the autumn or beginning of winter. 10,000 spindles at 14 leas per spindle per day equals about 4000 bundles per week; 3000 of which line yarn at 5 lb. per bundle = 15,000 lb. line divided by 60 lb. per cwt = 12 ton of flax fit for 4 lb. yarn. 10,000 ÷ 220 spindles in an arch = 45. This would require a mill about 18 arches long. If the reeling were done in the same building it should be 20 arches or 200 feet long. 12 ton a week = 600 yearly. We could hardly do therefore without larger warehouse room, which would not be amiss near the machinery shops.

The Mill and Engine would cost £20,000; the machinery, 10,000 spindles at 4£ = £40,000 would be lower than it has ever before cost. The flax and labour of 210,000 bundles at 8*s*. would be £84,000. It would therefore employ a capital about £150,000. The machine shops and tools might cost (and additional warehouse) £4000; the labour of the mechanics is included in the former cost of machinery.

If this plan of John Marshall II to spend £150,000 breathes optimism in their future as flax-spinners, it also shows how John Marshall II expected to conduct business. Although medium yarn prices had fallen, he believed the concern could be made more profitable by selling a larger output at a lower average profit. (On the basis of his current experience this would have been 1*s*. profit per bundle, a lower margin than any in the past thirty years.)[1] To increase the plant and its output, John II intended to divert that part of the capital in the business which his father used for speculative purposes, so that henceforth they would not set out to earn windfall profits. As a young man, under an obligation to follow in his father's footsteps as a flax-spinner, John II's attitude seems sensible. He realised that with the development of the trade, he would have to compete with rivals for as far ahead as he could see. This would require not only the continuous introduction of new methods and efficient operation, but also the exploiting of their accumulated resources in more mills and extra output. In this way the junior partners would be assured of adequate profits and Marshall and Co. by virtue of its size and progressiveness would maintain its reputation at the head of the trade.

In advocating this scheme, John II disturbed certain notions cherished by his father. The founder measured the success of a business not simply by its total profit but also by its return on outlay —'Profit per cent on capital of partners' or 'Returns...per spindle'.[2]

---

[1] J. Marshall II, 'Notebook', 1821–5, p. 63. If it could be spun, 50 lea line would yield a profit of 5*s*. a bundle on the basis of the prevailing price, October 1824. But the prices of yarns up to 30 lea had been falling for several years and were much less profitable than in 1820–2.

[2] See J. Marshall's 'Accounts', 1806–33, comprising six loose sheets at end of 'Experiments', vol. III, 'Spinning'.

A sensible businessman entered those ventures which promised the highest return on outlay. He thought that he had done this and thereby made a considerable fortune through large margins. If in time other opportunities seemed more lucrative than flax-spinning, those wanting to succeed should move into them. At the end of the war, however, John Marshall was fifty, too old to make a fresh start himself, and he looked forward to the day when his sons would take over the business. At the same time as a businessman bent on succeeding in his occupation he could not accustom himself to lower margins after 1815. He had decided therefore to do something about it in his own way.

After 1815 Marshall and Co. carried a much higher level of stocks per spindle than in the 1790's before war strangled trade. Some of this excess might be justified perhaps as a hedge against price movements, but this was not the main reason. At the end of 1817, for example, the firm carried over eight months' supply of flax compared with a usual peace-time level of three to four months; the following year, when prices temporarily rose, the business profited by £10 a ton on this stock. In this way, John Marshall offset the losses of the previous year despite a further fall in product prices. Again in 1823, as flax prices rose in the boom, Marshall bought heavily, only to find on this occasion that prices moved down the following year. Thus although flax prices in general fell for many years after 1813, Marshall thought that the vagaries of nature, the many grades of flax and the large number of markets, plus the resources which he had at his disposal, offered ample scope for speculation.

It was hardly surprising that he acted in this particular way. During the war he had bought flax successfully on a large scale and in 1814 he started to invest on his own account in government stock. To gamble with part of the mounting capital in the business, mounting because his partners did not draw their full measure of earnings, was only a further step in the same direction. In this way he might increase the firm's profits and in view of the prevailing partnership agreement this would augment *his* share of their total earnings as interest and profits. Rather than build a fourth mill at Water Lane when competition was lowering product prices and reducing margins and when there was no invention in sight that could be profitably developed, he used the firm's surplus capital to set up as a merchant.

With success, John Marshall would in the short run put more money into his own purse. But his son believed that in the long run it injured their trade; on the one hand it added unnecessarily to fixed costs (for the use of extra capital) and on the other they never had been and could not expect to be successful as merchants.[1]

In 1827 John II brought this matter to a head. Early in August whilst recovering from a severe illness at Brighton, John Marshall opened a letter from his son—into whose hands all business chanced to pass at that critical time—dutifully inquiring whether he wanted to gamble on a consignment of flax.

It is entirely a question for your decision: we are not obliged to take the flax, indeed Cummings could at the price sell it any day. We might gain nothing by taking it, but in my opinion could not lose. . . . It should be viewed as an outlay or investment of money: the money being yours, and the profit, if any, shared among us. It is in no way a speculation in the least degree connected with the well conducting of our manufactory. For my own part, I had as lieve be without as with it; we shall have enough to sell without it. Please to decide as you please. The last time I calculated it over, I thought that we should have 1000 tons to sell, without taking in the 130 ton about which Cummings is writing. Of this 1000, 200 is to remain at Riga, which leaves 800 to sell in Yorkshire; how we are to sell it, is not easy to say. We generally ask a top market price, if we tried a bottom market price perhaps the difficulty might be smaller. At any rate we have no chance of selling now, and we must lock it up in a warehouse and forget it I fancy; forget even to insure it. James has told you in what jeopardy 300 or 400 tons of our flax was in at Hull. We have had many a warning in the last year or two, we shall catch it soon.[2]

A month later the Baltic market opened for winter orders and dealers wooed reluctant buyers. John Marshall II grew a little fretful: 'We had intended to let our 200 ton remain at Riga during Winter: in my opinion we have more in our warehouse here than we can sell before May, when it can be shipped at a cheaper rate than now.'[3] He therefore proposed selling the Riga flax at prime cost for 'a good bill on a London Banker' hoping for £3 to £4 profit per ton. 'From

[1] J. Marshall II to J. Marshall, 16 September 1827.
[2] *Ibid.* 1 August 1827.
[3] *Ibid.* 9 September 1827.

present appearance there certainly appears but little chance of any
material advance in the price of flax.' The elder Marshall agreed,
whereupon his son took the opportunity to confess his profound
disagreement with the whole practice of speculating:

It would be much better to sell yarn than flax. . . . I agree with you that we
had better take £1 per ton profit on our flax lying at Riga rather than hold
it, if the new flax should possess good quality. At present we could not
sell to a profit according to Mitchell's last letter: we have therefore bought
about 1000 ton of flax on speculation which we could now buy on equally
favourable terms after being 6 or 9 months out of our money. It is but
rarely that it can answer our purpose to make a large speculation in flax.
It requires a range of information, and such a foresight of events as we do
not possess. Who could have thought that cotton would have so long continued at such immeasurably low prices? If we could have foreseen that circumstance, we might have saved ourselves the trouble of our speculation.[1]

John II declared that to his knowledge the business had not gained
from speculation since his entry in 1816; and he hoped his father
would refrain in future. It was too risky; John II, a young man with
only £25,000 of capital, did not feel confident about exploiting their
financial power like his father. Instead he preferred to be prudent,
concentrating more on concrete activities in the mills over which he
could effectively exercise a measure of control.

Soon after this incident, Marshall's sons took over the task of
buying flax and the firm's stocks declined, partly of course because
lighter yarns required less flax, but also because they trimmed
purchases to immediate needs. The commercial side fell to Henry
Cowper Marshall, a fourth son who entered as a trainee in 1828.
Having set his mind to anything, Henry would devise an impressive
system and assiduously follow it. For four years after 1828 flax prices
rose and each year he simply worked out a detailed schedule based
on what each mill would require of each grade of flax for the next
sixteen months and arranged to buy it in strict anticipation of consumption. The requirements themselves were nicely calculated from
orders received and expected, and related to the prices of yarn and
thread expected to prevail for each grade of flax in the next season.
It was mostly reasonable guesswork, which looked exact and con-

---

[1] J. Marshall II to J. Marshall, 16 September 1827.

vincing in figures. This is an extract from the final stages of the process in 1833:[1]

[Figures in tons of flax]

(Anticipated) Monthly consumption:	Leeds 50;	Salop 28
Consumption for 16 months	Leeds 800	
	Salop 448	
	1248	
Stock total, 14 Oct. 1833		
Leeds and Salop	418	
Deducting stocks, this leaves to be bought	830	
or say 800 tons		

This is not a large quantity and would be a fair supply, but considering the short crop, with probable great demand and high prices, we must run ourselves as near as we can. Say 6 or 8 weeks shorter into 1834 with a reduction in our consumption of 5 ton a month by using more baltic and spinning finer would allow of our buying 200 tons less, taking in all about 600 instead of 800.

John Marshall II thought 600 tons 'would be running it much too near—should not be much less than 800'. They resolved to buy 800 tons, and Henry then drew up a detailed market schedule.

Estimate [in tons] of purchase in different markets

[Grade of flax]	I	II	III		IV	V	VI
Courtrai	—	10	30	40 20			
Antwerp	—	10	20	30 80	90	100	30
Rotterdam					50	160	50
Ireland, England, etc.					20	40	20

We may divide the quantity amongst the months as follows:

	Courtrai	Antwerp	Rotterdam	[Rest]	Total
Sept.	5	25	—	—	30
Oct.	15	55	20	—	90
Nov.	20	70	45	10	145
Dec.	20	80	65	20	185
Jan.	15	60	70	30	175
Feb.	15	40	40	10	105
March	10	30	20	10	70

[1] H. C. Marshall, 'Notebook A', pp. 7, 15.

We are likely to fall most short of these (I and II) quantities in the last 3 months and therefore must order pretty near what we have set down to be taken before Xmas.

He thus bought cautiously, the risks of speculation outweighing any possible gains. In 1834 the forecast period was reduced from sixteen to twelve months, and they managed with even lower stocks. Then later that year when the crop failed, inflating prices and inflicting serious hardship on the industry, the business did not make a penny and the partners resolved to 'only buy what is absolutely required for use'.[1]

The two generations thus differed in their approach to business. John Marshall wanted above all to make as much money as he could for himself. He did so not because he was beset by avarice but because he considered it his job as a businessman. In the means he used to achieve this end, he remained flexible. If he received a check in any direction so that his return on outlay fell below the 15–20 per cent he considered worth while, he would look round for a more profitable opening. Sometimes this constant tacking brought Marshall into conflict with his partners, but before 1815 he never pursued any course harmful to the business. Large profits were turned into circulating capital and the resources of the firm grew. After the war, however, Marshall withdrew his own earnings to speculate in funds, investing heavily when spinning became less profitable than before. Simultaneously he jealously guarded his reputation as a businessman by seeking to revive the firm's fortunes through speculating in flax. As a result he allowed the business to slip. Until 1818, he made no strenuous effort to innovate; and he soon lost the services of his able assistants.

Such a lapse was not serious. Marshall felt confident that, with his experience and resources, he could re-equip the mills and forge ahead of any rivals once an important improvement was brought into the trade. Moreover, to some extent he was consciously withdrawing from the business to follow other interests. He had 'established manufacturing concerns, which...will provide an ample provision for my younger sons', and the transfer from one generation

[1] H. C. Marshall, 'Notebook A,' p. 4.

to the next was already taking place.[1] Furthermore, owing to his contact with the Benthamites, his experience of public office and the high proportion of children he employed, Marshall began to take a broader view of factory production in the 1820's. Hitherto he saw the mills as a machine to be driven efficiently without too much attention to the workers who passed the long days of their short lives in its throbbing atmosphere. Now Marshall considered the social aspect of factory life, introduced a two-shift system and schooling, and placed a fresh emphasis on the conditions of work. Nevertheless, even these new interests remained subordinate to the search for profit with the result that after the war he grew increasingly impatient with the fortunes of the business.

John II faced a formidable task following his successful father as manager of the firm. The latter expatiated no doubt on the qualities which bred success, but he could not communicate his instinctive flair for money-making. His precepts were humdrum, even misleading. Indeed the founder never confessed to himself just how he achieved what he did. Faced with the challenge of the post-war situation, John II concluded that his best course as a spinner lay in the continuous improvement and expansion of the plant and, compared with his father, he committed himself to a way of generating profit that was both more prudent and more rigid.

Transitions, particularly those which do not result in the separation of the participants within a short time, invite difficulties. John Marshall did not hasten to surrender his authority until he was in a position to withdraw most of his assets from the firm. After thirty-seven years in the trade, he enjoyed his legendary position as a great pioneer and the activity of management itself satisfied him. Therefore his sons, though inexperienced, grew impatient (as John Marshall had once been with his father) and gradually they sought to divest the founder of his power within the firm.

It was too early to see what the outcome would be. John Marshall ceased speculating in flax and allowed his son to start building a fourth mill at Water Lane. But whether John II, having embarked upon this course, would succeed better than his father remains to be seen.

[1] Marshall, 'Life', p. 24.

CHAPTER IV

WET SPINNING, 1826–1846

(i)

The recession in 1826 struck hard at the fortunes of the linen industry. In that year the United Kingdom's flax imports fell by more than a third, and three years later, when imports had risen to 46,000 tons, they were still below the volume of 1825.[1] For the first time, flax-spinners felt that their days were numbered owing to the competition of cotton goods. In some districts the industry sank into a state of permanent decline; yet elsewhere it recovered quickly, growing from strength to strength.

Eastern Scotland recovered most rapidly. Imports at Dundee in 1827 surpassed the high level of 1825. Within two years Scottish imports as a whole exceeded the volume of the boom and continued to rise. Linen cloth output, which declined 8 per cent in 1826, had fully recovered the following year when 350,000 pieces were made. Three years later output was up by a third. William Brown's prophecy that the Scottish industry would outgrow the English came near fulfilment. Before the 1820's Dundee's industry had grown slowly. The town's flax-spinners had less than a hundred steam horse-power when William Brown visited Leeds in 1821. Then a great many new mills were built. By 1823 the horse-power in Dundee's mills amounted to 178; in 1831 to 683; and in 1834, with 942 horse-power, Dundee was on a par with Leeds. Actually the town had more mills, smaller in size, spinning heavy yarns suitable for sail and sack cloth. Demand for these articles was both widespread and buoyant, and Dundee spinners did not jostle like their Leeds counterparts to supply a constricted market. Furthermore they used cheap, coarse Baltic flax whilst Leeds spinners clamoured for Flemish, and they had the further advantage that their products

---

[1] Unless otherwise indicated the statistical data used is derived from *Statistics of the Linen Trade* published by the Dundee Trade Report Association, 1855, plus the supplement of 30 December 1865; M. G. Mulhall, *The Dictionary of Statistics* (1892); *The Textile Manufacturer*, *The Irish Textile Journal* and the *Trade and Navigation Accounts*.

were fairly immune to cotton competition. Technically they lagged behind Leeds spinners and did not produce such fine, smooth yarn. They had, however, secured for themselves the heavy end of the trade, whilst English spinners concentrated on lighter yarns.[1]

In contrast with the Scottish industry, flax-spinning in the West Riding suffered a protracted and disheartening depression. Flax imports at Hull fell from 12,000 tons in 1825 to 7000 in 1826. Four years later the level of imports had barely risen. In part this was a consequence of spinning lighter yarns, but at the same time it indicates the very slow recovery of the Yorkshire industry. One major linen centre, Knaresborough, never recovered.[2] First the small dealers, who 'bought flax, dressed it, and employed mills to spin', failed. By 1827 large firms were 'making $4\frac{1}{2}$ to 5 days lately, but there are some weak ones that cannot last much longer'. Weavers left the town, many moving to Barnsley and, despite an influx of Irish, Knaresborough's population did not grow between 1821 and 1831. The recession was a fatal blow to an economy already undermined. As the Municipal Commissioners soon learned, it was the town's misfortune to lack cheap coal: 'The inhabitants of Knaresborough feel sensibly the difficulty of access to the Coal Districts; and state the want of this Mineral...as the principal drawback upon their commercial prosperity.'[3] Attempts to mine coal locally at Thornthwaite, Birstwith and Meg Yate did not prove commercial propositions. Two schemes for canals to join the river Ouse below York came to nothing. Knaresborough remained isolated from the coal regions, and the Commissioners prophesied pessimistically that 'expansion will depend on using water-power'. To say the least, this was a highly simplified explanation of the town's fate. But its decline was not averted even when rail communication came in 1847 and Knaresborough remained in a condition of arrested development for the rest of the century.

[1] Warden, *op. cit.* pp. 578–658, especially pp. 592, 617; D. Chapman, *Review of Economic Studies* (1938), pp. 33–55, 'the industries of Dundee and Leeds were complementary rather than competitive'.

[2] Fletcher, *op. cit.* pp. 118–19; *Report on the Borough of Knaresborough*, Sess. 1831–2 (141), vol. XL, p. 141; *R. Com. Rep. Handloom Weavers*, 1840 (43–I), (43–II), pp. 484–8, 499–505, 507; J. Marshall II, 'Notebook', 1825–7, p. 43, 13 January 1827, 15 March 1827; Grainge, *op. cit.* pp. 429, 451.

[3] *Report on the Borough of Knaresborough*, Sess. 1831–2, p. 141.

The most striking feature of this recession, and one with ominous implications for the future of West Riding spinners, was the success of cotton as a substitute for linen.[1] In 1820, when raw cotton prices began their precipitous descent, twice as much cotton was consumed as linen in Britain, and nearly half the cotton cloth produced in the country was sold at home. In the next twenty years raw cotton consumption increased fourfold, and although foreign sales of yarn and piece goods rose, more cotton goods were sold at home. Cotton prices fell by a third from 1825 to 1842 and domestic sales rose threefold. In competing with cotton goods, flax-spinners and linen-weavers laboured under three handicaps: first, they found themselves at an increasing disadvantage with regard to raw material costs; second, power-looms began to come into general use for weaving cotton in the 1820's; and third, cotton proved simpler and cheaper to spin. In the early 1820's cotton yarns half as heavy as the lightest flax yarns could be made by machinery. Only half as much capital per spindle was required by a cotton manufacturer, and since less time was taken in production, output per operative was higher. So cotton manufacturers were a threat to which flax-spinners never really found an answer. The cotton industry quickly recovered from the 1826 recession, cutting prices, accepting lower margins and keeping their growing plant fully occupied. Cheap cotton became a nightmare to linen manufacturers. In 1827 John Marshall II repeatedly complained that 'the price of cotton is again lower...so long as this continues we must expect that the consumption of linen will be a good deal encroached upon by cotton cloth', or 'cotton continues to pour in...therefore neither our raw material nor our manufactured goods can be high in price till cotton rises'.[2] Two years later, Edward Baines, addressing Barnsley weavers on strike against a cut in weaving rates, blamed their plight on the fact that 'cotton fabrics have of late come much into competition with linens, and one article

---

[1] Mulhall, *op. cit.* pp. 156, 280; R. C. O. Matthews, *A Study in Trade Cycle History* (1954), p. 129; W. J. Ashley (ed.), *British Industries* (1903), p. 147; L. C. Marshall, *The Practical Flax Spinner* (1885), pp. iii ff.; Greenwood, *Proc. Inst. Mech. Eng.* (1865), p. 123; J. G. Marshall, evidence for *Sel. Ctte. Rep. Exportation of Machinery*, 1841 (400), vol. VII, pp. 186–99; W. Charley, *On Flax* (1862), p. 83. See below, table 8 p. 315, for price relatives of cotton and flax.
[2] J. Marshall II to J. Marshall, 15 March 1827, 1 August 1827.

in particular, cotton shirting is now very much in request'.[1] The flax spinner who made medium yarns was exposed on both flanks: to the Scottish trade making coarse yarns on one side, and to the Lancashire industry making cheap cotton cloth on the other.

Early in 1826 the trading situation of Marshall and Co. appeared much the same as in recent years. After the raw material speculation of 1825 flax prices fell by a third, whereupon John Marshall bought over 1500 tons, 200 tons more than the previous year and the second highest purchase of his career, at an average price of £42·6. John II installed 1500 extra spindles, hired 237 additional hands and ran the Water Lane plant at full capacity, producing in 1826 222,000 bundles of yarn, 15,000 bundles more than in 1825. On average the cost of this yarn fell 21*d*. a bundle; flax costs dropped 29*d*. a bundle entirely owing to the lower price of raw material, and overheads rose by 8*d*. because John Marshall invested an extra £20,000 in the business for speculating and a new mill. Simultaneously yarn prices fell 22*d*. a bundle, and unit profits by 1*d*. Indeed the declared profits in 1826 amounting to more than £11,000 were at the same level as those of the previous year. By this reckoning the firm showed no ill-effects from the current disturbance in trade. But part of the profit for 1826 arose out of payments for sales made the previous year for cash in six months. The firm's sales began to decline towards the end of 1825 and fell a third the following year. Revenue was down by a quarter in 1826 and losses from bad debts stood at £5500, four times as much as in 1825. At the end of 1826 outstanding credits had fallen a third to £37,000 and stocks had trebled in value to £63,758. Marshall and Co. were not escaping the recession.

In view of the fact that parliamentary activities engrossed John Marshall in 1826, his son acquitted himself well. If next year the market improved, John II could expect to clear the extra stock at enhanced prices. But this did not happen. Cotton prices continued to fall and early in 1827 were half what they had been in 1825, so that Marshalls' sales fell steeply. In fact Marshall and Co. had more difficulty selling their yarns than other local spinners such as Hives

[1] *Leeds Mercury*, 3 October 1829.

or Titley. And for this John II was to blame. Recently the mills had spun increasingly lighter yarns, averaging 159 bundles to a ton of flax in 1825. But in 1826 only 147 bundles were spun. To increase output, particularly of tow yarns for the heavy end of the trade, John II had speeded up and overloaded the whole plant and as a result produced poor quality yarn. Explaining the episode to his father in September 1827, John II wrote: 'many a thousand bundles have we lost the sale of at Barnsley last winter which springs from our yarn not being good enough for their purpose.... This has been a gross blunder and never could have happened if I had visited Barnsley more frequently: they would have been pointing out the defects in our yarn and I should have found what was the cause.'[1] He had been too preoccupied with the new mill and his father's election to attend to such a minor detail as the quality of the firm's current output. Defending himself, he argued that 'I believe we were led into [making bad yarns] from the complaints of our Scottish and Irish customers, who had been accustomed to nothing but handspun yarns'.[2] Allegedly to satisfy these new customers, less twist had been put into the yarn and consequently it 'knotted in weaving'. By mid-summer 1827 the trade 'called up a tremendous cry in the country against our quality, which we in some measure have deserved; all the little spinners begin now to turn up their noses at our yarn'.[3]

Checked by cheap cottons and handicapped by a poor reputation, John II became appalled at the seriousness of their position in the spring of 1827. If, as he thought, cotton and therefore flax prices had reached rock bottom, their best course would be to raise the efficiency of the mills and reduce expenses. In March he reckoned that £10,273 a year could be saved on production costs, four-fifths of this amount at Water Lane. In the first place, if his father stopped speculating in raw materials, the cost of overheads (resulting from over-capitalisation) could be reduced by £1000. Second, by driving the machinery more slowly 'the waste would be small and though the frames would not turn off so much work, still it would be well done, and cost less in wages per bundle as well as having all the yarn on the bobbins instead of a great deal going on to the floor'.[4] In this way

---

[1] J. Marshall II to J. Marshall, 9 September 1827.   [2] *Ibid.*
[3] *Ibid.* 20 September 1827.   [4] *Ibid.* 15 March 1827.

John II expected a 3–6 per cent reduction in waste, and he hoped to save 3*d.* to 4*d.* in labour costs per bundle.

I have been looking over the cost in labour of spinning last year at Leeds and Salop, and am much shocked at the immense inferiority of the management compared with former years. I will have each overlooker up and let him see the account relating to his department, and show him what improvement we expect to arrive at this year, and tell him that his continuance in his place will depend on his exertions in promoting that result.[1]

By referring to his 'check accounts', John II indicated exactly where such improvements should be made. Mill *B* which had recently been reorganised for medium yarn spinning had settled to its new routine and improved its performance considerably during 1826. The standards of *A* and *C* mills at Water Lane would now have to be raised to the level of mill *B*. These proposals were 'a little overstated in some particulars, and at any rate ¼ or ⅓ of the year would be gone before the improvement could be effected. We ought at any rate to save £5000 this year in the waste and labour alone, and I will strive hard but we will accomplish it.'[2] Not only did John II initiate economies amounting to 8 per cent of total costs, but he also constantly urged James to modify the plant in order to improve their yarn. The latter, though harassed by his brother's persistence, devised a new system of preparing tow in 1827. Whereupon John II immediately placed an order with the Round Foundry for all the new machines which could be made within the year. The outcome of these efforts was that the Water Lane plant spun an extra 2000 bundles of yarn in 1827 with 264 fewer hands, and spun a ton of flax into 175 bundles so that their raw material purchases fell some two hundred tons. John II had done what he could to ensure the firm's recovery and put it in a position to gain from a revival of trade; 'that there will be a considerable demand...I have no doubt'.[3]

When by the autumn of 1827 Marshalls' sales still languished John II grew fretful. Having improved the firm's internal condition he scrutinised the market situation more closely.

We hear of the Barnsley people selling a good many linens; and I learn from Gott that the country trade was never so great in his recollection,

---

[1] *Ibid.*   [2] *Ibid.*

[3] *Ibid.* 1 August 1827.

nor ever at any time in so healthy a state...we have sold hardly any.... Surely this cannot continue without our participating in it. On the other hand, cotton wool is as cheap as ever, and Scottish goods: but if the lower class have better filled pockets, we may expect that they will begin to select rather stronger and more durable clothing....The Dowlas and coarse linen they [the Scotch] make, never can drive the Barnsley Dowlas for any long time out of the market: the people will not be satisfied with the poor raggy Scotch coarse linens, when they can afford to buy something better. There is something in a cheap mania: everybody has been bit with it lately, and perhaps amongst the rest, the purchasers of Scotch linens. I cannot help prognosticating the return, ere long, of a demand for good stout durable Barnsley linen. At the same time, I think the Barnsley people have had the opportunity of making as cheap linen as the Scotch, for I believe with our tow yarn they might have done it.[1]

However, the principal obstacle to Marshall's recovery was in fact the price of their sale yarn. Small spinners undersold Marshall and Co. 'in coarse yarns by 6*d*. or 1*s*. per bundle, and unless the demand for yarn increases soon so as to raise the prices of the little spinners to our level, we must go down to their level without doubt'.[2] In September John II informed his father, who decided the firm's prices, that 'the Barnsley people do not like to buy at 11*s*. 6*d*. for 13 lb. yarn; they would willingly give us 11*s*., and at that price would buy'.[3] The founder decided to await a change in the market and the dull state of trade weighed heavily on his son's mind. 'It would gladden me if stocks fell', he wrote, because further output could only be justified as 'production for stock'.[4] His efforts seemed to have been in vain. 'I am becoming very fidgety and low spirited.'[5] Late in September he became fatalistic: 'Jno Wilford [amongst the three largest houses in Barnsley] is beginning to want, and I think he will buy if our quality pleases him, which I rather fear.'[6]

In John II's view the remedy now lay with his father. He had endeavoured to expunge the effects of selling poor yarn; now their prices had to be reduced—'I think we have no alternative'—not least in order to dispose of the disproportionate quantity of tow which

---

[1] J. Marshall II to J. Marshall, 9 September 1827.   [2] *Ibid*. 1 August 1827.
[3] *Ibid*. 20 September 1827.
[4] *Ibid*. 16 September 1827. 'To spin for stock requires far more care and looking after than for immediate sale; in the latter case if you get wrong, your customers are not long in telling you and you get righted instantly.'
[5] *Ibid*. 20 September 1827.   [6] *Ibid*.

John II had produced the previous year.[1] With this stock out of the warehouse, John II would feel much happier. At the same time, in order to associate his father directly with their present plight, John II seized the opportunity to condemn fruitless speculation in flax.

On balance the firm's performance in 1827 was very satisfactory. Output rose slightly and manufacturing expenses fell by £8000. The principal saving, 9*d*. a bundle, arose from lower flax costs. Despite an increase in price of 30*s*. a ton, average raw material costs fell owing to the production of finer yarns. Simultaneously, John II saved £1285 on wages; by the end of the year the labour force had been reduced by 264 workers, mostly children, and the two-shift system was discontinued. The number of spindles per hand increased by a third and output by nearly a fifth, a performance unmatched for many years. In addition, overheads were £300 lower in 1827, equivalent to $\frac{1}{3}d$. a bundle, and John II anticipated lower fixed costs once his economy drive gained momentum. In 1827 Marshall and Co. made a total profit of £5592 or 6*d*. a bundle. And at the end of the year, when sales revived, John II felt his efforts had been worth while.

The following year he prudently pursued the same course. Flax prices rose by £8 a ton, so he drew on stocks and purchased 118 tons less than the previous year. Thirty-three hands were laid off; and with the installation of 700 extra spindles in the new mill, the average number per worker rose by a twelfth. A high proportion of medium yarn was spun, a ton of flax making on average 182 bundles. Sales regained the level of 1825, yarn stocks fell by £20,000, and profits amounted to £13,832, the equivalent of 1*s*. 4*d*. a bundle and the best return since 1824–5.

Both father and sons radiated optimism in 1828 and with good reason. Not only had they emerged from the recession, but behind the scenes a far-reaching change was being executed. The mill which John II had planned was to be equipped with a different kind of spinning frame. The new spindles were still too few to have much effect on output, but Marshall and Co. soon expected to spin only *fine* yarns.

The long flax fibre is composed of short ultimate fibres held together by a gummy substance, pectose. Up to the mid-1820's spinners

[1] *Ibid.* 11 November 1827.

drew out and twisted the long fibre, producing medium yarns up to 30 lea and even 50 lea. However, it had long been clear that progress toward finer machine-spinning would depend on twisting the ultimate fibres. To do this the gummy substance would have to be neutralised temporarily in the final drawing process and the flyer would twist short decomposed fibres. The method eventually adopted was to pass the roving through steam which neutralised the gum, and then draw the short ultimate fibres at a short reach of a few inches instead of the wide gap, perhaps as much as 24 in., used previously. Then the yarn could be spun more tightly with a greater concentration of twist, say forty to the inch for 200 lea line in 1828 compared with at the very most twelve to the inch for 30 lea line produced between 1805 and 1818 at Water Lane.[1]

Credit for this method has long been disputed.[2] A Frenchman invented the principle, and Leeds spinners found ways of turning it into a successful commercial proposition. Later in the nineteenth century when Marshall's successors sought to credit the Leeds industry with originating the new method, they were merely being defensive at the time of the firm's decline.

Since two possible consequences follow the wetting of flax by water the difficulty of finding out what happened in each case bedevils the reconstruction of events. Damped quickly, the effect is not to decompose flax into its ultimate fibres, but simply to produce a slippery roving which is easier to draw. Only thorough soaking or spraying with hot water produces a chemical action, parting the ultimate fibres and enabling very fine yarns to be spun. Quick wetting would facilitate the production of counts up to 60 leas; but beyond that, and especially for counts over 100, the *ultimate* fibres

[1] For an account of this process see Horner, *op. cit.* pp. 263 ff.; L. C. Marshall, *op. cit.* Part IV.

[2] H. Grothe, *op. cit. passim*; *Mémoire au Roi...sur la priorité due à la France dans l'invention des machines à filer le lin* (1844), pp. 9 ff.; *Invention de la filature mécanique du lin* (1850); *Sénat Rapport*, C. Dupin (1853); *Irish Textile Journal*, 15 June, 15 July 1887; *Textile Manufacturer*, 15 February 1885; Horner, *op. cit.* pp. 335–7. Several facts seem to be established by the evidence: (1) It is obvious that De Girard later claimed credit for improvements designed by others. (2) Kay used cold water to loosen the fibres, and James Marshall may have pioneered hot water, the method which, as the Factory Inspectorate Reports show, eventually became common. (3) By the 1880's, John Marshall's descendants claimed more credit for the achievement of their predecessors than the facts warranted.

are drawn and spun. At the same time, decomposed fibres could be and obviously were spun into yarns of less than 60 leas at the start, and this makes it difficult to discover what actually happened.

As early as 1789 John Marshall and afterwards others used cold water to make better rovings. 'Water had the desired effect of making the yarn smooth and strong, and saved about half the breakages—a roving spun wet breaking 12 times a day when a dry one broke 25 times.'[1] During the next twenty years he used water in several different ways, spraying the roving and dipping it in a trough. But he did not aim at producing a fine yarn, nor did he soak the roving before the final drawing in the spinning frame. Contesting the validity of Kay's patent in a court of law, Marshall attributed the fundamentals of the new method unreservedly to the Frenchman, De Girard: '[Kay] had no part in the discovery that the fibres of flax in a wet state are capable of being drawn to an extreme degree of fineness. That discovery was made and fully described by Horace Hall's specification.'[2] Horace Hall was the name under which two Frenchmen, Cachard and Lanthois took out a patent in May 1815. They had worked in De Girard's Paris factory and registered the method which their master offered for Napoleon's prize in 1810 and which he later practised in Austria and Poland without much financial success.[3] Hall's patent comprised machinery for dry gill roving, damp reducing and spinning. It claimed ambiguously that 'the hemp and flax becoming wetted is made more lax, and the fibres therefore *slip past each other* with greater ease'.[4]

A Leeds spinner, Robert Busk, the relative of a rich woollen merchant, acquired the patent conditionally for his exclusive use.[5]

---

[1] Marshall, 'Experiments', vol. I, June 1789; vol. II, August 1793, pp. 62–4; vol. III, January 1815, p. 65. The last experiment was carried out with the help of David Wood.

[2] Statement in the hand of John Marshall in connexion with the case of Kay v. Marshall, item 5 on the sheet.

[3] D. C. Long, 'Philippe de Girard and the Introduction of Mechanical Flax Spinning in Austria', *J. Econ. Hist.* vol. XIV, p. 21; A. L. Dunham, *The Industrial Revolution in France, 1815–48* (1955), pp. 249, 293–7. I can find no evidence to support Dunham's suggestion that Marshall lured one of De Girard's partners to join him; it seems unlikely because Marshall and Co. had no interest in that method in 1824.

[4] Patent 3855 of Horace Hall, 1814.

[5] The following paragraphs draw on a bundle of depositions made in July 1836 for Kay v. Marshall, especially those by J. Carr, J. Houseworth, W. Buckley, S. Coward, J. Milner, B. Brown and Dawson of Low Moor. J. Marshall II, 'Notebook', c. 1815,

He first operated in the lower part of a mill near Hunslet Moor and in 1816 two-thirds of his plant, around 1800 spindles, produced 500 bundles of fine yarn a week. The method used was kept a close secret. Younger of Sheffield and Dawson of Low Moor made the frames, and the latter who examined the machinery in London on behalf of Busk 'considered the principle of spinning from a wet roving decidedly new and important. I contemplated at that time entering into partnership with Mr Busk for the purpose of pursuing this invention.' Having proved the value of the machinery in practice, Busk sought to exploit his position and offered John Marshall an interest in the patent. The latter 'sent him some flax to spin for a specimen. We were then spinning no finer than 20 lea yarn, and for this coarse size wet spinning does not produce any great improvement and we declined the offer.' Marshall did not see Busk's machines, but he sent for a copy of the Patent and was 'perfectly aware of the nature of the invention'. Indeed he copied the gill frames specified by Hall and assisted by David Wood constructed an experimental wet-frame which did not satisfy them.

Meanwhile, Busk spun wet yarns locally known as 'French yarns', for more than two years. He made '25 to 60 or 70 leas on these frames at various reaches, chiefly 25 to 40 leas: sometimes as high as 100 leas: Mr Busk spun some little bits finer than 100 leas...when the flax was soft and easy to draw [he] had no difficulty; but frequently it was stubborn and the yarn much snarled'. In 1818 this mill was burnt down and, for the next four years before he left the trade, Busk reverted to spinning heavy yarns. He paid a forfeit for giving up the patent and scrapped the machinery.

Busk, who produced 25,000 bundles of fine yarn a year, gave up because 'the plan did not answer for any but fine yarns' and 'a small producer of fine yarn was not then wanted'. Weavers wanting fine yarns mostly dwelt outside England and bought from hand-spinners. Barnsley weavers objected to wet yarn at every turn. They complained of it 'breaking short as if there was no fibre in the flax'. They believed that linens made from light yarns would not be durable and would

27 July 1817, 'Mr Horace Hall having taken out a patent for a different method of preparing flax, which Mr Busk had adopted and said he found to answer, we got the specificatⁿ.'

not last more than a lifetime. One bleacher, Cawood, praised the yarn itself in the 25–40 leas range, but condemned it as too weak for bleaching. More serious as a handicap was the high price of the French yarn compared with that spun by mill-spinners in Leeds and by hand-spinners abroad. Probably this was a temporary phenomenon associated with the initial costs of production, although in 1821 John Marshall II who set his face against the new yarn reckoned wet-spinning to cost $4\frac{1}{2}d$. a bundle more on an output of 145,000 bundles.[1] However, in time the smaller quantity of flax used more than offset any rise in labour and machine costs. The most serious objection to Busk's method was in its defective application. Correct in principle, it fell short in practical details. The wet rovings if left overnight in cans tended to rot and become slack, with the result that there was a good deal of waste when they were transferred to the spinning frame. Moreover, Busk's machinery needed improving. To make the most of wet spinning, it was first necessary to prepare a fine roving. But this did not become possible mechanically until developments in gill frames and hackling machinery occurred in the 1820's. Finally, fine yarns required the carefully grown flax of Western Europe, not the coarse Baltic flax then in general use at Leeds.

In 1825 James Kay of Penny Bridge, Lancashire, revived wet spinning with a new patent.[2] His macerating process involved soaking rovings in cans of water and then drawing at a *short* reach. With improvements in gill frames and hackling, and with the flow of Flemish flax to Leeds, the technical chances of success had improved very much. Moreover, by that time, the local industry was under pressure from Scottish and Lancashire manufacturers to find a new product. So John Hives and Anthony Titley went to see Kay's new frames and pushed ahead with the new method.

[1] J. Marshall II, 'Notebook', 1821–5, 11 November 1821.
[2] Patent 5226 of James Kay, 1825. See Horner, *op. cit.* pp. 261–3; De Girard–*Manchester Guardian*, 2 December 1826; J. Marshall II to J. Marshall, 11 November 1827, 'I do not like us to think of giving the sanction of our name to what cannot in any sense be called a patent worthy machine....Kaye is intending to prosecute the infringers of his patent: he will find he has his work set.' Cf. Marshall Collection, Chancery Brief, Kay v. Marshall, 1836. Witness 18, R. Wetherall, stated that he was employed by Garseed, a Leeds flax-spinner, when Busk spun wet yarn which he saw and could remember; subsequently, he was employed by Crankshaw who helped Kay to exploit the 1825 patent. (When Marshall refers to *Crankshaw's yarns* he means those made by Kay's method.)

Hives's first experiment in June 1825 at the new mill on the Far Bank was not promising. Their head overlooker told John Marshall that 'the rovings from the reducing frames were steeped about an hour in water; there was great waste attending them by their entanglement in coming off the heap behind the spinning frame...[I] saw the yarn from this frame, it was all bad, uneven yarn...part was sold as waste along with other waste yarn to one Stevins or Stevenson in Holbeck'.[1] Others confirmed the failure. It was 'chiefly 60 leas, it was weak and appeared to be half rotten, besides being lumpy occasionally....I did not consider any of it fit to be used.' On Midsummer's Day, John Marshall II decided to find out for himself and went along to Hives's counting house where he learnt that 'all the yarn spun upon Kay's plan of maceration was worthless; that they did not in fact venture to sell any part of it.' Several spinners who took up Kay's patent met with no better luck. Such evidence seemed conclusive, and John II ignored eccentric correspondents like Joseph Steel of Halifax who claimed; 'I have been in possession of that [wet spinning] system as much as 10 years ago....I certainly should have pursued it, but my means fell short and I was obliged to abandon it just at a time when it might have done me good, and it has lain dormant with me ever since.'[2] At that time John Marshall II had committed himself to a different course. The demand for their medium yarn was brisk in 1825; and he pressed James to improve their preparing machinery so that the forthcoming mill could spin higher quality line and lighter tow yarn. For a brief moment John II had been curious about Kay's patent and he was relieved to find not only that it was not new, but also that it did not work. There was nothing in it to upset his plans.

Others persevered. When Hives replaced the soaking tins behind the frame by 'little troughs of water...near the top roller', he reduced most of the waste and snarling. 'The frame was then attended with very little trouble and the yarn spun well, with very few breakages. It was 60 lea yarn that they spun from 40 lea material...the best yarn of that size I ever saw.' Immediately Hives started to make fine

---

[1] Depositions, 1836, *loc. cit.*, of T. Robinson and Holmes, the head overlooker at Hives Old Mill in 1825. The other quotations in this paragraph are from the same source.

[2] Joseph Steel to Marshall and Co., 1825.

yarns of '60 leas on Kay's frame' and sold 50,000 bundles in 1825 and 70,000 bundles in 1826.[1]

James Marshall, who became a partner in 1825, was more curious than his brother about Kay's method. The system introduced by Hives would if practicable enable Marshall and Co. to develop a lucrative trade displacing the hand-spinners who made fine yarns on the Continent. Being responsible for the firm's machinery, James wanted to investigate the new process further, but for nearly a year this proved difficult owing to the demands of his brother and father for improvements in gill-roving and hackling. However, after accompanying his brother to Hives's mill in July 1826, James determined to copy Kay's frame.

We were shown some 40 and 60 lea yarn spun upon this [Kay's] system which was very fair yarn for the material it was spun from and was not weak.... We had some of it made into thread at Salop: it made good thread. Thompson of Darlington wove some of it, and gave a very favourable report of it. We determined to give this plan of spinning a fair trial.[2]

By August he had a frame at work at Water Lane and found that 'plain rollers with a four inch reach are practicable, and produce better yarn than our old plan: but that a large roving cannot be sufficiently wet to draw well and that a short draw appears essential.'[3] To ensure a thorough wetting and prevent lapping, he introduced two sets of water-pipes which sprayed the roving. This produced a good yarn, but 'we saw Hives sping frame which was spinning exceedingly well 60 leas; the yarn decidedly better than from our experimental frame'.[4]

[1] J. Marshall II, 'Notebook', 1825–7, p. 40, July 1826, p. 43, March 1827, and Depositions, 1836, *loc. cit.*; in a letter to the *Manchester Guardian*, dated 2 December 1826, De Girard, then in England, claimed 'the superiority of my process will be evident when it is stated that we commonly spin 120 leas to the pound, while the first spinners in Leeds do not exceed 42, except in experiments'. Though no spinner in Leeds produced yarns as fine as 120 leas, a few firms were manufacturing yarns lighter than 42 leas. See S. A. Marshall's letter in *Irish Textile Journal*, 1887, p. 5.

[2] J. Marshall II, 'Notebook', 1825–7, pp. 39, 43.

[3] *Ibid.* p. 40.

[4] J. G. Marshall, 'Notebooks', 1826–9, p. 5. Marshall and Co. were not then spinning wet yarns for sale; see Deposition, 5 July 1836 in Kay v. Marshall: 'We spun 300 Bdls 50–60 leas wet July to October 1827'. Marshalls thus started approximately two years behind Hives and Atkinson in wet spinning.

At this juncture James embarked upon a course different from that which his father would have followed. Not content to adapt Kay's frame for their purpose, he returned to first principles (as Charles Bage would have done) and sought to design a superior machine. He studied the effects of wetting flax, noticing what happened when fibres were quickly damped with cold water.

The principle of this mode of drawing a wet roving is that then it may, if of a small thickness, be drawn at a very short length. Even when the roving is only wet immediately previous to being drawn, this is the case. Here there is no time for any chemical action by which the fibres may be disposed to separate more easily; it appears probable that the only difference is the much better mechanical hold which the drawing rollers have on a wet roving which draws always to a solid tapering point, without any straggling fibres, and without the assistance of a conductor.[1]

To facilitate a chemical reaction, James wet the flax with hot water. In practice, 'we found a small copper steam pipe passed along the bottom of the trough...the most convenient mode of giving the heat.... This was a great improvement; roving was perfectly wet and we had no more snarled yarn...when the troughs were kept to a proper temperature.... The steam was let on 20 min before the mill started and the water heated.'[2] In addition he 'decided on using a finer and more delicate gill roving frame capable of producing a roving...such as could be easily wetted and drawn by fluted rollers', but finding the rollers overloaded, he lightened the weight on them. Then he applied the tow scale of twisting to wet yarns, which otherwise tended to become 'soft and oosey' when bleached. 'We then spun 120 leas upon it [the experimental frame] for some time, reach $1\frac{1}{2}$ inch, draw 8.'

That many troubles arose in operation was only to be expected. In January 1827 for instance, dirty river water clogged the orifices of the steam pipe, so James introduced filtering.[3] But by that time he felt confident that his frame would spin good fine yarn up to 80 leas, and in view of the depressed state of trade, he urged John II to hasten the completion of the new mill with a view to spinning wet yarns

[1] J. G. Marshall, 'Notebook', 1826–9, p. 1.

[2] *Ibid.* pp. 5–6. The remaining quotations in this paragraph are from the same source. See also J. Marshall II, 'Notebook', 1825–7, p. 41.

[3] J. Marshall II, 'Notebook', 1825–7, p. 42.

there. John II demurred. He had set his course, and intended to produce what he knew the local market wanted, namely higher quality medium yarns. Spinning wet yarns entailed an unnecessary risk in their already difficult situation. 'What is in our warehouse now is for sale 10 or 12 months hence': to make fine yarns 'we must push into some new trade that our last spun yarn may not interfere with the sale of our old spun yarn'.[1] Besides, their current orders for preparing machinery made it virtually impossible to obtain wet-frames at short notice. 'Our wants to supply our old establishment before we begin on a new one at all, and I am quite astonished at it, namely 73 machines costing £5450....This is as much machinery as the Foundry and Mirfin can well make for us during the remainder of this year.'[2] The most sensible thing in John II's view would be to continue along the lines they had already agreed upon.

If this gill roving and hackling machinery be really necessary to enable us to do our work well, it ought to be made in preference to any machinery for mill *D*. We shall make more money by doing what we do well, than by hurrying too fast into the making of an increased quantity of yarn....If our yarn can be improved, as I think it can, by light and careful preparation, this of all other times is the one in which we ought to be most active in promoting such an improvement....Our plan must be to let our spinning frames go leisurely along, making little or no waste, with the smallest complement of hands, and make our preparing do all it can to do its work well.[3]

He refused to speed up the availability of the new mill—'The Engine and foundations will be none the worse for plenty of time to set'— and resolved not to consider wet spinning until the following year, unless 'the proof of the great superiority of light preparing is not quite conclusive enough for you [his father] and James'.[4]

James flared up at his brother's brisk rejection of his advice on machinery. He believed that John II did not perceive the opportunities at hand and exaggerated out of all proportion the slight improvements made in preparing. Furthermore, by placing orders for machinery during James's absence, John II had encroached upon his brother's province. Deliberation gave way to a brotherly brawl,

---

[1] J. Marshall II to J. Marshall, 14 April 1827.
[2] *Ibid.*   [3] *Ibid.*
[4] *Ibid.*

whereupon John II told James bluntly that as it stood, the wet-frame was too defective to put into operation.

I cannot divine how you came to think me unmindful of the many brilliant discoveries for which we are indebted to you. Why, you are our witch, it is your vocation to invent and lay down the law in the construction of machinery. It is only in your absence that I presume to encroach on your department. If [you] will run away to watering places, and leave [your] place to be filled up . . . [you] must not grumble that [your] successors put in practice some of the best plans of their own. . . . I really cannot tax my memory with the recollection of having opposed the innovations which you so dearly cherish. . . . You must not suppose that this great attention to our line preparing is useless. But the construction of the fine Rovg. & the wet Sping. frame is exceedingly deficient. . . . The wet sping. frame is only wrong in its mechanical construction, but so much so that it is a very bad frame.[1]

A private note written in May 1827 shows that John Marshall II had not at that time been converted to the new method. He concedes that better preparing would not by itself make finer yarn; there was 'no remedy but depriving the fibre of that gluten which coats the fibre and prevents it from splitting'. This, he thought, could be done in any of three ways:

Boiling the flax frees it from this cement, but the waste is enormous, the expense of boiling very great, the hackling more expensive.

Stamping, which we practice . . . undoubtedly produces a fermentation, or at any rate a degree of heat that promotes the sub-division of the coarse fibres by freeing them from some of the gluten which cemented each fibre so firmly. This is accompanied by expense in stamping, extra wages for hackling, extra waste in hackling, more nobby tow, but we believe it to pay for this. A severe blow often repeated, or severe pressure often repeated seem to be all that is required in this principle.

A third method may possibly be found in the agency of steam. . . . One cannot imagine that the strick should be so matted together as though it had been subject to boiling, yet it is possible that it may derive some of the effects which it receives from boiling.[2]

There the matter rested. John Marshall II refused to introduce wet-frames except on orders from his father and at this point the elder Marshall fell seriously ill.

---

[1] J. Marshall II to J. G. Marshall, 27 April 1827.

[2] J. Marshall II, 'Notebook', 1825–7, p. 14, 5 May 1827; Cf. J. G. Marshall to J. Marshall, 21 February 1827, stating that wet spinning takes away the inducement to break flax.

Then at the end of September, John Marshall II unexpectedly favoured wet spinning. 'This is a trade that must be pursued most rapidly', he declared, 'or we shall lose the finest chance we have ever had since the time when you [his father] began spinning.'[1] He calculated that they would get 5s. 6d. profit from a bundle of 60 lea line, and 4s. 2d. from 50 lea tow. 'As soon as mill *D* is filled with machinery, I see clearly enough that the old mills must be emptied and all undergo a regeneration.'[2]

The reason for this change of mind can be surmised only from circumstantial evidence. In the first place, by the autumn of 1827, John II started to lose faith in his endeavours, and when his father refused to lower their yarn prices John II was ready to let initiative pass elsewhere. Second, in the interval between April and September, James improved his wet spinning frames though John II still thought that they were 'failing in some little things', particularly with respect to wooden rollers and troughs: 'we require the greatest delicacy in these frames and must have it. Wood is no friend, but the most bitter enemy of truth, on which account it is to be detested in every machine that has the most distant pretension to truth.'[3] Nevertheless the basic design seemed sound and the Foundry soon fitted copper rollers and cast iron troughs. Finally, and most decisive, John Marshall recovered from his illness and took a hand in the direction of affairs. Early in September, realising that his judgement was being borne out by events, James again urged the introduction of wet spinning and criticised their attitudes towards mechanical improvement.

It is of the greatest importance in new inventions not to attempt too much and get involved in too many new elements at once: to aim in the first edition at the attainment of the principal object, viz. a given effect on the material in the surest and easiest way possible; embracing as little that is new and untried as is practicable, and never grudging a little additional expense with the aim of insuring the main result. Always, however, rejecting refinements; and attempts to replace hand-labour too much with additional mechanical motions: and these in fact are the chief causes of expense. We have erred most egregiously against all these rules in our

---

[1] J. Marshall II to J. Marshall, 20 September 1827.
[2] *Ibid.*
[3] *Ibid.* 20 September 1827; and 9 September 1827, 'we are now spinning very good 60 lea yarn from our wet spinning frame'.

recent attempts at making new batting, hackling, spreading and wet spinning machines. When I recollect the innumerable errors in judgement that I have fallen into in the *manner* of *executing* these plans I am perfectly astonished; the more so as subsequent experience has confirmed the correctness of the principles I went upon at the same time that it has proved my application of them to have been extremely injudicious.... And though the chief errors have been mine they have often been very greatly increased by both you and John being bitten by the same mania of doing wonders all at once. When I have rashly rushed into a sea of difficulties, all created by haste and want of consideration and well-nigh foundered, then all at once came you and John upon my back each with a new plan which cannot wait; no, it must be tried forthwith. How very injudicious it was to waste our time in contriving half a dozen plans of wet spinning when Hives had proved that Kay's plan made good yarn. It was quite wrong also to meddle with the wet tow spinning now; we should stick to the line....[1]

John Marshall could not disagree with this view. Looking around, he saw how Hives, Titley, Lawson, and Walker, and Crankshaw exploited the new process and prospered, the first named using an empty corn mill until new premises could be built.[2] The founder, who knew better than anyone how a sudden technological change could produce wider margins, had no intention of remaining idle. Wet spinning presented the greatest opportunity of his career. Without hesitation, he shifted their resources into the manufacture of fine yarns and personally returned for a term of active duty.

Before the sale of fine yarns transformed the prosperity of the concern, the Water Lane mills sustained another trading setback. In 1829 their output fell 13,000 bundles and sales dropped £50,000. Profits, amounting to £4310, were the lowest in the past decade. This check, which illustrates how the firm as a producer of *medium* yarns depended on the local market, was caused by a strike at Barnsley. A small master-manufacturer there reduced the payment for drills from 12*s.* to 8*s.* a piece early in June, virtually forcing his weavers to apply for poor relief.[3] This action was justified on the ground that trade in 1829 was a third lower than in 1825. For four years Scottish goods had undermined Barnsley linen sales at home and cheaper

---

[1] J. G. Marshall to J. Marshall, 9 September 1827.

[2] J. Marshall II to J. Marshall, 16 September 1827, 11 November 1827. Lawson, Hives, Walker and Prest were spinning fine yarns in Leeds; Crankshaw in Lancashire; and Robinson in Knaresborough planned a new mill with 18,000 wet spindles.

[3] *Leeds Mercury*, 6 June 1829.

German products were preventing any progress in the continental markets which some Barnsley houses had recently tried to enter. Other employers soon followed Cooper's example and it was estimated that as a result weavers' earnings would fall by £52,000 a year.[1] In protest, the weavers went on strike and the struggle, embittered by the fact that many workers were Irish immigrants of Catholic faith, lasted for five months. Accordingly the demand for Leeds yarns fell sharply. When in October several small Barnsley houses in straitened conditions asked Marshall and Co. to grant longer credits, John II insisted on their original terms.[2] The firm's bad debts amounted to £6872 in 1829, the highest on record. But rather than dismiss hands who would soon be required for wet spinning, John Marshall reduced wages and also took the first step towards introducing a permanently shorter working week, which wet spinning requiring more concentration would soon make necessary.

To James, this setback was further proof if any were needed of the consequences of his brother's folly. It would not have happened if John II had introduced wet spinning in 1826. At the beginning of 1829, Marshall and Co. had only 2000 wet spindles, a sixth of their total; and the founder, convinced that 'wet spinning is a valuable invention; and we must try to make some profit of it', toured Ireland to seek customers for the fine yarns Marshall and Co. were beginning to produce.[3]

These episodes indicate defects in the firm's managerial arrangements which did not augur well for its future. When four of the founder's sons—John II, James, Henry and Arthur—entered the business, the prospects of competent management in the next generation seemed assured. Ideally each brother would be responsible for a particular aspect of the firm and become an expert in his own province. Whilst John II supervised the daily running of the mills at Leeds and attended to the commercial side, James kept an eye on Castle Foregate and looked after the firm's machinery. Then Henry, who became a partner in 1830, took over the commercial side, buying flax and selling yarn; and after John II's death in 1836, Arthur

---

[1] *Ibid.* 3 October 1829.   [2] *Ibid.* 12 October 1829.
[3] J. Marshall to J. Marshall II, 8 April 1829.

looked after the plant so that James could step into John's place. This specialisation should have improved efficiency; and with a measure of co-operation in pursuit of their common interest, the juniors should have conducted the business successfully.[1] But this did not always happen. The flaw lay not in individual incompetence or the misapplication of talent, but in the clash between differing personalities, a source of difficulty which could not be resolved with finality.

After becoming a partner in 1825, James claimed an equal voice in the conduct of affairs and thus alienated his elder brother. John II, who expected to inherit his father's position in the firm, though superficially a self-assured, detached and reasonable man, was acutely conscious of his limitations in business. Unlike his brother he had no flair for mechanical invention and machinery remained a mystery to him. And although he might speak aggressively after blundering —'I hope we are made of more gallant stuff than to flinch the spur', —he was always the first to despair of any improvement.[2] Family circumstances and personal temperament gave him a narrow outlook and hardened attitudes with the result that he clung assiduously to precedent in running the mills. Later James would also appear rigidly conservative but in the 1820's, apart from being tall like his brothers, he differed in most other respects. Compared to John II, he had a robust constitution; and he was an unusual character, at once talented and indifferent, lazy, stubborn, and impulsive. Though responsible for the firm's plant, he often awaited his father's instructions and then either passed the work on to his favourite manager at Salop or farmed it out to Leeds machine-makers. However, he displayed considerable ability once his interest was aroused. His notebooks show how methodically he conducted an experiment, setting forth the aim and removing irrelevant factors in a scholarly fashion; and his contribution to geology earned him a name in scientific circles. But the pursuit of knowledge for its own sake and the relegation of commercial considerations to second place ill-suited the needs of business. Moreover, being at first excluded from the

---

[1] Cf. W. N. Parker's view of success in German enterprises in the late nineteenth century, *Explorations in Entrepreneurial History*, vol. VII, no. 1, pp. 26–36.

[2] J. Marshall II to J. Marshall, 20 September 1827.

commercial side, he assessed the firm's performance in terms of plant with scant regard for the financial aspect. Nevertheless, by comparison with his brother, James was imaginative and adventurous; and because technical changes dominated the scene when he entered the trade, he soon undermined his brother's authority.

Having played the chief role in developing the firm's preparing machinery in the early 1820's, James subsequently rated his services to the business more highly than those of his brother. Hence his anger when his plans for mechanical improvements were rejected. At the same time, John II made several blunders including the sale of bad yarns, inadequate orders for machinery and the failure to perceive the importance of wet spinning; indeed his subsequent criticism of a local machine-maker could with equal force have been applied to himself—'He is keen enough in his sight when an object is brought within a short distance, but he cannot see it a long way off.'[1] By such errors John II injured his reputation at precisely the time James was advocating wet spinning, with the result that he found himself overruled by the other two partners.

Differences of opinion were to be expected and, providing they did not disrupt the conduct of affairs, might have proved beneficial. As the founder knew from experience, even hostile characters can co-operate smoothly in pursuit of a common end. But after expressing their various viewpoints, it was necessary to agree upon a joint policy and put it into operation. Should that prove impossible, someone had to go. But Marshall and Co. lacked this ultimate sanction. When James suggested that the partnership should be viewed as a cabinet, each brother running his own department and their father as Prime Minister, John II retorted 'Your parallel of His Majesty's ministers is only incorrect in one circumstance, rather an important one though; you were the ministry, and I, if you will give me the character, His Majesty's Opposition'.[2] Brothers might quarrel and if peeved neglect their work, yet one dare not dismiss another. Neither John II (nor later Henry) would implement policies formulated by James with which they disagreed. Instead, whilst jealously guarding their own departments against outside interference, they quietly neglected the

---

[1] *Ibid.* 11 November 1827.
[2] J. Marshall II to J. G. Marshall, 27 April 1827.

business. Thus the projection of family relationships and quarrels into the firm resulted at times in a passive resistance which led to indifferent management.

Apart from these conflicts, John Marshall was uneasy about the attitude of his sons towards business. He had derived great satisfaction from managing a firm and making money, and until his last days displayed considerable capacity for hard work. But his children, starting from a different position, had other goals. Their youth had been spent at Ullswater and Headingley, near those with position and substance. It was natural therefore that they spent much time in idle pursuits of the kind that their father had formerly frowned upon. John II's passion was race-horses; James liked fishing; all enjoyed hunting, climbing and foreign travel. As Dorothy Wordsworth noticed, John Marshall the calculating man of business became an indulgent, kind-hearted father in the family circle and encouraged his children to adopt a pleasurable way of life. When a guest arrived, for instance, they were expected to provide some hunting.[1] At the age of eighteen (the age at which John Marshall had entered his father's drapery business), these youths were placed in the mills at Water Lane, so that they could begin to prepare for their future livelihood. No doubt their father hoped that at least one would inherit his aptitude for business. But he was beset with misgivings.

John II thought that the business ought to be conducted on different lines, and made too many mistakes. James and Henry would absent themselves to visit spas or country relatives. As a result their father's letters remained unanswered and John II had to excuse this behaviour. 'Thinking you would not object to Henry's having another 10 days of shooting, he is going to Melmerby to-morrow in order to have it whilst his brothers are there. I did not think of it until James wrote about it, or I would have written to you before he went...a fortnight ago.'[2] Such signs perplexed the founder because he sensed the consequences for the business. But he could do little about it. To have reproached his sons would have defeated his ultimate purpose. Rather, he played the role of elder

---

[1] J. Marshall to J. Marshall II, 12 October 1829.
[2] J. Marshall II to J. Marshall, 9 September 1827. See also Selincourt, *op. cit.* 1821–30, pp. 288–9.

statesman, trusting that the next generation would profit by his example and heed his pontifical advice about the road to success. But seeing their father accumulate wealth without spending much time in the mills, the sons would draw their own conclusions. Already their future well-being had been assured and this reduced the need for them to acquire deep roots in the mills or town. For a while they devoted themselves dutifully to the concern, though without the zest their father had shown. None worked 12 hours a day and travelled in search of orders. Moreover none chose a wife from the local society. By the time they had reached forty, all moved to country houses in the Lake District, where they lived a quiet, civilised life. They were too wealthy to be interested in making more money and did not seek to distinguish themselves in other fields. The founder had reason therefore to feel ill at ease when he struggled to bring his sons into focus as gentlemen and mill-owners.

These weaknesses were more apparent than real in the late 1820's. Except under abnormal external conditions, large firms do not collapse suddenly. Marshall and Co. was strong enough to withstand a few setbacks, and even with very inadequate management it would have survived another twenty years. But the managerial difficulties of the late 1820's were resolved in the 1830's. During his lifetime the founder exploited his parental authority to lessen disputes, although such interference often had the effect of encouraging his sons to make common cause against him and deprived them of responsibilities which they should have shouldered themselves. More important in the early 1830's was the effective departure of John II from active management. Having fallen from grace, John II sought to restore his prestige by developing interests outside the business, especially politics. With his time divided between Keswick, Leeds and London, and his attention focused on the Corn Laws, factory reform and civil liberties, he lost touch with the mills. (At one public meeting where he was accused of maltreating certain workers he had no idea to what the speaker referred; afterwards he found out about the incident and defended himself in the press.)[1] Then in April 1835 a pulmonary disease recurred, compelling his retirement from active

---

[1] *Leeds Intelligencer*, 12 January 1832, and J. Marshall II's three draft replies.

affairs; eighteen months later he died after an operation at the age of thirty-nine.

Throughout the 1830's relations between the partners remained harmonious. There could be no disagreement about the path they had to follow and the exploitation of wet spinning required a considerable effort from all of them. James kept watch on the experiments of his rivals—Hives's superfine yarns and Titley's dyes—and developed a close association with Peter Fairbairn, a promising machine-maker whom the Marshalls helped to start in Leeds.[1] If the prestige of Marshall and Co. dwindled in the late 1820's, it rose again in the following decade, and the partners planned a mill bigger than that opened by Hives and Atkinson in 1833.[2] But the leadership problem was not resolved. It was difficult to foresee what would happen when the founder could no longer act as arbiter. Perhaps it was an omen that the partnership agreement concluded immediately after his death contained a clause for voting whenever difference of opinion arose.

(ii)

The introduction of wet spinning called for a second conversion and rearrangement of the entire plant within a decade. Optimistically, John Marshall II ordered a new frame in September 1827: 'Jackson of the Foundry...with such a power of hands...can really make our wet spinning frames fast enough.'[3] Within two months he changed his mind. 'The Foundry got on miserably slowly...they have only sent in one frame during five weeks....This will never do and we must try to get some assistance elsewhere.'[4] The delays the firm had faced when introducing gill frames began all over again. Every spinner in Leeds wanted new frames at the same time. At the

---

[1] J. G. Marshall to J. Marshall, 3 September 1832; J. G. Marshall, 'Salop Notebook', p. 30. They discovered Titley's method: 'We have a man...who worked for them. I set him to finish some thread their way. It was perceptibly more perfect than ours. But the labour was too great'—it cost approximately five times as much. For the start of Fairbairn's Wellington Foundry, see *Fortunes made in Business* (1887) by various authors, 2nd. ed., vol. II, pp. 262–3.

[2] See p. 202 below. For Hives's mill, see *Leeds Intelligencer*, 28 December 1833; J. G. Marshall to J. Marshall, 10 February 1833.

[3] J. Marshall II to J. Marshall, 9 September 1827, and in defence of the local trade, he added, 'I must assure you that most of the machine shops in Manchester turn out miserable work, very inferior in workmanship to ours'.

[4] *Ibid.* 11 November 1827.

beginning of 1828, only 700 out of 12,142 spindles at Water Lane were wet. But fifteen years later, only forty out of 30,444 spindles were dry. Twelve thousand old spindles had been scrapped and 30,000 new ones installed.

First to be equipped with the new machinery was mill *D*. This building, completed late in 1827 with the installation of a 70 horse-power engine from the Round Foundry, stood five floors high and had a superficial area of 2550 square yards. The total cost of fabric, engine and shafting amounted to close on £10,000. Early in 1828 a few wet spindles were at work there; at the end of four years when the mill had been filled to capacity, two-fifths of the firm's spindles could spin fine yarns. Long before that time plans for further expansion were in hand. The founder repeatedly exhorted his sons to exploit the demand for fine yarns as quickly as possible, and pointed to the path which they should follow: 'Our yarns from 80 leas upwards will soon *drive the handspun out* of the market. The hand-spun 120 leas and above are a higher price than ours and if we make suitable machinery we may sell a large quantity from 100 to 300.'[1] To accommodate more frames, they would strip the old mills and build new ones. Actually the small eighteenth-century mills to the north of Water Lane were unsuitable, and they decided to demolish mill *A* and to restrict production in mill *B* to a few coarse tow yarns. So, apart from mill *D*, that left only mill *C* for the new frames. Before the end of 1829, John Marshall had decided to build a third mill south of Water Lane, running parallel to Marshall Street and adjoining the two existing mills. 'As soon as the plan of the new building is settled, the boilers should be moved and everything prepared for having it at work in the autumn because it will save us so many removals to put the new machinery into it at once, and take down mill *A* in the spring of 1831.'[2] The new mill, *E*, stood seven storeys high and had 3000 square yards for machinery. Excluding power, which came from mill *C*, it cost £10,000. At the same time mill *C* was raised two storeys and a single tall structure—mills *C*, *D* and *E* —dominated Marshall Street. The extensions came into service in

[1] J. Marshall to J. Marshall II, 12 October 1829.
[2] J. Marshall to J. G. Marshall, 18 November 1829. At that time, incidentally, they were experimenting with mule-frames, which if adopted would have affected the alleys in the 'Cross-Mill'. But the scheme did not come to anything.

1831, but six years passed before the demolition of mill *A*. Early in 1833, after four years of reorganisation during which 21,000 wet spindles had been added and 5000 dry line-spindles scrapped, the partners foresaw the end of the expansion. James Marshall reckoned 'the necessity of pulling up directly, as far as possible in our machine making. . . . I propose to stop both Fentons and Gore after completing their present orders. . . . They have for some time sought orders everywhere and we have left them at perfect liberty, therefore I think we are equally free.'[1] By 1835 the firm had 90 per cent wet spindles and mill *B* alone housed old frames—3000 tow and almost 1000 line spindles.

Such an enormous conversion inevitably had repercussions on other processes. Both the quality and ratio of preparing machinery changed. Fewer old-style hackling machines were required to deal with the smaller quantity of flax consumed in fine-yarn production, and between 1828 and 1835 the number was halved. New, more efficient hackling machines such as the screw-gill machine designed by Peter Fairbairn of Leeds appeared in the mid-1830's, and in 1842 the firm introduced slide lever machines. Of more immediate impact was the invention of cylinder roughing machines which replaced manual labour in the roughing operation. The first one was installed in 1829, and by 1833 the firm had its total complement of 151. During the 1830's roving machinery also changed considerably. No sooner had the firm installed some circular gill frames in the late 1820's than Wesley, who had worked for Busk, told Fairbairn about 'a new principle of gill drawing' in return for £30. 'Fairbairn expecting to be repaid by us if we used it', James Marshall wrote, 'I agreed . . . thinking it very important to possess as soon as possible any new idea or hint that might affect our plans. . . for without excessive accuracy and delicacy in gill roving, I see no prospect of progression.'[2] After several years' preliminary work, Fairbairn produced a screw-gill roving machine which combed, drew and twisted the sliver into a rove and wound it on to a bobbin; and Marshall and Co. began to install these new machines.

[1] J. G. Marshall to J. Marshall, 10 February 1833.
[2] *Ibid.* 10 February 1833. Marshall and Co. installed their first circular gill roving machine in 1830 and had 163 in 1840. Also by 1840 they had eighty screw-gill roving machines.

Eight years of expansion, financed out of profits and savings on circulating capital, made Marshall and Co. the leading spinners of fine yarns in the country. The founder had been right in supposing that the system of wet spinning would bring substantial rewards. In the doldrums of the late 1820's profits at Leeds averaged less than £9000 a year (1826–30). For the next six years (1831–6) they came to £30,000 per annum. At Salop too, profits rose once the Castle Foregate mills were re-equipped. From 1826 to 1834 they averaged £7000 yearly, and from 1835 to 1839, £21,000. Thus after fifteen years of peace, a new invention enabled Marshalls to recover their wartime level of profit. Decennial earnings—profits plus income from rent and interest—which came to £439,000 for 1807–16 fell to £372,000 (1817–26), and then rose to £469,000 (1827–36) and £534,000 (1837–46). By the 1830's more partners claimed a share in the reward, but the second generation had no grounds for complaint. Two-fifths of the million pounds realised between 1827 and 1846 went to the founder and the rest to his sons. Not counting interest payments, John Marshall II received £90,000 before his death in 1836; and by 1846 James had over £220,000, Henry £200,000 and Arthur, a late-comer, £76,000: £10,000 to £15,000 a year was a very handsome income.

The partners' good fortune in having more resources than any other firm to develop wet spinning undoubtedly explains their success. Between 1827 and 1836 the number of spindles doubled whilst output rose by a fifth, from 220,000 bundles a year before 1831 to 260,000 a year during the next nine years. Spindleage naturally increased faster than output. Spinning finer yarns took more time—7 leas per spindle per day as against 14—and merely to have maintained the earlier level of output, extra frames would have been necessary. However, output rose by a fifth and profits by three-fifths. A large part of the gain came therefore from wider margins. From 1826 to 1829 the firm had its lowest rate of profit since its foundation, less than 10*d.* a bundle or 7½ per cent on turnover. Then the pendulum swung to the other extreme. The profit margin averaged 29*d.* a bundle from 1830 to 1836, a return of 22 per cent.

At first production costs continued to fall as they had ever since the war. In 1826 it cost the firm 138*d.* to spin a bundle of yarn, in

1830 105*d*. Concurrently, yarn prices came near to rock bottom in 1827, and fell very little farther in the following three years, so that margins began to widen, and if there had been no strike in Barnsley in 1829 total profits would have increased continuously. After 1830 output rose, and the sale of fine yarns began to influence margins. Production costs rose slightly to reach 114½*d*. in 1836; but the paramount influence in these years was the high price of fine yarns.

A heavy line or tow yarn was expensive to produce and unprofitable. In 1830, for example, 12 lea line yarn cost 15*s*. 9*d*. to make—12*s*. 3*d*. for flax and 3*s*. 6*d*. for spinning expenses. At the prevailing price of 15*s*., Marshalls lost 9*d*. on each bundle sold. By contrast, very fine 180 lea line yarn cost 8*s*. 5*d*.—3*s*. 5*d*. for flax and 5*s*. for spinning, owing to the extra labour and capital involved. These fine yarns sold for 14*s*. a bundle, yielding a profit of 5*s*. 7*d*. Within the range 60–100 lea line yarn, the firm made 3*s*. 6*d*. profit on a selling price of 12*s*. 6*d*. Likewise in 1833 light 6½ lb. to 10 lb. tow yarn cost 9*s*. to produce and sold for 12*s*. 3*d*., yielding a profit of 3*s*. 3*d*. a bundle. Accordingly, Marshall and Co. discontinued their coarse and many of their medium yarns, concentrating instead on the production of fine line and tow yarns.

Despite the fact that other Leeds spinners changed to the manufacture of fine yarns, the post-war situation in which over-production undermined prices was not repeated. Light yarn prices remained buoyant until the late 1830's. In 1828 120 lea yarn sold for 13*s*. 3*d*., and despite slight annual variations in price, there was no falling trend; in 1836 this yarn cost over 14*s*. a bundle. Prices remained high because the demand for these yarns increased faster than the output of the town's spinners and it was this which evoked John Marshall's appraisal of the situation as the greatest opportunity he could ever remember. Leeds spinners were no longer shackled to the Barnsley market, no longer at the mercy of competition from cheap, coarse Scotch linens, no longer paralysed by cotton goods. Instead, Leeds spinners displaced hand-spinners and flourished for a decade exporting yarn to Ireland and to the Continent where fine linens were preferred to cotton goods. In 1832 the United Kingdom exported 50 tons of yarn to the Continent; in 1836, 2000 tons; and in

1842, 13,000 tons. And these figures do not include the sale of fine yarns to the revived Irish linen industry.

Marshalls in 1835 sold 262,000 bundles of yarn (over 600 tons by weight). The firm no longer put much yarn out to local weavers, and at home their yarn sales had not risen above the level of the early 1820's when 130,000 bundles were sold annually, three-quarters of it at Barnsley. The whole addition to output, some 120,000 bundles, was exported in fairly equal parts to France and Ireland.

To expedite their entry into new markets the founder himself returned for a final spell of active duty. In August 1829 the great Leeds mill-owner and member for Yorkshire spent five weeks in Ireland prospecting for business.[1] Although Mulholland's mill in Belfast had been rebuilt for flax-spinning, Ireland had at that time virtually no machine-spinners and a rapidly expanding hand-loom industry. In the traditional weaving centres, Marshall noticed the rapid growth of merchant firms, some of which employed over a thousand weavers. Here was a market considerably larger than anything in England. So he made sure that the customers approved of his yarns, satisfied himself that they had reliable and energetic agents to handle their business, and concluded 'our connection here is making the progress we could wish...and the consumption of our yarns will be very great'.[2] At the same time he kept a wary eye on the sales of their rivals. At Belfast he called on a branch of Sadlers, the wholesale linen business which in the 1780's had been Marshall, Fenton and Co. In Ireland, this house 'sold £100,000 per annum, exclusive of Leeds', and all their yarns came from Hives and Atkinson, 'who must have made some concession to secure their order'.[3] So Marshall lost no time in telling his son to find out what practices were afoot. Equally serious was the success of Kay's yarn; 'Kay's yarns are improving and are sold in considerable quantities'.[4] Not only had the Lancashire spinner in conjunction with Crankshaw successfully invaded the Yorkshire yarn market in 1826–7, selling at Knaresborough, Darlington, Northallerton and Brompton, but since

[1] Marshall, 'Tours' (Ireland, 1829); J. Marshall to J. Marshall II, 2 October 1829. On this tour, Marshall was accompanied by William Wordsworth and J. G. Marshall. See Selincourt, *op. cit.* 1821–30, pp. 404–21.
[2] J. Marshall to J. Marshall II, 2 October 1829.
[3] *Ibid.* [4] *Ibid.*

then they had also made rapid headway both in Ireland and in Scotland.[1] No doubt Marshall took this into consideration when in the 1830's he decided to crush Kay by litigation. The latter asked for 6s. a spindle from wet spinners to use his patent, the validity of which John Marshall II denied in November 1827. After Kay had successfully prosecuted some small spinners, Marshall and Co. took up the challenge ostensibly on behalf of the whole industry, obliging other spinners to contribute towards their legal costs. They refused any compromise and five years of litigation, terminating in the House of Lords, won their case, though not before other firms in the industry felt that Marshall's ruthless pursuit and defamation of Kay had exceeded the bounds of reasonable justice: 'Kay has been a useful man to the trade . . . and if defeated eventually, it will be a generally received opinion that he was overpowered by the weight opposed to him.'[2]

In the 1830's James and his father showed considerable enterprise in aggressively advancing the interests of the business. Hearing of a demand for super fine (250 lea) yarns in France and the Netherlands, and 'perhaps England next as fashion spreads', James immediately demanded that Hives should tell him how to spin such fine counts.[3] Like his father he realised that their strength lay in the scale of their operations and accumulated resources. Others might invent new ways and introduce them sooner, but Marshall and Co. could re-equip and expand faster than firms like Hives and Titleys, mechanise more operations and engage a higher proportion of women. In addition they succeeded in retaining their supervisors whilst overseers elsewhere, such as Hives's mill manager, Temple, migrated, in his case to Lille.

The efficiency with which the mills were managed and the way in which the partners reacted to external changes in factor costs can be ascertained from a consideration of expenses. In 1827 the average cost of raw material in a bundle of yarn was $60\frac{3}{4}d.$; by 1833 it had

---

[1] J. Marshall II to J. Marshall, 9 September 1827; W. Renshaw to J. Marshall, 2 July 1836.

[2] J. Campbell to Messrs Marshall and Co., 10 August 1836, speaking also for Mulhollands; John Hives (in a letter to Messrs Marshall and Co. dated 16 July 1836) was reluctant to testify for his former partner at York Assizes. On the other hand, J. Marshall II had spoken against Kay's patent in 1827, see J. Marshall II to J. Marshall, 11 November 1827, note 2, p. 173 above.

[3] J. G. Marshall to H. C. Marshall, 24 May 1836.

fallen to 44¾*d*., and afterwards it rose, reaching 62½*d*. in 1836. Throughout this decade (1827–36) flax prices tended to rise. Marshalls paid £44 per ton in 1827 and £88 in 1836. There were two reasons for this steep increase. First, the price of flax rose everywhere as industrial demand outpaced supplies. The average price of flax in Britain, which stood about £40 in 1827, rose to £55 eight years later following a crop failure and an exceedingly heavy demand the next year. The second reason really explains why Marshalls paid £30 a ton more than the average price in the 1830's. Fine spinners did not use coarse Baltic flax which comprised the bulk of imports into the country. This cheap flax went to heavy-yarn spinners in Scotland. The mills in Leeds used Flemish and Dutch flax, carefully cultivated and cleaned but much more expensive. Demand for this flax rose substantially at a time when the size of the crop began to decline, and its price leapt up. When the depression of the 1840's curtailed demand, prices fell, and angry voices abroad protested that Leeds spinners, especially Marshall and Co., fixed the price of fine flax. Before that, however, Marshalls paid more for flax than they had been doing and along with other spinners began to explore the possibilities of alternative supplies from Egypt and New Zealand or substitute fibres such as China Grass. Notwithstanding the higher price of flax, its cost per bundle fell until 1833–4 owing to the growing impact of wet spinning. In 1827 Marshall and Co. had spun yarns up to 60 leas and made 175 bundles from a ton of flax. In 1834 they produced line yarns up to 200 leas and obtained 358 bundles. But in the next two years the average fineness fell to 339 bundles per ton in 1836 and the price of their flax rose £27 a ton or 45 per cent.

Labour costs fell and rose too, from 19½*d*. a bundle in 1827 to 17*d*. in 1830 and 18½*d*. in 1836. During the 1820's the management introduced two 6-hour shifts for children under thirteen. When the depression came, John II dismissed a third of the labour force, including a high proportion of children, and allowed the shift system to lapse. As a result average earnings rose until wage rates were reduced in 1829, and this was immediately reflected in lower labour costs. After 1830 the price of labour tended to rise. At the time, some industries in Leeds experienced labour shortages. New industry probably grew faster in the town of Leeds than the supply of hands, and employers had either to use less labour, substitute children and Irish for adult native labour, or pay more in order to obtain what they wanted. Unless they could pass higher costs on in the form of higher prices, businessmen would hardly favour the last course whilst others were at hand, and flax-spinners, who had not come off as well as other industrialists in the 1820's, did not hesitate to seek cheap labour. Despite an increase of between 3*d*. and 9*d*. in basic weekly rates for most spinners (which amounted to restoring the cuts of the late 1820's), average annual earnings at Water Lane remained constant at £15 per head in the early 1830's. This was due to changes in the composition of the labour force. Between 1830 and 1835 the firm took on a further ninety-one children under thirteen, thus raising the proportion of that age-group from 20 per cent to 28 per cent of the total working force. Again the partners devoted their attention to schemes for children: in 1833 a new infants' school was opened and an 8-hour day was introduced for those under eleven.[1] These young workers, costing only 3*s*. to 3*s*. 6*d*. a week, moved flax from one machine to the next, and where mechanisation displaced manual work they helped to tend machines. In 1836, when the Factory Act came into effect, Marshall and Co. began a two-shift system for children under thirteen who spent half their day at the factory school. After this the number of children employed was not increased; young girls between thirteen and eighteen were hired when the need arose for extra labour and from 1836 to 1838 they increased from 30 per cent to 34 per cent of the working force. Their price only amounted to between 4*s*. and 6*s*. a week, whereas boys aged sixteen cost 6*s*. 4*d*., and at twenty cost twice as much as a woman. Thus the firm met the local pressure towards higher wages by substituting cheaper labour.

Output per worker fell between 1827 and 1836 resulting in an upward pressure on labour costs. The number of hands increased by

---

[1] Hives and Atkinson followed suit; Horner, *Factory Inspectors Report*, 31 December 1836 (9), in 1836 (78), vol. XLV, p. 158. By 1843, 460 out of 700 children in the town's flax mills attended school half a day, see Saunders, *Factory Inspectors Report*, 1843, p. 28; it is interesting to note (in Saunders's *Report*, 13 July 1844) that Hives allowed four children over thirteen to spend half a day at the *National School* and receive full wages; and one pupil aged fifteen won a scholarship to York Training School. Such achievements no doubt confirmed mill-owners' views that some among the operative class had the ability to rise in the world.

a fifth from under a thousand in 1827 to over 1200 in 1832, remaining constant at that level until 1840. The number of bundles produced by a worker in a year fell from 226 in 1827 to 204 in 1836. This decline of 10 per cent is not surprising owing to the slower rate of spinning. Before the introduction of the new system, a spindle twisted 12 leas of yarn a day; in 1836 it produced about half this length. In its turn this reduction was partly due to a shorter working day. Before 1831 the firm nominally ran a 72-hour week. In that year it reduced its working week to 69 hours, and then in 1834 to 66 hours. The first of these reductions was taken on the initiative of the management, who thought wet spinning required extra concentration; they reckoned that the losses resulting from workers making poor yarns due to over-long hours were higher than any savings which could be made from spreading overheads over more time.[1] So to offset the fall in output per spindle and get the same output and value for money as they had formerly obtained from labour, the quantity of machinery each worker watched had to be considerably increased. The average number of spindles per head rose by about three-fifths, and in the spinning department labour costs fell $2\frac{1}{2}$ per cent despite shorter hours and higher earnings. But this gain was outweighed by what happened in other departments, such as hackling where productivity declined (due probably to the use of too many children) and labour costs rose, and productivity as a whole declined.

In summary: labour costs fell in the later 1820's owing to higher productivity and a reduction in wages. In the early 1830's when productivity tended to decline and wage-rates rose, the partners employed a higher proportion of children. This solution came to an end in 1836 and it became necessary once more to consider more drastic ways of curtailing rising labour costs.

However, reductions in unit expenses between 1827 and 1836 were caused principally by lower average fixed costs. Between 1827 and 1830 these fell 15d. a bundle (roughly a third) and rose 2d. in the next six years. These charges were abnormally high in 1826–7 before John Marshall II launched an economy drive. In the following three years, whilst output remained constant, overheads fell a third. Then

[1] J. G. Marshall, 'Salop Notebook'. 'Nor have I forgotten that the shorter time people work, the harder they work', J. Marshall II, draft speech for House of Commons, May 1833.

in the next six years, overheads grew faster than output. No clear relationship existed between the firm's fixed charges and the volume of output, chiefly because the former consisted of a changing miscellany of costs. In 1827 depreciation was added to overheads; in 1834, machinery repairs. One year the account would be swollen by bad debts; in another, the partners would agree to alter the price of rent, interest or depreciation.

Two important items determining the level of overheads were rent and interest, and something like half the saving realised between 1827 and 1830 can be traced to a reduction in these costs. Although the founder agreed to charge a rent of only $7\frac{1}{2}$ per cent on new outlays after 1824, with the completion of mill *D* the firm's fabric and engines were nominally worth £60,000 and the rent came to £5026 in 1829, about a twentieth of total costs. Since profits had been low for several years, and since John Marshall II questioned the value of the assets for which rent was charged, John Marshall reduced the rent by a third and drew £3404 the following year. Simultaneously, an effort was made to reduce the cost of capital; the partners agreed to accept $4\frac{1}{2}$ per cent in place of 5 per cent interest; and the quantity of capital also fell.[1] Although the cost of new machinery between 1826 and 1835 came to £99,000, the value of circulating capital fell after 1828 with the holding of smaller stocks. The combined value of fixed and circulating capital, which stood at £250,000 in the late 1820's, dropped to £175,000 in 1831. On the other hand, by charging depreciation and later maintenance on fixed capital, they offset the reduction in interest charges. Prior to 1827 there had been no systematic writing down of machinery. A new hackling machine in 1810 worth £20 was depreciated in a random manner, appearing as £17 in 1822 and £16 in 1830. From 1827 machinery was depreciated at $7\frac{1}{2}$ per cent per annum. (Several years passed before the valuations in the annual stock account coincided with the omnibus deduction of $7\frac{1}{2}$ per cent in the General Statement.) In 1827 depreciation added 4*d.* to the cost of a bundle of yarn and, as additions to fixed capital grew faster than its reduction by depreciation, this charge

---

[1] Reductions in rent and interest increased the sum available for distributed profit, which was to the advantage of the junior partners who earned no rent and whose capital was small.

gradually increased. But taken together, interest and depreciation costs fell between 1829 and 1830.

This combination of lower rent, cheaper capital, falling prices of such materials as oil and wood, and cheaper building repairs, together reduced average fixed costs to a low point by 1830. They amounted to £31,454 compared with £43,780 in 1827.

After 1830 general expenses rose, reaching £36,747 in 1836. Between 1831 and 1836 £12,000 was spent on the fabric, which raised the rent to £4436. After 1833 interest costs stopped falling, and total capital rose again to £200,000. Depreciation costs also grew, from £3974 (1830) to £6137 (1836). Maintenance costs increased, particularly for items of machinery, which were entered separately for the first time. The cost of gas, coal, oil and wood changed little. To avoid any rise in the cost of overheads per bundle of yarn, output should have grown as fast. In fact it failed to do so and overhead costs per bundle rose slightly. Thus by 1834 the partners looked for economies and, while some hands in the mills got higher wages, mechanics and travellers were either laid off or their salaries reduced.

To sum up: in the late 1820's reductions in wages, interest and rent lowered the cost of producing a bundle of yarn. Concurrently the cost advantages and disadvantages of wet spinning became apparent. Less circulating capital reduced interest charges, half the weight of raw material in a bundle of yarn reduced flax costs: on the other hand slower spinning reduced labour productivity. After 1830, as factor costs rose, James and Henry Marshall tried to exploit these advantages and to minimise the disadvantages. More child labour was introduced, the firm concentrated wholly on fine yarns, and a rising output almost, but not quite, overtook rising overheads. After the recession of 1827, the adoption of wet spinning and the withdrawal of John Marshall II, the remaining juniors guided by the founder had the situation well under control—lessening fixed charges, raising work loads, mechanising processes such as roughing, and securing cheap labour.

With buoyant yarn prices, a 20 per cent margin on turnover, a share-out (including rent and interest) of £50,000 a year, the founder and his sons tasted success. They had recovered the ground lost by the firm in the 1820's and felt very confident about their future.

(iii)

The Marshalls knew that their present prosperity would not last for ever. Speculations in 1836 alarmed the founder who thought prices must soon fall, as indeed they did the next year. At a deeper level, they watched new forces emerge which would undermine their position; the expansion of spinning at home in conjunction with the eventual contraction of markets abroad would again depress profits.

Competition would come in the first instance from spinners in Leeds. Scottish mills spinning Baltic flax, and later, Indian jute, produced non-competitive products. The reviving Irish industry, mechanised and localised in Belfast, a port of entry for imported coal, was still a far-off cloud. With only nine mills in 1837, none able to spin yarns as fine as Marshalls, Irish spinners made slight inroads on English yarn sales there.[1] The threat to Marshall and Co. lay nearer home, in Leeds. No new firms appeared in the dull years of the late 1820's, and six spinners passed out of existence. But by 1834, when Marshalls had completed their transition to wet spinning, thirteen new-comers had entered the trade. During the next five years ten new firms appeared, more than replacing the three casualties of the 1837 recession. In 1839 Leeds had thirty-one spinners situated either along East Street on the Far Bank or along Water Lane towards Holbeck. (The Mabgate district, a centre for spinners immediately after the war, declined owing to transport, water and site difficulties; in 1847 only three spinners had premises there.) In addition many existing firms, enriched by profits from wet spinning, removed to larger premises and built new mills. Alongside the river, Hives and Atkinson built a second towering structure in 1833, six storeys high and 163 ft. long, designed to employ 900 workers, and 'the largest building in the town used as a flax mill'.[2] Accumulated profits enabled Holdsworths to build Victoria Mills by the river Aire at Hunslet, and they increased their spindles from 4500 in 1838 to 8400 in 1842. Briggs, who began in 1834 with a few frames in an old house, built a mill two years later in Water Lane, and between 1838 and 1842 increased his plant from 600 to 3240 spindles. Other spinners who

---

[1] E. R. R. Green, *op. cit.* pp. 114–15.
[2] *Leeds Mercury*, 28 December 1833.

began in a small way during the 1820's now added to their machinery; Mark Walker and Morfitts had respectively 6000 and 4000 spindles by 1838. Wilkinson, a newcomer, rose spectacularly and eventually rivalled the largest firms: the son of a linen weaver, he rented a few rooms in Meadow Lane in 1825 at the age of twenty-six, and before 1840 he had accumulated £100,000, enough to build mills which carried 11,000 spindles in 1842 alongside the railway in Balm Road, Hunslet. By 1839 Leeds had fifty-nine mills with 134,000 spindles. Fixed and circulating capital amounted to £1½ million, and nearly 8000 hands were employed. Despite the manufacture of lighter yarns, flax consumption doubled in the decade, and the mills made 1½ million bundles of yarn a year. Half went to Barnsley, the rest overseas. Although Leeds yarns amounted to only a fifth of the United Kingdom's exports, they accounted for a very high proportion of the fine yarn sold on the Continent and in Ireland.[1]

This expansion raised no problem in the early 1830's when the demand for fine yarns was far from satisfied. But the growth of the Leeds industry in the late 1830's coincided with an impending change in market conditions. The probable reaction of the French government to a flood of yarn and linen imports hung like the sword of Damocles above the trade. Over three-quarters of Britain's yarn exports went to France. Bleached and coloured yarns paid a high duty, grey yarns carried in French ships escaped almost duty-free. From 1834 linen piece goods also paid less linen duty; and British exports of coarse and medium linens rose from 100,000 yards in 1830 and ¼ million yards in 1834, to 1 million in 1835 and 9 million in 1841. To liberals versed in the doctrines of contemporary political economy, the French consumer and weaver gained from such trade and specialisation. Furthermore, French linen imports would rectify Britain's unfavourable balance in the Channel trade, and improve French export opportunities. Nobody in France objected very strongly to the import of heavy cloth, which in the early 1840's amounted to less than 3 per cent of French production; the nature of the market precluded further substantial gains. French weaving firms, specialising in cambrics and damasks, welcomed cheap fine

---

[1] *Directories of Leeds*, Parson and White, 1830; Baines, 1834; Haigh, 1839. See also, H. C. Marshall, Lists of Leeds Spinners and Spindles, 1837–41.

yarns sent from England. Rural hand-spinners and a few native businessmen who set up spinning mills aided by English workmen and replicas of English machinery suffered most. At an inquiry in 1838, apart from regretting the peasant's plight, the commissioners reserved their real concern for the infant factory industry. British spinners thus foresaw the day when, to ensure the survival and growth of its mills, France would revive its hallowed policy of protection. But a *sudden* prohibition of fine yarns seemed unlikely because it would affect the country's weavers adversely, and prohibitive tariffs were not expected in the immediate future.[1]

If the output of fine yarns in Leeds increased and French demand diminished, a fighting market might develop. This made Marshall's sons think seriously about their future. James argued that the yarn trade, despite falling margins, offered an adequate return, and that the right course was to leave well alone. At the same time, since spinners could not look forward to making yarns any finer, he thought that they should experiment with new products to insure their future. In order to offset the consequences of any tariff, Henry considered setting up a water-mill in France between the Pas de Calais and La Somme. This scheme, like others to acquire flax mills in Scotland, never bore fruit. James, the elder brother, had his way, and proposed to expand the production of fine yarns (perhaps in order to maintain total profits as margins fell) and he also decided to develop two products of which they had some experience, thread and cloth.

In June 1836 James Marshall ordered four twisting frames for Leeds.[2] Next year the firm had 1200 spindles at work in *C* and *D* mills making thread. Since 1798 Marshall and Co. had made thread at Shrewsbury, and by 1825—possibly earlier—they had developed a market in the U.S.A. The founder noticed in 1829 how Lancashire spinners bought 25 lea Marshall yarn, twisted, bleached and wound it on spools, making 'beautiful thread [which] must take the market when it was known'.[3] Once the firm spun light yarns, it could if it wished make fine threads, which had so far been supplied by Scottish hand-spinners.

---

[1] H. C. Marshall, 'Notebook I'; Dunham, *op. cit.* pp. 295–9.
[2] J. G. Marshall to J. Marshall, 6 June 1836.
[3] J. Marshall to J. Marshall II, 12 October 1829.

As a commercial proposition, thread-making offered ample rather than spectacular profit. From 1830 to 1838 Marshalls had sold 3000 to 4000 dozens of thread each year in New York, bringing a net return of $13\frac{1}{2}$ per cent in a good year and 9 per cent in a bad one. James looked to the time when they could supply threads of all sizes, to sew leather, all kinds of cloths and for lace-making. They would encounter no technical difficulties and it offered a fresh opportunity for the partners to find an outlet within the business (if that was what they wanted) for the resources which they had been accumulating as fine spinners. Rather than expand thread output at Shrewsbury, Leeds, the centre of the flax trade and the residence of the partners, was chosen for this venture. The Castle Foregate mill continued to make thread, and later provided a brand name for the product, but no further extensions were made there. Benyon's Salop mill had been closed in the early 1830's, and Shrewsbury failed to realise the promise it had shown as a new industrial town a generation earlier. However, the real reason for introducing thread-making at Leeds was to diversify the output of the Water Lane mills. Except for Titley, Tatham and Walker of Water Hall mills, Holbeck, it would be, as the Marshalls realised, a new trade in the town.[1]

The proposals to make cloth showed rather more enterprise. Marshall and Co. had virtually withdrawn from the cloth trade when they stopped employing hand-loom weavers in the 1820's. At that time Scottish manufacturers began to develop a successful power-loom, and when Baxter, a leading Dundee spinner, began weaving a good stout cloth on power-looms in 1836 James reconsidered their position. They could employ girls on the looms and integrate yarn and cloth production under one roof. This would lower the cost of linens and bring the firm into direct contact with a wider consumer market. Besides, they were exasperated with the conservatism and high prices charged by Barnsley houses who failed to push their wares in foreign markets. As cloth sales rose abroad,

[1] Titley's had made thread in Leeds since 1818 at least, see Depositions, July 1836, Kay *v.* Marshall. See also J. Watson, *The Art of Spinning and Thread Making* (1878), p. 260. Fine spinning improved considerably the commercial possibilities of thread-making. In particular, the demand for thread rose with the introduction of the sewing machine, although a special grade of linen thread had to be manufactured for machining because ordinary thread was not sufficiently supple.

the partners saw their own opportunity; 'the demand for drills of all sorts is greatly increased'—James wrote in 1836—'particularly for exports in the United States, Italy and Spain'.[1] And they had the resources and reputation to speed them on this way.

This determination to advance along several fronts is reflected in their plan for extending the fabric. They proposed to build a warehouse, counting-house and a mill, larger than any in the town, which would be divided into three equal parts for making yarn for sale, thread and cloth. By May 1838 James had at hand two alternative plans. One, a design by Peter Fairbairn, was for a seven-storey warehouse and a six-storey mill, north of Water Lane on the site of the demolished mill *A*. The other, proposed by David Roberts, was for a single-storey building at the south end of Marshall Street.

The one-storey mill I have taken for the whole disposable area on mill *D* side, viz. Maclea's field and half the two next glebe lands that we have just bought, up to the line of Sweet Street continued. This street is pretty sure to be continued, and would form a good and direct communication east and west from Holbeck to Hunslet when completed....

[The proposed area of the one-storey mill was] 18,720 square yards. Deduct 2500 weaving and 1220 for waiting rooms, store rooms, passages, etc., leaving 15,000. Preparing 8000, spinning 7000. The proposed plan of having 6 feet frames gives 10 spindles per square yard at 2½ in. pitch 70,000 spindles, of these 17,000 spdle spinning for weaving, 18,000 spdle spinning for sale yarn, 18,000 spinning for thread, 17,000 twisting. Yarn to average 100 leas, 5300 Bdls per week.

[Cost of] Fairbairn's six storey mill [and Flax Warehouse] £30,835 [excluding a 400 h.p. engine, and covering only 13,392 sq. yards].

...the One Storey Mill if the whole area be occupied would take 80,000 spdls. spng *200* lea yarn 6,000 bundles per week, requiring 400 Horse Power....Estimate Expenses [including £6,852 for 7 storey Warehouse, Engine House, etc.,] £32,080.

After making some minor adjustments in order to secure a fair comparison, James concluded that:

6 storey mill 13,400 yards	£28,800
one storey mill 13,400 yards	24,300

A 1/7 th or £4000 in favour of the One Storey.

[1] J. G. Marshall to H. C. Marshall, 24 May 1836. See also Gill, *op. cit.* pp. 325–9; Warden, *op. cit.* p. 711, who states that Baxter at Dundee had power-looms as early as 1826.

...In no case could the One Storey be more expensive than the six storey. We have a model 1/3rd the full size and 6 feet high by 24 feet each way put up on boards in mill C yard by which we can compare accurately the light given on the two plans of mill. Light by the skylights [of the one-storey mill] though only half the area of the other windows is clearly and decidedly better and more uniform and there is no difficulty from shadows from its being too vertical:—the height of the room, number of skylights and reflected light from floor prevent this:—we have some machines set up in the shed to ascertain this:—I see no reason to doubt the practicability of fixing light shafts attached to the framework of the machines as is done in Cotton Mills driving a row of 3 or 4 or 6 frames; itself driven by gearing a belt from the main shaft in the tunnel underneath, so as not to require too frequent belts and uprights through the floor—The concentration of the One Storey plan I still think a great advantage for arrangement of work, overlooking, etc.....[1]

James won his father over to a one-storey mill. It would be cheaper, more functional, and its 'external appearance may be made to look extremely well quite as much so altogether as the six-storey plan'.[2] Shortly after 1839 the new structure, the second of its kind in the country, rose in Marshall Street.[3] In June 1840 its opening was marked by a great Temperance Tea for the firm's 2600 workers. Six months later machinery had been installed and the new mill began production.

The new mill, though only half the size James had forecast, was an imposing structure. It stretched 132 yards along Marshall Street and rose 32 ft. high. Half-way up the stone-faced walls, squat columns flanking the windows bore a massive entablature giving the appearance of an Egyptian temple. A few years later extensive offices (a more dignified name than counting-house) were added in matching style abutting the north end of the mill, and a columned warehouse in the yard of mill C. Behind its stylistic facade, Temple mill (as it became known) stretched 72 yards, and to the rear of the new offices, by the engine and boiler-house, rose a chimney disguised as Cleopatra's Needle. (It cracked in 1852 and was replaced by a conventional brick structure.) If the exterior seems pretentious, the single room inside covering two acres inspires a sense of awful vastness. A man feels small in such a place. Slender iron columns (also drain pipes

---

[1] J. G. Marshall to John Marshall, 24 May 1838.   [2] *Ibid.*
[3] The first mill on this plan was built by Mr Smith of Deanston whom J. G. Marshall knew, see *Institution of Civil Engineers, Minutes of Proceedings, Session 1842*, pp. 142–5.

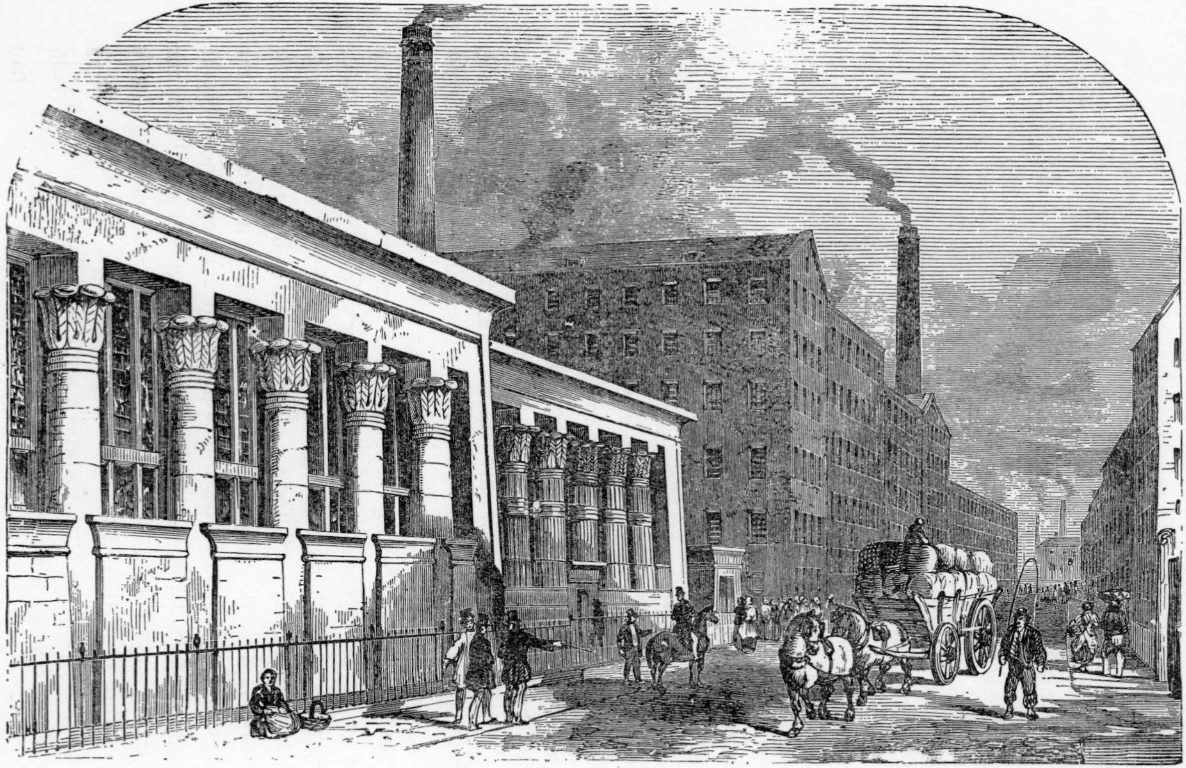

Fig. 2 (a). North view of the mills in Marshall Street, c. 1850.

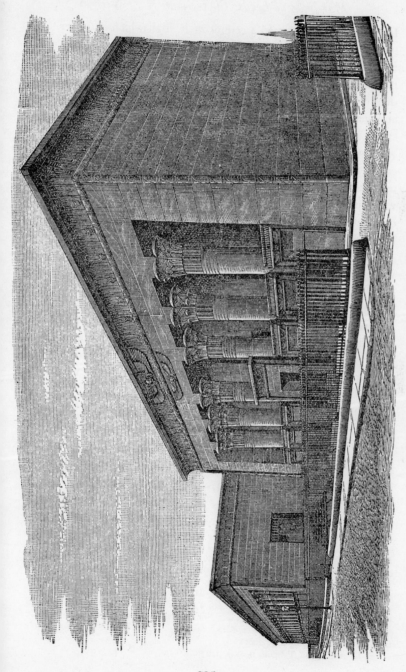

Fig. 2 (*b*). South view of the mills in Marshall Street, *c*. 1850.

from the roof) supported a ceiling 21 ft. high which had over sixty conical glass skylights 14 ft. in diameter and rising 10 ft. above the roof, 'like cucumber frames in a garden'.[1] By this means, light poured into the mill at all hours of the day, imparting a strange luminous quality to the great room, in grotesque contrast to the dark passages and shadows in the confined floors of the tall mills lower down the street. Underground in brick vaulted cellars ran a maze of passageways, some housing the shafting turned by a pair of 100 horse-power engines which drove the vast rows of machinery above. In one subterranean room a fan pushed steam-heated air into the mill, which was kept at a constant temperature and humidity. Farther along the cellars were tradesmen's shops, and private baths (each in a separate room) for the use of the hands (cold, free; hot, one penny). Above the building on the immense roof, 'a layer of earth, sown with grass, flourishes so well that sheep are occasionally sent to feed upon it'.[2]

Within a few years this temple of industry had acquired a legendary reputation. The Institute of Civil Engineers heard it described in technical terms and praised for 'the convenience of supervision, facility of access to the machines, the power of sustaining uniformity of temperature and moisture, the absence of air currents which are so objectionable in other mills, the simplicity of the driving gear, the excellent ventilation which is so desirable for the health of the workpeople'.[3] It appeared in fictional form as Mr Trafford's Mill in Disraeli's *Sybil*, 'one of the marvels of the district; one might almost say, of the country'.[4] In a town which seemed to be a 'forest of

[1] Whewell to sister, 29 September 1856; see also S.P.C.K., *The Manufacture of Linen Yarn* (*The Useful Arts no. 7*), 1846, pp. 29–32; *Leeds Mercury*, 13 June 1840; Fox Bourne, *op. cit.* p. 228. The mill and the offices, alleged to be 'an exact copy of the Temple of the Pharoahs at Philae', were perhaps inspired by the belief that ancient Egypt was the home of flax-spinning.

[2] S.P.C.K., *The Manufacture of Linen Yarn* (1846), p. 32. One noble lord in the *Proc. Inst. Civil Eng.* 1842, pp. 142–5, ventured the suggestion that such mills allowing cultivation on the roof would be important in future agricultural development.

[3] *Proc. Inst. Civil Eng.* 1842, pp. 142–5. The cost of Marshall's mill was greatly increased by the stone facing; at Deanston, Mr Smith's mill averaged 30s. per square yard. Mill *A*, built in 1790, cost 19s. 6d. a square yard; the fireproof warehouse of 1806, 43s. 6d.; and mill *C* 1815–17, 45s. For interior views of the Temple Mill, see S.P.C.K., *The Manufacture of Linen Yarn* (1846), p. 1; and H. Hamilton, *History of the Homeland* (1947), facing page 160.

[4] B. Disraeli, *Sybil* (Penguin Books), p. 179.

chimneys', the Egyptian obelisk stood out marking Marshall and Co. Besides being the most up-to-date building of its kind, a sign of Marshall progressiveness, the Temple Mill was an edifice of beauty both inside and out, an example of what industry would be like in the new society that was evolving. This was the peak of the Marshalls' achievement as spinners; they were justly proud of it as the ultimate symbol of the everlasting throbbing and clatter of machinery which had made it possible.

A few years later James and Henry, influenced perhaps by their clerical relations, thought it would be appropriate to erect a church for their employees. St John the Evangelist was built between 1847 and 1850 behind the Temple Mill, near Marshall's School in Sweet Street, to a gothic design of Gilbert Scott. Dr Hook, the Vicar of Leeds, officiated at its opening, and the sermon was preached by Dr Whewell, the Master of Trinity College. Within five years, Thomas Benyon, the son of John Marshall's former partner, had built the church of St Barnabas a few hundred yards away by his mill in Meadow Lane.

The cost of the extensions came to £52,474. A further £20,000 was spent on new plant: 7848 spinning spindles, 5640 twisting spindles, and preparing machinery. Nearly all the old dry spindles had been scrapped; and by 1846 the mills had 32,000 spinning spindles and 8000 twisting spindles.

Although this expansion sounds impressive, had the partners miscalculated? The new mill did not extend to Sweet Street. It was only half the size originally planned and carried only half the spindles it could house. Moreover, the extra yarn made was being turned into thread, and the manufacture of sale yarn had not increased. No cloth was woven and only after pressure from the elder Marshall in 1843 were six power-looms (36 in. to 45 in. broad) placed in the old *B* mill:

...It would be desirable to introduce [power-looms] if gradually for the sake of getting experience, but without expectation of much profit....I think we may look forward to the time when the yarns which are spun in England will be manufactured in England, and when that comes the weaving in spinning factories may be necessary.[1]

[1] J. Marshall to H. C. Marshall, 24 October 1843.

On the face of it, the Marshalls had not executed the plans put forward in 1836. Had something happened in the intervening years to interfere with their prosperity?

Between 1837 and 1846 the partners earned £534,244. Of this, £66,805 came as rent and £145,773 as interest on capital. Net profits amounted to £321,666, almost £40,000 lower than in the previous decade but still well above the post-war period. However, £183,693 came from Castle Foregate which had a capacity between a fifth and a sixth of that of the Water Lane mills but produced thread. Profit at Leeds came to only £137,973, substantially less than in the post-war decade. This concern made £30,000 a year from 1830 to 1836, £17,000 up to 1840, and then £6300 until 1846. In the year 1843 it declared its first loss for twenty-four years, a deficit of nearly £17,000.

Profits fell because yarn prices declined. Fine (200 lea) line yarn, which sold for 20s. a bundle in 1836, fell in price to 15s. in 1838 and 10s. by 1844. A medium (30 lea) line yarn brought 19s. in 1836, 16s. in 1838 and 11s. in 1846. In fact every grade plunged in price during 1837–8, and again between 1841 and 1844.

Production costs at Water Lane did not contract in anything like the same proportions. Between 1836 and 1842 the cost of making a bundle of yarn actually rose from 114½d. to 132d. and then it fell to 100d. by 1846.

The unit cost of flax rose by 3d. to 1841, after which it fell by 10d. The firm reversed the forces operating to determine flax costs in the previous decade. In the first place they began to make a higher proportion of heavier yarns. In 1836 a ton of flax was stretched into 339 bundles; by 1838, 383 bundles; by 1846, 340 bundles, and less in later years. From 1824 to 1834 tow yarns comprised a quarter of ouput; in the following decade, two-fifths. In 1837 the average size of their line yarn was 43 leas; in 1840, 35 leas; in 1860, 23 leas; and in 1880, 12 leas. The firm thus went full circle, and the turning-point came some time between 1838 and 1840. The manufacture of heavier yarns meant carrying more, but cheaper, flax, and a higher proportion of tow. Once more Marshall and Co. turned to the Baltic market, and since flax prices fell between 1836 and 1846 the cost of the extra fibre needed to make thicker yarn was just about cancelled out.

Under the stimulus of falling prices, the Marshalls reduced labour costs more substantially in this decade than at any other time. In the mid-1830's forces were at work which threatened to raise labour costs, yet the cost of labour per bundle remained constant at 20*d*. from 1836 to 1842 and then fell to a low point of 13*d*. in 1848. Between 1836 and 1842 spindleage rose a quarter, output and labour by a third. After 1842 a few extra frames were added, the labour force cut by a fifth (279 operatives) and output rose by a quarter (85,000 bundles). The weekly output per hand rose from four to six bundles and, despite a steady rise in average earnings from £16 in 1836 to £19 in 1846 (due chiefly to a reduction in the number of children employed), labour costs fell.

No change in hours of work took place which would account for the increased productivity. The next alteration in hours was a reduction to an 'eleven hour day' after the Repeal of the Corn Laws, which apparently inspired the concession.[1] James put classrooms at the disposal of the hands and urged them to use their free time for 'intellectual and moral improvement'. He also warned them to be prompt, work until the bell rang and stop loitering, if they wanted to avoid a cut in wages. As the reduction in hours followed several years of rising productivity, it seems that Marshalls chose to pay in kind rather than cash. During the previous decade, however, the actual time worked often fell short of the official 66 hours, especially after 1838. In practice the firm lost about 5 per cent of its operating time by the early 1840's and this makes the rise in productivity even more impressive.

Spinners' productivity rose because thicker yarns enabled faster driving. Between 1836 and 1846 output per spindle rose from 6·7 to 8·1 leas per day. The introduction of frames carrying 220 spindles in 1841 raised the number tended by an operative in the line department by 11 per cent. In the hackling section, earnings rose 11 per cent, output 69 per cent and labour costs fell 32 per cent. Many of the old hackling machines had been scrapped in the 1830's when the firm used less flax, and the remainder ran slowly to avoid excessively tearing the Flemish flax. Soon after 1836 Marshall and Co. again consumed 900 tons of flax annually, and a bottleneck built up. The

---

[1] Eleven Hours Time, Notice to the Workpeople of Messrs Marshall and Co.

number of flax-breaking machines was doubled by 1842 and processed 1300 tons a year; the number of workers employed for this task fell from eighty to fifty-four. In the hackling process itself, the firm installed twenty-eight new style screw-type machines in 1841, the number of workers remained constant, and productivity rose considerably as the new plant came into full use. Thus a smaller, older and more expensive labour force, making heavier yarn, tended more machinery and cut labour costs.

The real force behind rising costs until 1842 was swollen overheads. These increased by a half to reach £60,000 in 1842, about two-fifths of total costs. In the next few years they averaged £54,000, but a great burst in output reduced their incidence. Accordingly, unit overhead costs rose from 40*d*. (1837-40) to 48*d*. (1842) and then fell to 32*d*. (1846). In 1840 John Marshall reduced the rent by £1000, and in 1843 by a further £2500. Despite this, extensions to the fabric raised the cost of rent from 2·9*d*. to 4·1*d*. a bundle. On the other hand interest and depreciation charges fell. The rate of depreciation was raised to 10 per cent in 1842, but extra output overtook the rising cost, and depreciation fell from 6*d*. to 5*d*. a bundle. With a rising book-value for machinery and extra working capital, the burden of interest rose from £9000 in the late 1830's to £13,000 by 1842. For the first time since 1804 the partners borrowed from outside—nearly £60,000. But again, a rising output reduced the cost of interest from 10*d*. a bundle in 1840 to 7*d*. in 1846. In short, overheads rose as the extensions were built, equipped and brought into operation; and when output subsequently built up to 400,000 bundles they fell.

However, the slight reductions in cost after 1842 could not offset the considerable fall in prices. Profit margins on yarn narrowed and from 1840 became negative. It no longer paid to be a spinner. The threats to their security which the partners foresaw and planned to by-pass in the mid-1830's suddenly loomed large. Besides the competition of Leeds spinners, a maturing Irish industry reconquered the Irish trade and had a surplus to send abroad. The Ulster industry had two-thirds as many spindles as Leeds spinners; and it was growing fast.[1] Furthermore, in 1841 the long-awaited French tariff

[1] E. R. R. Green, *op. cit.* p. 114; Marshall Collection, Lists of Irish Mills and Spindles.

came. The import of heavy yarns and canvas was subject to a very high duty and Scottish exporters were adversely affected. Next year, Marshall and Co. met their day of reckoning. Between 1842 and 1847 the French virtually closed their market to foreign yarns.[1] Where Marshalls had paid 8s. 6d. to 18s., they faced duties ranging from 38s. to 132s. It became imperative for English and Irish spinners to find new outlets and Marshalls began to push their sales into Spain and Germany. Within a few years the sellers' market of the 1830's was transformed into a fighting market, overclouding the prospects of English spinners as John Marshall saw:

...flax spinning in Ireland has approached or rather arrived at an extent which brings it on a level as to profit with other trade. We have for some years seen that we could not compete with the Irish spinners in the lower sorts of yarns. Our greater experience may enable us for some years to supply them with yarns of 100 leas and upwards. Their low wages, supply of flax and saving in carriage, give them an advantage over us, and compel us to look out for other markets. The flax mills on the Continent are increasing, and no doubt will eventually supply their own manufacturers, but I think for some years to come, they will not supersede a large import of English yarns, which we should endeavour to get our fair share of. The revival of trade in Ireland will increase their home consumption of yarns, and prevent their sending so large quantities abroad, and there is nothing to prevent us from meeting them there on equal terms.[2]

Irish competition and French tariffs aggravated the depression which gripped the Leeds industry in the early 1840's.[3] In 1840, 5000 spindles went out of production; in 1841, 21,000. Seventeen spinners failed in two years, including all the firms established since 1836 and half of those established in the early 1830's. The large firms overshadowed the industry more than ever. In 1839 four firms each with over 10,000 spindles had 42 per cent of the town's capacity; and twenty-two firms had less than 5000 spindles. With the disappearance of many small spinners, the big four plus Wilkinson had 53 per cent of the town's spindles in 1842; two old and five new medium-sized firms had 27 per cent; and thirteen small firms had 20 per cent.

[1] H. C. Marshall, 'Notebook I'; W. Charley, *op. cit.* pp. 114-23, and Appendix III, pp. 159 ff.
[2] J. Marshall to H. C. Marshall, 24 October 1843.
[3] H. C. Marshall, 'Lists of Leeds Spinners and Spindles', 1837-41.

Henry Marshall, by then a leading local liberal, decided to take the lead in finding some collective way of alleviating the severity of the depression on the local industry. In July 1842, 16½ per cent of Marshalls' spindles lay idle, 12 per cent of the operatives had been laid off and the newcomers of the last decade who had jeopardised the prosperity of the industry had fallen by the way. Henry Marshall judged that the survivors, all old firms, wanted to remain in business, and he proposed that they should not 'work more than five days a week, commencing from 23rd of July, instant, until such time as a contrary resolution is come to by a meeting of flax spinners of Leeds— provided that not less than nine-tenths in amount of spindles concur in this agreement'.[1] Those in agreement possessed only 83 per cent of the town's spindles. Titley and four other spinners who had grown fast in recent years did not want to preserve the *status quo*. Consequently the attempt to collaborate fell through. In the winter and spring of 1842–3 Marshalls worked a 55 hour week, and did not resume a normal working week until 1844.

This scheme to promote a local agreement marks a new departure in the Marshalls' attitude towards the rest of the industry. It assumed that the period of revolutionary technical change having passed, Leeds spinners needed to collaborate in order to maintain their standing. Together they might decide on the price to be paid for West European flax or press for a political solution to their difficulties.[2] Yet efforts such as these could only prove abortive. The Leeds industry had not the slightest chance of controlling the growth of flax-spinning elsewhere and, even within Leeds, the belief in expansion was too strong to rally enough support for a policy of consolidation. Moreover, some spinners thought with justification that Henry Marshall was playing a double game. During the depression, Marshall and Co. equipped a new mill with 8000 spinning spindles, engaged 462 new hands and raised their output by 150,000 bundles. A go-slow policy would be to their advantage. Furthermore, a threadmaker like Titley noticed that Marshalls no longer confined themselves to yarn production. They had discontinued spinning many grades of fine yarn, sold much the same quantity at home and abroad

---

[1] H. C. Marshall, 'Leeds Spindles', 1837–41.
[2] T. C. Banfield, *Industry of the Rhine* (1846), part I, p. 23.

as they had ten years earlier, and turned their additional 150,000 bundles into thread. And within Marshall and Co., James, always a strong individualist, shunned collusion with other firms because he confidently envisaged their future enriched by an invention of his own.

As events turned out, thread-making provided Marshall and Co. with an avenue of escape. Their experience at Castle Foregate encouraged them to speed up thread production at Leeds. To make thread, to twist yarns and wind them on to spools, cost 8*d.* a bundle in extra labour and 2*d.* for machinery. The resulting product sold for 3*s.* to 4*s.* more than a bundle of yarn and provided a substantial profit. Of course falling yarn prices dragged thread prices down, especially the heavier kinds, but not enough to squeeze out all the profit. Marshalls sold a dozen thread in 1840 for 39*s.* 8*d.* and five years later for 37*s.* 8*d.* Few spinners made thread in 1840, and by entering the field early the partners hoped to repeat again their past success. In 1841 they sold 66,000 dozens of thread worth £134,000, much coming from Salop. Four years later they sold 86,000 dozens for £162,000; and in 1850, 98,000 dozens, but for only 34*s.* 5*d.* a dozen. By the end of the decade this trade too became competitive.[1]

Initially Marshalls' principal thread markets were large towns at home, where in 1841 they sold half their output. But their domestic sales, if they increased at all, did so very slowly. By 1850 less than a third of their thread output went for home consumption. They lost trade in London where they sent two-thirds of their thread, and also in Birmingham, Bristol and even Shrewsbury. In Manchester, Coventry, Liverpool and Leeds they made very slight headway. The second main market in 1841 was the U.S.A. There they sent 17,000 dozens: half direct to Boston and New York, the rest via wholesale houses in Manchester and Liverpool. Four years later they sent 21,000 dozens, consigning a larger quantity direct to their own agents in the U.S.A. By 1850 over 70 per cent went to American agents, but the volume of sales, which stood at 22,000 dozens, had scarcely increased. The third, and most important, thread market of the decade was central Europe. This soon overtook both the American

[1] H. C. Marshall, 'Notebook II', pp. 45–53.

and domestic markets in importance. In 1841 Marshalls sent 13,000 dozens to the Continent, mainly through H. S. Strauss, and a little through foreign merchant houses in Leeds. In 1845 they sold 30,000 dozens, and in 1850, 44,000 dozens. None went to France (at least directly); and consignments to Vienna, Magdeburg, and Leipzig accounted for more than half of their sales.

Thread sales to Europe saved Marshalls in the early 1840's from severe financial loss. After their success with wet spinning, they had taken too sanguine a view of the future in the mid-1830's, and were too slow introducing thread and weaving. As a result, they felt the impact of the depression more than might otherwise have been the case. However, when John Marshall died in 1845, his sons were beginning to realise that they could no longer survive solely as spinners of sale yarn.

(iv)

If the second generation of Marshalls had not done as well as they anticipated in the early 1840's, they were not paralysed by any doubts about their future success. Their misfortune was chiefly due to the depression and they could recover from such setbacks as they had done in the past.

Everybody expected boom to follow slump. Late in 1843 Saunders, the Factory Inspector, stated that 'the flax trade is still languid but there is every reason to believe this important article of Leeds manufacture will before long share in the general prosperity...and the large proportion of the population in this town dependent on that trade will enjoy with other operatives the advantages of more regular employment and higher wages'.[1] Low-level stocks and new Irish orders would initiate a revival. In the mid-summer of 1845 Saunders reported 'a very active trade', and the press confirmed this view; 'the flax-trade...last to feel the renewed activity in trade is now very active'.[2] New firms sprang up, and in 1846 Leeds had 198,000 spindles, more than ever before. Barnsley engaged an additional 200 weavers, who had left Knaresborough in search of more regular

---

[1] *Factory Inspector Report*, Saunders, 20 October 1843, p. 7.
[2] *Ibid.* 1 May 1845, p. 47; *Leeds Intelligencer*, 12 July 1845; *Leeds Times*, 28 June 1845.

work. The trade in fine drills flourished and a good harvest in 1845 brought raw material prices down.

The partners felt as confident as ever. Henry looked forward phlegmatically to a period rather less rewarding than the previous twenty years, but adequate for their needs; James radiated optimism. For ten years he had been carrying out experiments which he hoped would eventually enable them to turn coarse residual fibres into fine yarn. Later in the 1840's he developed China Grass as a substitute for flax. Both projects were long shots; but spinners everywhere needed a cheaper fibre or better utilisation of flax if they were to stem the advance of cotton. Once success attended these efforts the firm would reap a fresh fortune. James certainly did not feel that he was clutching at a straw. Before a Select Committee in 1841 he attributed the success of the Leeds industry to cheap machinery of the latest design; cheap local fuel and iron; excellent transport facilities; large units in both manufacturing and commerce; security of property and freedom of industry, 'the last is in my opinion by far the greatest cause of manufacturing and commercial prosperity; greater, in fact, than all the others put together'.[1] When Leeds spinners lost all other advantages he contended that the security of property and freedom of industry prevailing in this country were sufficient conditions to ensure their success.

That the Marshalls felt confident is a fact of some significance. Their satisfaction was inspired by a sense of their great accomplishments. No other spinner could match their fortune or compare with the scale of their operations. Strangers privileged to see their mills marvelled at their achievement in organisation, discipline, the flow of work, the comprehensive system of records.

But the Marshalls prided themselves not only on their mills, yarn and accumulated wealth, but also on the paternalistic interest which they took in the welfare of their operatives. John Marshall II had told the Commons in 1833 that 'Prosperity is not to be valued unless it be accompanied in the main by good physical and moral conditions of the work-people', and Marshalls featured prominently amongst

---

[1] *Sel. Ctte. Rep. Exportation of Machinery*, 1st Report, 1841 (201), vol. VII, evidence of J. G. Marshall, pp. 186–99, Q 2710; for the experiments, J. G. Marshall to H. C. Marshall, 20 April 1836, 13 April 1838; and papers relating to China Grass Experiments in the Marshall Collection.

those who cared for their hands.[1] Changing-rooms in the mills enabled workers to acclimatise themselves before leaving the hot interior for the cold street, stoves were provided to dry clothes, and baths. Since the 1830's, fans and air blowers changed the air every 20 minutes to maintain a temperature of 65–75 degrees Fahrenheit in the spinning rooms. Carding and hackling machinery was boxed up and much of the dust generated in these operations sucked out of the room.[2] When in 1832 attention was drawn to alleged physical strain in the mills, the Marshalls engaged a surgeon to attend twice weekly. As a result, to cite one instance, Margaret Kendall, a line spreader, who came to Marshall and Co. at the age of thirteen, was transferred to the reeling department and put on shorter hours when her back showed symptoms of deformity. In 1832 16 per cent of the workers were absent through illness, two-thirds of them for no longer than a week. For serious cases the firm arranged admittance to the Infirmary and treatment at the Dispensary. Only 1 per cent of working time was lost owing to illness.[3] Although such well-being plainly served the interests of the partners, they believed quite justly that it was also an advantage to the workpeople themselves. Their enlightenment and leadership brought benefits to all concerned. So they preached temperance, sponsored a friendly society, supported the distribution of allotments to the working-class, and provided education. As John Marshall II claimed, 'Are they [the manufacturing population] not infinitely better instructed than our agricultural population?...do you find in any other class so many persons who are able to raise themselves out of the class to which they were born?'[4]

[1] J. Marshall II, draft speech for House of Commons, May 1833; *ibid.* 17 June 1833, he stated 'the interest of the master [is] that the success of the business which he pursues should secure to his workpeople the enjoyment of their health, the attainment of education for their children, and the maintenance of orderly habits, together with regularity in their employment and at adequate wages'.

[2] *Factory Inquiry Commission, op. cit.* Copy in Marshall Collection, Queries 4–12.

[3] 'Labour Book', *passim*; *Leeds Intelligencer*, 12 January 1832.

[4] J. Marshall II, draft speech for House of Commons, May 1833. 'Sir, no one can go beyond myself in a sincere wish to promote the education of the labouring class, and I think I have proved it in my own neighbourhood. I rate its importance most highly.' When Dorothy Wordsworth sought a position for a young boy in the mills, J. Marshall II inspected the boy's copy-books to find out whether he was suitable and then offered him a trial at 7s. a week. However, when Mrs Jane Marshall heard her friend's request, she promised a much better job in the counting-house at the 15s. a week Dorothy Wordsworth thought necessary to live on. Selincourt, *op. cit.* 1821–30, pp. 284, 287, 297, 300.

The school was completely rehoused after 1832; in that year a separate infants' school was built, and ten years later a two-storey junior school behind the Temple Mill. There children were instructed in the New Testament, taught to read, write, and in a few instances advanced to arithmetic. In 1833 nine-tenths of the hands could read, two-fifths write and an eighth count. The women and younger boys were least proficient, and only half the 'mechanics' could count. Yet whatever the actual standards, the partners believed that they gave their hands an opportunity to better themselves, and James preached the need for compulsory public education. By 1860 nearly 600 half-timers attended their school; girls and boys were kept apart and in each of the ten classes the pupils were separated into *A* and *B* grades. The firm also equipped a mill library. In 1832 each of 112 readers borrowed an average of thirty books during the year for 1*s.* a quarter. And before the building of St John's Church, over three-quarters of the hands at Water Lane declared that they regularly attended a place of worship on Sundays.[1]

If such evidence is not necessarily a reliable guide to the condition of their workpeople, it at least reveals the Marshalls' intentions and the extent to which they thought that they were improving the lives of their employees. Basically they were trying to develop not only factories and products but also artisans worthy of the new society that was evolving. Whilst paying lip-service to the idea that able individuals should be given a chance to rise in the world, Henry and James thought particularly in terms of a sober, dutiful, self-respecting working-class.

As so often happens, confidence in their superior achievements made them contemptuous of others. They despised the squire who did nothing to improve the lot of his tenants. The poverty and seeming ignorance of rural life made much more impression on them than its friendliness, solidarity and stability. They disdained to treat seriously the rhetoric of prejudiced critics like Oastler who recalled that his father had been on a par with their grandfather in late eighteenth-century Leeds. They knew that the Factory King saw and felt just what he wanted to see and feel. 'I have often listened to the agonising complaints of your cast-off factory slaves. I have examined their

---

[1] 'Labour Book', *passim*; *J.R.S.S.* vol. II, 1839, pp. 32–3.

distorted limbs, their emaciated frames and seen how womanhood and manhood have in your mills been robbed of their bloom. I have assisted in conveying some of these victims to a Committee of the House of Commons.'[1] As for the 1831 Committee, John Marshall II rejected its findings. 'The evidence of last year was entirely ex-parte evidence and it was always considered so at the time; and it was understood that those who took a different view of the subject would have the opportunity of establishing their opinion by evidence and by facts.'[2] It was absurd to depict their mills as a den of vice, 'a nursery of thieves and dissolute women'.[3] Inevitably, distasteful incidents did sometimes occur. But only a mischievous and ignorant person would represent them as characteristic of mill life. The Marshalls had an excellent record and disdained such criticism. They scorned the wild emotions roused at the hustings, nor would they argue with taunting clerics who claimed 'not very much experience in this practice of dissenters political economy, nor indeed of chopping logic'.[4] The plain fact was that the physical shortcomings of town life—overcrowding, inadequate sanitation, the lack of open spaces—were not due to the machination of the mill-owner, and the Marshalls were prominent amongst those who sought to improve this state of affairs.

In fact they were advancing so successfully in the world that when they chose to defend themselves they were not apologetic but aggressive. They were the great improvers, who formed the Leeds Social Improvement Society, led in parliamentary and municipal reform, generously supported the Infirmary, undertook to maintain the Botanical Gardens, and took the lead in installing smoke burners to lessen the pall of smoke that overclouded the town.

Never doubting themselves, they did not hesitate to explain in a didactic manner to the Factory Commissioners some of the immutable principles governing business.[5] Asked what effects would follow a re-

---

[1] R. Oastler to W. Marshall in the *Shropshire Conservative*, 19 June 1852.

[2] J. Marshall II, draft speech for House of Commons, 5 July 1833.

[3] *Shropshire Conservative*, 19 June 1852; Oastler attributes this remark to Mr Blaydes, a leading banker in Leeds.

[4] *Leeds Intelligencer*, 12 January 1832.

[5] The following paragraph is based on the *Factory Inquiry Commission*, Marshall's copy, Q 37. (Printed version, *Factory Inquiry Commission*; Supplementary Report, Part 2, North-eastern District, C. I, pp. 75–9, Sess. 1834 (167), vol xx.)

duction in hours, John II replied that their raw material and interest on working capital accounted for 50 per cent and 18 per cent respectively of production costs; wages and interest on fixed capital accounted for 18 per cent and 14 per cent. A reduction in hours from 69 to 58 without a cut in wages would raise the cost of production by 6 per cent. Shorter hours would increase the cost of fixed capital to $16\frac{1}{2}$ per cent, so that to keep production costs constant, wages must be reduced by a seventh on the given quantity of yarn, 'but as the quantity produced each week is also reduced one seventh by the reduced hours, the weekly wages of the workpeople must be reduced by two-sevenths, or upwards of one fourth'. The alternative, a reduction in the cost of capital, would check capital accumulation hence expansion, and then the demand for labour would decline. In a job calling for physical strength, a 10-hour day would be sufficiently long and might raise productivity, but the output of machine-minders could not increase likewise since 'the velocity [of a machine] does not admit of such an increase as would compensate to any great extent for diminished hours of labour'. They were reasonable men whose logic was irrefutable. What they did was for the best interests of all concerned. Shortly afterwards John Marshall II declared in Parliament, 'We must take care to avoid legislating... in such a manner as to cripple the productive power of our manufacturers and so diminish the very source from which the work people have to look for their wages and permanency in employment. The House must at once see that if the working hours are reduced from 69 to 58...',[1] and so on.

Nor were they well-disposed to newcomers in business. Most of the crimes against humanity of which they were accused should

---

[1] J. Marshall II, draft speech for the House of Commons, May 1833. This is of course the specious talk of those in authority arguing that they are motivated by the general interest. Marshall and Co. could easily have paid higher wages, but to have done so would have reduced their own resources and run counter to their belief in a structured society with social inequality. The refusal ironically brought its own nemesis, not so much because the issue kept on smouldering and burst into flame, but because in this particular case cheap labour *inter alia* led them to neglect improving machinery. English industrialists were slow to appreciate the disadvantages of cheap wages and often a sudden restriction of labour by decree (e.g. the Act forbidding women and children in mines or that providing for elementary education in the 1870's —both inspired by humanitarian motives) was necessary to jolt businessmen into substituting capital and raising labour productivity.

properly have been attributed to the small upstart employers who neglected their workers' welfare and devoted no time and money to public service. The Marshalls strongly denied having exploited child labour. The low productivity of the early nineteenth century and the age-composition of the population made it essential for children to work. The only issue was, at what age? Marshall and Co. said eleven, and generally adhered to this in practice. They resented being tarred with the same brush as the unscrupulous employers who hired children at nine or even younger.[1] Within the flax trade too there was implicit in their actions an assumption of rectitude and the prestige attaching to leadership. When Marshall and Co. challenged Kay's patent and his claim to a royalty of 6s. a spindle, they masqueraded as saviours of the industry. 'We are fighting their battle as well as our own.' And when some spinners in the trade hesitated to contribute towards the legal expenses of Marshall and Co. in what turned out to be five years of litigation, John Marshall suggested that 'it might be convenient to both Kay and us, by suspending our proceedings, to leave them to pay for their new machinery to Kay'.[2]

Social position accounts for much of their self-assurance. They were more than local worthies; they belonged to a well-connected, socially elevated family. In the early 1840's the founder and his wife gave up the struggle for wealth and status, spending their last years quietly at Hallsteads 'very much by themselves'. Sometimes John Marshall hankered after the social and business world, but infirmity prevented any return. He had to draw his satisfaction from the achievements of his children, and they made marks in society which augured well for the family in the years ahead.

Apart from Ellen, an invalid, and Arthur, the youngest child, all Marshall's offspring had married before he died in 1845. Five weddings took place between 1838 and 1842.

Henry at the age of twenty-nine married Catherine Lucy Spring-Rice, youngest daughter of the Chancellor of the Exchequer. This alliance was greatly welcomed by John Marshall, and Henry himself

[1] J. Marshall II, draft speeches for Commons, 17 June 1833, 5 July 1833; *Factory Inquiry Commission*, Marshall's copy; *Factory Inspector Reports*, Saunders, 14 May 1846, p. 12, and 1 July 1842, p. 36. All the culprits were small spinners.

[2] J. Marshall to J. Marshall II, 9 May 1836.

gained immediate prominence in local liberal circles, became an Alderman and then Mayor of Leeds in 1843. By that time he had a growing family and wanted an alternative residence to Weetwood Hall, their house on the northern outskirts of Leeds. So he bought an island from General Peachy's widow at the north end of Derwent-water, near the estate of his late brother at Keswick. In the centre of Derwent Island's few acres stood a small square house built in 1785 by Pocklington, a Newark merchant. On to this building Henry added east and west wings. His wife, who loved flowers, bestowed great care on laying out the gardens; and round the edge of the island (except on the south lawn) they planted a windbreak of trees. From the study window, Henry looked across the lake to the fells of Borrow-dale. From the Italian-style balcony of the drawing-room, placed on the first floor to overlook the trees, they saw Catbells, Grassmoor and Grisedale Pike. In this house, amidst the natural splendour of the Lakes, Henry spent much of his remaining years. The isolation of an island had its inconveniences but money smoothed them away. Water-pipes were laid under the lake. There was a fleet of boats to ferry people and provisions from the mainland, including a squat boat to carry coal and another to convey coffins to St John's Churchyard. Underneath the house, in ill-lit cellars with iron columns and arched roof just like a mill, lived nearly a score of servants, moving in an inferior world, along backstairs or out by a concealed passageway overlaid as a garden that vanished into the trees. Confined to the island, the servants found life irksome and left when they could. But replacements could soon be brought from Leeds. It was an expensive and pleasurable style of life: Henry spent £5000 a year on his houses. In addition, he soon had to educate five boys and to care for an infirm wife whose health failed after bearing eight children in eleven years.[1]

James reached his fortieth year before marrying Mary Spring-Rice in 1841. Before long they too had a family, two boys and two girls, and moved between Headingley House in Leeds and Monk Coniston Park in the Lake District, which James had bought as a country residence in 1838 whilst still a bachelor. There he converted an outbuilding nearby into a laboratory and, as Whewell phrased it,

[1] Derwent Island Collection, *passim*; *Yorkshire Post*, 17 October 1884; *Leeds Mercury*, 16 October 1884.

'geologized' frequently with Adam Sedgwick, the Professor of Geology at Cambridge. Another frequent visitor, besides William Whewell and Sedgwick, was Sir John Herschel, the Cambridge astronomer, whose daughter later married James's nephew. In addition to his interest in science, James held advanced views on both education and the franchise, and for a time he played an active part in politics. In Leeds he inherited the political mantle of his late brother and father, and in 1847 he was returned to Parliament as an advocate of compulsory education after a hard contest with Joseph Sturge. However, his radical proposals for electoral reform alienated many liberals and in 1852 he gave up his seat. Like most members of the family, James did not speak well in public, and thinking the business needed him, he gave up his political career. From then on he resigned himself to 'influencing the councils of the party' behind the scenes, coming before the public eye only as a J.P., or Deputy Lieutenant of the county.[1]

Two months after James's wedding, Lord Monteagle himself married John Marshall's eldest daughter in April 1841.[2] (Subsequently these two families were united by further marriages, like that of Monteagle's son to William Marshall's daughter.) Mary's marriage was a surprise. It almost seemed as if she and her sister Cordelia would remain spinsters. During their twenties the family had been leaving provincial town society, but had not been accepted by the gentry to the extent of marriage. So Mary and Cordelia accompanied their father on his social rounds, and indulged their artistic interests, but did not marry—until they were forty.

Cordelia's turn came in the autumn of 1841, when she married William Whewell, Professor of Moral Philosophy at Cambridge. Whewell, like John Marshall, had risen ostensibly by his own efforts,

[1] *Leeds Mercury*, 24 October 1873; *Yorkshire Post*, 25 October 1873; Mayhall, *op. cit.* vol. III, p. 585; Whewell to sister, 24 September 1857; J. S. Mill, *op. cit.* p. 218; J. G. Marshall, *British Association*, 1858, p. 184.

[2] For the career of Thomas Spring-Rice, who was member for Cambridge after 1820 and subsequently Chancellor of the Exchequer in Melbourne's second administration, see *D.N.B.* LIII, p. 427. Whewell wrote to his sister, 12 November 1841, that Monteagle worked at his office twelve hours a day starting a 17.30 a.m.; but hard work did not make him a successful minister. For the activities of Marshall's daughters, see Selincourt, *op. cit.* 1821–40, pp. 404, 567, 882. Their interests extended to painting, music and writing poetry; and Wordsworth himself wrote a sonnet to Cordelia, *Yarrow Revisited*, p. 230.

and he was as successful in his own way as Thomas Spring-Rice, gradually approaching the summit of his ambitions as first one and then another university colleague died. This tall, handsome man, so very able and urbane, was extremely lonely. After being elected to a fellowship at Trinity in 1818 and making a reputation for himself as a scientist, Whewell moved in upper-class circles and lost contact with his own kin, lower middle-class folk who were not well-off and lived in a small town on the Lancashire side of the Lakes. Occasionally he returned north, and through the Wordsworths he made the acquaintance of the Marshalls, 'well-connected', 'excellent, amiable, plain mannered...north country people'.[1] Cordelia agreed to marry him, and surrounded by Marshalls and Monteagles 'all of them as you see our relations, soon to be', the ceremony took place in October 1841. None of his family attended the wedding, for he considered them an embarrassment: having duly conveyed the invitation that they might come (they dwelt nearby), he contrived to the point of ultimately deciding for them that they should not be present.

Within a month of the wedding, Peel appointed Whewell to be Master of Trinity in succession to Christopher Wordsworth. 'This office is the summit of my ambition, and one which my friends have always thought me likely to obtain.'[2] Cordelia exchanged the tranquility of Hallsteads for the activity of the Master's Lodge. There she gave full rein to her interests in floral painting and choral music, collected materials for a biography of her husband, and entertained a stream of distinguished visitors, including the young Queen: 'I hardly have time to get a look at her—besides which I can't stare her in the face—I haven't courage enough.'[3] Her French dressmaker and the round of visits to the Marquis of Northampton, Lord Lyttleton and Lord Braybrook gave vicarious enjoyment to Whewell's sisters. But, unhappily, Cordelia soon became a chronic invalid, confined to their cottage at Lowestoft where she was comforted by her niece, and Whewell relapsed into pathetic loneliness.

Marshall's youngest daughter Susan married last, in 1842. The

---

[1] Whewell to sister, 18 June 1841, 22 June 1841, 26 August 1841, 7 September 1841, 28 September 1841, 25 August 1842. See also W. Whewell, *D.N.B.* LX, p. 454.

[2] Whewell to sister, 16 October 1841.

[3] Mrs C. Whewell to Miss Whewell, 20 October 1851, 10 April 1844; Whewell to sister, 7 May 1842, 23 February 1843, 17 October 1843, 24 March 1856.

affair lacked the renown and lustre of the preceding alliances, for Frederick Myers was a young man of promise rather than achievement. He came from an academic background, and in 1837, when a Fellow of Clare College, was invited to become Vicar of Leeds. Acceptance of a living was the next step in the career of a young don and it was a considerable honour to be offered Leeds. But he refused, apparently on grounds of age, and Dr Hook went to Leeds instead. The Marshalls, wanting a priest for their new church of St John at Keswick, persuaded Myers to go there. He agreed, and although technically without a parish, soon gained a reputation for outstanding parochial work. His benefactors provided the resources for him to found an infants' and girls' school at Keswick, start lectures for adults, and in 1849 he used a legacy from John Marshall's wife (who died in 1847) to start a public library.[1]

The number of Marshalls grew rapidly. Mary and Cordelia had no children, but the other seven marriages produced thirty-eight Marshalls, Elliotts, Temples and Myers. 'We seem to have so many relations', Whewell wrote. Thirty years later, when the fourth generation appeared, 111 Marshalls lived in the Lake District counting only the male side of the family.[2]

They were numerous and also wealthy. James Marshall drew over 85 per cent of his earnings from the mills between 1836 and 1847, an average of £11,000 per annum. Part of each year, the Marshalls lived in their town houses at Leeds or London, and the rest of the time they spent at Hallsteads, Monk Coniston, Derwent Island, Patterdale, and later other houses in the Lake District. Conscious of their rapid social rise, and late to marry, Marshall's children were strongly attached to one another. They moved freely and frequently between the family houses, and nephews and nieces spent their youth together. Henry, with a passionate attachment to numbers, measured the height of the growing flock each year.[3] And there

---

[1] Whewell to sister, 18 August 1842, 12 August 1856; Bulmer, *Directory of Cumberland* (1901), pp. 401 ff.; F. Myers, *Lectures on Great Men* (London, 1856), delivered 1840–4.

[2] Derwent Island Collection, *passim*.

[3] *Ibid.* Compared with their parents, John Marshall's sons were tall; H. C. Marshall, in measuring the third generation, was presumably imitating those physicians who measured mill children to prove their healthiness and mental capacity, e.g. *Factory Inspector Report*, Horner, 31 December 1836, p. 23.

always seemed to be social gatherings at one or other of the houses. With an entourage of scholars introduced by Whewell, and later social reformers like Josephine Butler, with the poets Southey, Wordsworth, later Swinburne and Rawnsley, the Marshalls set off to walk the fells, to boat, fish and hunt. Whewell was proud to belong to such a family. 'We made a great figure at Ambleside, turning out with two carriages...the Ambleside people did us the honour of assembling to look at us.'[1] As a family they used their considerable influence to help one another. Lord Monteagle introduced James Marshall, Temple and Whewell at Court in 1842. And if Whewell could not obtain a job in the Customs, he could offer a 'place as tutor with nominal duties only'. In a society where connexions played a predominant part in family success, the Marshall clan was well-placed in Cambridge (where besides the relationship with Whewell, Lord Monteagle's eldest son was Master of Downing), Leeds and the Lake District. In London, their influence was much more circumscribed. Whewell had some authority for instance in Westminster School by virtue of his office; but when the Marshalls set afoot inquiries about Christ's Hospital, he scanned the list of governors and excused himself from further action on the grounds that he did not personally know any of those Londoners.[2]

In the late 1840's the third generation of Marshalls started their education.[3] From 1849 William, James and Henry sent their sons to Arnold's Rugby and then on to Whewell at Trinity College, Cambridge. (Temple sent his son to Harrow and the widowed Mrs Myers found a cheaper school, Cheltenham.) For the most part, they read classics and maths. Henry's son, John, had a very good academic record; others distinguished themselves more as athletes. But all were well-mannered young gentlemen, perhaps fond of ancient literature or keen on climbing. In due course the eldest son in each family would inherit his father's house; the rest would seek a livelihood in the mills and with luck accumulate enough to buy an estate in the Lakes. The young Elliotts, Temples and Myers sought

---

[1] Whewell to sister, 22 September 1850.
[2] *Ibid.* 13 April 1842, 24 September 1842, 31 December 1851, 12 December 1854, 3 January 1856, 6 May 1858.
[3] *Ibid.* 2 June 1854, 20 August 1856, 29 October 1863.

respectable posts (as Whewell put it) in the university, army, or Indian service.

Meanwhile, as the children grew up, their parents, endowed with substantial means, gratified their own pleasures. They enjoyed the countryside, watched birds, 'geologised', tended their gardens and estates, sailed on the lakes, fished for pike, trout and salmon, and indulged their tastes for reading. Some delved into the history of the estates which they had acquired. Henry went to considerable trouble supplying the Meteorological Office with data from Leeds and Derwentwater.[1] After 1850 they began to migrate each summer to the Continent. 'We have a sort of colony here [at Krenznach]', Whewell wrote in September 1852. Next year, he told his sister '. . .several of Cordelia's brothers and sisters are visiting and are also going abroad this summer. Henry Marshall sets off soon. . .and James and his wife are to come to Krenznach again. Then I believe that William Marshall also intends to travel in the same direction, so that our whole clan will be in motion.'[2] They lived like lotus eaters in the land 'in which it seemed always afternoon'.

John Marshall had founded a family more exacting in its requirements than the firm. His children enjoyed high material standards and extensive social connexions, interests which, if any conflict should arise, they would serve rather than those of the firm.

However, as the Marshalls did not share William Wordsworth's melancholy view of the times, only two things could jeopardise the existence and fortunes of the clan: inadequate resources and social misfits. Neither seemed probable in the mid-nineteenth century. Their accumulated resources guaranteed them means for a long time ahead. The personal cost of estrangement would inhibit tendencies towards individual rebelliousness. One son defied his mother and ran away to sea, another wed a foreign girl and lived abroad; both became

[1] Derwent Island Collection, *passim.* Note also at Derwent Island the books in the library bearing on the education of the third generation and relating to special pursuits such as angling, bird-watching and gardening.

[2] Whewell to sister, 10 April 1852, September 1852, 2 May 1853, 14 July 1853. The plea was invariably connected with health; e.g. J. G. Marshall's wife, Whewell to sister, 24 September 1842; or in 1858 when J. G. Marshall left for six months in Italy, Whewell to sister, 6 October 1858.

outcasts. Perhaps a more subtle danger lay in the women chosen by marriage to become the mistresses of the family. Yet marriages were not lightly entered into when the future of a family was at stake; a mother saw to that—if she were alive. Certainly when John and Jane Marshall died, it looked as if their descendants would be fine country gentlemen, members of the governing classes and mill-owners for a very long time to come.

CHAPTER V

THE FINAL PHASE, 1846–1886

(i)

Leeds flax-spinners believed that after the depression of the early 1840's their former prosperity would return. But it never did. 'The greater part of the flax-spinning machinery' in the town stood idle in October 1846, and seven mills 'wholly unoccupied'.[1] Unemployment spread during the following year to affect the town's woollen industry. And flax-spinners were last to share in the subsequent revival of trade. Early in 1849 production 'remained languid notwithstanding the very low price of raw material' because manufacturers carried large stocks. Late in the year Saunders reported that 'the flax industry...has partaken largely of the increased demand for goods'. Leeds spinners ran their mills at full capacity, twisting thread and weaving 'railway covers and revolutionary blouses'. Seven newcomers replaced six firms which had given up since 1845. But it was a false start. Thread exports had not yet risen above the level of 1844, and by 1851 mills were again 'turning off hands and stopping frames'. Flax imports at Hull fell from 16,000 tons in 1849 to 11,000 tons in 1851.

Apart from a few rare intervals of prosperity induced by war in Russia, America and France this chronicle of chronic misfortune could be continued for another twenty years. Leeds spinners could no longer make ends meet. The number of firms and hands steadily diminished after 1851. The reduction in flax supply owing to the Crimean War was a serious blow, though accumulated orders brightened up trade for a few years afterwards. When civil war broke out in the United States exports there fell, but the subsequent cotton famine gave flax-spinners a great opportunity. The Belfast, not the Leeds industry, however, gained most from this catastrophe.[2] Flax imports into

---

[1] *Factory Inspector Reports*, Saunders, April–October 1846, p. 30; April–October 1847, p. 29; April–October 1848, p. 107; April–October 1849, pp. 28–47; April–October 1850, p. 47; October–April 1850–1, pp. 41–58; *Leeds Times*, 28 June 1845.

[2] W. O. Henderson, *The Lancashire Cotton Famine* (1934), p. 10; J. Combe, *Suggestions for Promoting the Prosperity of the Leeds Linen Trade* (1865), *passim*; Gill, *op. cit.* pp. 315 ff.;

Hull declined in the early 1860's. Many small spinners in Leeds had gone out of existence, and in 1861 Benyons became the first casualty amongst the large firms.[1] For twenty years Thomas Benyon's successors had allowed this business to run down, and several consecutive years of poor trade in the late 1850's made it impossible to raise further credit. Their liabilities stood at £52,000 (including £20,000 for Riga flax); their assets at £17,500—£7500 in plant, £5000 in yarn stocks and £5000 due from debtors. Eventually, thanks to a donation from a retired member of the family who had put his money elsewhere, the firm paid its creditors 10s. in the pound. By 1866 only eighteen spinners survived in Leeds; in 1867 thirteen; in 1872, after two good and two bad years of trade, ten were left. Morfitt and Wilkinson had gone. Five large firms—Marshalls, Hives, Briggs, Titleys and Holdsworths—with 105,000 spindles and nearly 8000 hands, and five tiny firms, each with only a few frames, remained to gain from the temporary plight of the French industry following Prussia's invasion. Between 1875 and 1879, 120,000 spindles went out of operation in England, half of them in Leeds. Holdsworths closed; then Briggs and in 1881, Hives—the only two Leeds firms to expand their spinning plant after 1842. Hives normally employed 3000 in their three mills; but in the late 1870's when extreme depression gripped the Leeds industry they had only 200 workers.[2] Two large and six small spinners remained, employing 3500. In 1886 Marshall and Co. closed, and a few years later, Titley, Tatham and Walker.

During the contraction of the Leeds industry, flax-spinning flourished elsewhere. The number of spindles in Leeds barely increased in the generation after 1840. Yet in England as a whole they doubled, reaching nearly half a million. In Ireland, they increased four times to reach a million. Expansion on a similar scale occurred in France. In Belgium, spindleage doubled to exceed a quarter-million;

Warden, *op. cit.* p. 417; L. C. Marshall, *op. cit.* pp. iii ff.; W. Charley, *op. cit.* pp. 84 ff.; H. Cox (ed.), *British Industries Under Free Trade* (1903), p. 43.

[1] Mayhall, *op. cit.* vol. II, p. 24; *Leeds Intelligencer*, 2 March 1861, 16 March 1861; Benyon documents in the custody of Dibb Lupton and Co., Leeds.

[2] Estimate of Spindles in Leeds, March 1872, by H. C. Marshall and R. Tennant (Marshall Collection); *Textile Manufacturer*, 1881, p. 182. (The initial development of Holdsworths as flax-spinners was probably associated with Fairbairns; see *Fortunes in Business*, vol. II, p. 266.)

and in Germany, Austria and Russia, there were nearly a million mechanical spindles by 1870. James Marshall acknowledged this contrast at the British Association meeting in 1858: 'the extension of flax-spinning has of late been more rapid in other quarters than the town of Leeds'.[1] After the Napoleonic War, Leeds had a very high proportion of the world's mechanical spindles. It had only a fifth of the United Kingdom's spindles in 1850, and an eighth in 1880 when the Continent had more spindles than the British Isles.

The same story of expansion elsewhere holds also for weaving. Leeds had 500 power-looms in 1856, a quarter of those in the United Kingdom. Subsequently very few more were added, although in England there were 5000 such looms by 1870. Scotland had 10,000 in 1879. Ireland, where the power-loom came into use slowly, had 5000 in 1861, overtook Scotland during the cotton famine, and had 30,000 looms by 1900. And there were by 1880 as many power-looms on the Continent as in the United Kingdom.[2]

From the 1880's, the flax industry everywhere languished and entered upon a long period of secular decline.[3] Many firms failed in Scotland. Despite wishful thinking that there were 'no dangerous symptoms of decline' the number of spindles in Ulster diminished, and the mills crawled along on short time. In western Europe too, the industry ceased to grow. Belgian as well as Irish spinners considered migrating, mostly to the U.S.A.[4] But the stagnation of the Leeds industry occurred whilst spinning and weaving grew in Belfast, Lille and Ghent, and before the European linen industry as a whole contracted in the face of insurmountable economic obstacles.

[1] J. G. Marshall, *British Association, 1858, op. cit.* pp. 184–8; Mulhall, *op. cit.* pp. 280–2; *Irish Textile Journal*, 15 August 1886; *Textile Manufacturer*, 15 July 1881, 15 December 1884; J. Marshall to H. C. Marshall, 24 October 1843.

[2] Combe, *op. cit.* p. 4; Gill, *op. cit.* pp. 325–9; Charley, *op. cit.* p. 88; Warnes, *op. cit.* p. 265; Cox, *op. cit.* pp. 55–61.

[3] Cox, *op. cit.* pp. 40 ff.; W. J. Ashley (ed.), *British Industries* (1903), pp. 126 ff.; Charley, *op. cit.* pp. 136–7; *Textile Manufacturer*, 1880, p. 394; *ibid.* 1884, p. 431; *ibid.* 1896, p. 202. In 1880 the *Textile Manufacturer*, p. 314, contained an article on Linen versus Cotton, which concluded—'It will thus be seen that, where durability is concerned, linen certainly carries the palm, and that it cannot be replaced by cotton for many articles of luxury in body linen; but that as soon as there arises the question of lightness and of sanitary consideration, it must give way to cotton'. Linen 'will never approach cotton' in price and hence the demand for it must be severely limited.

[4] Cox, *op. cit.* p. 57; *Textile Manufacturer*, 1885, p. 501.

The Final Phase, 1846–1886

The town's spinners attributed their decline to a variety of causes:[1] the French tariff of the 1840's and the erection of tariff walls elsewhere later on; the native flax crops which allegedly helped their rivals in Ulster and Flanders; and the lower wages and longer hours of foreign operatives. Accustomed to thinking in competitive terms, Leeds spinners argued that their competitors had cost advantages which they could not meet.

It is important to know how businessmen assessed their chances. What they thought was happening influenced what they did. Therefore their view is important in any explanation of what happened. This is not to say of course that the forces which they singled out were as important as they seemed at the time, if indeed they were important at all. The way in which businessmen read the situation was not the same thing as what was really happening. They may not consciously have been aware of some facts, or for their own peace of mind they may have taken them for granted. Their explanations in this connexion would be those which presented their decline in the most favourable light. But were they sufficient in fact to account for the stagnation of the Leeds flax industry?

Before the Select Committee in 1841 James Marshall stated that Leeds spinners had been very successful owing to excellent machinery, cheap coal and iron, good transport, large-scale operation, and 'security of property and freedom of industry'.[2] No contemporary would have argued with him. And he expected that these advantages, except the last, would disappear. This was already happening as anyone could see who compared the recent development of the Leeds and Belfast industries.

---

[1] L. C. Marshall, *op. cit.* p. viii; *Textile Manufacturer*, 1886, p. 30; J. G. Marshall, *British Association 1858*, *op. cit.* pp. 184–8; G. E. Stead, *The Decline of the Flax Industry in Leeds*, reported in the *Yorkshire Post*, 6 December 1896; Notice to the Workpeople of Messrs Marshall and Co., who left their work on Monday, 4 March 1872, para. III; *Belfast News Letter*, 7 March 1872; Marshall Collection, 'Book Concerning the 1872 Strike', p. 40; *Leeds Express*, 11, 12 March 1872, in which Samuel Sykes wrote, 'I feel convinced myself that if the remaining flax-spinners in Leeds are compelled to work at so great a disadvantage, as they will apparently have to do in case the workpeople get all they desire, that the trade will eventually die out in this town'.

[2] J. G. Marshall, evidence in the *Sel. Ctte. Rep. Exportation of Machinery*, p. 187, Q 2710. Marshall and Co. never complained of tariffs at that time; in fact they claimed that they could undersell foreign spinners in Europe.

Relatively cheap coal and iron, and superior local transport facilities became much less important by the mid-nineteenth century. In the early nineteenth century, coal cost four times as much in Belfast as in Leeds; by the mid-century the Leeds price was 8s. a ton plus delivery and in Belfast imported coal cost between 8s. and 12s. a ton. Leeds producers still had a margin in their favour, even when their coal came by rail from farther afield, but the difference was now fairly small.[1] The advantage derived from the exploitation of local ore also diminished; by the 1860's local deposits were almost worked out and Leeds foundries relied more on pig-iron brought from the northeast. The disparities in transportation that existed between regions in 1800 diminished in the next fifty years. Leeds manufacturers were at the hub of a well-developed transport system in 1800 when freight was expensive everywhere. At that time the Irish network converged on Dublin and changed only when Belfast emerged as a new commercial capital. Even then roads and services in Northern Ireland did not compare with those in northern England. But communications with the interior were not too important for the reviving Irish linen industry. Two-thirds of the industry was localised in Belfast, which obtained its coal and much of its flax by sea. Freight to Liverpool cost no more than consignments from Leeds to the east or west coast. Leeds spinners may have been nearer the English market, but railways helped to equalise costs in this respect, and the growing importance of export markets put Belfast and Leeds spinners on an equal footing[2].

By 1850 the average firm had 6000 spindles in Belfast, Leeds and Belgium. Many of the concerns in all three centres had more than the 4000 spindles reckoned by William Charley to be the minimum economic size. In 1860 Belfast and Liége had mills as large as those of Marshalls and Hives. In one respect the Irish industry operated on a larger scale, since both sections of the industry—mill-spinning and hand-loom weaving (in the 1840's)—were localised at the port of Belfast.[3] A similar integration never really took place in England despite John Marshall's prophecy. Leeds spinners continued to send

[1] R. Baker, 'The Industrial and Sanitary Economy of Leeds', 1858, in *J.R.S.S.*, vol. XXI, p. 441; H. C. Marshall, 'Notebook', II, p. 107; P. Fairbairn evidence in *Sel. Ctte. Rep. Exportation of Machinery*, p. 219, Q 3249–50; Banfield, *op. cit.* vol. II, p. 164.
[2] Green, *op. cit.* pp. 46 ff.
[3] Charley, *op. cit.* p. 83; L. C. Marshall, *op. cit.* p. ix, put the minimum economic

yarn twenty miles south to Barnsley, and they had little control over the weaving end of the trade.

The factor that decisively narrowed differences was the use in Ireland and Europe of cheap Leeds machinery. Spinners elsewhere could for the first time operate with similar production ratios to those used in Leeds. This terminated a real advantage that had so far favoured Leeds producers. Once they no longer kept their machines to themselves (and the day of sharing could have been postponed), Leeds spinners had to keep technically on the move. Not only would they have to remain interested in improvements but they would also have to apply them with as much vigour as in the past.[1]

The sale of local machinery to spinners in other towns was due to the divergent interests of Leeds machine-makers. As the flax industry grew, specialists in machine-making evolved, such as Fenton, Murray and Wood, March and Maclea, Mirfin, Cawood, Taylor Wordsworth, all of whom were in business by 1825. Spinners no longer made their own machines, contenting themselves with the maintenance of their plant. Thenceforth these engineering firms set the technical pace for the industry. By 1841 there were eighteen machine-makers with a capital of £300,000 in the town and, according to Peter Fairbairn, Leeds was 'the seat of the chief flax machine establishments, I may say of the whole world'.[2]

size of a firm at 8000 spindles twenty-three years later. H. C. Marshall, List of Irish Firms and Spindles, 1851, shows the following size of Belfast spinners:

Over 10,000 spindles	15 firms
5000–10,000 spindles	21 firms
1000–5000 spindles	38 firms
less than 1,000	2 firms

The largest firm, Mulholland, had 25,164 spindles. For the United Kingdom as a whole, the average size of flax-spinners in the three constituent countries was:

		England	Ireland	Scotland
1850	Labour	140	300	150
	Spindles	2700	4700	1650
1860	Labour	142	260	190
	Spindles	3200	5650	1670

See also *Textile Manufacturer*, 1884, p. 543.

[1] J. G. Marshall, *Sel. Ctte. Rep. Exportation of Machinery*, p. 194, Q 2824–7, stated that in the previous twenty years spinners replaced machinery owing to improvements, not because it had worn out.

[2] *Ibid.* P. Fairbairn evidence, p. 210, Q 3098; see also W. Marshall, 'Report on a Tour in Yorkshire and Scotland', 1817, p. 31, in which he states that Murray's machines were superior to any made in Ireland or Scotland.

Once local spinners had installed wet spinning machinery, their orders dwindled to a replacement demand. This was the situation reached by the late 1830's on the eve of the government inquiry into machinery exports. Machinists whose capacity had grown rapidly sought business beyond the town. In 1833 James Marshall, referring to Fentons, wrote 'They have for some time sought orders everywhere...and we have allowed them to use our models'.[1] Fairbairn, who employed 500 hands and £50,000 in capital, could produce machinery worth £60,000 to £70,000 a year and wanted to sell in continental markets.

At the time machine-makers outside Leeds could not make comparable machines. The few manufacturers in Ireland produced nothing more complicated than spinning frames.[2] This would have placed the Irish flax industry at a great disadvantage if spinners had been unable to buy preparatory machinery in Leeds. So a one-way traffic developed which lasted until the 1850's when Belfast engineering firms, reinforced by English talent and capital, gained in competence and versatility. 'Three Leeds gentlemen located in Belfast, Messrs Combe, Horner, and Catton, have been increasing their endeavours during the past ten years to bring the hackling machine to the highest pitch of perfection.'[3] After 1860 Leeds spinners began to buy hackling machinery in Belfast.

Continental spinners also depended heavily on Leeds machinery in their early days. Despite smuggled models and the migration of English mechanics, lack of skill and the small size of continental firms hampered development. Foreign firms did not catch up technically before 1850, after that Leeds spinners started to buy machines abroad.

Thus in 1840 Leeds spinners would not gain from a more extensive trade in flax machinery. Such sales enabled outsiders to begin their careers as spinners with plant which had taken over a generation to bring to perfection, and this undermined the near-monopoly of the town's spinners in the production of fine yarn. Any manufacturer in Leeds with a plant more than ten years old might soon be at a

---

[1] J. G. Marshall to J. Marshall, 10 February 1833.
[2] P. Fairbairn, *Sel. Ctte. Rep. Exportation of Machinery*, pp. 210–11, Q 3096, 3100; p. 220, Q 3253; Green, *op. cit.* p. 99.
[3] *Leeds Express*, 27 March 1872; Charley, *op. cit.* p. 80; H. D. Traill, H. Duff and J. S. Mann (eds.), *Social History* (1902–4), vol. VI, pp. 594–5.

disadvantage. But Fairbairn argued that by exporting spinning frames in addition to the carding and hackling machinery already sold abroad under licence, he would actually be helping Leeds spinners. Free trade was, he submitted, a destructive weapon. As long as exports were restricted, foreign machine-makers such as Schlumberger in Alsace or Escher, Wyss and Co. in Zürich, would develop. 'The great thing we want to prevent is the establishment of machine shops on the Continent.'[1] If this were to be achieved, the prosperity of Leeds machine-makers would be assured. But short of a subsequent restriction on the export of textile machinery, it is difficult to see how Leeds spinners would gain. Fairbairn, secure in an imperfect market, promised the local flax industry first call on all new models and a superior repair service at hand. This would certainly have helped the industry in its competition with producers elsewhere. But it rested on the assumption that Leeds engineers would specialise on and improve textile machinery. In fact many of them, including Fairbairn in the 1850's, increasingly developed interests in other fields of engineering and no longer gave Leeds spinners the advantage which they had enjoyed in the past.

James Marshall agreed at the time to free trade in machinery but for more realistic reasons than Fairbairn's. He believed that although Leeds spinners would lose yet another of their past advantages as a result of such commerce, they could use their experience and accumulated resources to maintain their position in the trade. There was no reason why they should not devise new methods. So long as they kept a flexible and progressive attitude towards business, they might expect to do as well in the future as they had in the past. Marshall therefore remained optimistic. Not many shared his views, nor were they matched by his own practice. In particular he refused to share *his* methods with producers in Leeds or elsewhere. No stranger saw Marshall's 'mode of using machinery'.[2] Nonetheless,

---

[1] P. Fairbairn, *Sel. Ctte. Rep. Exportation of Machinery*, p. 221, Q 3267. There was perhaps an element of personal interest in Fairbairn's desire to prevent the growth of Escher, Wyss and Co. Murray Jackson, son of a second-generation partner in Fenton, Murray and Jackson of the Round Foundry, became manager of Escher, Wyss and Co. See Kilburn-Scott, *op. cit.* p. 81.

[2] J. G. Marshall, *Sel. Ctte. Rep. Exportation of Machinery*, p. 195, Q 2839–42. Cf. J. G. Marshall to H. C. Marshall, 19 August 1854, bemoaning the fact that Fairbairn

in the circumstances James Marshall took a sensible view. The machine-makers of Leeds would in any event sell their machinery to spinners elsewhere. This must be accepted as a fact. Nothing could be gained from bemoaning it. It would be more useful to see what its implications were for their future; what advantages, if any, it would bring. It might be hoped that the development of machine-making would lead to fresh inventions and perhaps to cheaper plant. When this happened, Leeds spinners must be the first to innovate.

The sharing of these advantages—coal, transport, scale, and machinery—meant that in future, so far as these factors were concerned, spinners everywhere were on more equal terms. Leeds spinners would no longer thrive at the expense of hand-spinners. To become *primus inter pares* they would have to sell more vigorously and keep in front with methods. This should not have been difficult in view of their long start.

However, Leeds producers looked at the new situation with a jaundiced eye. Basing their views on the same facts as James Marshall, they reached a different conclusion. Like him, they attributed their greatness to cheap coal, machinery, and so on, and they saw these advantages, on which their success allegedly rested, vanishing. Whereas Marshall at first regarded the new situation as a challenge, others saw only the deterioration from more favourable days, and this crippled their sense of confidence.

The loss of these advantages affords no objective reason why Leeds manufacturers should not have maintained their position in the trade until its general decline at the end of the nineteenth century. Nevertheless in the more difficult situation of the 1840's they began to feel that their greatness lay in the past and by the 1850's they regarded their prospects sourly. Having decided that spinners elsewhere had all the advantages, they complained that tariffs, or imported raw materials, or higher wages and fewer hours were the causes of their relative and absolute decline.

enabled other spinners to buy the latest machinery and so catch up with them, though he adds that they had only themselves to blame for being apathetic. Sometime between 1833 and 1836 Marshall and Co. changed from buying machinery off the Round Foundry to dealing chiefly with Fairbairn.

Complaints that foreign tariffs injured trade began in the 1840's after French action. Duties designed to protect native producers certainly affected trade with such countries as France and later Germany. However, in the absence of preferential treatment or physical controls, all exporters, Irish, Flemish, and English alike, encountered the same difficulties. In transatlantic trade, particularly that with the United States, so long as linen goods were in demand and so long as no native industry developed, flax products at some stage of processing had to be imported and all European producers faced the same scale of tariffs. The fundamental point is whether markets grew or declined after 1840, and whether Leeds spinners retained their share of the trade.

The Leeds *yarn* trade grew initially by supplying Barnsley weavers. In the 1830's spinners sold fine yarns in Ireland and France. Not counting sales to Ireland, United Kingdom yarn exports rose from 0·1 million lb. worth £9000 in 1830 (about ½ per cent of the declared value of linen exports) to 17·7 million lb. worth £823,000 in 1840 (about 20 per cent of linen exports). In 1842, 29 million lb. of yarn were sent abroad. At that point the French imposed a higher tariff which drastically reduced imports. Between 1842 and 1843 United Kingdom yarn exports to France fell by two-fifths. In 1832, 70 per cent of the yarn exported went to France; in 1841, 83 per cent; in 1851, 5 per cent and in 1884–6, 7 per cent. This would have been a very severe blow, had it not been for other opportunities. But the drop in foreign yarn sales was not calamitous. Yearly United Kingdom exports between 1840 and 1846 ran at 23 million lb.; between 1850 and 1856 at 20 million lb.; and in the 1860's more yarn was sold abroad.[1]

British spinners compensated themselves in new markets. They sold yarn in central Europe; Germany, Holland and Belgium took 16 per cent of United Kingdom exports in 1841, 45 per cent in 1851, and the same proportion in 1884–6. An important trade developed with Mediterranean countries in the 1840's; by 1851, Italy and Spain took 44 per cent of United Kingdom yarn exports; and in 1884–6, 36 per cent. Not until 1870 did United Kingdom yarn exports fall appreciably; and even in 1884–6 they ran at 17 million lb.

[1] *Statistics of the Linen Trade, passim; Irish Textile Journal*, 1886, p. 105.

The French tariff was not fatal to yarn exports, and venturesome spinners, particularly those in Belfast, found alternative markets. Leeds spinners did so too; but the volume of their sales languished. By 1884 'England had given up putting Belgium on her export lists', and Leeds spinners had lost ground in the home market.[1] 'Irish and particularly Belgian yarns have been sold for some time back in Leeds, Barnsley and other linen manufacturing places in England, at considerably under Leeds spinners prices; and this is likewise the case throughout the linen manufacturing districts of the Continent to which we formerly exported large quantities of yarn.'[2] Price-competition and energetic salesmanship, not tariffs, crippled Leeds yarn sales.

Dwindling yarn sales would not have been significant if Leeds producers had sold thread or linen cloth instead. Fine and coarse linen thread was wanted for making shoes, carpets, books, harness, net, lace and clothes (although cotton suited sewing-machines better).[3] In the 1840's most Leeds spinners began to produce thread, and they sent a large proportion abroad. Thread exports doubled in the 1830's and again in the 1840's. Marshalls exported 70 per cent of their thread in 1850, chiefly to the growing markets of central Europe. For the trade as a whole slightly over half the exports went to Europe and the rest to North America. In 1854–6 the declared value of thread exports averaged £359,000: thirty years later they came to £340,000. Judging by overseas sales, British thread-makers had a buoyant market until the 1870's. Then the high price of linen and the more extensive use of cotton thread, along with the imposition of tariffs to protect new native thread-makers, narrowed the market without much immediate prospect of alternatives. Some producers chose to move: 'High tariffs in the United States put an end to British thread exports: the result being that the principal makers of linen thread in the three kingdoms have established their own works in the States, importing their flax hackled... from the parent works

---

[1] *Textile Manufacturer*, 1884, p. 543. The view expressed here for Belgian supremacy is too naïve. Sacking and sailcloth would not have been manufactured from Flemish flax.

[2] *Leeds Express*, 12 March 1872.

[3] Greenwood, *Proc. Inst. Mech. Eng.* (1865), p. 120; Charley, *op. cit.* p. 85. Combing facilitated the manufacture of very fine thread.

in these countries.'[1] But until the late 1870's English spinners had a good run in this minor market.

The decisive market was that for linen goods. At the beginning of the nineteenth century the United Kingdom linen industry made less than 100 million yards of cloth a year. Half was sold at home; the rest abroad. In the next fifty years linen production rose four-fold. The volume of domestic sales increased five times; exports nearly trebled.[2] The home market grew faster than foreign sales until the mid-1820's, when some sections of the industry felt the effects of widespread competition from cotton goods, which supplanted some of the lighter linens in the home. The *per capita* consumption of cotton cloth rose quickly, whilst that of linen remained fairly constant; thus the demand for linen increased more slowly keeping step with population growth.[3] Momentarily in the 1840's when most textile producers faced hard times, linen manufacturers regained some ground, owing perhaps to the introduction of power-loom weaving. However, during the 1850's the domestic market for home-produced linens collapsed, shrinking to half its former size. At the same time the *per capita* consumption of cotton doubled. Ticks, ducks, handkerchiefs, sheeting, shirts and cloth for summer trousering were all produced more cheaply and better coloured in cotton. Sailcloth too was in less demand than it had been formerly. Whereas in 1800 twice as much cotton cloth was sold at home as linen, the difference by 1860 was elevenfold.[4]

The impact of substitution went even farther. At the heavy end of the trade, flax manufacturers found it increasingly difficult to compete with jute goods after the mid-century. By 1850 jute accounted for a third of the raw material used in Dundee, and jute yarn sold for 1s. a bundle less than tow yarns of equivalent weight. Home sales

[1] W. J. Ashley (ed.), *British Industries* (1903), pp. 142–3; see also H. Cox, *op. cit.* p. 57; Charley, *op. cit.* pp. 85–6; *Textile Manufacturer*, 1883, p. 147.

[2] Charley, *op. cit.* p. 30; J. G. Marshall, *Sel. Ctte. Rep. Exportation of Machinery*, p. 197, Q 2894.

[3] Presumably much of the increase in lower-class income was spent on the cheaper kinds of textiles with the result that the home demand for cottons rose faster than that for linens.

[4] Cox, *op. cit.* pp. 49, 50–2, suggests that drapers' margins were too high, that demand for sailcloth fell after the mid-century, and that linens were inferior to cotton in design and finish.

rose until 1880 and after 1870 an export market grew up in jute yarn and cloth.[1]

Owing to the inroads made by cotton and jute, the home market for native linens contracted absolutely after 1850, and a generation later it absorbed only about 100 million yards, the same quantity as it had taken soon after the Napoleonic wars. Foreign sales, however, continued to increase. After the removal of bounties which could no longer be justified, exports grew from 65 million yards in 1831–5 to 84 million yards in 1851–5. Early in the 1870's exports exceeded 200 million yards, equal to peak home sales a generation earlier.

Cloth sales in Europe remained fairly constant around 10 million yards annually, though the shares taken by various countries changed. In 1827–30, 90 per cent of the linens sent to the Continent went to the Mediterranean area, especially Spain and Portugal. When their former colonies in South America no longer bought through Spain and Portugal, this trade waned. British producers sent cloth instead to France, Germany and Italy. Exports to France rose from 80,000 yards in 1827 to 8 million yards in 1842. The tariff ruptured this trade, and only 1·3 million yards went to France in 1851.[2] However, between 1830 and 1850 sales in the German market rose from 70,000 to 4 million yards and in the Italian market doubled. In the generation after 1850, the pattern of exports to the Continent changed very little. France imported the same quantity in 1884–6 and Germany, then becoming industrialised, took a little less.

Cloth exports rose chiefly through sales in the rapidly growing U.S.A. and British colonial markets. Duties on imported flax stifled an incipient American linen industry early in the nineteenth century, and European manufacturers found the expanding United States economy to be their best market. In 1827–30 the U.S.A. bought 31 per cent of the United Kingdom's linen exports; in 1849–53, 42 per cent; and in 1884–6, 49 per cent. United Kingdom manufacturers sold almost as much linen there as in the home market. The

---

[1] Warden, *op. cit.* ch. 3, and p. 632.

[2] The French tariff was specific, and its incidence heavier when prices fell; the U.S.A. imposed an *ad valorem* tariff and Leeds firms tried to evade its mounting impact by consigning at a discount. This caused difficulties with the U.S. Customs; *Textile Manufacturer*, 1883, p. 426. (Tariff levels were mostly between a third and two-fifths on price.)

other principal markets, buying the 94 million yards of United Kingdom linen sold outside Europe in 1850, were the West Indies and South America. Exports there came to 37 million yards in 1850, the lion's share going to Brazil. In the following generation the United Kingdom's exports to this area fell to 27 million yards. On the other hand sales increased in imperial markets. Australia took 10 million yards (1884–6) and Canada nearly 5 million. Altogether, cloth exports rose until the 1870's, and then began to sag. But in the mid-1880's they still stood higher than the level of 1850. There was no decline to a permanently lower level of exports until World War I. So far as native products were concerned, considering both home and foreign markets together, the demand for linens grew until 1850, remained constant, and declined after 1880.

Thus the market for United Kingdom flax goods of all kinds did not contract until late in the nineteenth century. Many Leeds spinners adjusted to the changing market situation by making thread and cloth. But the town's industry shrank *before* the United Kingdom industry as a whole faced a diminishing market.[1]

Despite the fact that growing foreign markets actually offset the fall in home sales, Leeds manufacturers blamed tariffs and the market situation generally for their misfortunes. They thus sought some form of protection to preserve the dwindling home market for themselves. The trouble was that they could no longer compete.

When the Leviathan firm of Marshall and Co. was being established, there were thousands upon thousands of tons of linen yarn imported into England...as well as thousands of tons of linen fabric...and yet that firm could compete with them....How is it that Messrs Marshall and Co., and other Leeds flax spinners talk so much about competition?[2]

They talked about competition because they believed their plight arose from higher costs due to factors beyond their control. They thought that they could not compete because their mills used imported flax and their hands had higher wages and shorter hours than workers elsewhere.

---

[1] In 1853 thirteen out of the town's twenty-eight spinners made thread. Measured by spindles, the decline began in the late 1850's; by labour, after 1851; by the number of firms, after 1843. Cf. W. Schlote, *British Overseas Trade* (1952), Table 15, p. 149. British exports of flax yarn and fabric would have been higher if importers had not imposed tariffs to protect their infant industries.

[2] *Leeds Express*, 15 March 1872.

In the long run, a deficient supply of flax probably sealed the fate of linen producers everywhere. Like wool, but unlike cotton, flax is reared in a temperate clime. Like cotton, but unlike wool, it requires much labour. Where cheap or slave labour existed outside Europe, the climate was unsuitable. In temperate zones outside Europe labour was too scarce. High labour costs and lack of technical change meant that flax remained a European peasant crop. Its production never increased to anything like the same extent as that of wool or cotton. So, by comparison, flax remained expensive, and this handicapped the industry.

However, since the Leeds industry shrank whilst growth occurred elsewhere, was the supply of flax in any way responsible for its early downfall? Did English spinners suffer as the native crop declined?

During the Napoleonic wars English flax production rose to 4000 tons, half of which was reared in the north-east. Subsequently, it shrank to a few hundred tons after the mid-century. Likewise in Scotland the wartime crop of 1000 tons halved.[1] These contractions evoked protests from writers who believed agricultural development to be the panacea for current economic ills.[2] John Warnes, a stalwart opponent of free trade, wanted the unemployed to rear flax in the 1840's. He forecast a crop of 100,000 tons, which would allow English spinners to dispense with imports. Later, in 1862, Dewar argued that if each farmer in England and Wales grew five acres of flax, they could produce half a million tons, enough to provide jobs for Lancashire's unemployed operatives. Flax-spinners in Leeds gave such schemes very lukewarm support because they did not foresee any useful results. They knew full well that home-grown flax would be comparatively expensive owing to labour costs. And for that particular reason, home-grown flax was never important for English spinners. They depended on cheaper imported materials. From 1800 to 1815, during the French war, over three-quarters of

---

[1] Warnes, *op. cit.* p. 75; W. Marshall, *op. cit.* pp. 13–14, 31–2; *Textile Manufacturer*, 1881, p. 219; G. P. Bevan (ed.), *British Manufacturing Industries* (1876), W. Charley on flax, pp. 60–1.
[2] Warnes, *op. cit.* pp. 26, 52; Warden, *op. cit.* p. 732; Vargas Eyre, *The Possibility of Reviving the Flax Industry in Great Britain* (Supplement of the *Journal of the Board of Agriculture*, 1914), *passim*.

the United Kingdom's flax imports came from Russia. After the war the proportion stood at two-thirds for forty years. Before 1840 between 80 per cent and 90 per cent of the exports from Riga, the world's largest market, went to Britain. A similar situation prevailed at St Petersburg and Archangel. The smaller ports, Narva, Revel, Pernau, and Libau, consigned their entire shipments to the United Kingdom. After 1840 French and Belgian spinners entered the Baltic market; but in 1850, when British spinners took about a seventh of their imports from western Europe, 83 per cent of Russian exports went to Britain, only 1 per cent less than in 1825.

With regard to the requirements of Leeds spinners, this picture requires modification. In the second quarter of the nineteenth century, nine-tenths of Dundee's flax imports came from the Baltic and nine-tenths of the United Kingdom's tow imports went into Scotland. Hull imports in 1848–52 comprised 58 per cent Baltic and 42 per cent Flemish and Dutch. In absolute terms, Dundee took more than twice as much Baltic flax as Hull; and Hull imported six times as much Dutch and Flemish flax as Dundee. These figures simply reflect the fact that Dundee made heavy and Leeds light goods; but the supply of flax in western Europe was more limited and the demand for it greater, consequently it cost more than Baltic flax.

If English spinners depended on imported flax, how did their competitors manage? The Irish reared a medium-quality flax which increased in value as better methods of dressing spread in the nineteenth century. After the French wars the crop covered 120,000 acres. During the tragic 1840's it shrank to a half. But it recovered its former size during the Crimean War and in 1863 reached a peak at 300,000 acres, 6 per cent of the farming area. From the late 1870's the acreage under crop declined, and by 1900, 50,000 acres were sown, without any significant rise in yield to compensate for the loss.[1]

A similar trend occurred in western Europe. The French crop, covering a quarter-million acres in 1840, declined in the last

---

[1] Charley, *op. cit.* pp. 36–7, 130–3; Bevan, *op. cit.* p. 60; L. C. Marshall, *op. cit.* p. iii; J. Marshall, 'Notebook', 1790–1830, p. 66; *Textile Manufacturer*, 1885, p. 50. There is no evidence of much improvement in yields; cf. Arthur Young, *General View of the Agriculture of the County of Lincolnshire* (1799), p. 158; Bevan, *op. cit.* p. 60; *Textile Manufacturer*, 1880, p. 315. Whilst the average performance of farmers gradually improved as in Ireland, there was no advance over the best yields obtained in the early nineteenth century.

quarter of the century. In Belgium the cultivated area remained constant around 100,000 acres. Banfield noticed the recent neglect of flax growing in western Germany in 1846, and a conference in Frankfurt in 1841 ascribed the decline of the native linen industry in part to inadequate local flax supplies.[1]

The neglect of flax culture in the west was due to economic, not technical, reasons.[2] Land could be put to more profitable use. As the agricultural scene changed, the large-scale farmer avoided a crop so expensive in labour and fickle in performance; '....it being a crop that depends so much on a good or bad season; in general 30 to 50 stones per acre. I have 70 stones grown and from a bad season, I have seen the crop not worth reaping.'[3] Western farmers did not find it worth while to compete with Baltic peasants, and implicit in schemes to revive flax cultivation in England or Germany was a system of tariffs to protect native farmers.

Only in Russia did the crop expand, though somewhat erratically. In the mid-1860's peasants there produced 150,000 tons; in the late 1870's, 250,000 tons, and just before World War II, 600,000 tons. Thus Russia raised a third of the world's flax in 1860 and four-fifths in the later 1930's.[4] The net effect of this decline in the western crop and expansion in the east was a very gradual and modest rise in the world's flax supply from half a million tons in the early nineteenth century to three-quarters of a million in the 1930's.

As flax cultivation declined and flax spinning increased in the west, spinners relied more and more on Baltic flax. In 1880 Belgium imported 60 per cent of the flax she used, and France even more. In 1886, the *Irish Textile Journal* stated that 'more than 80 per cent of the flax spun in Germany is of Russian growth, in England and

[1] Banfield, *op. cit.* vol. I, pp. 26, 50; *Leeds Mercury*, 31 May 1845; Warnes, *op. cit.* p.100.

[2] Vargas Eyre, *op. cit.* p. 52; Charley, *op. cit.* p. 130; Warnes, *op. cit.* p. 100, quotes a letter from Marshall and Co. dated 28 November 1842: 'The demand...has been increasing and ...there has not been a corresponding increase in the quantity of land sown...hence the prices have risen considerably'. *Factory Inspector Reports*, Baker, October–April 1863, p. 48 'flax [is] decreasing everywhere whence we have hitherto been accustomed to be supplied'. Banfield, *op. cit.* vol. I, pp. 26, 50, ascribed the German decline to the absence of a protective tariff, and noted that famous crops such as the one at Ravensburg were deteriorating.

[3] Warnes, *op. cit.* p. 78; Charley, *op. cit.* p. 24.

[4] L. C. Marshall, *op. cit. passim*; W. S. and E. S. Woytinski, *World Population and Production* (1953), p. 615; *Textile Manufacturer*, 1880, p. 312.

France I dare say 50 per cent. This being the case it will be almost impossible for Continental and British spinners to do without Russian flax.'[1] By the 1870's spinners everywhere in the west depended on Baltic flax, and those who survived in Leeds laboured under no special disadvantage. Like the rest, they paid about 5 per cent more on their flax for insurance, storage and shipment, and nearly 20s. a ton for an export duty which Russia began to charge.

Was it probable then that Leeds spinners had been at a disadvantage earlier—in the generation before 1870—when the infant industries of Ireland, Belgium and France had native crops which they could use? There is no straightforward answer to this question.[2] In the first place, native crops in the west did not fully meet the requirements of home spinners anywhere. Each region reared different qualities of flax and although machines worked wonders, a great deal depended to start with on the actual fibre used. Furthermore, there was an economic side to the utilisation of fibres. Potential yields had to be set against price. To take an example: if Irish spinners had relied on native flax they would not have found it worth while making heavy yarn in the 1840's, nor could they have spun yarns finer than 80 leas.[3] Thus although (apart from famine years) Ireland usually raised enough flax to meet home requirements, she exported a sixth of her crop and imported between a quarter and two-fifths of her flax (mostly from the Baltic) in the early 1850's. Similarly, had they relied on home-grown flax, Belgian spinners would not have made heavy and medium yarns. Between 1850 and 1853 Belgium exported on average 12,000 tons of flax a year and imported 4500 tons, at a time when home consumption ran around 15,000 tons. Consequently, even in the mid-century there was considerable movement of flax between countries; and as the demands of native spinners grew after the mid-century without any corresponding rise in native flax production, the proportion of imported

[1] *Irish Textile Journal*, 1886, p. 107. In 1880 Belgian spinners imported nearly two-thirds of their flax requirements, see Bevan, *op. cit.* p. 62.

[2] J. Marshall to H. C. Marshall, 24 October 1843; P. Fairbairn, *Sel. Ctte. Rep. Exportation of Machinery*, p 220, Q 3255–57; L. C. Marshall, *op. cit.* p. vi. All allege that Irish spinners had an advantage in this respect in the 1840's.

[3] P. Fairbairn, *Sel. Ctte. Rep. Exportation of Machinery*, p. 220, Q 3257. Irish spinners depended on imported flax for fine yarns, and simultaneously Leeds spinners reverted to using more Baltic flax. See *Statistics of the Linen Trade, passim.*

flax from the Baltic rose. Leeds spinners were at no overwhelming disadvantage. Indeed, it is doubtful whether they suffered at all. Spinners in western countries who relied on home-grown flax used a fibre more expensive to produce than the Baltic flax to which Leeds spinners increasingly returned. English spinners never fully supported schemes for rearing flax at home. They wanted a cheap raw material. Hence it does not seem likely that Leeds spinners suffered any particular disability by bringing flax from afar.

Their real anxiety, *au fond*, was universal amongst linen producers, namely the price of flax compared with that of other fibres.[1] Demand increasing faster than supply exerted a pressure on price before the mid-century. Cotton and wool became cheaper; flax never fell below its post-war price. Hence the search for new areas of cultivation, all of which were of course a long way off. In 1829 a small quantity of New Zealand flax (encouraged by the colonial bounty scheme) came on to the market and spinners hoped for more. But only a few thousand people lived on those islands at the time. More encouraging were reports that French-Canadians preferred linen goods and might venture into growing flax. However, before long English spinners learned that 'in British North-American colonies hand labour is too expensive for large investment in flax growing'.[2]

Regional flax supply associations formed after 1850 wanted Indians to grow flax. The Leeds Association formed in 1859 bemoaned the shrinking home crop and stagnant level of imports. Its members agreed that increased sales depended above all on cheaper flax and decided that 'the Punjab... presents a fine field for [such] enterprise'. Native labour cost 3*d*. to 4*d*. a day; and the Association called upon the government to build canals for irrigation.[3]

These schemes fostered hopes but brought no practical results. Nor did China Grass turn out to be a suitable substitute; it could not be spun wet and it was expensive to cultivate. The only way to reduce material costs was by adulteration, and Leeds spinners were

---

[1] Charley, *op. cit.* pp. 129–35; Warnes, *op. cit.* p. 100; *Textile Manufacturer*, 1880, p. 164. Raw material prices dominated J. G. Marshall's view of the situation in the 1850's.

[2] *Textile Manufacturer*, 1880, p. 157; Charley, *op. cit.* p. 132; *Leeds Mercury*, 12 March 1861.

[3] *First Report, The Leeds Flax Supply Association*, 1859. For Ireland, see Bevan, *op. cit.* p. 61.

second to none in this art. For a generation they had managed to spin finer and finer counts from a particular grade of flax. After 1840 they shifted to inferior fibres, reflected in the composition of imports at Hull. Between 1848 and 1852, 82 per cent of the fibres imported were flax, 5 per cent tow and 13 per cent hemp; between 1860 and 1864, 64 per cent were flax, 17 per cent tow, and 19 per cent hemp.

Were high wages any more decisive as an explanation of the stagnation of the Leeds industry?

Labour costs, never more than a fifth of total costs at Marshalls, were the product of two forces: efficiency (depending on equipment and effort) and wages. These two aspects can be usefully considered by distinguishing between several situations that evolved before 1870.

In the generation *before* 1840, when the market for yarn and cloth grew, no English spinner had cause to complain about foreign wages and hours. Ever since the end of the French war, young women spinners in Leeds had received a subsistence wage of 6s. weekly. This may have been a little more than their counterparts received in Belfast or Lille. But the difference did not matter. There were few mill-spinners outside Great Britain, and Leeds producers competed chiefly with foreign hand-spinners who worked at home for a low remuneration. These domestic workers earned part of their livelihood by other means, and the rates for this job fell under pressure from mill-spun yarns. However, once a particular grade of yarn could be spun effectively by machinery, the decisive point in the long run was not a difference in wage levels between mill- and cottage-spinner so much as the enormous variations in productivity. It took a hand-spinner nearly four weeks to produce a bundle of yarn. A mill operative, attending between twenty and 400 spindles, spun five to a hundred bundles a week. Mill-spinners had superior production ratios in the order of 20:1 to 400:1. This comparison perhaps overstates the case, since it omits the cost of capital and the labour involved preparing the rovings. A line-spinner at Marshalls in 1840 produced sixteen bundles a week; if preparers were included, the average output per head falls to four. Even then labour cost per bundle of line including hackling came only to 18d.; by comparison, a hand-spinner who received 6*s*. in wages (and in Ireland they once received this rate) would be paid over £1 for a bundle of yarn. When hand-spinners' earnings fell to only 1*s*. a week the labour cost per bundle amounted to 3*s*. 6*d*. —and this assumes that they undertook the task of preparing as well. Thus as long as Leeds spinners had a near monopoly of mechanical methods they could not complain about hours and wages elsewhere. In fact John Marshall II boasted that Leeds spinners earned more than German spinners, and the management on its own initiative shortened hours. Indeed, when in 1833 he objected to a legal limit on hours, he argued the case not on grounds of foreign competition and long hours abroad, but on the injurious effect it would have on capital accumulation at home.[1]

It was after 1840 that criticism arose over foreign hours and wages. In the generation before 1870, when the economy of Leeds began to change fundamentally, wages rose and hours fell generally in most industries. Hitherto Leeds had been a *one-industry* town. In 1841 two-fifths of its workers were in textile mills, wool more than flax. By 1871 less than a fifth worked in mills. The number of men employed in them declined absolutely after 1851, and the number of women did not increase beyond the 12,000 employed in 1851. Instead men took jobs in new industries, especially engineering, which employed the largest proportion of males in the town after 1860. This industry, and others such as tanning, printing and transportation, paid higher wages than the mills. Consequently, flax-spinners had no alternative but to raise the wages paid to their male employees. This caused little anxiety, however, for they used a high proportion of child and female labour whose price remained low until the 1870's. Then the needle trades offered a new opening, employing 9000 women in 1881. At the same time children had to attend school and were no longer available for mill work. But throughout, low wages for women and children persisted because they were, from a family point of view, marginal workers. It was worth their while working

[1] L. C. Marshall, *op. cit.* p. 137; Charley, *op. cit.* p. 81; S.P.C.K., *The Manufacture of Linen Yarn*, p. 25; Horner, *op. cit.* pp. 251–3; *Textile Manufacturer*, 1888, pp. 105, 159; *Leeds Intelligencer*, 12 January 1832, 28 March 1840; *Factory Inquiry Commission, Supplementary Report*, Part 2, C. I., North-eastern District, p. 77, shows Marshalls claiming to pay wages a third above the level prevailing abroad and competing successfully owing to skill and superior machinery which reduced costs.

for low wages and this reinforced the established attitude towards such labour, namely that it was cheap. Consequently, as male labour became more expensive, flax manufacturers used more women. Women made up 64 per cent of the industry's labour force in Leeds in 1841, 70 per cent in 1861, and 78 per cent in 1881. Except for workers in the shoddy trade, no other group of workers in Leeds received such a low average wage in 1858. Between 1840 and 1870 their hours had fallen 6 per cent and wages had risen 13 per cent. The industry thus secured the cheapest labour in town.[1]

Using such labour created difficulties that were to be expected. Sometimes hands could not be obtained: '...when all branches of trade are sufficiently active to create a demand for labour, I am not surprised that flax mills should experience difficulty in obtaining a supply of hands'.[2] John Marshall had lost touch with the local scene when he rebuked his son in 1843 for offering higher wages to secure reelers. More serious in the long run than occasional shortages was the tendency for children, a fifth of the labour force, 'not [to be] brought up into the trade in as large numbers as formerly'.[3] Manufacturers had to rely more on young women and unskilled men, many of whom were Irish immigrants. This resulted in indifferent work, strained industrial relations, and helped to produce a crisis in the early 1870's. Moreover, because they could manage with cheap labour, Leeds spinners were reluctant to introduce more capital and higher workloads. They lacked this particular incentive to change their ways. One spokesman for the men put the point bluntly when he stated that until the masters paid the same wages as other factories, they would never run their mills satisfactorily.[4]

Of course more important than having the cheapest (and perhaps the worst) labour in town, was having lower labour costs than Belfast and Ghent producers. In the 1830's Irish mill-spinners got about a third less than their Leeds counterparts, and John Marshall referred to this in 1843 as a handicap for Leeds manufacturers. After the

[1] W. G. Rimmer, 'Leeds and Its Industrial Growth; The Working Force', *Leeds Journal*, vol. XXV, no. 3, pp. 87–90; J. Thomas, *A History of the Leeds Clothing Industry* (1955), *passim*; R. Baker, *J.R.S.S.* vol. XXI, pp. 436–42.

[2] *Factory Inspector Report*, Saunders, 1 May 1845, p. 47.

[3] Meeting of the Employers and Employed, 7 March 1872, in Marshall 'Strike Book', p. 40; J. Marshall to H. C. Marshall, 24 October 1843.

[4] *Leeds Express*, 1 April 1872.

famine, Henry Marshall noted that Irish wages were on a par with those paid in Leeds. In 1872 Irish (and Scottish) operatives received 8s. to 9s. 6d. a week compared with a *rate* of 6s. 3d. in Leeds.[1] When some allowance has been made, Leeds manufacturers paid wages that were lower, or certainly no higher, than their competitors elsewhere in the British Isles. Naturally they never complained about *cheap* Irish and Scottish labour. Instead they protested against foreign, especially Belgian, wages. There, the mill hands subsisted on 'black bread...potatoes...and chicory', working a 72-hour week for three-fifths as much pay as an English operative.[2]

But how did Irish spinners who paid more than English firms manage to compete with such low Belgian wages? The answer lies in the fact that wages are only part of labour costs. Different levels of wages cannot alone stand as an explanation, and for that reason they do not account for the decline of the Leeds industry. The quality of labour and the quantity of capital also help to determine labour costs.

The application of machine-spinning in other countries after 1840 had an important bearing on labour costs. Each Irish spindle in 1853 averaged eighteen bundles of yarn a year; since 1846 Marshalls had not managed much over twelve. The late and simultaneous introduction of the power-loom into several countries meant that in weaving each began with the same technical advantage. A weaver at Marshalls tending one loom, in 1870, made 90 yards of cloth in a week, three times as much as a hand-loom weaver; ten years later she made 125 yards. In some Irish mills, operatives watched two looms and turned out 240 yards of cloth in a week.[3] Producers everywhere were potentially on the same technical terms and at this point a lead in productivity depended on differences in skill, work-loads and quality of plant.

In Belgium where labour was abundant and cheap, it was used

[1] L. C. Marshall, *op. cit.* p. 206; H. C. Marshall, 'Notebook', II, p. 107; *Leeds Express*, 18 and 23 March 1872.

[2] *Leeds Express*, 13 and 23 March 1872; L. C. Marshall, *op. cit.* p. viii; *Belfast News Letter*, 7 March 1872.

[3] Charley, *op. cit.* pp. 36, 92 ff., 97. Output per worker would depend not only on work loads and plant efficiency, but also on the type of yarn or fabric being produced. My general point here is simply that as regards plant, manufacturers were technically on equal terms.

wastefully. 'Three or four men are employed to do the same quantity of work that one is compelled to perform in this country.'[1] Perhaps the large limited liability companies of Ghent and Liége had higher labour costs than Leeds. In Ireland lower labour costs were the result of up-to-date plant and skilful, if more expensive, labour. Even higher labour costs incurred by slower sorting proved worth while because they produced a considerable increase in the yield of line.

The efficient performance of sorting is considered in Belfast to be the very life of the flax spinning trade. There are many thousands of men there at their occupation earning respectable wages. Their daily task is about 80 lb. of flax of medium quality, and 100 lb. of flax of coarse quality. In finer sorts, say from 100s to 300s, their days work is from 45 lb. to 25 lb. By careful attention to dressing over the sorting hackles, and his knowledge of the qualities of flax, the skilled workman is able to separate all the finer sorts which the flax is capable of producing, and every pound of a finer sort is a gain of from 2d. to 3d. to the master. Where there are 50,000 lb. of line dressed in a week, and flax costing £70 to £100 per ton, what a quantity of money can be lost by the careless performance of sorting. In some Leeds flax mills, the sorting is done while the flax is in the rough state, in others it is performed by girls utterly ignorant of the business, whilst in others it is done by unskilled men who may be found labouring this week in a foundry and the next week sorting. The latter class tear through the flax in the most destructive manner, doing as much in two days as a skilled sorter should do in a week. The cost of hackling, sorting, etc., to a Belfast spinner is more than double the amount paid for the same in Leeds...but it is a fallacy to suppose that cheap labour in hackling produces cheap line. If it does, then the Leeds spinner must gain the difference, which in large firms would amount to thousands of pounds yearly. But it is said he can't compete with the Belfast spinner and his profits are smaller. It is no doubt quite true. It is the inevitable result of obsolete machinery and conservative ideas as to the perfection of their system of working.[2]

The final sentence puts the matter in a nutshell. Until their wage rates rose sharply in the 1870's, Leeds spinners installed little new machinery and did not step up work-loads. A correspondent to the *Leeds Express* wrote in 1872

I know a firm in Belfast who have not a single machine now working that they had in 1863. I know a firm in Leeds, who, until a few months ago, had

---

[1] *Leeds Express*, 15 March 1872.   [2] *Ibid.* 27 March 1872.

not a single hackling machine that was not from fifteen to twenty-five years old. In the former, Flemish flax, costing about £80 a ton, yielded on an average 74 lb. of dressed line per hundredweight, a difference which in a few months would pay for the cost of the improved machine.[1]

Leeds spinners made little progress before the 1870's towards the introduction of piece-rates. Nor did they buy the excellent new roving and hackling machinery which economised labour and improved yields.[2] They were anchored to their past, so rigidly conservative that their equipment and the quality of workmanship fell behind achievements elsewhere. As a result the efficiency of capital and the quality of labour in Leeds mills declined at precisely the time that improvement was needed most. 'It is a well known fact that several of the old established firms in the spinning trade who failed, was in consequence of being unwilling to go with the age, by introducing improved machinery into their mills, and thereby losing their established status in the market.'[3] Perhaps they had ceased to be competitive in cost terms. They believed this to be the case for reasons which do not bear much scrutiny. At the very least, they had lost confidence. The expedients they adopted and their fatalistic outlook ruled out the possibility of a comeback. Despite the fact that 'those large and respectable firms which are left...made every improvement', their effort, when it came in the 1870's, was too late.[4]

From this analysis of the reasons commonly advanced for the decline of the Leeds flax industry, it appears that its stagnation was not a straightforward matter of higher costs beyond the control of spinners. Nevertheless, the town's producers viewed the situation in

[1] *Leeds Express*, 27 March 1872.
[2] Charley, *op. cit.* pp. 79, 83; Greenwood, *Proceedings of the Institute of Mechanical Engineers*, 1865, pp. 103-22 *passim*.   [3] *Leeds Express*, 15 March 1872.
[4] Marshalls' costs rose after 1840, owing mainly to rising flax costs. In contrast, Belfast costs tended to fall, L. C. Marshall, *op. cit.* p. iii. Nevertheless, Leeds and Belfast spinners were not always competing with each other; the former specialised in warp yarns and the latter in weft, and in addition there was a considerable cross-traffic in yarns for finishing, especially at Leeds. The main points in this complex situation are that Leeds spinners declined whilst growth occurred elsewhere, and that Leeds and Belfast producers differed in two respects: (1) in the relative age of their machinery, and (2) in the intensity of its use. When flax-spinning declined everywhere later in the nineteenth century, there were complaints that Irish spinners fell behind those in Belgium in machinery, and that flax-spinners generally fell further behind cotton manufacturers. See *Textile Manufacturer*, 1896, p. 281; 1898, p. 402.

defeatist terms. The system which they had evolved in the 1830's, they believed to be the acme of progress. In the lean years that followed, they clung to it faithfully making only a few fitful changes and sought to blame outside factors for their distress. At the same time, when they had to meet competition on equal terms, deal in more complex factor and product markets, and incorporate small improvements rather than major technical changes, spinners like Marshall and Co. gradually lost faith in free trade and competition and sought help from outside. They formed associations with impractical goals and, being increasingly enmeshed in politics, thought of political solutions: a tariff, empire flax produced with government aid, a subsidy to facilitate the spread of power-looms on the scale achieved in Ireland during the cotton famine, and an end to further legislative concessions for the operative class. Their old framework of liberal economic ideas seemed inadequate. Once the pioneering days of rapid change and falling costs were over they wanted new rules which would guarantee their perpetuation. But they developed no worthwhile notions as to how to succeed by their own efforts, and at the root of their infirmity was the failure to adjust their outlook to changing conditions.

The relative decline of the Leeds flax industry was not due, as Marshall's sons eventually believed, simply to tariffs, imported flax and high wages. More important was neglect, indifference, defeatism, even open hostility within firms based on the family. The growing Belgian spinners and many Irish firms were organised by the later 1860's on a joint stock basis which probably produced greater managerial flexibility, although this did not necessarily save them from stagnation later in the nineteenth century.[1]

(ii)

In the twenty-five years after the founder's death, the size and composition of the plant at Water Lane changed considerably.[2] Spinning

[1] *Textile Manufacturer*, 1884, p. 543; L. C. Marshall, *op. cit.* pp. vii–ix. Despite their misgivings about the future of the local flax industry, no Leeds spinners ventured into a different business after 1840, and many insured their future by investing in coupon-incomes.

[2] At Castle Foregate, the number of twisting spindles increased from 3630 in the mid-1840's to 4450 in the late 1860's. But in general no expansion took place at the

spindles did not increase beyond the 32,000 operating in 1845. After 1852 this side of the business was reduced. The production of warp and tow yarn for sale was discontinued and 5000 spindles had gone by 1855. A further 7000 spindles were scrapped in the five years after 1873. Consequently although the firm could in theory, and occasionally in practice did, spin 400,000 bundles a year, after 1872 its effective output ran around 250,000 bundles.

There were at least two reasons why the partners did not want to reduce drastically the output of yarn before the 1870's, despite the fact that its production generally ceased to be profitable after the early 1840's. The plant was there and Marshall's sons regarded themselves primarily as spinners. Not all counts were unprofitable every year, and the composition of the output could be varied to gain from this fact.[1] The possibilities were there—at least until the 1870's, when first-quality line yarns doubled in price compared with the 1840's and 1850's making it impossible to compete with cotton and jute. Another reason for maintaining a high level of yarn production was the conversion of between a third and a half into thread and cloth.

The number of twisting spindles for thread-making increased from 7000 to 10,000 between 1846 and 1852. In 1850 the firm turned 180,000 bundles of its yarn into thread. But the expansion stopped there. In 1860 Marshall and Co. used only 130,000 bundles, and in the following two years dismantled 2000 twisting spindles. A decade later they scrapped 2000 more spindles, and used only 80,000 bundles of yarn for thread.

It would not have been surprising if Marshalls had reduced their thread production in the late 1870's. The trade became so difficult that even makers of cotton thread complained. When prices tumbled after 1877, Marshall and Co. turned only 50,000 bundles of yarn into thread. But they had removed two-fifths of their plant before this. In the 1840's thread-making offered a large margin and they de-

---

Salop plant after the early 1820's. See W. G. Rimmer, 'The Castle Foregate Flax Mill', *Transactions of the Shropshire Archaeological Society*, 2nd series, vol. LVI, pp. 49–68.

[1] The secret was simply to make extreme counts. 'It is on the extreme counts of yarn—very coarse or very fine—that most money is to be made, as the prices paid for these yarns are disproportionately higher, on account of little competition existing at the ends of the trade.' See *Textile Manufacturer*, 1880, p. 424.

veloped this side of the business at Leeds as well as at Shrewsbury. There are signs that they subsequently tried to exploit the market by the device of a trade mark. By offering a wide range of colours, different sized spools, and special finishes for sewing machines, they claimed that 'Marshall and Company...pride themselves...on producing the exact style of yarn required for every sort of thread'.[1] New markets were sought ranging from Canada to Australia and New Zealand; and foreign buyers were granted substantial discounts, a device which led to friction with the United States Customs over valuation for duty.

But the fact was that once other spinners entered this trade and a fighting market evolved, Marshalls made little headway. Thread prices fell—a quarter in the 1840's, a fifth in the late 1850's. Marshalls' costs rose, partly because of the finishing touches they added, but principally because the cost of their yarns increased. Consequently, their margins narrowed and thread-making did not prove as promising as they had hoped. They added no more spindles, and cut production in the late 1850's.[2]

The production of cloth increased too after 1846. There were twenty-six power-looms in 1847 and 241 in 1884. In the late 1840's when the partners sought a new balance of production, they not only developed thread-making but also doubled the number of looms. In 1850 the firm turned 25,000 bundles of yarn, $6\frac{1}{2}$ per cent of its output, into cloth. In 1857 after two years of very poor trade, the partners added forty looms, and another forty during the American Civil War. After 1860 the weaving section used 50,000 bundles of the firm's yarns, and in addition from 1856 the partners bought between 2000 and 4000 bundles a year outside. (During the strikes of 1872, the mills used 14,000 bundles made outside and 37,000 of their own manufacture.) A final addition to loom capacity was made between 1873 and 1876, and by the 1880's the firm's weaving depended heavily on imported yarns.

As long as the demand for linens remained buoyant the partners stood to benefit from producing cloth. They extended their market by

[1] *The Journal of Domestic Appliances and Sewing Machine Gazette*, 1 October 1882, p. 16.

[2] *Textile Manufacturer*, 1887, p. 206. The thread trade had been a losing proposition for the past forty years.

dealing direct with the general public through such shops as Shoe-breads in Tottenham Court Road, and the integration of weaving with spinning lowered costs. In 1853 they produced 268,000 yards (5500 pieces); between 1862 and 1868, they averaged 800,000 yards, and in 1882, 700,000. The linens made were chiefly of the heavier kind. Before 1860 they produced ticks and drills in equal proportions. Then more huckabacks, so far a marginal product, were made. In the mid-1860's output comprised 45 per cent ticks, 34 per cent drills, and 13 per cent huckabacks. By 1879 the proportion of ticks had risen to 51 per cent; drills and huckabacks had fallen to 24 per cent and 10 per cent respectively. In addition small quantities of sheeting, towelling and ducks were occasionally woven.[1] Much of the linen was exported to the Mediterranean, North America and, through Strauss Brothers and Sons, to central Europe. It proved a quite profitable venture. Between 1853 and 1862 the cost of making a piece of cloth came to £2·42 and it fetched £2·77, yielding a margin of 7s. on an output of 10,000 pieces a year. Even in 1880–2 when yarn and thread were unprofitable, cloth cost £3 and sold for £4 a piece. This explains why the firm kept up the level of its linen production to the end.

Despite these adjustments Marshalls became unprofitable after 1850. In twenty-one of the last forty years before 1886 the business ran at a loss. The attempt to diversify output in the late 1840's did not save the firm from losing £100,000 in the 1850's, and it could not have withstood a drain for long on that scale. The firm's prospects were bleak until civil war in the United States revitalised the local linen trade. But in the 1860's the partners made a profit of only £6000 a year at Leeds and lost £5000 in Salop. (This does not mean that Castle Foregate alone was unprofitable. Much of the Water Lane yarn and thread was sent to Salop for twisting and finishing. These items passed through the Leeds books without loss, and the subsequent reckoning was debited to the Salop account. Therefore no special emphasis should be placed on the losses registered by the smaller plant.) During boom conditions Marshall and Co. made less

---

[1] Marshall and Co. wove plain linens from 1 to 4 yards wide. In 1846 they had one Jacquard loom and added four more ten years later, but only a small proportion of the cloth was produced on them.

than 1 per cent on turnover and this was largely the result of one year's trading, 1864, when net profits exceeded £40,000. By this time, the founder's sons had become fatalistic about profits, regarding them like a harvest as beyond their control. In the 1870's the firm made £3000 a year at Leeds and lost £4000 in Salop. It still kept going, struggling along on what remained of the great resources which had formerly been accumulated. But in the decade after 1876 a trading deficit of over £100,000 piled up and the founder's grandsons decided to stop production. In all, between 1847 and 1886, Marshall and Co. made a profit at Leeds of £99,000 and a loss in Salop of £181,000 giving a *net* loss of £82,000.[1]

At the founder's death in 1846 Marshall and Co. had been in a strong position. New rivals and trade barriers clouded the horizon but his sons felt confident about the future. The world demand for their products was not falling and they could compensate for lower sales in one market by finding customers in another. Yet for forty years the firm wasted away, losing its former power and prestige. Why?

It is clear even on the basis of slight evidence that one weakness was an unenterprising sales policy. If the alliance between Leeds spinners and Barnsley weavers had once been profitable, it was no longer so. Because Marshalls' connexions made it easy to secure orders there, the larger part of their sale yarns still went to weaving factories in Barnsley until the 1870's. But Barnsley linens could no longer compete with those made in Belfast; so this trade and the demand for Leeds yarn fell. And even more disturbing, the surviving Barnsley houses began to use cheaper yarns produced elsewhere. In order to gain access to new markets Henry Marshall, who directed sales, sold thread and cloth abroad through commission agents. Using the specialist services of a merchant house was not without advantages, but it restricted the firm's choice of markets (omitting, for instance, those in south-eastern Europe) and certain agents pushed the products of competitors harder than Marshall's own. To some extent this was the result of a genuine preference for the goods of other firms on grounds of quality, delivery and, above all, costs. But agents

[1] These figures gloss one item. In 1871 the partners ceased to charge interest as a cost of production and from their point of view lost a further £16,000 a year.

could also be influenced by margins of commission, and it was significant that Christopher Empson, who was brought into the business as a commercial expert in 1849, advised Henry to offer a bonus to the more aggressive sellers. Henry characteristically ignored the suggestion. A few years later his brother suggested 'you must both speak and act so that both your agents and competitors may be thoroughly convinced'.[1] But what could he usefully do? Travel abroad on business in order to ascertain at first hand overseas market conditions? Employ salesmen and increase the burden of their fixed costs? Trade had become very tough in the 1850's and their products were too expensive. But the problem of high costs was not Henry's but his brother's affair. If Henry's lukewarm attitude towards sales was one serious defect, the reaction of customers to Marshalls' prices both at home and abroad indicates that the trouble lay deeper.

A second reason for the firm's unprofitableness was the composition of its output. Despite very considerable changes in the late 1840's— the extension of thread-making and the introduction of power-loom weaving—the firm had an average annual deficit of £15,000 between 1851 and 1856 at Leeds and Salop. Half the firm's yarn became thread and yielded approximately half the firm's revenue. But thread prices in the early 1850's were much lower than they had been in the mid-1840's, and income from this source fell by a third. Slightly more than two-fifths of the firm's yarn was sold direct to customers, and although yarn prices remained fairly steady in the early 1850's, production costs at Water Lane rose by more than 1s. a bundle. Spinners in Leeds and elsewhere had caught up with and surpassed Marshall and Co. in the quality of their top-grade yarns and threads, making the same article at a lower cost. Cloth production alone remained profitable. But only a fifteenth of the firm's yarn was woven into cloth, and in the early 1850's income from this source averaged only £16,000 or one-twelfth of total revenue.

---

[1] J. G. Marshall to H. C. Marshall, 19 August 1854. 'The general tone of your letter is desponding, it would seem as if you scarcely hoped to do more than avoid being decidedly beaten. Now in commercial as well as military affairs there is a great deal of "Pluck". You must go in with a determination to win and take any quantity of punishment necessary for that purpose.' (In the margin alongside this cant, H. C. Marshall, in response to the allusion to the offensive against Russia, wrote: 'What has that [i.e. Pluck] got to do with it.') H. C. Marshall's 'Notebook', II, p. 107, shows his despondency.

In this predicament the partners had to choose between three alternatives—or two if they intended to remain in business. First, they could concentrate entirely on producing linens which were profitable. An investment of £20,000 would buy the additional looms and accessories required to weave the whole of their yarn output. All they needed was some extra capital and an agreement to make cloth; but neither proved easy to obtain when it came to the point. Second, and more fundamental (unless they purchased yarns from outside in the event of becoming weavers), was the need to find a cheaper way of manufacturing yarns and improving their quality. They had to do this to remain in business as spinners and thread-makers. James told his brother as much when he realised the enormity of their problem in 1854. It was not so much the general flatness of trade which disturbed him

but independent of, and beyond that, the course of events for some years shows me decisively that we are in a very critical position. What is the general cause? I say it consists in the trade at large having *come up* to us in quality and reputation of their production, having got the very same machinery which we first introduced, and learnt how to use it through Fairbairn, who learnt from us; besides their own improvements in various ways, probably most in economic production of good fair yarn and thread.—We have been nearly at a stand for some time. Our only chance in my opinion is in the enterprise, skill and judgement with which we lead the way in a new set of improvements. We must do over again what we did after Wet spinning was introduced. And what I am now specially insisting upon is that we must use these improvements in the *first place* to establish clearly the *superiority* of our *quality* of production.[1]

The average cost of producing a bundle of yarn at Marshall and Co. rose from 119*d.* in 1847 to 165*d.* in 1869, much faster than the average for other prices in the economy. The chief cause of this rise was higher raw material costs, which increased by 36*d.* to 109*d.* per bundle. Unfortunately there is no record of what Marshall and Co. paid for flax, but ever since 1840 flax prices increased and in the late 1860's generally stood a third higher than 1847. However, more expensive flax was only part of the reason for higher material costs.

[1] J. G. Marshall to H. C. Marshall, 19 August 1854. Phrases such as 'falling behind' and 'in the rear' constantly recur in this correspondence. See also *ibid.* 11 March 1853, 28 August 1857.

Indeed the firm began to use a higher proportion of tow and codilla and introduced combing, all of which should have had the effect of lowering costs. Another, more important, reason for pushing materials costs up so much was the production of heavier yarns. The firm made over 330 bundles from a ton of raw material in 1847 and 235 bundles, a third fewer, in 1869. Roughly speaking, flax costs rose in the early 1850's because of heavier yarns (owing to the diversification of the firm's output) and in the later 1860's because of higher flax prices.

On and off for almost a generation raw material costs had been the principal stumbling block to the industry's prosperity. Ever since the late 1830's James Marshall had very sensibly sought a way out of this impasse for fine spinners. For many years he experimented with China Grass and this work gained a medal for Marshall and Co. at the Great Exhibition.[1] But China Grass never became a commercial or technical success. Not only was it expensive to raise, but James mistakenly treated it like line yarn instead of carding and spinning dry like tow. In the mid-1850's, when the firm again produced a higher proportion of heavier yarns, he abandoned China Grass and concentrated on reducing the cost of flax. In 1856 he bought a farm at Patrington, near Hull, from his brother William in order to steep undressed Baltic flax by chemicals. This flax was 20 per cent cheaper than dressed flax and James hoped to economise considerably on the expense of steeping. His experiments, he hoped, would have the effect of 'diminishing the cost of material per bundle.... The moment...we ascertain that the plan will answer we have the means...of going into it extensively. And in my opinion this is an experiment to be pushed "*vi et armis*" with sleepless energy by day and night if it be possible—for every week, day, hour, that can be gained is a great gain.'[2] Six months later he still persisted: 'I firmly believe yet that here is to be a main foundation of any success

[1] P. S. Horsman, experiments On the Preparation of China Grass, 1840–52; Greenwood, *Proceedings of the Institute of Mechanical Engineers*, 1865, pp. 123–8 *passim*. At the Great Exhibition, 1851, Hives and Atkinson received a medal for yarns, Holdsworth and Titley for threads, and a Barnsley firm for fancy linens. Marshalls were also commended for attaining medal standard with their threads. See Charley, *op. cit.* App. 1, pp. 139–51, for a full report.

[2] J. G. Marshall to H. C. Marshall, 15 February 1856. He proposed to process 1250 tons of flax a year. After eighteen months, James and Arthur Marshall who jointly ran the venture agreed to dispose of Patrington; J. G. Marshall to H. C. Marshall, 28 August 1857.

of M and Co. in carrying on a profitable business in our line of fine yarn and threads'.[1] However, nothing came of these efforts. Flax prices fell enormously for three years after 1856 and James decided to give up his trials and sell the farm. He made no further attempt to reduce raw material costs, and by the late 1860's they had risen by 73 per cent per bundle above the level of the mid-1840's.

With regard to the cost of flax or its substitutes, nearly all spinners laboured under the same disadvantage. In the long run Marshall and Co. probably had more scope to prove their superiority by keeping the level of their overheads and labour costs below that of their competitors. But despite James's intentions, they were not particularly successful in raising the efficiency of their plant. Between 1847 and 1869 overheads rose by 4*d*. a bundle to 36*d*. and labour costs by 6*d*. to 20*d*.

Mounting overheads were not at this period due to increases in rent. Only £40,000 was spent on the fabric after 1845. A reeling-shed (subsequently used as a warehouse) and a shed for steeping China Grass (later used for carding) were built alongside the Temple Mill in 1854-5. In the 1860's stables, warehouse and calender shed were added. By the mid-1850's, the plant needed a little extra energy and the 70 horse-power engine installed in mill *D* in 1827 was compounded with a new 30 horse-power engine in 1859: seven years later, a 40 horse-power engine was compounded with the 70 horse-power engine, fifty years old, in mill *C*. The eighteenth-century mill *B* north of Water Lane was demolished in 1852 and the site abandoned; the open cooling reservoirs were filled in and replaced by an underground culvert to the river. The increase in rent which followed this modest outlay on fabric was offset by frequent partnership agreements to charge less: and the rent was reduced to £4700 in 1853, to £5100 in 1858, to £4670 in 1875, and to £3600 in 1880. In addition, in the late 1870's the Temple Mill and other buildings were sublet and ceased to be a net expense. Despite this, the rent charge for mills and engines erected between forty and seventy years earlier was 3½*d*. a bundle in 1880.

Overheads rose owing to the cost of extra capital. As the firm bought more flax for heavier yarn, held a wider variety of finished

---

[1] J. G. Marshall to H. C. Marshall, 13 September 1856.

goods, and financed sales farther afield, the amount of its circulating capital rose from around £150,000 to £200,000. And notwithstanding the fact that little was spent on machinery after 1858, the plant was revalued frequently in the following decade and in theory the partners added £45,000 to their capital. Simultaneously they decided to reduce the rate of depreciation from 10 per cent to 7½ per cent in 1858 and to 5 per cent in 1862, theoretically doubling the life of the plant. Accordingly, capital and interest charges grew. In 1860 the total capital amounted to £274,000 and interest at 5 per cent cost nearly £14,000, or 9*d*. a bundle.

Labour costs in both the spinning and hackling processes also rose between 1849-53 and 1864-68. During this period a spinning operative's output fell 22 per cent (whilst hours remained fairly constant); her earnings rose 6 per cent; and labour costs rose 37 per cent. To what can this fall in output per worker be attributed? Was it a consequence of ageing machinery? In the generation after 1846 Marshalls installed 6000 *new* spinning spindles; 4000 with a 3-in. pitch in 1847 and 2000 in 1862. Compared with the previous generation, this was a much slower turnover of physical plant. But as Greenwood, a Leeds machine-maker, stated in 1865, 'Scarcely any improvement has been made in spinning frames for a great number of years and they are practically the same as employed a few years after the introduction of wet spinning'.[1] As the firm shifted to coarser yarns, output per spindle rose by 12 per cent. Nevertheless the use of old frames did matter when competitors used new ones. In 1862-3 when Marshalls installed seven new frames each carrying 300 spindles, this together with the fact that they had scrapped 5000 old spindles raised the average number of spindles per frame from 135 in 1850 to 156 in 1870. The size of frame helps to determine the productivity of labour, and until the late 1870's the firm had a small proportion of large frames. However, the point at issue is not why productivity failed to rise but why it fell. It did so because of an increase of labour. Where there had been seventy spindles per operative in the mid-1840's, in the late 1860's there were forty-five. The ratio of capital to labour fell, offsetting the increase in output per spindle: productivity declined. Why labour

---

[1] Greenwood, *Proc. Inst. Mech. Eng.* 1865, p. 122.

in spinning increased from 1849 to 1853, and again after 1860 is open to conjecture. The striking fact about the swollen numbers in the 1860's is the employment of children, mostly girls under thirteen, in the spinning-room. The most probable explanation is that in order to raise output in the early 1850's and in the early 1860's— the only occasions when the firm's output of yarn exceeded 400,000 bundles—the partners had to bring into operation machinery which had been laid on one side, old machinery which required a higher ratio of operators. In short, they hired more labour to make fuller use of the plant. Faster driving became possible because a larger proportion of heavier yarns were made, so that in the line department a spindle averaged 8·39 leas per day in 1844-8, and in 1859–63 the figure was 9·41 leas. In the tow department, a spindle produced 8·14 leas a day from 1844–48, and 11·51 leas in 1859–63. Rather than invest in new equipment when a seller's market developed, the partners thought that they could afford the higher labour cost that would result from the operation of unused old plant.[1] To have lowered labour costs, it would have been necessary to acquire larger frames.

In the hackling operation between 1849–53 and 1864–68 a worker's output fell by a third measured in bundles (or a tenth by weight, owing of course to the production of heavier yarns). Earnings did not fall, with the result that there was a 70 per cent increase in labour costs. Early in the 1840's the partners had been quick to install the latest hackling machinery. In 1847 they scrapped over half the older machines and put in new Marsdens. James Marshall wrote in 1856 as if he had the situation well in hand. A new

---

[1] A supplementary explanation would be that productivity fell owing to an increase in the number of part-timers. Just as Marshall and Co. shifted to the employment of more young women in the later 1830's, they engaged more juveniles after 1850.

Children employed	Half-time	Full-time
1837	165	—
1851	376	164
1861	572	195

Since productivity was calculated by dividing output by all the workers in a department, the inclusion of part-timers would lower the average performance. At the same time, they should also have reduced average wage levels. But this did not happen (see Table 18, p. 326 below) so that this explanation seems less likely than the former. The increase in child labour was probably greatest in the hackling department.

machine had just appeared which raised the yield of line and dispensed with hand-feeding for the spreading frame.

We have got in three of Fairbairn's Sheet Hackling and the fourth is nearly ready.... They are good machines... but in the meantime, a Mr. Lowry of Manchester has brought out a patent improvement on the Sheet Hackling. ...We have a machine at work, I think it promises very well, and is likely to combine the advantages of the other two classes of hackling.... I think there is no department in which a greater opening exists for improvements to tell directly on profits than the hackling processes connected with it.[1]

The firm got Lowry to modify twenty-six of the Marsdens and as a result saved £10 a ton. But as James wrote, 'this is yet to be applied to a very large proportion of our consumption'.[2] New machines were added only as they were needed to cope with a growing volume of flax. By 1868 they had nine Lowry machines, a Combe, and a Horner from Belfast. Hence in the later 1860's a third of the plant was old, a third modified by Lowry, and a third installed since 1850. They could have done better than this, and economised on labour as Belfast firms apparently did. Even so, output per worker increased almost enough to offset a slight rise in average wages, and labour costs for machine-hackling remained fairly constant. To explain the *decline* in productivity in this department, it is necessary to consider the manual processes of sorting, jobbing and cleaning. In order to handle a growing volume of flax, the numbers engaged in these operations increased in the later 1850's and early 1860's. Concurrently average wages declined, suggesting the use of more unskilled or juvenile labour. Output per worker fell sharply in the later 1850's, rising a little but not so fast as wages in the 1860's. Unfortunately, the record is not complete enough to be certain what happened. Coarse flax would not need such careful handling; yet a decline in output per worker may perhaps reflect more careful work. But if as the evidence suggests the partners resorted to cheap labour for these preliminary manual tasks, they may not have been serving the best interests of the business.

Thus there are signs that labour costs rose owing to the numbers

---

[1] J. G. Marshall to H. C. Marshall, 13 September 1856; Greenwood, *Proc. Inst. Mech. Eng.* 1865, pp. 107–11 *passim*.

[2] J. G. Marshall to H. C. Marshall, 28 August 1857.

and quality of the working force and also because the firm's machinery was not so up-to-date as it had once been. Spending on plant declined after 1846, amounting to only £88,000 in the following twenty-six years, the lowest annual average since the post-war decade. Moreover, the larger part of this sum was spent before 1858 on twisting-frames, power-looms, and combing machines.

What happened then to James Marshall's intention to restore the fortunes of the firm by 'a new set of improvements'? As in the case of raw materials, he tried and failed. Uppermost in his mind was a scheme to introduce combing machinery, 'out of this we must purchase a renewal of our *good name*'.[1] Taking advantage once more of French ingenuity he installed ten combing machines in 1854. Two years earlier, Schlumberger had succeeded in upholding in Britain the patent of the combing machine which he had bought from Heilmann. Leeds spinners went to inspect the machine immediately. In September 1852 Thomas Lawson reported favourably to Hives and Atkinson on its usefulness for combing tow.[2] Next month Marshalls despatched a cargo of tow to Strassbourg for a demonstration. At this point, whether by accident or design, things went wrong. Their agent reported that Schlumberger 'had not any combing at work in Flax; they had broken the crank of their Steam Engine which drives the flax mill, and had adapted the flax combing to Silk.... They have not been able to adjust it so well to Flax as to other materials.'[3] Marshalls quite reasonably asked that a machine be sent to Leeds for trial. This the machine-makers 'would not listen to: they already had offers from very respectable parties in England. They proposed that we should agree provisionally upon terms...they undertaking not to offer it in the meantime to any other parties.'[4] This put Marshalls in a difficult situation. Schlumberger wanted (and got) £20,000 for flax combing, £30,000 for wool, and

[1] *Ibid.* 12 August, 1854.

[2] T. Lawson to Hives and Atkinson, 16 September 1852; Schlumberger and Co. to Messrs Marshall and Co., 9 September 1852. See also J. Burnley, *History of Wool and Woolcombing* (1889), pp. 221–41, 434.

[3] J. G. Marshall to A. Marshall, 29 August 1852; T. Ainsworth to Messrs Marshall and Co., 22 October 1852.

[4] J. G. Marshall to A. Marshall, 29 August 1852. It seems likely that just as in 1819 when Marshalls joined with Benyons and Titley in trying out the gill frame, they collaborated with Hives to test the usefulness of combing in 1852.

the same for cotton. Marshall and Co. could leave it; share it with others; or keep it to themselves.

What James would decide depended on his view of how useful the machine would be in restoring the reputation and fortune of Marshall and Co. To transform the plight of the firm it would have to produce one and probably two results. First it must enable him to spin yarns out of tow comparable in every respect with those spun out of line. 'They showed me yarn, spun they assured me from the same tow I saw, and which they sold as good line yarn....'[1] A little extra cost in combing and he would spin a smooth yarn that would make fine thread out of cheap tow. James had dreamed of something like this. Second, he hoped to replace hackling by combing. This would be a long-term effect. 'It is rather premature to form a judgement...for some purposes it probably may...but not I think for all purposes.' But he thought it not unreasonable that in the future they would

obtain from our finer hackled line and tow taken together, a far better material for finer spinning than we have ever yet obtained.... In endeavouring to get a fine fibre by hackling, we entirely spoil the best part of the flax which is alone capable of affording the finer fibre we want. We break it so short and cut it so severely, that all the finest fibre is worked out into the tow; and not only so, but it is made into such short fine tow that great part is actual waste.[2]

All this was speculation, but James, anxious to introduce an improvement, took a chance on acquiring the exclusive use of Schlumberger's combing machine. 'Everything turns on the real value of the invention; if it is what it professes, I do not see how we can do otherwise.'[3] In 1856, Marshall and Co. had seventy-four machines worth £20,000 at work, and up to 1861 (when Lister's patents expired) they paid £15,485 in royalties.

But the process failed to come up to James's expectations and Marshall and Co. did not repeat the gains which had come in the

---

[1] J. G. Marshall to A. Marshall, 29 August 1852. J. G. Marshall still thought that the firm led in innovations and held the first position in the trade in fine yarns. He also thought that a patent would save the 'time and trouble of perfecting the system'. On 21 October 1853 J. G. Marshall and P. Fairbairn registered a patent of a provisional nature, no. 2432, comprising modifications to the Heilmann machine.

[2] *Ibid.* 29 August 1852.

[3] *Ibid.*

past from sudden technological change. Indeed, combing produced no perceptible improvement at all in the firm's fortunes during the later 1850's. Since the introduction of rotary gills in 1849, a higher proportion of tow yarn had been transformed into thread and less offered for sale. After 1855 tow sales came to an end, presumably because all the tow was combed with a view to thread-making as James intended. In 1856 he boasted that they would gain £5000 a year from combing and obtain 100 lea thread from inferior flax.[1] The records do not show what happened. But between 1856 and 1860, when the firm spent over £35,000 on this machinery, its thread sales fell off and after 1858 tow yarns were again offered for sale in increasing quantities. Combing clearly failed to produce commercial results and, as more emphasis was placed on weaving, the manufacture of light tow yarns was discontinued. The subordinate hope, that the firm would use combing in place of hackling machines, never materialised. After 1861 Marshalls bought a few new machines from Fairbairns and Taylor Wordsworth, and ten years later they had seventy-six on their books. But the machines stood idle for many years and in 1874 all those made under Schlumberger's patent were scrapped.

After 1858, when it became apparent that James Marshall had failed to redeem the business by chemical retting and combing machinery, the partners should have tried other methods to improve their situation. Only a small proportion of the hackling and spinning machinery had been modernised in the past decade; or, in view of the profit made from cloth sales they might have converted the plant entirely to weaving and sought to establish a leading position for themselves in that field. But because the firm was ceasing to be profitable, any substantial outlay would have to come from the partners' own pockets, and they were reluctant to make great sacrifices. In 1857 James offered to sell his London residence and other property in order to raise £10,000: 'if it was really wanted I must of course

---

[1] J. G. Marshall to H. C. Marshall, 13 September 1856. Earlier he described combing as 'our sheet anchor', *ibid.* 19 August 1854; see also *ibid.* 15 February 1856. Combing produced finer thread from cheaper fibres, but its impact on the fortunes of the firm was not preponderating except perhaps in the negative sense of arresting the rate of decline. Primarily the fate of Marshalls turned on their fortunes as spinners of high-class yarns, and thread-making remained a subsidiary activity.

provide it'.[1] In general, the partners demurred to liquidate their other assets in order to invest in the mills. The £50,000 spent on machinery between 1847 and 1856 had brought little return and they were no longer optimistic about the firm's future prospects. As a result it proved difficult for the first time in more than half a century to raise risk capital for the business. Spending on new plant fell very low after 1858, old prime-movers were compounded to provide extra power, and economies were carried to such a pass that boilers with no more than a few years' life left in them were reinforced to carry an increase in steam pressure to save the cost of new ones.

The result was that the performance of Marshall and Co. declined relative to that of other spinners. Their labour and overhead costs were no lower in the 1860's than they had been a generation earlier; and owing to chronic trading losses they had no profits out of which they could improve the plant, and this aggravated their predicament. The great engine was being allowed to run down.

In the last analysis managerial fatalism and paralysis sealed the fate of Marshall and Co., although the final day of reckoning was postponed by civil war in the United States and later by the efforts of the founder's grandsons. During the founder's lifetime there had been signs that his sons would not prove capable of managing a large business successfully. Try as they would to imitate their father, they did not share his satisfaction in business as a way of life and they lacked his overriding ambition to become rich and distinguished. Besides making a considerable fortune out of wet spinning, the second generation had their future well provided for by incomes from other sources and they valued other activities more highly than business. When they were married and reached middle-age, they put other interests ahead of the firm: politics, foreign travel, a country life. Accordingly their presence in the mills became infrequent. John Richardson at Water Lane and Edward Parry at Castle Foregate could be trusted to look after the mills. Rightly believing that their plant was the most up-to-date in the world, it seemed reasonable to suppose that little would be gained from their continuous attendance at business. An occasional trip to Leeds in the later 1840's enabled

[1] J. G. Marshall to H. C. Marshall, 28 August 1857.

them to keep an eye on the installation of the power-looms and twisting spindles that had been decided upon before John Marshall died. James, who was elected to Parliament in 1846, lived chiefly in London when he was not at Coniston or abroad, and frankly confessed that 'Whilst in Parliament I am aware that I have given a greatly diminished amount of time to the business; I think I was fairly entitled to take such a position...if I wished it'.[1] Henry did not aspire to high political office, but much of his time was spent at Derwent Island, or serving as a director of the Leeds Northern Railway and attending to his investments in land and funds.

Accordingly, Marshall's sons modified their attitude towards the mills. Thinking that they had reached the acme of progress as spinners they became conservative and perhaps fatalistic. Business ceased to be an integral part of their lives. The enjoyment of their wealth and position became more important. As a result, what they expected from the firm underwent a gradual change. All the brothers had accumulated large amounts of capital in the business before 1846; James had £83,000, Henry £123,000 and Arthur £40,000. Each year they could count on upwards of £15,000 as rent and interest to be shared out between them. In addition there would be profits which were very welcome, but in a sense peripheral. Ever since the late 1830's trading profits had been falling, and in the fair years of the later 1840's when Henry earned £9000 a year from the business £8000 came from interest and rent. They thus became absentee rentiers, and this contributed to their apathy as managers.

In 1853, after two years of heavy trading losses amounting to £36,000 coupled with an obvious fall in the firm's prestige, James decided that something drastic must be done. Whereupon he resigned from Parliament, explaining to Henry '...you must admit that I acted with decision in retiring from that position as soon as I found it was my duty to take that step. You of course will have understood pretty well that it was not mere considerations of health that led me to that step; but seeing that our concern wanted my personal labour and attention.'[2] It was then that James, attributing their past success

[1] *Ibid.* 11 March 1853.
[2] *Ibid.* Cf. *ibid.* 23 August 1854, where J. G. Marshall stated that even allowing for flat trade 'independent of, and beyond that, the course of events for some years shows me decisively that we are in a very critical position....The large losses for two or three

to innovation and price competition (features common enough in a period of rapid change), sought unsuccessfully to put the firm back on this course. At the same time he endeavoured to arrest the drain on the firm's resources. Ever since the founder's death, both he and Henry had withdrawn far more than their earnings from the business.[1] Between 1846 and 1856 Henry took out an average of £15,000 a year and James £14,000. Such drawings together with the apportionment of losses reduced the value of their capital in the firm. Between 1849 and 1854 Henry's capital fell by £38,000; £13,000 was swallowed up in three years of loss and £25,000 augmented his earnings from other sources. Between 1846 and 1858 James almost halved his capital. Only Arthur, a bachelor, took out less than his current earnings in the mill. By drawing on this scale, James and Henry made serious inroads on the firm's working capital so that in 1856 James, then wanting to buy combing machinery, persuaded his brothers to agree to take out nothing further, not even interest and rent for the next few years. But their restraint lasted only two years and after 1858 Henry recommended a policy of window-dressing which began with an upward revaluation of the plant and a reduction in the rate of its depreciation.

Despite this energetic effort by James to revive the business, he failed for reasons other than the impracticality of his technical contributions or the shortage of capital. Compared with his father, James foundered because he would not persevere, because he was unwilling to put everything into business, because he neglected details and, in later life, lacked vision. Like his brothers he sensed a growing gulf between himself and those he employed. All the partners felt uneasy, even guilty at times, about the contrast between their wealth and the condition of the hands. As a result they dealt increasingly through

years together is proof of that.' On 19 August 1854, he wrote to Henry that he was 'determined...at whatever cost of care and money...to keep at all hazards our old place of ranking first in the market'. The business had fallen behind badly since the late 1840's, compared to Irish and Belgian spinners; and Strauss, their London agents, had been rubbing salt in their wounds.

[1] During his first decade as a partner, James drew only a fraction of his earnings from the firm, about £1000 a year; then between 1836 and 1847 he withdrew nearly nine-tenths of his earnings, about £12,000 a year. Henry's drawings remained modest until after his father's death, amounting to slightly over £3000 a year between 1831 and 1846, about a third of his earnings. Arthur withdrew some £1200 a year, an eighth of his earnings, during his first decade as a partner.

the mill manager—even when, on critical occasions, they might have appeared personally. And James tried to delegate this side of the business to Henry, claiming that only by doing so could he concentrate on the experiments which would be so vital for the firm's future prosperity. Everything depended on his success and must be subordinated to it.

Henry was disgusted with his brother; 'a strange notion must have been in his mind of what the general management consists in'.[1] He saw James as 'being of late absorbed in experiments of a doubtful importance', and this reinforced Henry's natural inclination to keep aloof. His wife had been ill for several years and he seldom came to Leeds. The year after her death in 1853, he left England for Germany soon after Easter, returned to Derwent Island in August, staying there until the end of the year. In fact he became a recluse, contenting himself with business interests outside the mills and preferring to avoid his brother. At bottom, he resented James's claim to control the business. All three had equal shares until 1871; but Henry had most capital in the concern and he bridled when James as the eldest claimed the right to dictate. Henry abhorred being asked for his own views on general policy simply to have them overruled summarily by James, who nonetheless expected him to 'assist in that which you disapprove'.[2] He refused to be a lackey in James's high-handed ill-judged schemes, and stayed away.

For his part, James, sensitive to his own deficiencies and indignant at Henry's attitude, badly needed help to make the business 'prosperously and profitably conducted instead of working to a loss as at present'[3]. Characteristically he reproached Henry in a forthright manner:

[1] Comments of H. C. Marshall on letter, J. G. Marshall to H. C. Marshall, 11 March 1853. See also *ibid.* 19 August 1854, where Henry complained that James failed to reach his objectives, and objects to the latter's moralising and lack of realism.

[2] J. G. Marshall to H. C. Marshall, 11 March 1853. Henry's isolation after his wife's death was subject to versification by his younger son:

> He yearns to sit in garb of sorrow,
> 'Neath his Blossoms precious sway,
> All night long, thus each tomorrow,
> Finds him sleepier than today.

(Marshall Collection at Derwent Island.)

[3] J. G. Marshall to H. C. Marshall, 11 March 1853.

I place in the first rank of importance a better understanding and a more hearty and active co-operation amongst ourselves. We are far too much isolated each in our own departments, not acting in harmony, nor rendering mutual assistance as we ought to do. More especially I think does this remark apply to yourself. I do not recollect another instance of a principal partner in our concern before, taking so little active share in the *general practical management* of our concern taken as a whole.[1]

Henry had apparently attended to the erection of a few new out-buildings, looked after 'matters of Trustee management for which we are jointly responsible', and (with considerable foresight) favoured further development in the weaving department much to the dismay of James.

But in the great mass of work to be done in carrying on the main manufac-tory, personal superintendence of the personnel, of the material, of the machinery in the mills, the introduction and working out of improvements of whatever description, in which hitherto all the principal partners have taken an active part, it seems to me that we are grievously in want of your [Henry's] active personal thought, attention, and assistance. For the most part you pass over all those matters as if you had no responsibility or share of work to do in them,...and content yourself with general remarks as to results, thinking you have done enough when you have pointed out defects in what exists, or suggested doubts and difficulties in the way of any plans for improvement suggested or actively worked out by myself or Arthur. Mind I am not saying that all the blame of this rests with you. I am not making these remarks with a view to exonerating myself and throwing the blame on others for what is past. I am aware that there is a blame on all sides; what I am anxious to secure is a right understanding and better co-operation for the future.[2]

The collaboration which the founder had managed to secure during his lifetime became unattainable after his death. To complete the picture, neither James nor Henry would co-operate with Arthur. James praised his youngest brother as 'zealous, hard-working, [giving] close attention to the business', but confessed that he was sorely tried by Arthur's irritability.[3] Arthur was rather simple, without talent and very conscious of his inferiority. He had according to his birthright been fitted into the firm and, keeping himself timorously apart, pretended to do some useful work. By comparison

[1] J. G. Marshall to H. C. Marshall, 11 March 1853; see also *ibid.* 19 August 1854.
[2] *Ibid.* 11 March 1853. [3] *Ibid.*

his brothers seemed successful men of the world taking everything easily in their stride; and, confusing their appearance with their achievement, Arthur was envious. So he too held aloof, resenting any interference from his brothers. As James told Henry, 'This carping, uncomplying temper in Arthur as respects you is very greatly owing to that very isolation and want of active interest and co-operation into which you have fallen. You would find it greatly diminish the moment he felt you were working alongside him instead of merely criticising what he does. I always find it so.'[1]

Unable to secure co-operation from Henry—'you seem disposed to let things slip on much as usual'—James might well have ignored his brother and managed the business alone. In fact as regards policy James had dictated what went on for at least a decade, and by bringing Christopher Empson into the firm in 1849 and Reginald Marshall five years later, Henry thoughtfully provided substitutes to do his work for him. But James, who shared Henry's distaste for business, expected his brother to put in at least as much work as he did. 'In your plans... I cannot perceive that you have what I should consider an adequate perception of the amount of *extra* personal exertion that is due from each of us.'[2] Moreover James frankly did not trust the juniors to make and introduce improvements or to devise a system of piece-rates which the hands would accept. These tasks, which urgently needed attending to if business was to be recovered, required the experienced judgement of a senior and, lest he became overburdened, the senior was to be Henry. But even Henry's compliance would not have ended the matter because he always acted 'in rather too isolated a manner'. Even more than his active effort, James wanted his brother's moral support. Henry's indifference towards James, and hence as James thought towards the business, became increasingly distressing when first one and then another of James's schemes miscarried. 'Certainly you have concurred [in James's plans] but only in a lukewarm manner. You may think them rash and speculative; but still once we are decided...it seems strange to me you should take so little personal interest in them.'[3] By 1857 James was very fretful, 'I have never complained of your impatience at the repeated

[1] *Ibid.*   [2] *Ibid.*
[3] *Ibid.*

failures to reach the success I am aiming at.... I wish you would estimate more fairly what has been really done...and then you would look forward: not without anxiety I grant, but not so gloomily as you do.'[1] After two years of further loss in 1855–6 amounting to £62,000, James began to despair. Combing machinery had not saved the situation; and he stopped his steeping experiments, offering to sell Patrington. He had lost confidence in his methods, and wearied with his brother's criticisms he gave up, deciding that the time had come for him to withdraw from an active business life. After declaring in public that the Leeds flax industry was stagnating he retired to Monk Coniston, and spent much of his time in Italy.[2] At the time of his death fifteen years later, he had almost passed from living memory in Leeds.

James had tried and failed. His gradual withdrawal at the end of the 1850's gave Henry a chance to rescue the firm. With his interest in weaving he might have transformed Marshall and Co. into producers of cloth. But only forty looms were installed in the early 1860's. One difficulty was raising capital internally. Another was that James, who considered Marshall and Co. to be first and foremost spinners, would have opposed such a scheme. At least Henry might have tried. But he had been away from the factory too long and felt too old to return to a way of life that he found repugnant. Overcome by boredom, he had no desire to pull James's chestnuts out of the fire and did not intend to put his own in.

By default, control of the mills at Leeds slipped more and more into the hands of John Richardson, the manager. He had joined the firm along with Marshall's sons in the 1820's and enjoyed their confidence. Like them, he remembered the good old days and clung meticulously to old methods. As the effective control over appointments

[1] J. G. Marshall to H. C. Marshall, 28 August 1857.

[2] Cf. Whewell to sister, 6 October 1858. Health reasons took James to Italy for six months. The correspondence between James and Henry is important for other reasons. It shows that they seldom came face to face with each other. Communication by letter took a day in the Lakes or a week from Europe to reach the recipient. This meant a considerable delay which could on occasion be very detrimental to the business; see the episode of the strike 1871–2, below, when letters crossed in all directions and it proved difficult to bring about a meeting at which some decisions could be taken. Not only the personalities of the partners, but also the mechanics of conducting business conspired to injure the firm.

passed into his hands, he soon placed his brother and other friends into prominent positions with salaries of between £300 and £500 a year. The only member of the family continuously on the spot, living just outside Leeds, was the son of the late John Marshall II, Reginald Dykes Marshall, who joined the business after leaving Trinity College in 1854. Reginald was twenty-two then, ten years older than any of Henry's or James's sons; three years later in 1857 he became a partner without any capital, an unenviable position because in view of the firm's losses he got no income. So the following year Henry transferred £6000 to his nephew's account, thus assuring him of £300 a year. But the slight interest Reginald had in the business was extinguished by his uncles who refused to grant him any authority, and his earnings were pitiably small on the threshold of matrimony. At the end of his mother's life, he would one day inherit his father's estates and he looked forward to this.

Thus the firm suffered from creeping managerial paralysis. Henry objected to James's authority only a little more than he disliked working with Empson or Arthur. James, having failed in what he set out to do, had decided to withdraw. Henry had no intention of returning to the mills and Arthur had no desire to wrest control himself. The juniors, who were closer to the mills, were not allowed to introduce alterations which they thought would improve the business. Authority resided in the two seniors, both splendidly isolated in the Lake District or even more inaccessible in foreign parts, both content to draw their share of rent and interest, and both willing to avoid quarrels by remaining aloof. Such control as they chose to exercise from time to time was confined to the particular parts of the business which nominally came within each brother's province. In practice, little was done; the piece-rates which James had wanted were not introduced, and by neglecting labour relations and allowing Richardson too much power, especially over appointments and promotions, they stored up trouble for the future.[1]

---

[1] Cf. *Leeds Express*, 15 March 1872. As in the founder's day, the partners continued to reward the most efficient workers with an extra 1*d*. or 2*d*. a week. However, by the 1870's this radical newspaper suggested that these small sums granted by absentee plutocrats were an insult. J. G. Marshall reacted to such attacks by suggesting co-partnership schemes (which started in the district at least as early as the mid-1860's) in order to re-establish a more harmonious relationship with the hands.

If the firm had continued to incur losses on the scale of the 1850's, the partners would have been compelled to take more radical decisions in the 1860's. They were saved, however, by the course of external events. The civil war in the United States brought linens into prominence as a substitute for cotton cloth and offered a tremendous opportunity to spinners, unlike anything since Napoleon's blockade. Imports of flax, tow and codilla into the United Kingdom increased by 40 per cent in the period 1862–5 over the previous four years. At Water Lane the plant that had been laid on one side was brought into use, the labour force raised to over 2500, and for a couple of years the firm spun over 400,000 bundles of yarn. In the three years from 1862 profits at Water Lane amounted to nearly £80,000, or *net* of Castle Foregate's losses to nearly £70,000. This unexpected turn of events gave the business a reprieve and provided the partners with the means to buy new plant. However, Henry decided to withdraw all he could, and between 1863 and 1867 he took £98,000 from the firm, nearly £30,000 more than his earnings in those years. And though James withdrew only £33,000 which was less than his earnings, and Arthur hardly anything at all, most of their recent gains were devoured by Henry, and none of them was invested in renovating the plant. The number of spinning spindles was allowed to decline in the late 1860's and new machines were bought sparingly to replace only what was absolutely necessary.

After the war the need to consider the firm's future receded so far as the second generation was concerned. In the later 1860's their sons became of age and assumed their inheritance. After a transitional period, the safe-keeping of the business would be vested in the third generation. For a time Henry even took a more active role in the firm's affairs. His two sons, being older than their cousins, came into the business a few years earlier, and in order both to shield them from his brother and to secure their future ascendancy Henry began to influence what went on. But his interest was purely dynastic and did not extend to the plant and its performance.

The tragedy of Marshall and Co. lies in the behaviour of the founder's sons in the twenty-five years after his death. First they sacrificed the business to other ends. As James wrote to Henry in

1853, 'Surely you and I, and through us, our concern have done enough already in both money and time to make it necessary to meet our further expenditure with great strictness'.[1] When money was required to improve the prospects of the firm, they hesitated to dip into their pockets. Indeed they had become rentiers counting on a fixed annual tribute from their outlays in real estate, in funds, and in the firm. Such a situation would not have been to the detriment of the business if the second generation had felt the same consuming passion for business as the founder. But they were less interested in making money than in spending it. Consequently they devoted less time to the mills so that they could undertake other activities after 1840, and their negligence suggests a growing dissatisfaction with business as a full-time occupation.

At first they thought it was safe to place their other interests in front because Marshall and Co. were unquestionably the greatest flax-spinners in the world. But in the early 1850's when it became obvious that the firm was slipping, they failed to improve matters. This was their second defect. James made a commendable effort to reduce costs once he realised their plight but his schemes went astray. If he had considerable scientific talent, he was also a poor business-man. Prejudice prevented him from extending weaving and he made no real effort to modernise the plant. If most of his ideas were fundamentally sound, he tended to concentrate on them at the expense of other equally important considerations, and he sadly lacked the ability to achieve the results he aimed at in practice.

James's efforts were worthy but pathetic; those of Henry were negligible. A strong antipathy towards James, and family misfortunes reinforced his melancholy disposition; in addition to which he had misgivings about the casuistry involved in defending the condition of their workers. In practice he attended to the commercial side with the minimum of effort. However, even if Henry had been more energetic and enthusiastic he would have been no more effective than James. For if James's vision was limited by virtue of his early duties in the mills to the improvement of plant, Henry lacking experience of that side of the business failed to appreciate the need for technological advance. In a peculiar way he was as unrealistic as James.

---

[1] J. G. Marshall to H. C. Marshall, 11 March 1853.

Henry had a passion for statistics, and on becoming a partner in 1831 he had introduced a very elaborate system of accounts and checks which occupied him throughout the year.[1] These recorded in summary form almost every dimension of the firm capable of measurement, and their extent and repetition suggest that compilation became an end in itself and not a tool to facilitate the conduct of business.[2] This misplaced enthusiasm did not matter because the founder continued his own accounts. But after John Marshall's death the partners had no succinct Profit and Loss or annual check account. Instead Henry provided a mine of information, which if it had been digested or communicated to his brothers would have proved useful. But Henry was not communicative, and James found difficulty in following Henry's figures. As he complained on one occasion, 'I do not understand how the account of orders...is made up so large'.[3] There was fortunately no disagreement over profits. These were still calculated by the balance of assets over liabilities at the annual stock-take. But Henry's devotion to figures reflected his remote, somewhat phlegmatic, attitude towards business. By filtering the performance of the firm in such a way, he readily confused the shadow of his own creation with the substance. He never looked closely at what was going on and when he decided that a particular policy was desirable, for instance the extension of weaving, he lacked determination and was not prepared to meet the personal cost that would have been called for to push it through.

Finally, in addition to their indifference and shortcomings as businessmen, the partners failed to co-operate in their common interests. The advantages that might have arisen from specialisation were outweighed by the disadvantages. At best each partner restricted himself to his own special province; at worst they left their duties in abeyance. Henry's records provided an overall view of the firm's position and James believed that he held its destiny in his hands. But the kind of solution that might have come from their

[1] For H. C. Marshall's passion for figures, see Concerning some Commercial Monkeys, below, p. 289, and his papers, e.g. 'Altitudes Book', in the Derwent Island Collection.

[2] The indexes in these ledgers, very little of which survive, indicate their scope. The annual series begin in 1849 and carry quinquennial averages for the previous twenty years. J. Marshall, 'Notebook', 1820–33, carries an itemisation of the basic accounts kept under this system, dated January 1831.

[3] J. G. Marshall to H. C. Marshall, 13 September 1856.

joint endeavour did not materialise because they could not work in harness together. James found such a simple matter as meeting face to face difficult to arrange: 'I am especially desirous that before we are both absent abroad we may have sufficient time together at Leeds to originate and set to work some of the larger improvements that are likely to tell upon the main results of the concern in the way of profit and loss, as well as of character and standing in the trade.'[1] Henry treated such overtures with suspicion, and the mutual confidence required for successful collaboration was utterly lacking.

Times were hard and the mills no longer made a profit. With each bad year, frost spread deeper into their hearts and they dissipated their inheritance. At the same time despite their boredom and distaste for business, they were attached to the firm like a child to its playthings. They venerated a great deal, perhaps too much, the daily round and physical reality of the mills and the family achievement which they symbolised. Because they envisaged Marshall and Co. as a family firm they refused even to consider raising money outside in order to modernise it, and they clung all too tenaciously to their past methods and success. Beyond such feelings, however, the mills could not be closed because the founder's sons held them as if in trust for his grandsons. But when they came to discharge their duty, the greatness of Marshalls as a firm had gone. The scales had turned decisively against its recovery as rot spread deeper into every corner of the business.

John III and Stephen, Henry's two sons, left Cambridge in the early 1860's and with capital transfers of £10,000 each from their father entered the partnership in 1867 and 1871 respectively. James's eldest son, Victor, who was by all accounts a very colourful character, had his patrimony assured and kept out of the business. But his younger brother, James Garth Marshall, joined the partnership at the age of twenty-eight in 1871 with a capital of £7000 from his father.

With so little interest-bearing capital and with no share in the rent, the junior partners faced beggarly prospects and soon grew dissatisfied. To appease them the seniors inserted clauses in the

[1] *Ibid.* 11 March 1853.

articles of partnership guaranteeing the juniors some income. The first, included in 1861 to succour Christopher Empson and Reginald Marshall, stated that 'the three seniors shall guarantee to the two junior partners, that their share of profits, over and above the credits in their accounts by way of interest on capital, shall not on the average of the three years be less than their respective shares of an annuity of £10,000 for each year of this term'.[1] The next agreement, drawn up during the cotton crisis, decreed that the two juniors would receive 'to the extent of their shares an average amount of not less than £12,000 annual profit' during the three-year term. In 1867 the seniors guaranteed 'a surplus to be divided among the junior partners as their share of profit, in the proportion of their shares, of not less than £2000 per annum over and above the 5 per cent on... capital'. (No partner could draw more than £125 per share a year: and the juniors had thirty-four shares out of 100.) After 1871 interest payments were discontinued and no further concessions were made to the juniors except in respect of their liability for losses.

No one was satisfied when it came to sharing out poverty, least of all the third generation, most of whom were near thirty and had wives and children to provide for. What they derived from the business would never secure them a place in the same social circles as their parents and grandfather. Reginald came off best. He had been the first to enter the firm and left perforce along with Empson when his cousins appeared on the scene. Between 1862 and 1864 his capital grew from £8600 to £14,900, and by 1870 stood at £20,500. He earned £8000 as interest (helped by periodic revaluations of plant) and £14,000 as profit (having paid £600 towards losses and gained in 1870–1 from the 'guarantee clause'). But an income of less than a thousand a year at the age of thirty-eight was not exciting. He gladly withdrew his capital and retired to Keswick where he spent the rest of his days looking after his father's estate. Four years after joining the partnership the capital of John III had grown by only £900. He had earned £1800 as interest and £1500 as profit (half under the 'guarantee clause'); his drawings amounted to £600 a year. James Garth came off worse. In three years after 1871 he received £1400 as his share of profit and withdrew half of it, not enough to

---

[1] 'Leeds Ledger', 1806–70 (bk. IV), pp. 285–7 and (bk. IX) pp. 3–9.

meet the cost of his widespread interests in local politics, music, education and travel.[1]

The situation of John Marshall's grandsons was far from promising. They had social position but not the means to maintain it. If they were fortunate, they might in due course inherit sufficient for their lifetime. Meanwhile they could expect little from a run-down firm. Lacking the tie which bound their parents to the founder, the third generation actively despised the firm whereas their fathers had merely neglected it.[2] In their eyes, it was a great sham. Not only were they appalled with the problems to be faced but they were also aghast at the trust placed in Richardson, the mill manager. The unhealthy atmosphere of the mills repelled them. But even if they had been keen businessmen—which they were not—ready to start introducing improvements, they soon discovered that their parents intended to retain control just as the founder had done in his day.

Christopher Empson left in 1870 and Reginald Marshall two years later, taking £53,000 out of the business. The remaining juniors began to grow rebellious, and simultaneously relations with the hands deteriorated disastrously. The second generation was about to reap what it had sown.

Apart from three brief stoppages in 1819, 1829 and 1852, there had never been any serious labour troubles at Water Lane. Of course Marshalls paid low wages and any gains that accrued went to capital. But they had a good reputation as employers during the founder's day. Afterwards their lenience made them popular. When trade was dull, they worked a short week rather than dismiss hands who might be difficult to secure again.

In the autumn of 1871 when trade showed signs of reviving, the operatives demanded a 10 per cent pay increase.[3] On Friday,

---

[1] *Yorkshire Post*, 2 September 1874; *Leeds Mercury*, 2 September 1874.

[2] See the cartoon on p. 283, from the Derwent Island Collection. It depicts dragon Marshalls springing from the house on Derwent Island and devouring people in the mills. This indicates a contempt for business as a mode of plunder.

[3] The following section is based on correspondence between partners; 'Minutes of the Meetings of the Leeds and District Association of Factory Occupiers', 1872–5, kept by S. A. Marshall; and the 'Strike Book', a collection of cuttings and comments kept mainly by S. A. Marshall. Together these sources present the *management's* reaction to the events of 1871–2.

11 August, 600 girls, a quarter of the labour force, staged a protest strike to support this claim. Next day they returned to work. The following Monday a few hundred left the mills after dinner to demonstrate in the street. Richardson went out to threaten them without success. Stephen, one of the two junior partners on the spot, watched from a window. Next day he closed the mills.

In a letter to his father he claimed that a one day lock-out would bring the girls to their senses.[1] But the source of the trouble lay deeper than a mere wage claim which Stephen was prepared to concede—'we shall in any case have to advance spinning wages'—at 3*d*. a week. He traced the unrest to Temple Mill, 'as bad a lot of men as we have', particularly the foreman 'who by his own incompetence and barefaced neglect of duty has done more than anything else to ruin *A* mill'. On their side the men objected to the intrusion of the new juniors who wanted to introduce changes and they were using the girls to achieve their own object, a retention of the *status quo*. Stephen wanted to resort to 'violent measures'. He proposed the public dismissal of the Temple foreman in such a way as to ruin him and the replacement of all the existing overlookers by new men. This was easier said than done. He confessed that 'we have no man in *A* spinning who is at all likely for the supreme command there', and the men 'felt that we have no one ready to replace them with'.

James and Arthur, the other seniors, received copies of this letter. James, who saw a spark of hope, wrote to Henry in support of Stephen's belligerent if rather inconclusive proposals.[2] But Henry, Arthur, and Reginald, the other junior at Leeds, recoiled from such cavalier treatment. 'My firm belief', the latter wrote, 'is that ten words from one of us on the mill steps...would have prevented this business'.[3] The thought uppermost in their minds was 'it comes upon us at a bad time as regards trade because there are certainly signs of a revival'.[4] Nothing would be gained by interference. Instead they wanted to avail themselves of the profit which had unexpectedly come their way, for all three knew how difficult this had become of late. To be prompt with their deliveries, the

---

[1] S. A. Marshall to H. C. Marshall, 14 August 1871.
[2] J. G. Marshall to H. C. Marshall, 15 August 1871.
[3] R. D. Marshall to H. C. Marshall, 15 August 1871.
[4] *Ibid.*

most sensible course of action would be to placate the hands by raising their wages. It was tiresome, but expedient. On Wednesday, 16 August, the mills were reopened. Arthur hurried to Leeds from Hallsteads and prevented his nephew from going ahead with his radical schemes. To reach a settlement, he met a deputation of hands

Fig. 3. Cartoon: the mill-owners of Derwent Island seizing the profits of the Water Lane and Castle Foregate mills.

and agreed to negotiate, not about a 10 per cent rise which he considered to be beyond the means of the firm but on an allied question of hours. If both sides could agree on Saturday working time, then they would consider some improvement in wage-rates.

These talks dragged on for days, and as each day passed the chances of a settlement narrowed. The hands learnt how much other operatives earned in local and far-off mills and their restlessness increased. The *Leeds Express* added fuel to the fire by contrasting the poverty and insecurity of a worker's life with the spending and luxury of their absentee employers.[1] Attitudes hardened and the hands stood by their 10 per cent demand.

On his side Arthur had prolonged the negotiations because he wanted a family conference to settle what he judged to be the most serious labour unrest within memory. He called one for Saturday, 19 August, at Keswick, within easy reach of most partners. But James offered only to go to Leeds. So the meeting was arranged there for the following weekend. James dallied again, protesting that his domestic affairs had priority, and offered to go only 'if really wanted'. At the same time he changed his mind about what they ought to do. 'Looking at the general state of trade and wages we may have two to five years of brisk trade, and advancing wages; and if we get into a great or obstinate dispute with our people may be crippled all that time.... Our dispersed hands would supply the other Flax Spinners.'[2] Henry had a painful leg which made it difficult for him to leave Derwent Island, and the juniors were in no hurry to set off for Leeds. Arthur grew fretful, feeling that some definite offer had to be made to the hands, and in the absence of the other partners, he had to reach a decision by himself.

Since there had been no rise since November 1865, he proposed to raise wages liberally, but individually. In this way the trouble-makers in the Temple Mill could be punished, and James and Stephen would not repudiate what he had done. Arthur certainly writhed at the responsibility he had shouldered alone; 'I am sorry that John did not arrive this forenoon, but I hope to have done the best under the circumstances'.[3] Next day, Friday, 25 August, Richardson communicated the offer to the hands, who rejected it and gave a week's strike notice.

Two days later, two junior partners reached Leeds. John III did not conceal his impatience at the summons. 'We want to get away on Wednesday if we can, and certainly if there is nothing to be done

[1] *Leeds Express*, 18 August 1871.

[2] J. G. Marshall to H. C. Marshall, 25 August 1871. James wanted to remain near his eldest brother William, who lay ill at Patterdale and died on 16 May 1872. See *Leeds Mercury*, 21 May 1872.

[3] A. Marshall to H. C. Marshall, 24 August 1871.

except to determine the scale of the advance we might as well have stayed at Coniston.'[1] In the absence of James and Henry, the conference was a one-sided affair. Even John III wrote to his father, saying 'I wish we could have had your confirmation'. However, after some discussion, a policy emerged.[2] Henry's sons still wanted a radical reshuffle. They argued that the hands had put themselves in the wrong by walking out in the first instance and must expect punishment. Arthur and James's son favoured conciliation in order to take advantage of the trading situation. They compromised. Wages would be increased 1s. a week, about the 10 per cent asked for; and for the present they would not dismiss or lower the wages of the overseers in mill *A* but they would endeavour to promote amenable young men to responsible positions with a view to introducing changes in the future. In addition, Arthur warned his nephews that 'the rearrangement may call for rather more mill supervision from ourselves. I think for the next month or so, it will require us to go into that line.'[3]

The meeting ended on Wednesday (30 August) and everyone left for the Lakes, except the two youngest partners, Stephen and James Garth, who were to put the proposals into effect. The wage increase averted the impending strike. But the young men selected for promotion refused for reasons varying from their own or their wife's health to an outspoken aversion towards mill *A*. Short of some dismissals—which they had agreed to avoid—Stephen felt he could do nothing except perhaps recruit and train outsiders for supervisory posts. Finally, as proof of their presence in the mills, the junior partners decided to open an Attendance Book. They proposed to be present thirty-nine weeks a year and in order to qualify for a day's attendance they had to sign in before 11 a.m.—'except Saturday—when *attendance* at all might count as half a day'.[4] This did nothing,

[1] J. Marshall III to H. C. Marshall, 28 August 1871.
[2] The main issue concerned the rearrangement of the mills. H. C. Marshall and A. Marshall were against it, and J. G. Marshall who had been for it changed sides suddenly, see J. G. Marshall to H. C. Marshall, 23 August 1871. The third generation favoured a change. See J. G. Marshall to H. C. Marshall, 23, 25 August 1871; A. Marshall to H. C. Marshall, 19, 21, 24, 26 August 1871; J. Marshall III to H. C. Marshall, 28, 30 August 1871; S. A. Marshall to H. C. Marshall, 28, 29 August 1871; R. D. Marshall to H. C. Marshall, 31 August 1871.
[3] A. Marshall to H. C. Marshall, 30 August 1871.
[4] J. Marshall III to H. C. Marshall, 5 March 1872.

however, to settle the question of responsibilities. James disagreed that the juniors should be left a free hand. He had no qualms about telling Stephen what to do when he took over the line-repairing department; and Henry regarded this interference with his son's activity as a personal affront. As in the past, the senior partners were ready to revive old feuds, argue about their rights, and do nothing whatever to help the business or their successors. In June 1872 James agreed to allow the boys free scope in managing their own departments, 'subject only in more important matters to the cognizances and approval of the other partners'.[1] He was concerned of course to keep a voice in the firm's affairs. His capital had dwindled and his son had little enthusiasm. It looked as if the mills would pass entirely under the control of Henry and his family. At the same time, as a result of his own experience, James tried to prevent each junior from becoming engrossed in his own little province.

The junior partners entering the management should have free scope each in his own department to arrange it generally, and make experiments with the view to improvements according to his judgement and his own responsibility...all parts of the business will be open to the inspection and suggestions as to change or improvements, by all the partners.[2]

To the juniors it seemed as if the second generation were bent on stifling the efforts of their successors. The destructive chaos of piece-meal responsibility, the endless quibbling about where initiative should end and interference began, thus continued unchecked. And so far as labour relations went, the unimaginative settlement that had been patched up in 1871 brought no real satisfaction to any party.

In October 1871 the local engineering industry conceded a 9-hour day and John III declared that this gave spinners a 'case for voluntary and prompt action'.[3] To compensate their male employees for the longer hours which they worked, Marshalls granted an 8 per cent wage increase. As soon as this issue had been settled, the hands pressed for Saturday work to end at 12.30, a point outstanding from the earlier negotiations. John III hurriedly consulted nearby spinners and agreed 'to anticipate the demand...and concede the point with good grace....By acting at once we had the appearance

[1] J. G. Marshall to H. C. Marshall, 26 June 1872.   [2] *Ibid.*
[3] J. Marshall III to H. C. Marshall, 15 October 1871.

of giving it without pressure.'[1] The seniors had counselled the juniors to avoid disputes which would injure trade. But no sooner had the latter capitulated to current demands than their seniors were indignant, holding that the business could not afford both higher wages and shorter hours. The wage rise of 2 September would add £5200 to costs in a full year and to reduce expenses the partners agreed to forgo interest amounting to £16,000 a year on their capital from 1 January 1872. Marshall and Co. had gained very little from the dislocation of the French linen industry in 1870–1 and the seniors became very anxious about the survival of the firm.

As usual, James had some ideas. For the first time he made the momentous proposal that Marshalls should spin jute. But his brothers did not take him seriously; Marshall and Co. were flax-spinners. Secondly, he wanted the firm to engage a fresh set of hands, workers from the countryside who had little to do in winter and would accept lower wages. (Perhaps he had in mind docile farm labourers from the Coniston district.) However, the other partners did not for a moment relish the idea of replacing even the present labour force with unskilled strangers from afar. Finally James emphasised the obvious need to raise productivity. Wherever possible work-loads should be raised and the hands paid piece-rates. Other tasks such as the cleaning of machinery might be made more efficient by subcontracting.

A head cleaner responsible with a gang at wages fixed by us, on recommendation of head cleaner. Number employed fixed in like manner....Of course there will be some difficulty in fixing what is cleaning, what repairs. ...If they economise on the sum fixed, to have half the difference as profit.... That is the most practicable way for us to introduce the principle of partnership between ourselves and the work people.... Then each gang of cleaners would have the opportunity of making profit on the job by diligence and good work. They would keep down useless numbers and send away useless hands themselves.[2]

John III and Stephen wanted to start piece-rates where output could be immediately and easily examined and recorded. They proposed to introduce the system in roving, spinning and weaving. To

---

[1] *Ibid.* 18, 20 October 1871.
[2] Copy of J. G. Marshall's suggestions, 23 October 1871. The operatives suspected any general introduction of piece-rates, because, with a reduction in hours, their earnings were likely to fall. See 'Strike Book', 6 February 1872.

encourage workers to watch three instead of two sides, John III suggested a 25 per cent increase in pay from 7s. 3d. to 10s. 6d. a week. But he shied from subcontracting, feeling that it assumed 'a capacity for management [in the ganger] which I am sure is very rare, and would probably make a man's fortune if he set up in business on his own account'.[1]

Although one of James's proposals—that concerning piece-rates—bore fruit later, in the short run the discussion led nowhere. The seniors preferred to coerce the hands by threats largely based on a picture of the firm's vulnerability to unfair foreign competition. The workers refused higher loads without more pay. The junior partners were more than ever convinced that both their uncles and the hidebound overseers must go. Otherwise they would leave themselves.

On 4 March 1872, a two-month strike began. It was part of a widespread movement for a 54-hour week without a reduction in pay. The senior partners at Marshall and Co. were no longer anxious for peace because, contrary to their former expectations, trade had fallen off and a four-day week had been imminent for some time. The juniors welcomed the break as an opportunity to alter the machinery and prepare a new system of working. The family was unanimous. They would only reduce hours along with wages. Henry Marshall, placing himself at the head of the trade, returned to Leeds and rallied almost a hundred local firms to present a solid front against the operatives' demands; in short they agreed not to hire strikers from each other's mills. And his son Stephen's policy was summed up as meeting 'brute force with brute force'.[2]

After a few weeks some impoverished male workers left the town.[3]

[1] J. Marshall III to H. C. Marshall, 27 October 1871.

[2] *Leeds Express*, 27 March 1872. The third generation welcomed the strike as an opportunity to engineer the changes they wanted. On 16 February 1872, ten days after a petition from the town's textile operatives, there was a meeting of Leeds spinners, who on 8 March 1872 formed 'the Leeds and District Association of Factory Occupiers'. H. C. Marshall was elected chairman and S. A. Marshall one of the four secretaries. Soon a National Federation of such groups was suggested to meet organised labour on equal terms; and in London on 10 November 1874, over fifty delegates met, representing employers with over a million operatives. See 'Minute Book', pp. 49–51.

[3] 'Strike Book', pp. 29, 31, 45, 87, 93, 103, 134–6. This contains a full account of the collection for and the dole paid to the strikers. The first payment, at the end of nine days, amounted to £270 and was distributed at the rate of 4d. to 1s. 4d. for women and children, men receiving nothing.

Others eked out a miserable existence on doles of a few pence paid by the strike committee. Fortunately, from a human point of view, women and children who comprised the majority of the strikers were supported by other wage-earners. At the same time, the large firms rescued small ones whose credit payments fell due. The atmosphere was very bitter, the gulf wide.

At the end of March some weak links broke. Several small firms agreed to shorter hours for the same pay and took back their hands. Early in April Marshalls made overtures, offering to compensate workers from 3*d* to 2*s*. a week for working longer hours (intending of course to raise work-loads), but the partners refused to re-engage the strike leaders. On 9 April 400 children returned, and those still out stoned the mills, the first mass hostile act in the street since the Chartists came to town in 1841. Late in April when every other mill had restarted, the hands came back. Marshall and Co. had a new reputation as 'the scrubbiest employers in or within twenty miles of Leeds'.[1]

The outcome was a victory for the junior partners. The agitators never came back, and the senior partners withdrew. The third generation could if it wanted at last try to repair some of the damage to profits and status incurred during the past twenty-five years, unless it was now too late.

The rigid conservatism of the seniors, their refusal to copy competitors and raise resources outside as a private or public company, and the wide gulf between the two generations was parodied by one junior at this time under the title

CONCERNING SOME COMMERCIAL MONKEYS[2]

Once upon a time a set of monkeys of different kinds associated themselves for the purpose of making and selling jam. Jam was quite unknown in Tartary where they lived, when first they set up business; at least in its artificial state. All that ever came to market was collected from holes in the rocks or from the beds of rivers; so these monkeys turned a pretty

---

[1] 'Strike Book', p. 101. (Strikers' meetings were held in the Co-operative Hall, opposite Marshall's mills.) Cf. Mayhall, *op. cit.* vol. 1, p. 484.

[2] This document, based on Swift's parody, was discovered at Derwent Island at a late stage by the author and confirms many points dimly apparent in the other evidence. It is in the hand of J. Marshall III, and internal evidence indicates that it was written sometime in October/November 1871. The names in brackets indicate the persons referred to.

penny, and got very fat. Some people say the fat got into their heads. However, as other animals learnt the art of making jam, and how much gravel could be put in it without anyone finding it out, our friends became by degrees less busy; and they naturally began to look out for some new means of attracting customers. One principle at all events had been instilled into these monkeys, it was this that when they wished to find things they should look straight before their noses and not cast chance glances here and there, upwards and downwards. Now the wise old monkey who taught them this unfortunately did not tell them that they ought to move their noses round to another direction when they found after close examination that nothing whatever lay before them. He took it for granted that they would understand this—Unhappily they didn't understand it. So it fell out, that having their noses irrevocably fixed in one direction, through their misinterpretation of the wise old monkey's precept and seeing that what they wanted to find in order to restore their business, did not happen to lie in the direction in which their noses were trained, it was easy to see that as long as this state of things continued their affairs would not improve.

After a time the younger monkeys [the third generation] began to lose their respect for the precept seeing that it led to nothing tangible, and they began to try and slew round the three old monkeys, who stood in a row with their twelve legs planted solidly in the mud, in order that they might catch sight of certain interesting objects which were quite apparent to the young monkeys. However they were obliged to desist from their attempt as it made the old ones choke in such an awful manner that some people thought the end of the world was come. The young monkeys were very different in manners and appearance—the youngest was rather a dandy and had a gold tassel at the end of his tail. His name was Huzzy [James Aubrey Garth Marshall], and sometimes he used to try and ride on a donkey. Next to him came Raddy [Stephen Albert Marshall], who had read several books and got them mixed somehow, he was always dead certain about all matters which other people doubted, on the other hand he never was sure of anything that seemed plain to the rest of the world. He was a very fine young monkey but he wore a very common tassel. After him came a very grave and important monkey he was by no means old tho not in the first bloom of youth, but he looked as old and as wise as he conveniently could. He used to keep himself in a very low den to prevent the hair growing too thick on the top of his head. He was a great scholar and could do washing bills in Flemish. This monkey was called 'The Bloke' [John Marshall III]. The next was 'Ruggy' [Reginald Dykes Marshall], he was a fine monkey and he too had a gold tassel, his only fault was that he was continually turning sharp round as if he imagined someone was standing on his tail; when he found no one behind him, he used to bite an inch off his tail, and then go on with his work, but he was never thoroughly comfortable and happy. He was the elder of the young monkeys. The youngest of the three elder monkeys was called 'Hunks' [Arthur Marshall], he made himself exceedingly busy with everything. He had an unpleasant way of bringing his elbow sharply round into the pit of the stomach of anyone who came to ask him questions or give him information. Consequently he got very little information, and nobody dared to ask him for anything. The middle monkey was called 'Old Harry' [Henry Cowper Marshall], he was a fine old monkey and amused himself by collecting all the figures he could and reducing them to pounds shillings and pence. When he couldn't get enough figures he used to invent some out of his head. His roar was terrible, but he never bit anyone, and in his own den he was quite affable. The eldest monkey was very scientific, his name was Bumblebrug [James G. Marshall], and he was excessively fond of squirts. He squirted almost everything and even insisted on squirting the jam which was a most unlikely thing to benefit by such a process. It was very difficult to prevent him from squirting when once he had got his squirt and a pail of water handy. It was also very difficult to prevent Old Harry from doing sums out of his head and making the clerk monkeys do fancy sums which he used to set them, and which they used to work out with wonderful perseverance. The pity of it was that they had no reference to the jam. And it was very difficult or rather impossible to prevent Hunks from going round the stores pulling off all the labels and altering them. He wasn't a stupid monkey by any means but as he never communicated much with the other monkeys and always insisted on putting his finger into every pot of jam on the premises it was only natural that confusion should arise. One of the worst features of the shop was a head undermonkey [John Richardson] who had been at his post a long time who not only kept his nose pointed always in the same direction but had acquired the habit of resolutely shutting his eyes. The old monkeys used to depend on him for information about what was going on in the shop, and you may imagine what sort of information he gave them.

If the aptitude of the founder's sons for business was such that they effectively ruined the firm, what would happen when it reverted to the third generation?

Two changes in the partnership at this juncture made it easier for John III and Stephen to start afresh if that was what they wanted to do. In 1873 James Marshall died and the following year his son, James Garth, was killed mountaineering in Switzerland.[1] Their interest in the business, amounting to £47,000 and a third share of the

---

[1] *Leeds Mercury*, 24 October 1873, 2 September 1874; *Yorkshire Post*, 25 October 1873, 2 September 1874.

rent, passed to the eldest son Victor and his two sisters. None had any claim or desire to enter the partnership. Each year they collected their part of the rent and interest on £20,000 which they left in the business, receiving 4 per cent according to the agreement governing a deceased partner's capital. In this way Victor earned over £1000 a year whatever the state of trade, without any share in management. In 1880 his sister Julia put £8000 in the business for a few years on the same terms. However, not only did the Monk Coniston family leave the partnership but the surviving seniors, Henry and Arthur, withdrew entirely from the scene, whilst continuing to provide nearly all the firm's capital resources. After 1873 John III became the largest shareholder, and by 1876 he and Stephen held three-fifths of the shares. Once in control, they removed the overseers who had previously obstructed their plans and made Richardson retire with a gift of £1000.[1]

With the way clear for action, John III and Stephen tried to revive the fortunes of the firm on a smaller scale. They immediately reduced the size of the plant in both Salop and Leeds. In the Castle Foregate mills, they halved the spinning and twisting spindles. At Water Lane, they dismantled 6000 spinning spindles leaving 20,000, left the thread spindles unchanged, and added ninety looms to the 151 already there in 1871. In addition part of the premises at Water Lane was leased to two weaving firms whom Marshall and Co. supplied with yarn. Thus the character of the plant and its output changed. Yarn production fell from 375,000 bundles in 1870–1 to around 250,000 by 1876. Since the 1830's the firm had sold about 200,000 bundles of yarn a year; in 1880 it sold less than 100,000 and much of it went to Messrs Rhodes and Fox. Furthermore, after 1878 thread production was curtailed and the firm twisted only 50,000 bundles of yarn, about half the amount used in the 1850's and 1860's. The quantity of yarn used for weaving remained constant at 50,000 bundles, additional requirements being met by outside purchases.

This reorganisation had the effect between 1873 and 1878, and again in 1882, of scrapping the oldest machines. In addition John III

---

[1] Richardson was replaced by Wilson whom the junior partners had sought to elevate since late 1871; J. Marshall III to H. C. Marshall, 28 October 1871.

spent heavily on new plant, £52,000 in a decade. He installed 202 new preparing machines, fifty-two new spinning frames carrying over 9000 spindles, ten Catton hackling machines and ten Horner Duplex. At the closing-down sale in 1886 the auctioneer described the plant as 'the most modern and improved construction...supplied within the last few years by Messrs S. Lawson and Sons; Combe, Barbour, Combe; Fairbairn, Kennedy and Naylors'.[1] Its sole shortcoming was that it had only one new Unsworth twisting frame (out of thirty-one operating), which according to an advertisement could double output. But this omission was perhaps not so important because thread output diminished in the later 1870's.

Along with new machines, the partners introduced higher workloads and piece-rate payments. By 1880 three-quarters of the weaving department and a quarter of the spinning department were paid piece-rates. In weaving, the number of operators did not increase proportionately with the looms. On average, seven girls attended five looms in 1870 and eight looms in 1881. Output per head rose nearly a fifth in spinning. The average size of frame increased from 156 spindles in 1870 to 200 in 1882, each operative watching more spindles. In the hackling process between 1869-73 and 1879-83 output per worker rose over 90 per cent measured in bundles. The total labour force shrank faster than output, from 2500 in 1870 to less than 1300 in 1878 and to 1100 by 1885. Thus John III and Stephen transformed the plant as their elders should have done twenty years earlier.

Despite these changes labour costs did not fall. Indeed fewer hours and higher wages which were partly responsible for accelerating this long-overdue change tended to push up labour costs. The price of labour rose precipitously in the 1870's. An overseer who earned 23s. in 1871, 8d. more than in 1851, was paid 30s. in 1880. A spinner who earned 5s. 4d. in 1833, 6s. in 1871, received 9s. in 1880. At the same time the beginning of compulsory education terminated the use of cheap child labour, and reinforced the need to

---

[1] Marshall Collection, Auction Catalogues, 19–25 October 1886. For Catton hackling machines see L. C. Marshall, *op. cit.* pp. 21–2; the Unsworth twisting frame is advertised at the end of the same work. The quality of the plant remaining at the end was very uneven; for example, out of fifty-two wet spinning frames, two-thirds carried 220 spindles each and a third 132 spindles.

redeploy workers or raise work-loads. In 1870 Marshalls employed 500 children; in 1878 a hundred; and in 1885, three. The number of working hours also lessened. In 1871 the firm had reduced the 60-hour week which had been in force for twenty years to 58½ hours. John III was not prepared to go farther than this, and after the strike in 1872 paid between 6*d.* and 2*s.* a week 'compensation' for 'overtime' beyond 56 hours. But in 1874 he conceded a 56-hour week. The overall effect was that where in the 1830's the firm ran on average 3500 hours a year, in the 1870's it ran less than 3000.

Increasing efficiency and rising wages neutralised one another, and labour costs remained constant at 20*d.* a bundle. What happened in practice varied with each department. In hackling where the situation was aggravated by the disappearance of child labour, wages rose 120 per cent and labour costs 20 per cent. The principal gain was in weaving. There labour costs rose in the mid-1870's owing to a decline in productivity which followed the shorter working week and to higher average wages when child labour came to an end; but between 1878 and 1882 average wages were reduced by a sixth and productivity rose by an eighth, with the result that labour costs in weaving were at their lowest since 1869. In spinning during the 1870's, earnings rose a third and labour costs an eighth; indeed shorter operating time reduced the output per spindle by 2 per cent. However, after 1880 this was reversed; faster driving increased the output of yarn per spindle by a fifth and 7*d.* was knocked off weekly wages.

A similar effort was made to reduce overhead costs. In 1875 and again in 1880, John III and Stephen lowered the rent charge to £4670 and £3600 respectively. After 1871 there were no more revaluations of plant and no further interest payments on partners' capital. This saved £12,000 a year. On the other hand the cost of fuel, mechanics' wages and repairs rose. But the most important fact was that fixed costs were spread over a reduced output. Unit overheads rose with the contraction of 1878 and fell only after sub-letting and strenuous economies after 1881 on white-collar costs, repairs and fuel. In all, between 1869 and 1883 overheads fell by 6*d.* to 30*d.*

Flax costs per bundle fell a quarter in this last period. The price of flax dropped 40 per cent. Between 1876 and 1882 Marshalls paid an average price of £63 a ton. At the same time the firm made a smaller proportion of light yarns for sale or thread and obtained only 139 bundles from a ton of flax.

The net effect of all these changes—cheaper flax, lower overheads, and constant labour costs—was a substantial fall in the average cost of yarn from 165*d*. in 1869 to 134*d*. in 1883.

But the effort came too late. From 1871 to 1875 average yarn costs and prices came closer together than at any time since the 1840's. The partners made a profit of £12,000 a year for five years, about 5 per cent on sales—less than the margin made in the depression of 1826–9. Then in the late 1870's flax markets sagged. Flax prices fell later and less than cotton so that the demand for linen goods sank, and producers everywhere sought refuge from the new situation. Thread and yarn were no longer profitable at Marshalls. Between 1876 and 1881 the business lost £90,000 on an annual turnover around £120,000. The deterioration in trade dashed the efforts of John III and Stephen. Yet they had hoped for too much if they expected to repair the neglect of years in a short time. New machinery alone could not do this. They had to contend with the resistance of an increasingly adult labour force which fought doggedly against piece-rates and heavier work-loads; and in this respect John III and Stephen reaped the seed sown by their elders. Moreover, the firm was financially weak. No sooner had they ploughed back profits to buy new plant, than heavy losses ate into their assets.

At best they were marking time. A decade passed without much return for their efforts. According to the partnership terms in force after 1872, the first charge on declared profit was 5 per cent interest to the extent of each partner's capital, and only after that had been met was the residual to be divided according to the number of shares each partner held. Thus the major part of the profits declared between 1872 and 1876 went to the retired seniors despite the fact that they were minority shareholders.[1] And the chronic losses that occurred after 1876 were shouldered by all the partners until 1880

[1] For partners' shares, see Table 2, p. 312. In 1876–8 the distribution was as follows:

	Shares	Capital
H. C. Marshall	15	£114,375
A. Marshall	25	£120,870
J. Marshall III	30	£16,414
S. A. Marshall	30	£12,163

when the surviving seniors accepted them. The result was that John III and Stephen each had a capital of just over £1000 in 1872, and no more than £2000 ten years later; and in the intervening years John III had drawn £1000 a year and Stephen £400. Nor did their prospects show any signs of improving—except in one respect. Henry Cowper Marshall died in October 1884. Apart from inheriting his property and stocks his sons took over his assets in the firm worth nominally about £112,000. His death severed the last formidable link with the past which he represented. The partners could if they wished close the firm. John III who had inherited Derwent Island wanted to do this. Though only forty-four, he had no desire to continue in business any longer than was necessary, not least because of the delicate state of his health. It would be prudent to retire while he could still salvage enough to live on. Another few years of heavy loss and there would be very little left. Stephen wanted to reorganise the firm as a public company; but his brother disagreed. As an alternative, he considered closing the mills in England, transferring the new machinery to the United States and reopening in New Jersey or Connecticut. To weigh up his prospects he crossed the Atlantic, and then decided to give up the idea. Possibly he noticed signs of concentration in the thread industry there which did not augur well for his success.[1] Just as likely he disliked the business atmosphere in the New World:

In this horrible country of notions
And Barnum and Buncome and Puff,
His affections and tender emotions
Are reckoned unreasoning stuff.[2]

Trade was very bad in 1886 and in the previous decade the business had lost £97,000. The labour force was gradually reduced and late in the year the partners ceased production.[3] The plant and premises in Leeds and Salop passed into the hands of an auctioneer who sold

[1] *Textile Manufacturer*, 1883, p. 19; 1886, p. 30. *The Commonweal*, 10 July 1886, contains an attack on 'capitalists...resolved to follow their profits'. See also Green, *op. cit.* p. 115.

[2] *To Daisy*, in the hand of S. A. Marshall (Derwent Island Collection).

[3] The first notice of closure appeared in the *Textile Manufacturer*, 15 December 1885, p. 561. See also *Yorkshire Post*, 4 March, 27 May 1886; *Hunslet and Holbeck News*, 28 August 1886; *The Commonweal*, 10 July 1886 attacks Marshall and Co. for granting pensions worth in all only 29s. a week. There is no ledger record of this, but the partners made gifts to senior workmen amounting to £844 at Water Lane and Castle Foregate in 1886–7.

them for a mere pittance.[1] The Marshalls left Leeds. Arthur lived out his days at Hallsteads; John III went to Derwentwater; and Stephen bought Skelwith Fold, near Windermere. Each had sufficient for his lifetime, though nothing on the scale of the press report which described Arthur as a millionaire and the junior partners as having 'trifling fortunes of a few hundred thousand each'.[2]

After an existence of nearly a century, the firm of Marshall and Co. passed from the scene. In a different way its decay was as momentous as its rise. A great accumulation of business resources, a going concern with a universal reputation, dwindled to a shadow of its former power and prestige in little over a generation. Instead of protecting their business interests and evolving a self-repairing structure, Marshall's sons decided in middle-age to coast on their inheritance and dissipated the assets which the founder had built up.

(iii)

Marshall and Co. sank into decline because of defective management. The partners developed attitudes incompatible with the energetic conduct of business and gave priority to other interests. Of course even in the founder's day the firm had provided the means for social and political advancement; but then its well-being was never seriously sacrificed to other ends. By contrast, having made their fortunes, Marshall's sons thought in the 1840's that they could safely neglect the mills and, instead of searching methodically for profit and improvement as their father had always done, they collected whatever the mills happened to offer, regarding profits with the fatalism of a peasant awaiting the harvest. Although its great size and resources long ensured the firm's continuance, under such unenterprising management its end was only a matter of time. When the mills closed, linen goods were no longer wanted as they had been in the past; but

[1] At the auction, 19–25 October 1886, the machinery and equipment (including four muskets) at Water Lane brought £12,343; see S. A. Marshall's annotated Auction Catalogue. The plant's book value on 2 January 1886 was £52,751. The sale of the land and fabric in fourteen lots between 1886 and 1899 yielded £44,918. In addition, the partners sold the Shrewsbury mill and machinery and their houses in Leeds. Thus they probably obtained above £100,000 when they went into liquidation.

[2] *The Commonweal*, 10 July 1886. Arthur Marshall's wealth probably amounted to not more than £300,000.

after the founder planted the family's roots in the Lakes, the business began to suffer at the hands of his sons. When the Temple Mill was constructed—the climax of their achievement as spinners—the great engine inside was already underdrawing itself to destruction. Doubts about the future, family quarrels, political activities—all conspired to deny the firm adequate leadership. James and to a lesser extent Henry were aware that the business and their reputation as spinners sorely needed attention. But their efforts were limited and unsuccessful. No agreement was reached on an alternative use of resources. Instead each partner acquired assets outside the business to provide for his own and his family's needs. Therefore in the last analysis Marshall and Co. declined owing to social barriers which could not be surmounted.

The family did not for long maintain the social and political pre-eminence it had reached by the 1840's. Shortly after the founder's death 'dark shadows fell on one side and another'.[1] Only one of Jane Marshall's children had died in infancy—'never surely was there a Mother who had so little sorrow in the bringing up of eleven children'. But many of the survivors suffered from chronic ill-health later in life, needed continuous medical care and watering at spas, and died early in middle-age.[2] John II had died in 1836; within twenty years, Julia, Dora, Cordelia and Ellen had been buried. Then in the early 1850's, Henry lost his wife, and Susan Myers her husband. A third of Marshall's children or their partners had died by 1855, and two-thirds of the households of the second generation were headed by widowers or widows. To some extent this meant that individuals and households drifted apart more than they might otherwise have done after the founder died, and Hallsteads lost its significance as the family home. Although none suffered a drastic lowering of standards because John Marshall made ample provision for all, prospects within the family differed considerably. Susan Myers, left with three young sons, moved into a smaller house at Blackheath and chose less expensive schools; relatives expressed sympathy in what must have seemed to them a fall in status. Dora's

---

[1] Whewell to sister, 20 July 1851.
[2] Selincourt, *op. cit.* 1831–40, p. 696.

children, left to the care of Colonel Temple, evoked more pity for they were cut off from the family. Along with social dispersion went geographical spread; grandchildren left for Canada, India and service in the Navy.[1] Such inevitable changes account for the parting of many ways; but they fail to explain why some households in the clan, in particular those on the male side remaining in the Lakes, did not maintain the family's pre-eminence.

Whatever their abilities, Marshall's four surviving sons were not ambitious men, driven to accumulate wealth as their father had done. Apart from William they did not seriously contemplate public service, nor apparently did they seek social advancement. They had reached the farthest point of their ambition and had no social objective in view. Henry insinuated this when towards the end of his life he pictured himself as a member of a new middle-class gentry, fixed in their station not by virtue of their birth and position as landlords but on account of their fitness as leaders in the new industrial society.[2] Whatever the merit of such a view, it suggests that Henry Marshall had fulfilled his social aspirations, and his efforts were directed to holding on to what he had. Politically there had been a time in the late 1830's and 1840's when James and Henry played prominent roles in the cause of Leeds liberalism and might have gained distinction as men of party. But despite their connexions, neither emerged as spokesman for any coherent interests and their careers were brief. In part, they lacked the personal qualities which make for political success. More fundamental, they marched out of step on questions such as the franchise, and later free trade and Home Rule; for this reason they would not have gathered a following. Instinctively they withdrew to their own corner of the country, and took more interest in the events of their nearby market towns than in the affairs of Leeds or the nation where their names soon passed from memory. Their purpose was to maintain an assured income, to indulge very civilised tastes, to uphold a social position in the Lakes. Consequently, in their later years they became as fiercely conservative there as in the mills. Henry, in particular, brought his influence to

---

[1] Whewell to sister, 25 December 1851, 29 May 1852, 6 May 1858, 9 December (no year).

[2] H. C. Marshall, *Presidential Address*, Social Inquiry Society of Ireland, 19 June 1883.

bear against changes in the local scene. He opposed a railway, however discreetly disguised, along the edge of Derwentwater despite the fact that it would have led to the development of minerals on his property. He organised campaigns against trippers from the towns who violated the peace of his sanctuary. And as if to protect Derwentwater from intruders, Marshalls acquired more property around the lake at Borrowdale, Hawse End and Hibbert's Island.[1] Yet notwithstanding such activities, changes took place: as their business waned, as liberal politics lost their meaning, as strangers broke into their seclusion, and as friends passed away, a melancholy permeated their thought. 'The sun'—one said—'on this world used to shine.' In the 1870's the third generation of well-educated, capable, urbane young gentlemen claimed their inheritance. They valued business as a way of life less than their parents, for the second generation had a sentimental if somewhat misguided attachment to the mills. Their sons had no such feeling, and at the earliest opportunity severed their connexions with Leeds to settle down as country gentlemen living on interest and parental estates. Reginald Dykes Marshall acquired Castlerigg Manor and played an active role in the local life of Keswick for forty years. Stephen lived quietly at Skelwith Fold and John III on the Island. (Henry's two younger sons entered professions: Francis, a master at Harrow, kept his association with the Lakes by building a house at Hawse End; William, on the other hand, became a partner in a firm of London architects.)

Those who lived in the Lakes, though not as rich as their fathers, had ample wealth for their needs. In 1890 before disposing of the mill property in Leeds, John III had assets of £100,000: three-fifths was in stocks—£15,000 railways, £20,000 foreign bonds, and £4000 in recent shipping lines and telephones; the other two-fifths consisted of property, mostly farms and houses around Keswick. From dividends and rent—some assets brought no return—John III received £3626 in 1889 and £3828 in 1890. Living quietly on the Island, which was the first charge on his purse, had cost his father an average

---

[1] Derwent Island Collection: papers relating to H. C. Marshall's opposition to the 'Braithwaite–Buttermere Railway', 'the Lake District Vandals', and many other aspects of local life. In the last quarter of the nineteenth century, Keswick became a popular holiday centre. Jackson's *Directory of Cumberland and Westmorland* (1880) shows that a quarter of those listed as tradespeople in the town were proprietors of lodging houses.

of £790 a year between 1879 and 1883; this included servants, boatmen, half a ton of coal weekly, and every item of household expenses.[1] Sufficient remained therefore to educate sons at Rugby and King's, to spend much time in Madeira (for health reasons), and to increase his investments. What John III did not do after the style of his father was to run more than one household and participate in public life. In the 1870's, before leaving Leeds, he devoted time and money to the new Yorkshire College and also to Adel Reformatory School; but later he refused to become a parliamentary candidate and restricted his activities to the bench and the Cumberland County Council. Health, perhaps death, diminishing means and political uncertainty conspired to prevent the third generation from taking an active role in politics. There had never been a strong tradition in the family to encourage the pursuit of high public office. And their economic interests, confined to safeguarding the security of their assets, required no political protection at that time. The decline of landed power above and the encroachments by the lower middle-class and artisans from below did not threaten their station in life whatever inconvenience it may have caused. By inclination and family tradition, the third generation associated with humanitarian reformers, and mocked the mounting assaults on the bastions of conservatism.[2]

> ...Sweeps to be Lords, on my life!
> Sitting with Salisbury,
> Cranbrook and Halsbury,
> Devonshire, Portland and Fife!
>
> Shades of the Percy and
> Howard cry Mercy! and
> Spare our immaculate Cross!
> Only to think of it!
> We're on the brink of it,
> Blank irretrievable loss.
>
> ...Better be ending us
> Make a *clean sweep* of the lot!

[1] Derwent Island Collection: 'Bundle of Accounts', containing 1890 estimate of property and income; memo of dividends 1894; Abstract of Expenses at Derwent Island, 1879–83; capital sums received and invested 1887–8.

[2] 'Poem', in the hand of S. A. Marshall. For obituaries of J. Marshall III, see the *Textile Manufacturer*, 1894, p. 339; the *Leeds Mercury*, 28 July 1894, described him as 'a cultivated gentleman'.

In the next generation the houses in the Lakes were abandoned. After Arthur's death in 1898, Hallsteads was sold; the other households lived comfortably off coupon-incomes until the First World War. Then they left the Lakeland scene. In part, taxes and inflation reduced their incomes and imperilled the stability of their ways. But they still had sufficient wealth to linger awhile had they chosen to do so. Rather, the Victorian society of the Lakes passed away and Marshalls lost their place in it.

Just as the family had withdrawn from Leeds, its various households withdrew increasingly from public life in the Lake District at the end of the century. Neighbours left and newcomers probably did not survive long enough to repair stable social relationships. On Derwent Island, John III who died in 1893 was survived by his widow for thirty-five years. As a newcomer to Cumberland society she had sense of purpose more positive than many around her, and she hoped that at least one of her three grown-up sons would achieve something worth while in his lifetime. To this end she used her extensive connexions to push their names forward for public office in the county.[1] But the sons did not share their mother's ambition. John IV was a cripple who lived mostly at home until his death in 1923. Charles escaped, eventually renouncing his patrimony, and settling on the Continent. Denis, who remained a bachelor, returned to Sedbergh where his mother had sent him to school, as a master. In the mid-1920's the Island was inhabited by an ageing invalid and when Emma Marshall died in 1929, Denis, who had settled at Sedbergh, installed a caretaker to look after the house. Like his brother and other members of the family, he no longer felt that he belonged in the Lakes.

Before, or shortly after, the Second World War, when the great mills at Water Lane and Castle Foregate were used by a maltster, printers and mechanics, the family's houses had become hotels, hostels, schools and National Trust property. The vandals from the towns whom Henry Marshall had tried to keep at a distance looked

---

[1] The eldest son died in 1891 at the age of twenty-six from scarlet fever. For E. E. Marshall's activities, see the Derwent Island Collection. H. L. Clarke, *History of Sedbergh School, 1525–1925* (1925), *passim*. The travels of D. Marshall can be followed from the postcards which he sent to his mother, who preserved them in an album. See also Burke's *Landed Gentry* (1952), pp. 1709 ff.

at Borrowdale from Friar's Crag or rowed noisily round the Island. The name of Marshall no longer evoked much response in the Lakes, the paintings on the walls of former Marshall houses bear faces that are unknown, and store-cupboards carry stocks of linen made nearly a hundred years ago by a firm whose name has long been forgotten in Leeds.

APPENDIX

PRODUCTION AND CAPITAL: TABLES AND FIGURES

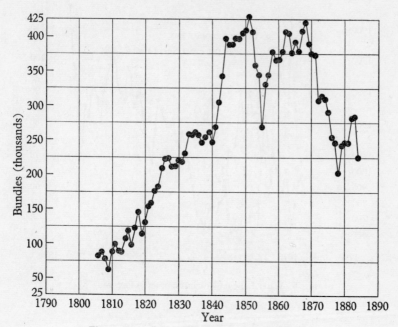

Fig. 4. Water Lane mills: output of yarn, 1806–84.

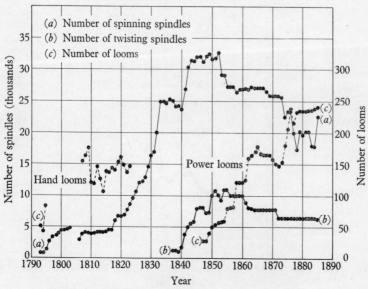

Fig. 5. Water Lane mills: spindles and looms, 1793–1884.

307

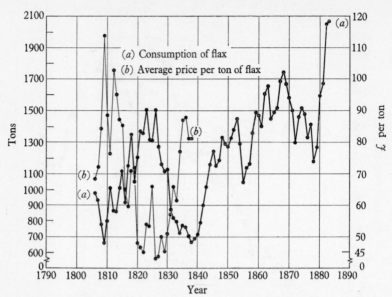

Fig. 6. Water Lane mills: consumption of flax, 1806–83.

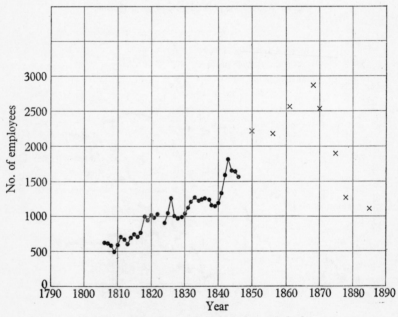

Fig. 7. Water Lane mills: labour-force, 1806–46.

308

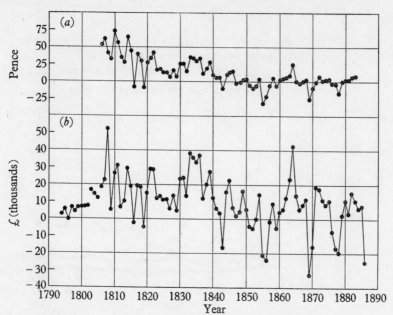

Fig. 8. Water Lane mills: (a) average profit or loss per bundle of yarn and thread, (b) total trading-profit or loss.

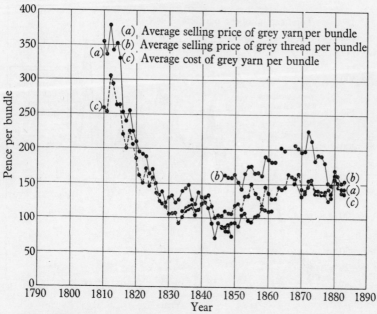

(a) Average selling price of grey yarn per bundle
(b) Average selling price of grey thread per bundle
(c) Average cost of grey yarn per bundle

Fig. 9. Water Lane mills: average price and cost per bundle of yarn, 1810-83.

309

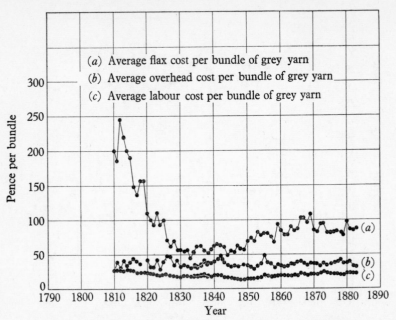

Fig. 10. Water Lane mills: average cost of flax, labour and overheads per bundle of yarn, 1810–83.

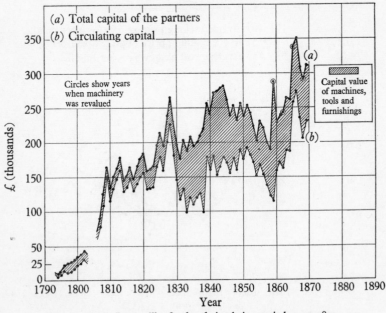

Fig. 11. Water Lane mills: fixed and circulating capital, 1793–1870.

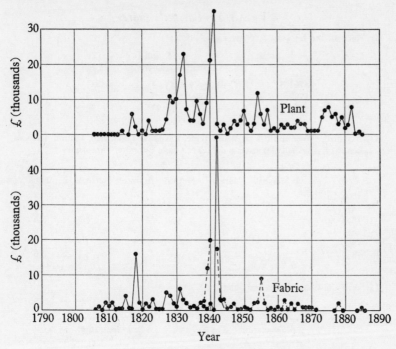

Fig. 12. Water Lane mills: annual spending on fabric and plant, 1806–85.

TABLE I. *Partners' capital at Water Lane mills*
(*before allocation of previous year's profits*)

	J. Marshall £	T. and B. Benyon £	Total £
1794 (May)	10,423	3,706	14,129
1795 (Jan.)	9,011	6,084	15,095
1796	9,635	12,889	22,524
1797	11,861	18,673	30,534
1798	10,686	18,103	28,789
1799	15,154	21,958	37,112
1800	16,942	23,974	40,916
1801	19,230	19,684	38,914
1802	21,046	22,730	43,777
1803	24,812	27,081	51,893
1804	31,396	12,004	43,400

TABLE 2. *Partner's shares*

(I) Marshall and Benyons of Water Lane, Leeds:

	John Marshall	T. and B. Benyon	Total
1794–5	1	1	2
1796–7	2	3	5
1797–1804	9	11	20

(II) Marshall, Hives and Co. of Water Lane, Leeds: *and* Marshall, Hutton and Co. (after 1815, Marshall, Atkinson and Co.) of Castle Foregate, Shrewsbury:

	J. Marshall	Hives	Hutton	Atkinson	John Marshall II	Total
1804–10	10	1	1	—	—	12
1811–12	19	2	2	1	—	24
1812–14	35	5	5	3	—	48
1815–19	6	2	—	1	—	9
1820–2	5	2	—	1	1	9
1823	5	—	—	—	1	6

(III) Marshall and Co. of Leeds and Salop:

Number of Shares

	2nd Generation					3rd Generation					
	John Marshall	John Marshall II	James Marshall	Henry Marshall	Arthur Marshall	C. Empson*	Reginald Marshall	John Marshall III	Stephen Marshall	James Garth Marshall	Total
1824–9	5	2	1	—	—	—	—	—	—	—	8
1830–2	6	3	2	1	—	—	—	—	—	—	12
1833	7	4	3	2	—	—	—	—	—	—	16
1834–5	4	3	3	2	—	—	—	—	—	—	12
1836–9	2	Died	3	3	1	—	—	—	—	—	9
1840–3	1		2	2	1	—	—	—	—	—	6
1844–50	Retired		1	1	1	—	—	—	—	—	3
1851–7			8	8	8	1	—	—	—	—	25
1858–66			3	3	3	2	1	—	—	—	12
1867–70			22	22	22	19	10	5	—	—	100
1871			10	19	19	Retired	19	19	9	5	100
1872			12	23	23		Retired	23	12	7	100
1873			10	15	20			23	20	12	100
1874–5			Died	15	20			23	23	19	100
1876–8				15	25			30	30	Died	100
1879–83				15	25			30	30		100
1884				Died	25			30	30		85
Liquidation					2			1	1		4

* C. Empson was the only outsider with a share in the partnership after 1823.

In 1879, the senior partners agreed to accept all trading losses, each taking a half. In 1884, losses were shared between all partners, in the ratio: A.M., 2; J.M.III, 1; S.A.M., 1.

TABLE 3. *Distribution of assets at Water Lane mills, 1793–1803*

	Land, engines, fabric £	Machines £	Stocks of flax and finished goods £
1793 (April)	5,770	3,726	10,658
1793 (Dec.)	5,814	3,131	5,687
1795 (Jan.)	6,499	5,198	7,610
1796 (Jan.)	14,729	7,811	14,805
1797 (Jan.)	12,746	14,735	11,657
1798 (Jan.)	13,436	13,882	13,134
1799 (Jan.)	12,447	13,050	17,032
1800 (Jan.)	14,095	12,567	23,543
1801 (Jan.)	14,243	11,713	25,464
1802 (Jan.)	18,484	12,794	31,663
1803 (Jan.)	20,454	13,461	26,841

TABLE 4. *Yarn sales at Water Lane, 1801–39 (in 000's of bundles)*

1801	38	1811	83	1821	128	1831	200
1802	57	1812	65	1822	124	1832	248
1803	?	1813	84	1823	104	1833	264
1804	?	1814	93	1824	220	1834	219
1805	42	1815	99	1825	187	1835	240
1806	63	1816	81	1826	148	1836	252
1807	62	1817	91	1827	200	1837	161
1808	64	1818	100	1828	242	1838	284
1809	55	1819	90	1829	192	1839	228
1810	71	1820	128	1830	263		

Note. This series together with that for thread and cloth in Table 5 are derived from extremely fragmentary records, and are intended to show the composition of the firm's products and the state of the market. In conjunction with the firm's annual stock-take, they indicate broad movements in the stocks of finished goods. Yarn sales alone cannot be set against the production of yarn in order to determine stocks, because some of the yarn produced would be woven into cloth and some twisted into thread.

TABLE 5. *Yarn, thread and cloth sales at Water Lane, 1853–82 (expressed in 000's of bundles)*

	Yarn	Cloth	Thread		Yarn	Cloth	Thread
1853	217	21	151	1868	252	65	98
1854	133	25	165	1869	229	47	66
1855	127	23	123	1870	269	47	62
1856	239	23	105	1871	305	50	69
1857	195	30	125	1872	174	40	67
1858	218	43	93	1873	182	61	65
1859	176	45	122	1874	183	67	32
1860	229	40	127	1875	188	58	35
1861	203	52	102	1876	167	58	24
1862	283	62	104	1877	151	47	15
1863	229	?	95	1878	115	50	20
1864	181	57	99	1879	120	54	58
1865	259	45	88	1880	117	50	77
1866	208	53	99	1881	122	52	62
1867	185	57	114	1882	105	57	67

Note. (*a*) Cloth sold was manufactured both from yarn spun at Water Lane and also from yarns bought on the market, e.g. in 1866, 54,000 bundles of the firm's own yarn and a further 14,000 bundles bought outside were converted into cloth. In the same period, the equivalent of 53,000 bundles of yarn was *sold* in the form of cloth.

(*b*) Most of the thread went to Castle Foregate for finishing. Often it is difficult to know how much was thread and how much was yarn in these transactions between the Leeds and Salop mills.

Like the previous series, these figures illustrate the diversity of the Water Lane output and the condition of the yarn and cloth markets.

TABLE 6. *Yield of line after hackling 1 cwt. of flax at Water Lane*

Year	lb.	Year	lb.	Year	lb.
1806 (1st half)	47·6	1818	56·9	1835	48·9
(2nd half)	46·1		57·9	1836	49·9
1807	46·8	1819	58·3	1837	48·6
	49·2		57·2	1838	48·8
1808	50·1	1820	53·1	1839	49·8
	54·4		55·4	1840	48·4
1809	56·5	1821	56·7	1841	49·5
1810	56·4		54·4	1842	53.0
	53·9	1822	51·8	1843	58·1
1811	52·1		52·8	1844	58·3
	51·7	1823	54·0	1845	59·7
1812	54·8		54·2	1846	64·0
	56·0	1824	53·4	—	—
1813	58·6	1825	53·1	1873	54·9
	55·8	1826	55·7	—	—
1814	55·6	1827	56·0	1878	64·0
	60·4	1828	51·7	—	—
1815	56·7	1829	48·9	1882	68·7
	55·3	1830	49·6	—	—
1816	57·1	1831	49·2	—	—
	55·3	1832	49·2	—	—
1817	57·1	1833	49·6	—	—
	58·1	1834	48·6	—	—

TABLE 7. *Bundles of yarn spun from a ton of flax at Water Lane*

Year	Bundles	Year	Bundles	Year	Bundles
1806	110	1832	344	1858	338
1807	112	1833	398	1859	298
1808	105	1834	438	1860	302
1809	115	1835	423	1861	329
1810	126	1836	418	1862	308
1811	118	1837	407	1863	295
1812	121	1838	474	1864	316
1813	125	1839	461	1865	310
1814	125	1840	423	1866	304
1815	128	1841	412	1867	296
1816	125	1842	413	1868	292
1817	127	1843	413	1869	284
1818	127	1844	415	1870	289
1819	130	1845	385	1871	300
1820	127	1846	412	1872	288
1821	139	1847	409	1873	262
1822	141	1848	360	1874	246
1823	144	1849	383	1875	238
1824	168	1850	392	1876	235
1825	192	1851	391	1877	212
1826	180	1852	356	1878	211
1827	213	1853	301	1879	234
1828	222	1854	330	1880	188
1829	233	1855	316	1881	179
1830	261	1856	353	1882	168
1831	302	1857	361	1883	167

Note. This table shows—as a measure of average fineness—the number of bundles of yarn in a given weight, that is, a ton of spun yarn. It does *not* show the number of bundles per ton of raw material. That series, though parallel in trend, is lower because in the spinning process raw flax loses about a seventh of its weight owing to wastage and drying.

Cf. C. R. Porter, *Progress of the Nation* (ed. F. Hirst, 1911), pp. 227–8.

1806–20 average 11 lea yarn.
1821–30 average 11–27 leas.
1831–40 average 27–40 leas.
1841–50 average 36–28 leas.
1851–60 average 35–28 leas.
1861–70 average 30–25 leas.
1871–80 average 27–17 leas.

TABLE 8. *Index of cotton and flax prices (1782–90 = 100)*

	Cotton	Flax		Cotton	Flax
1782–90	100	100	1841–50	22	89
1791–1800	104	107	1851–60	25	115
1801–10	67	190	1861–70	58	123
1811–20	68	165	1871–80	28	112
1821–30	32	98	1881–90	23	89
1831–40	31	100			

SOURCE: M. G. Mulhall, *The Dictionary of Statistics* (1892), pp. 471 ff.

TABLE 9. *Composition of the labour force at Water Lane mills by age and sex*

Year …	1831 M	1831 F	1832 M	1832 F	1833 M	1833 F	1835 M	1835 F	1836 M	1836 F	1837 M	1837 F	1838 M	1838 F	1847 M	1847 F
Age																
Under 13 (Under 9 / 9–11)	5	—	112	162	11	9	120	245	115	85	94	71	135	161	93	219
(10–15 / 12–15)	—	—			187	320										
(16–21)	237	269			138	414										
13–17	88	272	142	398	—	—	128	363	142	516	200	567	138	448	101	537
Over 18	—	—	191	312	—	—	175	286	115	320	—	—	128	316	264	664
Over 21	125	43	—	—	139	126	—	—	—	—	—	—	—	—	—	—
Totals	455	584	445	872	466	878	423	894	372	921	—	—	401	925	458	1420
	1039		1317		1344		1317		1293		—		1326		1878	

Year …	1850 M	1850 F	1856 M	1856 F	1861 M	1861 F	1868 M	1868 F	1870 M	1870 F	1875 M	1875 F	1878 M	1878 F	1885 M	1885 F
Age																
Under 13	228	218	217	224	251	347	327	306	267	258	113	307	31	77	1	2
Females over 13	—	1386	—	1371	—	1519	—	1705	—	1526	—	1138	—	884	—	814
Males 13–17	100	—	109	—	135	—	146	—	121	—	62	—	32	—	56	—
Over 18	288	—	256	—	311	—	390	—	358	—	275	—	243	—	242	—
Over 21	—	—	—	—	—	—	—	—	—	—	—	—	—	—	—	—
Totals	616	1604	582	1695	697	1866	863	2011	748	1784	450	1445	306	961	299	816
	2220		2177		2563		2874		2530		1895		1267		1115	

TABLE 10. *Time worked at the Water Lane mill*
(quinquennial averages)

	Hours per day		Days per year
1806–8	11	51 min.	311
1809–13	12	19	324·6
1814–18	12	20	323·4
1819–23	11	50	308·2
1824–8	11	48	?
1829–33	11	38	311·2
1834–8	10	56	309·8
1839–43	10	36	309·4
1844–8	10	20	310
1849–53	9	38	310·6
1854–8	9	17	305·4
1859–63	9	40	307
1864–8	9	35	303
1869–73	9	20	297·8
1874–8	—		294·5
1879–83	—		285·2

TABLE 11. *Marshall's mills, Leeds: Average annual earnings of labour engaged in the manufacture of yarn (i.e. hackling, preparing, spinning and reeling departments)*

Average annual earnings for all operatives

Year	£	Year	£
1810	20½	1827	18½
1811	21	1828	17
1812	18¼	1829	17½
1813	20	1830	15½
1814	22¼	1831	14¼
1815	22¼	1832	15
1816	19½	1833	15
1817	19	1834	15
1818	15½	1835	15½
1819	14½	1836	16
1820	13½	1837	16½
1821	16¼	1838	17½
1822	14½	1839	18
1823	—	1840	18
1824	17½	1841	17½
1825	18	1842	17½
1826	15½	1843	17

TABLE 11 (*cont.*)

Marshall's mills, Leeds: Average weekly Wages:

Year	Men		Girls and Women		Children	
	s.	*d.*	*s.*	*d.*	*s.*	*d.*
1831	19	10	5	3	3	2¾
1836	21	6	5	5½	2	10¾
1840	21	8	5	11½	2	5¾
1841	21	9¾	5	9¾	2	4¾

This information was sent to Samuel Smiles for the *Leeds Times*. To explain the reduction in female and child wages, the firm added the following explanation:

> The increasing proportion of children employed half-time under the Factory Act in the latter years is the cause of the decline in their wages.
>
> An increased proportion of the younger class of girls and women employed in 1841 causes the wages of that year to be lower.
>
> The wages of the men afford a fair comparison: there not having been any material variation in the description of employed.

Average weekly rate of wages at Marshall's mills, Leeds, 1851

	Men		Boys	
Males:	*s.*	*d.*	*s.*	*d.*
Overlookers	22	4	—	
Mechanics and cleaners	19	3½	6	6½
Labourers, jobbers, storemen	16	4	6	7½
Packers and warehousemen	17	10½	7	7½
Females				
Weavers	10	5	—	
Winders, warpers, twisters and dressers	8	7	—	
Yarn thread reelers	6	4	—	
Thread twisting	5	4	—	
Yarn spinning	5	2¼	—	
Line and tow preparing	5	7	—	
Children	Full-time		Part-time	
Hackling	4	3¼	1	8

Weekly wage rate

	1851		1861		1871	1880
	s.	*d.*	*s.*	*d.*	*s.*	*s.*
Overlooker	22	4	23	4	23	30
Weaver	10	5	9	3	?	11
Spinner	5	2¼	5	7	6	9

Marshall's mills, Leeds: Weavers' average earnings

	s.	*d.*		*s.*	*d.*
1863	10	0 (60-hour week)	1873	12	1
1864	9	10	1874	11	8 (56-hour week)
1865	9	6	1875	12	0
1866	10	0	1876	12	6
1867	10	8	1877	12	7
1868	10	8	1878	14	0
1869	10	5	1879	12	6
1870	10	9	1880	13	1
1871	11	0 (58½-hour week)	1881	13	1
1872	12	9	1882	12	1

TABLE 12. *Total earnings of the partners from Water Lane and Castle Foregate (in £'s)*

	Leeds Profit	Salop Profit	Leeds Interest	Salop Interest	Leeds Rent	Salop Rent	Total
1804/5	18,015	6,865	1,532	511	2,000	1,500	30,423
1806	18,233	6,520	1,662	709	2,000	1,518	30,692
1807	22,708	8,646	2,340	1,063	2,075	1,518	38,350
1808	52,581	15,963	3,375	1,607	2,075	1,534	77,135
1809	5,028	10,795	6,043	2,523	2,330	1,534	28,253
1810	25,374	5,790	6,555	3,280	2,392	1,534	44,925
1811	31,295	9,401	7,665	2,810	2,554	3,095	56,820
1812	6,725	6,358	8,827	3,220	2,554	3,585	31,269
1813	9,791	5,243	8,855	3,628	2,583	3,708	33,808
1814	29,824	6,851	7,797	4,210	2,592	3,722	54,996
1815	19,114	5,570	6,602	4,332	2,958	3,722	42,298
1816	−3,464	186	7,191	5,069	2,986	3,722	15,690
1817	20,085	9,285	5,343	4,963	3,100	3,722	46,498
1818	19,046	879	5,927	4,338	3,893	3,727	37,810
1819	−4,930	2,365	7,234	4,239	3,697	2,808	15,413
1820	14,423	1,496	7,476	4,183	3,688	2,808	34,074
1821	20,808	3,890	6,757	4,133	3,941	3,155	42,684
1822	28,443	9,850	6,819	2,898	4,192	3,220	55,422
1823	11,959	6,738	7,177	4,041	4,207	3,216	37,878
1824	13,632	13,972	7,617	3,768	4,207	2,355	45,551
1825	11,228	10,744	9,448	3,733	4,207	2,355	41,715
1826	11,112	9,639	c. 9,000	c. 2,123	4,207	2,355	38,446
1827	5,592	11,023	c. 9,000	c. 3,330	4,552	2,378	35,875
1828	13,832	5,483	9,503	3,852	4,872	2,378	39,907
1829	4,310	2,161	7,517	6,743	5,026	2,378	28,135
1830	23,623	6,607	7,749	6,121	3,403	1,585	49,089
1831	23,948	7,325	7,771	3,063	3,940	1,585	47,632
1832	13,442	1,540	7,070	5,482	4,181	1,585	33,270
1833	38,374	11,066	8,196	2,336	4,297	1,618	65,887
1834	35,851	11,655	7,064	4,501	4,331	1,674	65,075
1835	32,661	14,991	7,980	4,325	4,413	1,749	66,119
1836	37,383	20,788	9,562	2,608	4,436	1,749	76,526
1837	11,497	22,977	9,969	2,239	4,436	1,749	52,867
1838	18,672	26,088	8,543	5,910	4,436	1,749	65,468
1839	27,520	23,431	9,337	6,439	4,556	1,920	73,202
1840	12,415	13,136	10,737	3,940	3,555	1,920	45,703
1841	6,645	23,916	9,672	5,564	3,555	2,039	51,392
1842	3,280	16,085	11,116	3,229	7,235	2,069	43,013
1843	−16,921	7,781	6,937	8,722	7,280	2,121	15,920
1844	15,049	16,447	8,152	8,575	4,700	1,300	54,223
1845	22,364	13,044	9,098	5,424	4,700	1,300	55,930
1846	6,235	14,119	c. 9,000	c. 5,317	4,700	1,300	40,670
1847	1,423	4,419	c. 9,000	c. 5,936	4,700	1,300	26,779
1848	3,918	9,805	c. 9,000	c. 5,380	5,378	1,348	34,828
1849	16,421	15,192	c. 9,000	c. 5,758	5,378	1,348	53,096
1850	5,363	20,341	c. 9,000	c. 5,366	5,378	1,348	46,797
1851	−4,673	−13,837	c. 9,000	c. 5,354	5,378	1,348	2,571
1852	−6,397	−10,743	c. 9,000	c. 4,119	5,378	1,348	2,705
1853	−1,192	−7,071	c. 9,000	c. 3,288	4,660	1,770	10,454
1854	14,175	−831	c. 9,000	c. 3,528	4,660	1,770	32,301

TABLE 12 (*cont.*)

	Leeds Profit	Salop Profit	Leeds Interest	Salop Interest	Leeds Rent	Salop Rent	Total
1855	-21,339	-8,483	c. 9,000	c. 4,033	5,422	2,041	-9,325
1856	-24,377	-8,289	7,301	5,478	5,560	2,054	-12,273
1857	-2,854	-3,923	8,067	3,925	5,560	2,054	31,429*
1858	10,793	-743	7,847	4,661	5,100	1,900	29,558
1859	-6,702	-4,234	10,436	3,304	5,100	1,900	10,435
1860	3,243	-5,090	9,850	4,098	5,100	1,900	34,915*
1861	4,999	-8,799	8,914	4,650	5,100	1,900	17,764
1862	12,469	976	10,415	4,056	5,100	1,900	34,916
1863	22,680	-4,692	11,778	2,563	5,100	1,900	50,810*
1864	42,537	-1,356	11,679	4,294	5,100	1,900	64,154
1865	13,595	-3,757	13,902	4,167	5,100	1,900	34,907
1866	5,063	-2,196	13,942	4,411	5,100	1,900	37,570*
1867	7,820	-11,057	13,092	4,024	5,100	1,900	20,879
1868	11,638	-902	12,000	5,255	5,100	1,900	34,991
1869	-33,047	-10,092	12,426	5,504	5,100	1,900	-28,209*
1870	-15,919	-7,210	12,424	3,985	5,100	1,900	271
1871	19,125	1,196	—	—	5,100	1,900	27,934
1872	17,045	1,630	—	—	5,100	1,900	25,675
1873	11,020	-8,511	—	—	5,100	1,900	9,508
1874	8,153	-1,562	—	—	5,100	1,900	13,591
1875	10,201	4,384	—	—	4,670	1,597	20,852
1876	-7,538	1,488	—	—	4,670	1,597	218
1877	-16,840	-5,177	—	—	4,670	1,597	-15,750
1878	-20,096	-12,062	—	—	4,670	1,597	-25,891
1879	1,886	-4,548	—	—	4,670	1,597	3,585
1880	10,966	-16,930	—	—	3,600	1,200	-1,164
1881	2,429	-23,660	—	—	3,600	1,200	-16,431
1882	15,743	-14,940	—	—	3,600	1,200	5,603
1883	10,845	-7,933	—	—	3,600	1,200	7,712
1884	5,516	-5,787	—	—	3,600	1,200	4,529
1885	7,145	-4,072	—	—	3,600	1,200	7,866
1886	-25,186	-18,661	—	—	3,067	1,022	-39,758

Note. (*a*) Interest payments on partners' capital were discontinued as a prime cost during 1871.

(*b*) The starred totals for 1857, 1860, 1863, 1866, and 1869, take into account profits and losses owing to machinery revaluations.

(*c*) An approximate division of interest-income for Leeds and Salop has been made for the following years: 1826-7, 1846-55.

TABLE 13. *The estate of John Marshall (in £'s)*

Year	Business	Property	Securities	Loans	Less Debts	Net Estate
1793	10,546	2,480	—	649	11,296	2,180
1794	9,970	2,480	—	430	9,476	3,405
1795	12,578	2,400	—	314	9,094	6,198
1796	11,652	2,400	—	255	8,658	5,849
1797	13,296	2,200	—	248	7,670	8,074
1798	17,009	1,200	—	606	9,598	9,217
1799	19,829	1,200	—	—	5,230	15,799
1800	27,256	1,200	—	328	5,453	23,331
1801	30,268	1,200	—	194	5,211	26,451
1802	35,458	2,336	—	406	4,989	33,211
1803	27,617	2,336	—	10,078	5,080	39,941
1805	85,200	—	—	234	11,792	73,642
1806	103,397	—	—	187	9,005	94,579
1807	129,382	—	—	354	5,495	124,240
1808	192,319	—	—	323	6,117	186,526
1809	212,032	—	—	231	4,855	207,408
1810	244,283	—	—	362	4,637	240,008
1811	271,406	9,980	—	1,931	3,704	279,613
1812	282,425	13,890	—	2,724	3,004	298,855
1813	274,368	25,230	24,041	2,648	2,915	323,373
1814	246,355	39,830	74,001	5,850	2,542	363,494
1815	265,728	42,830	80,751	7,891	2,620	394,580
1816	245,814	52,230	100,251	8,088	2,988	462,795
1817	238,086	52,200	134,291	7,826	1,797	430,606
1818	255,551	59,700	140,861	8,797	2,114	462,795
1819	254,751	60,200	147,950	8,846	2,115	469,632
1820	225,420	62,200	192,843	7,700	—	488,163
1821	215,712	62,200	230,000	8,000	—	515,912
1823	244,336	62,200	235,050	5,305	—	544,536
1825	259,087	66,500	289,000	4,000	—	628,587
1827	336,672	76,500	162,944	4,000	—	580,116
1829	268,874	76,500	253,852	2,000	—	601,226
1831	234,340	76,500	308,641	10,000	—	629,481
1832	211,144	77,000	302,463	2,000	—	592,607
1833	207,000	77,000	323,972	4,000	—	611,972
1834	191,830	77,000	350,825	4,000	—	623,689
1835	183,235	77,000	393,700	20,000	—	673,935
1836	167,391	77,000	389,259	63,000	—	696,650
1837	183,439	77,000	403,725	63,000	—	727,164
1838	218,000	77,000	383,711	68,000	—	746,711
1839	179,214	77,000	393,751	67,000	—	716,965

Note. After 1820, personal loans and debts were entered as a single credit item. The sudden increase in 1836 is due to the inclusion as outstanding loans of railway shares that no longer paid. In addition to the above distribution of assets, John Marshall made gifts to his family, consisting of money, property and stocks, worth at least £150,000 between 1824 and 1840.

TABLE 14. *John Marshall's earnings from the mills at Water Lane and at Castle Foregate, 1805–44 (in £'s)*

1805	28,039	1825	30,322
1806	26,317	1826	28,468
1807	32,718	1827	27,407
1808	65,030	1828	32,136
1809	24,364	1829	22,784
1810	37,030	1830	29,837
1811	44,292	1831	28,160
1812	25,769	1832	21,101
1813	27,749	1833	34,084
1814	43,100	1834	24,182
1815	31,382	1835	27,123
1816	16,465	1836	22,650
1817	34,754	1837	17,705
1818	28,335	1838	21,687
1819	13,664	1839	24,216
1820	24,054	1840	14,182
1821	28,224	1841	16,103
1822	35,473	1842	16,061
1823	23,885	1843	13,681
1824	32,009	1844	15,044

TABLE 15. *Capital and earnings of three second-generation partners at Water Lane and Castle Foregate, 1825–60 (in £'s)*

James Garth Marshall

	Interest	Rent	Profits	Capital
1825	421	—	2,747	8,446
1826	528	—	2,595	10,598
1827	650	—	2,077	12,788
1828	752	—	2,414	15,078
1829	872	—	809	17,485
1830	931	—	5,038	18,679
1831	1,183	—	5,212	23,716
1832	1,471	—	2,497	28,954
1833	1,569	—	9,270	31,460
1834	2,003	—	11,877	40,162
1835	2,725	—	11,913	54,648
1836	3,341	—	17,724	67,006
1837	2,895	—	11,491	58,059
1838	3,468	—	14,920	67,965
1839	4,077	—	16,984	81,770
1840	3,780	—	8,517	75,812
1841	3,680	—	10,187	73,810
1842	3,912	—	6,455	78,453
1843	3,918	—	−3,047	78,576
1844	3,675	—	10,499	72,308
1845	4,129	1,167	11,803	82,802
1846	4,574	2,000	6,784	91,733

TABLE 15 (*cont.*)

	Interest	Rent	Profits	Capital
1847	4,508	2,000	1,948	90,406
1848	3,827	2,242	4,574	76,755
1849	3,541	2,242	10,537	69,682
1850	3,651	2,242	8,586	73,230
1851	3,621	2,242	−5,923	72,611
1852	2,916	2,242	−5,485	58,488
1853	2,518	2,143	−2,644	50,493
1854	2,583	2,143	4,270	51,810
1855	2,638	2,488	−9,543	51,898
1856	2,550	2,537	−10,888	51,138
1857	2,076	2,537	−2,259	41,627
1858	2,250	2,333	2,512	45,117
1859	2,691	2,333	−2,576	53,958
1860	2,630	2,333	−336	51,751

Henry Cowper Marshall

	Interest	Rent	Profits	Capital
1830	249	—	2,519	5,000
1831	366	—	2,606	7,338
1832	517	—	1,249	10,163
1833	572	—	6,180	11,468
1834	872	—	7,918	17,497
1835	1,307	—	7,942	26,206
1836	1,610	—	17,724	32,291
1837	2,525	—	11,491	50,634
1838	3,117	—	14,919	61,336
1839	3,749	—	16,984	75,182
1840	4,479	—	8,517	89,828
1841	4,815	—	10,187	96,556
1842	5,340	—	6,454	107,101
1843	5,709	—	−3,047	114,491
1844	5,769	—	10,499	113,513
1845	6,156	1,167	11,803	123,459
1846	6,522	2,000	6,784	135,789
1847	6,931	2,000	1,948	138,992
1848	6,916	2,242	4,574	138,708
1849	6,971	2,242	10,537	137,174
1850	5,886	2,242	8,568	118,051
1851	5,427	2,242	−5,923	108,846
1852	5,042	2,242	−5,485	101,109
1853	4,873	2,143	−2,644	97,726
1854	4,951	2,143	4,270	99,292
1855	5,243	2,487	−9,543	103,394
1856	5,374	2,538	−10,888	115,003
1857	5,586	2,538	−2,259	112,026
1858	5,793	2,333	2,512	116,070
1859	5,751	2,333	−2,576	115,346
1860	6,023	2,333	−336	118,519

Note. Profits of £2,500 and £3,828 should be added in 1857 and 1860 on account of machinery revaluations.

TABLE 15 (*cont.*)

Arthur Marshall

	Interest	Rent	Profits	Capital
1836	249	—	5,908	5,000
1837	574	—	3,830	11,521
1838	716	—	4,973	14,093
1839	964	—	5,661	19,324
1840	1,255	—	4,259	25,170
1841	1,327	—	5,094	26,617
1842	1,563	—	3,227	31,349
1843	1,753	—	−1,532	35,156
1844	1,758	—	10,499	34,592
1845	2,295	1,167	11,803	46,020
1846	2,991	2,000	6,784	59,994
1847	3,497	2,000	1,948	70,133
1848	3,637	2,242	4,574	72,950
1849	4,246	2,242	10,537	83,540
1850	4,829	2,242	8,568	96,847
1851	5,294	2,242	−5,923	106,162
1852	4,589	2,242	−5,485	92,028
1853	4,370	2,143	−2,644	87,632
1854	4,424	2,143	4,270	88,722
1855	4,508	2,487	−9,543	88,697
1856	3,971	2,538	−10,888	79,646
1857	3,760	2,538	−2,259	75,400
1858	3,881	2,333	2,512	77,830
1859	4,295	2,333	−2,576	86,130
1860	4,458	2,333	−336	87,718

Note. Profits of £2,500 and £3,828 should be added in 1857 and 1860 on account of machinery revaluations.

TABLE 16. *Capital and earnings of two junior partners, at Water Lane and Castle Foregate, 1858–70 (in £'s)*

	R. D. M.			J. M. III		
	Interest	Profits	Capital	Interest	Profits	Capital
1858	—	837	7,257	—	—	—
1859	362	858	6,293	—	—	—
		S. o. G.				
1860	320	859 } 1,164*	9,705	—	—	—
1861	484	–317	8,625	—	—	—
1862	430	1,120	11,782	—	—	—
1863	587	1,499 } 957*	14,879	—	—	—
1864	741	3,432	18,455	—	—	—
1865	920	819	17,967	—	—	—
1866	913	239 } 779*	18,439	—	—	—
1867	919	–324	18,401	495	–162	9,500
		S. o. G.			S. o. G.	
1868	917	1,074	18,147	474	537	10,777
		S. o. G.			S. o. G.	
1869	904	1,015	19,311	537	507	11,115
		S. o. G.			S. o. G.	
1870	962	588	20,536	554	294	10,963

* Share of profit in machinery revaluations. S. o. G. Share of Guarantee.

TABLE 17. *Annual output per spindle, measured in bundles of yarn spun, at Water Lane mills*

1806	24·9	1832	11·1	1858	14·2
1807	22·3	1833	10·4	1859	13·6
1808	19·0	1834	10·5	1860	13·6
1809	15·3	1835	10·6	1861	14·0
1810	22·6	1836	10·1	1862	15·1
1811	25·6	1837	9·8	1863	14·8
1812	21·7	1838	10·4	1864	13·8
1813	21·6	1839	10·7	1865	14·5
1814	26·4	1840	10·5	1866	13·9
1815	27·7	1841	10·1	1867	15·1
1816	21·4	1842	10·1	1868	15·9
1817	27·2	1843	10·9	1869	15·2
1818	29·0	1844	12·7	1870	14·5
1819	17·0	1845	12·5	1871	14·4
1820	19·6	1846	12·1	1872	11·9
1821	22·3	1847	12·7	1873	12·2
1822	20·7	1848	12·4	1874	13·8
1823	20·4	1849	12·4	1875	12·5
1824	19·1	1850	12·9	1876	10·8
1825	19·6	1851	13·5	1877	12·5
1826	18·4	1852	12·4	1878	11·7
1827	18·4	1853	12·3	1879	12·1
1828	16·4	1854	11·8	1880	12·7
1829	14·8	1855	9·8	1881	12·3
1830	13·5	1856	12·1	1882	14·1
1831	12·8	1857	12·6	1883	15·9

TABLE 18. *Spinning—costs and productivity at Water Lane mills*

Period	Labour cost per bundle (pence)	Labour earnings per week s. d.		Output per man per week (bundles)	Leas per spindle per day	Spindles per hand		Time (average hours per week)
						Line	Tow	
1824–8	5·64	—		11·8	12·2	32	29	—
1829–33	5·62	5	9	12·3	7·2	57	46	69·22
1834–8	5·47	6	6	13·2	6·7	64	58	65·39
1839–43	4·85	6	7	16·2	7·6	71	63	63·38
1844–8	4·39	6	7	17·9	8·3	71	64	62·00
1849–53	4·41	6	1	16·5	8·6	64	51	57·48
1854–8	4·66	6	3	16·0	9·1	59	39	55·44
1859–63	5·09	6	4	14·9	9·4	52	45	58·12
1864–8	6·03	6	5½	12·9	9·6	45	43	57·36
1869–73	6·32	7	0½	13·4	9·6	46	41	55·51
1874–8	6·83	8	6	15·1	9·4	50	49	—

TABLE 19. *Hackling—costs and productivity at Water Lane mills*

	Workers' output		Workers' earnings (weekly) s. d.		Labour cost	
	Bundles weekly	Cwts. weekly			Per bundle (pence)	Per cwt. (pence)
1824–8	16·1	—		—	6·3	—
1829–33	16·9	1·34	5	3	3·8	47·47
1834–8	16·6	0·95	5	3	3·8	66·57
1839–43	14·8	0·98	5	1	4·1	62·68
1844–8	27·3	1·87	5	10	2·6	37·32
1849–53	19·8	1·69	5	9	3·1	36·01
1854–8	13·3	1·53	5	3	4·7	40·96
1859–63	13·3	1·38	5	6	5·0	46·42
1864–8	13·8	1·53	6	0½	5·3	47·70
1869–73	14·3	1·69	6	6¾	5·2	46·71
1874–8	23·2	3·23	10	7	5·3	44·40
1879–83	27·6	2·68	14	6	6·5	65·75

BIBLIOGRAPHY

1. Manuscript Sources

At the Brotherton Library, Leeds
Gott Papers, 1792–1837.
Marshall Collection, 1788–1886.

At the Leeds Public Library, Archives Department
Apprentice Register of the Leeds Workhouse Committee, 1726–1809.
Business records of Wilson and Sons, Linen Merchants at Water Lane, Leeds, 1754–1832.
Leeds Corporation Court Book, vol. III, 1773–1835.
Leeds Quarter Sessions, Order and Indictment Book, 1784–1809.
Miscellaneous account books of a merchant trading in linens, etc., at Leeds and Glasgow, 1773–1813.
Poor Rate Assessment Books for the Township of Leeds, 1713–1805.
Valuation Book of the Township of Hunslet, 1823–4.

At the Leeds Reference Library
A compilation of facts illustrative of Methodism in Leeds, 1735–1835, by John Wray.
Rusby, J., compiler: Pedigrees and arms of the Leeds Families. 1892.

At the Yorkshire Archaeological Society, Leeds
Papers relating to Edward Armitage of Farnley Hall.

At Aireborough Urban District Council Offices, Rawdon
Records of Yeadon Township: Minute books, 1765–1857; Overseers Accounts, 1753–1842; and Miscellaneous deeds, accounts and reports, 1688–1752.

At the Baptist Church, Rawdon
Church Book, 1715–1810.

At the Baptist Church, Gildersome
Church Book, 1749–1807.

At the General Register Office, Somerset House
Non-Parochial Registers of Leeds Chapels for the period 1730–1837.

At Derwent Island, Keswick
Notebooks, letters and accounts of various members of the Marshall family.
Correspondence of William Whewell to his family, 1811–64.

At Shrewsbury Reference Library
Letters of Charles Bage to William Strutt, 1802–18.
Deeds relating to the Castle Foregate Flax Mill, 1796–7.

Bibliography

At Birmingham Public Library
The Boulton and Watt Collection: letters of Marshall and Co., 1789–97.
At Darlington Reference Library
MSS. History of Darlington by W. E. M. (no date).

2. GOVERNMENT PUBLICATIONS

1744   *Report from the Select Committee on the Petition of the Dealers in, and Manufacturers of, Linens.*

1751   *Report from the Select Committee Appointed to Examine…the several Petitions of the Manufacturers of, and Traders and Dealers in, The Linen Manufactory.*

1773   *Report from the Select Committee Relative to the State of the Linen Trade in Great Britain and Ireland.*

1817   *Report from the Select Committee Relating to Machinery for the Manufacturing of Flax.*

1822   *Report from the Select Committee on the Laws which Regulate the Linen Trade of Ireland.*

1825   *Report from the Select Committee on the Linen Trade of Ireland.*

1831–2   *Report from the Commissioners on the Proposed Division of Counties and Boundaries of Boroughs; Knaresborough, by H. W. Tancred.*

1834   *Factories Inquiry Commission*, Supplementary Report, Parts 1 and 2.

1840   *Handloom Weavers' Commission*, Assistant Commissioner's Reports, Parts 2 and 3.

1841   *Reports and Minutes of Evidence from the Select Committee on the Exportation of Machinery.*

1852   *The Report from Sir Robert Kane to the Chief Commissioner of Works, on the Preparation of Flax.*

1886   *The Depression of Trade and Industry Commission*, First Report, Appendix A; Second Report, Minutes of Evidence and Appendix Part 1.

1894   *Report by E. H. Osborn, Factory Inspector, upon the Condition of Work in Flax Mills and Linen Factories in the United Kingdom.*

The Census of Population, annual Reports of the Factory Inspectors, and the Trade and Navigation Accounts have been used as indicated in the text.

3. NEWSPAPERS AND PERIODICALS

The Leeds Express.
The Leeds Intelligencer.
The Leeds Mercury.
The Textile Manufacturer.
The Yorkshire Post.

Bibliography

4. DIRECTORIES AND MAPS

1790 *Universal British Directory* (2nd edition).

1797 Ryley, J. *The Leeds Directory.*

1800 Binns and Brown. *A Directory for the Town of Leeds.*

1807 Wilson, G. *A New and Complete Directory for...Leeds.*

1809, 1814, 1817 Baines, E. *Directory...of Leeds.*

1822 Baines, E. *Directory of the County of York.*

1826 Parson, W. *General and Commercial Directory...of Leeds.*

1830 Parson, W. and White, W. *Directory of ...Leeds and the Clothing District of Yorkshire.*

1830 Pigot and Co. *Directory of Yorkshire.*

1834, 1839 Baines and Newsome. *General and Commercial Directory...of Leeds.*

1837 Pigot and Co. *Directory of Leeds.*

1837 White, W. *History, Gazetteer and Directory of the West Riding.*

1839 Haigh, T. *A General and Commercial Directory...of Leeds.*

1842, 1847, 1853, 1857, 1861, 1866, 1870, 1875, 1894 White, W. *Directory and Topography of the Borough of Leeds and the Whole Clothing District of the West Riding.*

1845 Williams, J. *Directory of the Borough of Leeds.*

1847, 1849 Charlton, R. J. *Directory of the Borough of Leeds.*

1851 Slade, W. and Roebuck, D. I. *Directory of the Borough and Neighbourhood of Leeds.*

1872 Porter, T. *Topographical and Commercial Directory of Leeds.*

1876, 1878, 1882 McCorquodale and Co. *Topographical and Commercial Directory of Leeds and Neighbourhood.*

1881, 1886, 1888, 1893, 1897, 1899, 1900, 1906, 1910, 1914 Kelly's Directories, Ltd. *Directory of Leeds.*

1880 Jackson. *Directory of Cumberland and Westmorland.*

1901 Bulmer. *Directory of Cumberland.*

1770 Jefferys, T. *A Plan of Leeds.*

1815 Giles, N. and F. *Plan of the Town of Leeds and its Environs.*

1831 Fowler, C. *Plan of the Town of Leeds.*

1850 *Ordnance Survey Map of Leeds.*

5. BOOKS, PAMPHLETS AND ARTICLES PUBLISHED BEFORE 1900

Baines, E., jr. *The Life of Edward Baines.* London, 1859.

Baker, R. On the Industrial and Sanitary Economy of the Borough of Leeds in 1858. *J.R.S.S.* vol. XXI. 1858.

Banfield, T. C. *Industry of the Rhine.* Part I. Agriculture. London, 1846.

Bourne, H. R. F. *English Merchants,* 2 vols. London, 1866.

Bibliography

Bradley, T. *The Old Coaching Days in Yorkshire.* Leeds, 1889.

Bremner, D. Hemp, Flax and Jute. *Great Industries of Great Britain,* 3 vols. London, 1878–80.

Brown, R. *Flax: Its Culture and Preparation in Scotland, Ireland and and Flanders.* Glasgow, 1851.

Brown, W. *Information Regarding Flax Spinning at Leeds.* 1821. (In Leeds Reference Library.)

Burland, J. *Memoirs of William Wilson.* London, 1860.

Burnley, J. *The History of Wool and Woolcombing.* London, 1889.

Charley, W. T. *Flax and its Products in Ireland.* London, 1862.

Charley, W. T. *Flax and Linen in British Manufacturing Industries.* Edited by G. P. Bevan. London, 1876.

Claussen, P. *The Flax Movement,* 3rd ed. London [1851].

Combe, J. Description of a Flax Mill Recently Erected by Messrs Marshall and Co., at Leeds. *Institution of Civil Engineers, Minutes of Proceedings.* London, 1842.

Combe, J. *Suggestions for Promoting the Prosperity of the Leeds Linen Trade.* Leeds, 1865.

Defoe, D. *Tour through England and Wales.* London, 1724–6.

Deman, E. F. *The Flax Industry: Its Importance and Progress.* London, 1852.

Dodd, G. *The Textile Manufactures of Great Britain.* London, 1851.

Douglas, Mrs S. *The Life...of William Whewell.* London, 1881.

Dundee Trade Report Association. *Statistics of the Linen Trade.* Dundee, 1855, and Supplement, 1865.

Dupin, C. *Rapport [pour le Sénat] fait au nom de la Commission chargée d'examiner le projet de loi qui confère...des pensions aux héritiers de feu Philippe de Girard, inventeur de la filature mécanique du lin.* Paris, 1853.

Encyclopaedia Britannica, 3rd ed. Edinburgh, 1797.

Fairbairn, W. *Treatise on Mills and Millwork,* 2 vols. London, 1861–3.

Farey, J. *A Treatise on the Steam Engine, Historical, Practical and Descriptive.* London, 1827.

Favier, A. *The Textile Nettles; Rhea or Ramie.* London, 1882.

Fletcher, J. S. *History of Harrogate and Knaresborough.* London, 1920.

Fordyce, W. *A History of the County Palatine of Durham,* part 1. Newcastle upon Tyne, 1855.

Fortunes Made in Business: A Series of Original Sketches. By various authors, 3 vols. London, 1884–7.

Girard, P. de. *Mémoire au Roi...sur la priorité due à la France dans l'invention des machines à filer le lin.* [Paris, 1844.]

Grainge, W. *The History and Topography of Harrogate and the Forest of Knaresborough.* London, 1871.

Greenwood, T. Machinery Employed in the Preparation and Spinning of Flax. *Proceedings of the Institute of Mechanical Engineers.* 1865.

Bibliography

Grothe, H. *Philippe de Girard, l'inventeur de la filature mécanique du lin.* Berlin, 1873.

Hargrove, E. *The History of ... Knaresborough,* 7th ed. Knaresborough, 1832.

Hearth Tax Return (Skyrack Wapentake), 1672. *Publ. Thoresby Soc.* vols. II and IV; 1891, 1895.

Higgins, W. and Sons. *The Growth, Treatment and Manufacture of Flax into Linen.* Salford, 1851.

Hulbert, C. *The History and Description of the County of Salop.* Shrewsbury, 1837.

Hunter, J. Familiae Minorum Gentium. *Publications of the Harleian Society,* 4 vols., XXXVII–XL. 1894–6.

Hunter's 'Church Notes'; St John's, Leeds. *Publ. Thoresby Soc.* vol. II, 1891.

Invention de la filature mécanique du lin; [lettres] à M. le Ministre du Commerce et de l'Agriculture. Paris, 1850.

Jackson, R. *The History of the Town and Township of Barnsley in Yorkshire, from an Early Period,* 2nd ed. London, 1858.

Leeds Corporation, Statistical Committee. Report upon the Condition of the Town of Leeds and its Inhabitants. *J.R.S.S.* vol. II. 1839.

Leeds Flax Supply Association. *First Report.* Leeds, 1859.

'Letter from a merchant who has left off trade to a Member of Parliament in which the case of the British and Irish manufacture of linnen, threads and tapes is fairly stated....' London, 1738.

Lister, T. A Sketch of Barnsley, it Mineral and Manufacturing Products.... *Proc. Geological and Polytechnic Society of the West Riding of Yorkshire,* vol. III. 1857.

Longstaffe, W. H. D. *The History and Antiquities of the Parish of Darlington.* Darlington, 1854.

Marshall, J. *A Digest of all the Accounts Relating to the Population, Production, Revenues...of the United Kingdom of Great Britain and Ireland,* 2 parts. London, 1833.

Marshall, J. G. Sketch of the History of Flax Spinning in England, Especially as Developed in the Town of Leeds. *Report of the 28th Meeting of the British Association for the Advancement of Science.* London, 1858.

Marshall, L. C. *The Practical Flax Spinner.* London, 1885.

Marshall, W. Report on a Tour through Parts of Yorkshire and Scotland in May, June and July 1817. *Minutes of the Trustees of the Linen and Hempen Manufacturers of Ireland.*

Matthewman, A. E. 'Old Leeds', newspaper cuttings: Leeds industries past and present—flax spinning. (In Leeds Reference Library.)

Mayhall, J. *The Annals and History of Leeds and other Places in the County of York,* 3 vols. London, 1878.

Bibliography

Minshull, T. *The Shrewsbury Visitor's Pocket Companion; or Salopian Guide and Directory*. Shrewsbury, 1804.

Mortimer, T. *A General Commercial Dictionary*, 3rd ed. London, 1823.

Mulhall, M. G. *The Dictionary of Statistics*. London, 1892.

Murray, J. *A Treatise on the Art of Weaving*, 2nd ed. Glasgow, 1827.

Murray, J. *The Phormium Tenax; or, New Zealand Flax*. London, 1836.

Owen, H. *Some Account of the Ancient and Present State of Shrewsbury*. Shrewsbury, 1808.

Pickles, W. *The Flax and Tow Spinner's Complete Calculator*. London, 1850.

Reasons for Encouraging the Linnen Manufacture of Scotland and Other Parts of Great Britain. By the author of *The Interest of Scotland Consider'd*, etc. London, 1735.

Rees, A. *The Cyclopedia*, 6 vols. London, 1819–20.

Repertory of Arts and Manufactures.... *Trans. of the Philosophical Societies of all Nations*, vols. I–VII. London, 1794–7.

Sharp, P. *Flax, Tow and Jute Spinning*, 2nd ed. Dundee, 1886.

Slater, P. *History of the Ancient Parish of Guiseley*. London, 1880.

Society for Promoting Christian Knowledge. The useful arts and manufactures of Great Britain, no. 7: *The Manufacture of Linen Yarn*. London, 1846.

Stead, G. E. The Decline of the Flax Industry in Leeds. *Yorkshire Post*, 6 December 1896.

Taylor, R. V. *The Biographia Leodiensis*. Leeds, 1865–7.

Trustees of the Linen Manufacture [of Ireland]. *Copies of Several Exemplifications of Patents Passed in Great Britain Relative to the Machinery for Spinning Flax*. Dublin, 1796.

Ure, A. *A Dictionary of Arts, Manufactures, and Mines*. London, 1839. And 7th edition, by Robert Hunt, London, 1878–9.

Ure, A. *The Philosophy of Manufactures*. London, 1835.

Visitors' Handbook to Knaresborough, 3rd ed. Knaresborough, 1854.

Wardell, J. *The Antiquities of the Borough of Leeds*. London, 1853.

Warden, A. J. *The Linen Trade, Ancient and Modern*. London, 1864.

Warnes, J. *On the Cultivation of Flax*. London, 1846.

Watson, J. *The Art of Spinning and Thread Making*. London, 1878.

Watson, J. F. *Report on the Preparation and use of Rheea Fibre*. London, 1875.

Wilkinson, J. *Worthies, Families and Celebrities of Barnsley and the District*. London [1883].

Yarranton, A. *England's Improvement by Sea and Land*, 2 parts. London, 1677–81.

Young, A. *General View of the Agriculture of the County of Lincoln*. London, 1799.

6. RECENT BOOKS, PAMPHLETS AND ARTICLES

Bannister, T. The First Iron-Framed Buildings. *Architectural Rev.* 1950.

Beckwith, F. The Population of Leeds during the Industrial Revolution. *Publ. Thoresby Soc.* vol. XLI, part 2. 1948.

Burke's Genealogical and Heraldic History of the Landed Gentry. London, 1952.

Carter, H. R. *Modern Flax, Hemp and Jute Spinning and Twisting.* London, 1907.

Chapman, D. The Establishment of the Jute Industry: A Problem of Location Theory? *Rev. Econ. Stud.*, vol. VI. 1938.

Clapham, J. H. *An Economic History of Modern Britain,* 3 vols. Cambridge, 1926–38.

Clarke, H. L. and Weech, W. N. *History of Sedbergh School, 1525–1925.* Sedbergh, 1925.

Clow, A. and N. L. *The Chemical Revolution.* London, 1952.

Cox, H. (ed.). *British Industries under Free Trade.* London, 1903.

Crump, W. B. (ed.). The Leeds Woollen Industry, 1780–1820. *Publ. Thoresby Soc.* vol. XXXII. 1929.

Dictionary of National Biography.

Dunham, A. L. *The Industrial Revolution in France, 1815–48.* New York, 1955.

Eyre, V. The Possibility of Reviving the Flax Industry in Great Britain. *Supplement to the Journal of the Board of Agriculture,* 1914.

Gameson, F. R. Charles Bage, 1752–1822. *The Shropshire Magazine,* June 1954.

Gayer, A. D., Rostow, W. W. and Schwartz, A. J. *The Growth and Fluctuation of the British Economy, 1790–1850.* Oxford, 1953.

Gill, C. *The Rise of the Irish Linen Industry.* Oxford, 1925.

Green, E. R. R. *History of the Lagan Valley, 1800–50.* London, 1949.

Heaton, H. *The Yorkshire Woollen and Worsted Industries.* London, 1920.

Henderson, W. O. *The Lancashire Cotton Famine, 1861–1865.* Manchester, 1934

Hipperholme Grammar School, 1648–1948. Compiled by J. W. Houseman. Hipperholme, 1948.

Hoffmann, W. G. *British Industry, 1700–1950.* Translated by W. O. Henderson and F. H. Chaloner. Oxford, 1955.

Horner, J. *The Linen Trade of Europe.* Belfast, 1920.

Hutchins, B. L. and Harrison, A. *A History of Factory Legislation.* London, 1911.

Johnson, H. R. and Skempton, A. W. William Strutt's Fireproof and Iron-Framed Buildings, 1792–1812. Paper read at the Institution of Civil Engineers, 1956.

Bibliography

Long, D. C. Philippe de Girard and the Introduction of Mechanical Flax-Spinning in Austria. *J. Econ. Hist.*, vol. XIV. 1954.

Mantoux, P. *The Industrial Revolution in the Eighteenth Century.* London, 1928.

Matthews, P. W. *History of Barclay's Bank, Limited.* London, 1926.

Matthews, R. C. O. *A Study in Trade-cycle History.* Cambridge, 1954.

Moore, A. S. *Linen: From the Raw Material to the Finished Product.* London, 1914.

Moore, A. S. *Linen.* London, 1922.

Morris, J. The Mayors of Shrewsbury. *Trans. Shropshire Archaeological Soc.* 4th series, vol. IX, 1923.

Palliser, J. H. *Rawdon and its History.* Rawdon, 1914.

Patterson, R. L. The British Linen and Flax Industry. *British Industries.* Edited by W. J. Ashley. London, 1903.

Pressnell, L. S. *Country Banking in the Industrial Revolution.* Oxford, 1956.

Pringle, A. V. *The Theory of Flax Spinning.* Belfast, 1949.

Rimmer, W. G. The Castle Foregate Flax Mill. *Trans. Shropshire Archaeological Soc.*, vol. LVI, 1959.

Rimmer, W. G. Leeds and its Industrial Growth. No. 4: The Working Force. *Leeds Journal*, vol. XXV, 1954.

Rimmer, W. G. Middleton Colliery, near Leeds (1770–1830). *Yorkshire Bull. Econ. Soc. Res.* vol. VII, 1955.

Schlote, W. *British Overseas Trade from 1700 to the 1930's.* Translated by W. O. Henderson and W. H. Chaloner. Oxford, 1952.

Schroeder, L. W. *Mill Hill Chapel, Leeds, 1674–1924.* Leeds, 1924.

Scott, E. K. (ed). *Matthew Murray.* Leeds, 1928.

Skempton, A. W. The Origin of Iron Beams. *Actes du VIIIe Congrès International d'Histoire des Sciences*, 1956.

Speight, H. *Nidderdale.* London, 1906.

Thomas, J. A History of the Leeds Clothing Industry. *Yorkshire Bull. of Econ. Soc. Res.* Occasional paper, no. 1. Hull, 1955.

Traill, H. D. and Mann, J. S. (eds.). *Social England*, 6 vols. London, 1902–4.

Turberville, A. S. and Beckwith, F. Leeds and Parliamentary Reform, 1820–32. *Publ. Thoresby Soc.* vol. XLI, part 1, 1946.

Wadsworth, A. P. and Mann, J. de L. *The Cotton Trade and Industrial Lancashire.* Manchester, 1931.

Ward, G. The Education of Factory Workers. *Economic History*, 1935.

Weyman, H. T. Members of Parliament for the Borough of Shrewsbury. *Trans. Shropshire Archaeological Soc.* 4th series, vol. XII, 1929–30.

Wilson, C. *Anglo-Dutch Commerce and Finance in the Eighteenth Century.* Cambridge, 1941.

Woodhouse, T. and Brand, A. *A Century's Progress in the Jute Manu-facture, 1833–1933.* Dundee, 1934.

Woodhouse, T. and Milne, T. *Jute and Linen Weaving.* Manchester, 1904.

The Letters of William and Dorothy Wordsworth, edited by E. de Selin-court. *Early Letters, 1787–1805*, Oxford, 1935. *Letters...the Middle Years, 1806–1820*, 2 vols. Oxford, 1937. *Letters...the Later Years, 1821–[50]*, 3 vols. Oxford, 1939.

Woytinski, W. S. and E. S. *World Population and Production.* New York, 1953.

INDEX

Aberdeen, 56
Accounting methods, 73, 121–2, 146, 151–2, 196, 256, 278
Adel Reformatory School, Leeds, 301
Ainsworth and Vallet, 52
Aire Navigation, 33, 34
Apprentice house, Castle Foregate, 55, 110
Arkwright, Richard, 7
Armitage, James, clothier, Leeds, 18, 37
Atkinson, John, partner with Marshall, 66, 70, 93, 94, 112, 115, 137, 143, 148–9, *see* Hives and Atkinson
Atkinson, Moses, flax-spinner, Leeds, 125
Australia, 241

Backhouse, J. J., linen merchant, Darlington, 6, 9
Bage, Charles, partner of Marshall and Benyons, 51 n., 54, 58–60, 62–3, 65, 105, 137
Baines, Edward, editor of *Leeds Mercury*, 68, 69, 98, 111, 164–5
Baptist Meeting House, Rawdon, 11, 40
Barnsley: bleaching, 51; growth of linen industry, 126–8; linen weaving, 3, 7, 163, 167–8, 181, 201, 214; market for Leeds yarn, 47, 87, 129, 134, 136, 166, 172, 191, 199, 233, 257; strikes, 145, 164, 180
Baxter, linen manufacturer, Dundee, 201
Beckett and Co., bankers, Leeds, 37, 97
Belfast linen industry, 8, 131, 198, 232, 233 n., 234
Belgium, 192, 229
Benson and Braithwaite, flax-spinners, Ambleside, 57
Benyon, Benjamin, partner with Marshall, 44, 47, 54, 58, 60–6 *passim*, 110
Benyon, Thomas, partner with Marshall, 44, 47, 54, 58, 60–6 *passim*, 69, 109, 116 n., 135, 138
Benyon, Thomas, jr., 207
Benyons and Bage (later Benyon and Co.), flax-spinners, Leeds, 51, 65, 124, 125, 136, 229
Berthollet, C. L., 51
Bingham, P., 105
Bischoff, James, woollen merchant, Leeds, 98, 102

Bleaching, 46, 50–3, 110
Booth, Sarah, 14, 21, 23 n., 36
Bounties, 4
Bridgenorth, 54
Briggs, Emanuel and Co., flax-spinners, Leeds, 198, 229
Boulton and Watt, 35, 45, 55, 64 n.
Bower, Joshua, crown-glass manufacturer, Hunslet, 18
Brompton, 88, 191
Bromsgrove, 3
Brougham, Henry and James, 111
Brown, William, flax-spinner, Dundee, 83, 88–9, 118, 119, 125–6, 129, 130–3
Busk, Robert, flax-spinner, Leeds, 171–2, 173 n.
Butler, Josephine, 225

Cachard and Lanthois, flax-spinners, 171
Calverley, Sir Walter, 11
Canada, 241, 246
Canvas, *see* Weaving: types of cloth
Capital: circulating, 44, 47, 74, 147, 196, 262; fixed, 44, 47, 56, 70, 85, 118, 147, 196, 210, 262, 265, 297 n.; sources, 36–7, 40, 46–7, 55, 56, 60–1, 66, 189; withdrawals, 270, 276
Cardigan, James Brudenell, 5th Earl of, 98
Carlisle, 3, 4
Carlyle, Thomas, 89
Cartwright, Edmund, 29, 49, 138
Castle Foregate Mill, 44, 54–5, 56, 110, 135, 143, 201, 253 n.
Cawood, M. and Sons, machine-makers, Leeds, 233
Cawood, S., bleacher, Barnsley, 173
Chaptal, M., 53
China grass, 193, 215, 246, 260
Cleveland, 3
Cloth, *see* Weaving: types of cloth
Cloudsley and Stephenson, linen merchants, Leeds, 11
Clyde valley, 4
Coal, 34, 130–1, 163
Coal-gas lighting, 86
Coates, flax-spinner, Ripon, 57
Colbeck, Ellis and Willis, flax-spinners, Fewston, 133

337

Index

Holbeck, Leeds, 34
Holdsworth, W. B. and Co., flax-spinners, Leeds, 198, 229
Hook, Rev. Walter Farquhar, Vicar of Leeds, 207
Hornby, Bell and Birley, flax-spinners, Egremont, 57-8
Horsman, P., manager at Castle Foregate, 120, 123
Hull, 76, 77, 124, 126, 132, 157, 163, 228, 229
Humble, Richard, steward at Middleton colliery, Leeds, 18
Hutton, William, partner with Marshall, 66, 70, 115 n.

Ireland, 3, 4, 8, 56, 130, 191, 198, 210-11, 229, 230, 243
Italy, 240

Jackson, Murray, engineer, Leeds, 235 n.
Jackson, Richard, engineer, Leeds, 186
Jute, 239

Kay, James, flax-spinner, Preston, 170 n., 173-5, 191-2, 220
Kendrew, John, flax-spinner, Houghton, 9, 23
Kidderminster, 54
Knaresborough: linen industry, 2, 3, 4, 7, 47, 125, 163; decline, 133-4
Königsberg, 37

Labour: children, 105-6, 108-9, 119, 132, 169, 193, 194, 209, 220, 263 n., 294; composition of labour-force, 106, 119, 145, 194, 249, 263; duration of work, 79, 80-1, 119, 135, 161, 169, 195, 209, 212, 219, 249, 294; education, 105-6, 108-9, 161, 194, 209, 217; management of, 119-21, 216-17, 293; mill club, 121, 216; numbers employed, 37, 56, 79, 80-1, 118, 165, 169, 193, 195, 212, 263, 293; religion, 207, 217; strikes, 281-9; wages and earnings, 83, 84, 120, 131, 145, 146, 193-4, 209, 248-50, 262, 293-4
Lake District, 68, 99-102, 116-17, 221, 300-3
Lancashire, 3, 8, 125
Lancasterian School, Leeds, 105
Land, Water Lane, 33, 45, 63, 64, 66, 297 n.
Lawson, Samuel, 125, 130
Lawson, Samuel and Sons, machine-makers, Leeds, 293

Lawson, Thomas, engineer, Leeds, 265
Lawson and Walker, machine-makers and flax-spinners, 180
Leach and Hardcastle, bankers, Bradford, 95
Lead mines, Wharfedale, 94
Leeds: Corporation, 13, 18; growth, 10, 12, 33; industrial diversification, 193, 248; linen industry, growth, 124-6, 198-9, decline, 211-12, 214, 228-30, causes, 231-53 *passim*; linen merchants, 13; society, 18-19, 112; textile-machine industry, 233-5
Leeds and District Association of Factory Occupiers, 288
Leeds and Liverpool Canal, 34
Leeds Flax Supply Association, 246
Leeds Library, 68
Leeds Literary and Philosophical Society, 104, 105
Leeds Mechanics Institute, 105
Leeds Mercury, 68, 111
Leeds Social Improvement Society, 218
Leicester, 3
Liége, 232, 251
Linen industry, 2-9, 228-30, 232
London, University of, 105
Lowry, George, flax-spinner, Manchester, 264

Manchester, 3 n., 186 n.
March and Maclea, machine-makers, Leeds, 233
Marshall family: Yeadon, 10-11; John Marshall's children, 224-7; Lake District, 298-303
Marshall, Arthur, youngest son of John Marshall, 269, 272-3, 283, 292
Marshall, Christiana (*née* Hibbert), 114
Marshall, Cordelia (Mrs Whewell), 222-3, 298
Marshall, Ellen, 118, 298
Marshall, Henry Cowper: character, 224, 257-8, 277, 299-300; commercial manager, 158-60, 181; scheme for spinners' co-operation, 212; marries, 220; Mayor of Leeds, 221; Derwent Island estate, 221; withdrawals of capital, 270, 276; relations with James, 271-4, 277-8; accounting method, 278, 291; in control, 286; spinners' leader in strike, 288; withdraws from firm, 292; death, 296

339

Index

Marshall, James Aubrey Garth, 279–80, 291

Marshall, James Garth: character and interests, 182–3, 222, 299; wet spinning, 170, 176–7; manager, Castle Foregate, 181, Water Lane, 200 ff.; experiments, 215, 260–7; on Leeds industry, 215; marries, 221; belief in free trade, 235; reluctance to invest, 267–8; absences, 269; withdrawals of capital, 270; relations with Henry, 271–4, 277–8, 286; retires, 274; death, 291

Marshall, Jane (née Pollard), wife of John Marshall, 68, 99–101, 216 n.

Marshall, Jane Dorothea (Mrs Temple), 117, 298

Marshall, Jeremiah, John Marshall's father, 11, 13, 22

Marshall, John (1661–1745), 11

Marshall, John (1765–1846): character, 15–17, 19–21, 97, 99–100; schooling, 14; Benthamite leanings, 21, 105; enters father's business, 22; inheritance, 22–3; spins flax, 23–5; partnership with Fenton and Dearlove, 26, 36; partnership with the Benyons, 44, 46, 58–66 *passim*; invests at Castle Foregate, 56; separates from the Benyons, 63–6; junior partners, 66–7; social interests, 67–9, 91–2, 103–4; marriage and family, 68, 99, 224–7; flax speculations, 72–8, 93–4, 156–8; organisation of mills, 88–9; achievement in 1815, 88–90; outside investments, 92, 94–6; earnings, 93, 96; fortune, 97; Hallsteads, 99–102; residence in London, 104–5; attitudes towards education, 105–10; M.P., 110–13; settlements on children, 114–18; business attitudes, 155–6; wet spinning, 179–80; new markets, 181, 191; comparison with sons, 184–5; litigation with Kay, 192

Marshall, John II, 93–4, 109, enters business, 115; Derwentwater Estate, 116–17; manager at Water Lane, 141–2, 149, 165 ff.; views on flax speculation, 157–8; wet-spinning, 174, 176–8, 179; relations with James, 182–3; interest in politics, 185; death, 186; on hours of work, 219

Marshall, John III, 279, 280, 292, 296, 300–1

Marshall, Julia (Mrs Elliott), 118, 298

Marshall, Mary (née Cowper), 13, 19, 56

Marshall, Mary (Lady Monteagle), 222

Marshall, Reginald Dykes, 273, 275, 280–1

Marshall, Stephen, 279, 282–6, 292, 296

Marshall, Susan (Mrs Frederick Myers), 224

Marshall, Victor, 279, 292

Marshall, William, eldest son of John Marshall, 114, 260, 284 n.

Middleton Colliery, Leeds, 12, 34

Mill club, 121

Mill Hill Unitarian Chapel, Leeds, 14, 40, 68, 98

Mill library, 109

Milton, Viscount, *see* Fitzwilliam, Earl

Mirfin, Thomas, machine-maker, Leeds, 177, 233

Monteagle, Baron, *see* Spring-Rice, Thomas

Morfitt, John, flax-spinner, Leeds, 199, 229

Morpeth, George William Frederick Howard, Viscount, 111

Mulholland, Andrew, flax-spinner, Belfast, 191, 233 n.

Murdock, William, engineer, 35

Murray, Matthew, engineer, 29–30, 31–3, 42, 44, 46, 49, 59, 60, 84, 139 n., *see* Fenton, Murray and Wood

Myers, Rev. Frederick, 224

Naylor, William, merchant, Leeds, 33

New Grange, Headingley, Leeds, 67, 98, 102, 116

New Zealand, 246

Northallerton, 87, 125 n.

Oastler, Richard, 217–18

Owen, Robert, New Lanark mills, 57, 110

Paisley, 55

Parliamentary History and Review, 105

Parry, Edward, manager, 268

Partners: relations between, Marshall, Fenton and Co., 38–40; Marshall and Benyons, 60–5; Marshall and Co., 119–23, 141–3, 148–61, 166–9, 174, 176–86, 192, 197, 200–3, 207, 215–20, 254, 257–79 *passim*, 281–92 *passim*, 295–8; terms of agreement, Marshall, Fenton and Co., 26, 36; Marshall and Benyons, 44, 61, 63, 65; Marshall and Co., 66, 70, 115, 261, 269, 279–80, 291–2, 295

Patrington steeping establishment, 260

Petersfield, 111

340

Index

Plant: machinery, 36, 46, 65, 79, 81, 82, 84, 85, 136, 147, 152, 188, 207, 210, 262-4, 293, 297 n.; reorganisation, 82, 85, 139-42, 167, 187-8, 292

Pollard, William, 37, 68, 95, 99

Pontefract, 112

Porthouse, Thomas, flax-spinner, Coatham, 9, 23, 84

Portugal, 240

Preparing: carding, 25 n., 27, 32, 36, 42-3, 141; combing, 138, 265-7; gill frames, 139-40, 142, 152, 172, 173, 188; hackling, 25 n., 28, 30-1, 83, 84-5, 137-8, 141-2, 173, 188, 209-10, 234, 263, 293; steeping, 260-1

Prest, flax-spinner, Leeds, 180 n.

Productivity, average, 83, 131, 146, 195, 209-10, 262-4, 294

Profits and losses, 37-40, 47, 56, 61, 63, 69-71, 72-4, 79, 80, 81, 118, 143-4, 145, 148, 165, 169, 180, 189, 208, 256-7, 276, 295

Rawdon, 10, 14

Rawnsley, Rev. Hardwicke Drummond, 225

Reading, 3

Rhodes, Abraham, Leeds, 40

Rhodes and Fox, linen manufacturers, Leeds, 292

Richardson, J. and J., bleachers and merchants, Belfast, 148

Richardson, John, manager at Leeds, 268, 274, 281, 282, 284

Rider, David, Leeds, 45, 64

Riga, 243

Roberts, David, engineer, Leeds, 202

Robinson and Dearlove, flax-spinners, Leeds, 134, 180 n.

Russell, John, 98

Russia, 3, 243, 244

Rye, 111

Sadlers (i.e. Fenton, Sadler and Sadler), 191

St Barnabas Church, Leeds, 207

St John the Evangelist Church, Leeds, 207

Schlumberger and Co., machine-makers, Alsace, 265-7

School at Water Lane, 105, 194, 216-17

Scotland, 3, 8, 55-6, 162, 168, 230

Scotland Mill, see Fabric

Scott, Gilbert, 207

Sedgwick, Adam, 222

Shrewsbury, 54, 201

Smoke abatement, 218

Somerset, 3, 125

South America, 241

Southey, Robert, 117, 225

Spain, 240

Spinning: competition from hand-spinners, 24-5, 50, 87, 126, 130, 247-8; competition from other spinners, 87, 124-6, 128-9, 130-4, 147-8, 166, 168, 191, 198-9, 210, 229-31; competition from substitutes, 134, 164-5; consumption of flax, 37, 74, 118, 159; costs, 25, 42, 71, 81-2, 129, 144, 147, 165, 166, 189-90, 199, 208, 219, 259, 295; experiments, 9, 27-9, 30-3, 42-4, 49-50, 138-42, 171, 175-8, 215, 260; frames, 9, 36, 46, 80, 81, 146, 153, 209, 262, 293; machine-makers, 129-30, 152, 233-5; output of yarn, 37, 47, 71, 79, 80, 81, 118, 135, 136, 142, 145, 165, 167, 180, 189, 191, 254, 276, 292; output per spindle, 146, 195, 209, 262, 263, 294; output per worker, 83, 146, 169, 195, 209, 247, 262; spindles, spinning, 36, 45, 46, 56, 80, 136, 139, 142, 153, 165, 169, 181, 187, 188, 189, 207, 254, 262, 291; spindles, twisting, 200, 207, 254; yarn, grades of, 42, 48, 50, 71, 78-9, 80, 82, 127, 135, 140-1, 142, 146, 166, 169, 170, 172, 175 n., 190, 193, 208, 260, 295; yarn markets, 47-8, 78, 87-8, 127-8, 130, 172, 190-1, 211, 237-8; yarn prices, 72, 80-1, 128, 129, 135, 140, 144, 147, 148, 168, 190, 208; yarn, see also Weaving and Thread

Spring-Rice, Catherine Lucy (Mrs Henry C. Marshall), 220

Spring-Rice, Mary (Mrs James G. Marshall), 221

Spring-Rice, Thomas, first Baron Monteagle, 220, 222-3, 225

Steam-engines, 35, 45, 46, 55, 56, 86, 131, 135, 139, 143, 187, 200, 261

Steel, Joseph, 174

Stockton-on-Tees, 3, 4, 30

Strauss, Brothers and Sons, merchants, 256

Strauss, H. S., 214

Strutt, Jedediah, 51 n., 54, 59

Sturge, Joseph, 222

Swinburne, Algernon Charles, 225

Sykes, Samuel, 231

Tariffs, 210-11, 237, 238, 240

Temple, Sir Granville, 117

341

Index

Temple Mill, *see* Fabric, Water Lane
Tennant, James, flax-spinner, Leeds, 84, 124
Tennant and Knox bleaching powder, 53
Thread: costs, 213; markets, 55, 213–14, 238; output, 80, 213; prices, 213, 255; yarn consumed, 254, 258, 292
Titley, Anthony, 138, 139, 173
Titley, Tatham and Walker, flax-spinners, Leeds, 109, 124, 180, 186, 201, 212, 229
Tottie, Thomas William, Leeds, 69

United States, 200–1, 213, 240, 256, 276

Wade's Trustees, Leeds, 98
Walker, Mark, machine-maker and flax-spinner, Leeds, 180, 199
Warnes, John, 242
Warrington, 1
Water-powered mills, 27, 35, 56–7, 133–4
Watt, James, jr., 17, 49, 64 n.
Watts, Alaric, editor of *Leeds Mercury*, 17
Weaving: costs, 256; hand-looms, 25, 30, 36, 53, 79; markets, 4, 5, 29, 239–41, 256; output, 29, 37, 80, 143, 250, 256; power-looms, 29–30, 137, 143, 230, 255, 292; prices, 143; types of cloth, 37, 53–4, 79, 143, 256; yarn consumed, 53, 79–80, 143, 255, 258, 292
Weetwood Hall, Leeds, 221
West Indies, 4, 241
Wetherall, R., mill-hand, 173 n.
Whewell, Rev. William, Master of Trinity College, Cambridge, 102, 207, 221–2, 223, 225

Whitaker, Dr Holme, 114 n.
Whitehaven, 3, 4
Whitely, James, dyer, Leeds, 26
Whitwell, William, manager at Castle Foregate, 123
Wigan, 51
Wilford, Jonathan, linen manufacturer, Barnsley, 168
Wilkinson, John, flax-spinner, Leeds, 199, 229
Wilson, J. and Sons, linen merchants, Leeds, 13
Wilson, William, linen bleacher, Barnsley, 6
Wood, David, engineer, Leeds, 20, 49, 118, 123, 137, 138, 149, 172; *see* Fenton, Murray and Wood
Wood, Rev. William, minister of Mill Hill, 14 n.
Wordsworth, Dorothy, 17, 68, 101, 113, 216 n.
Wordsworth, Taylor, machine-maker, Leeds, 233, 267
Wordsworth, William, 116–17, 191 n., 222, 225, 226
Wright, Joseph, flax merchant, 40, 65

Yarn exports, 190–1, 199, 237
Yarn imports, 3, 5–6, 41, 56, 71, 72, 76, 127, 255
Yeadon, 10
Yorkshire, West Riding, 10, 12, 125 n., 163–4
Yorkshire College, 301
Younger, Matthew, machine-maker, Sheffield, 172